Lecture Notes in Computer Science 6956

Commenced Publication in 1973
Founding and Former Series Editors:
Gerhard Goos, Juris Hartmanis, and Jan van Leeuwen

Myra B. Cohen   Mel Ó Cinnéide (Eds.)

Search Based Software Engineering

Third International Symposium, SSBSE 2011
Szeged, Hungary, September 10-12, 2011
Proceedings

 Springer

Volume Editors

Myra B. Cohen
University of Nebraska-Lincoln
Department of Computer Science and Engineering
Lincoln, NE 68588-0115, USA
E-mail: myra@cse.unl.edu

Mel Ó Cinnéide
University College Dublin
School of Computer Science and Informatics
Dublin 4, Ireland
E-mail: mel.ocinneide@ucd.ie

ISSN 0302-9743   e-ISSN 1611-3349
ISBN 978-3-642-23715-7   e-ISBN 978-3-642-23716-4
DOI 10.1007/978-3-642-23716-4
Springer Heidelberg Dordrecht London New York

Library of Congress Control Number: 2011935251

CR Subject Classification (1998): D.2, D.4, D.1, F.1

LNCS Sublibrary: SL 2 – Programming and Software Engineering

Typesetting: Camera-ready by author, data conversion by Scientific Publishing Services, Chennai, India

Printed on acid-free paper

Springer is part of Springer Science+Business Media (www.springer.com)

Message from the General Chair

It is my great pleasure to welcome you to the Proceedings of the Third International Symposium on Search-Based Software Engineering, SSBSE 2011, held in the beautiful surroundings of Szeged, Hungary. This year, for the first time, SSBSE 2011 benefited from co-location with a major event, ESEC/FSE, through which we hope to widen our community and welcome many new faces.

Search-Based Software Engineering (SBSE) continues to be an exciting and challenging field to work in, and one that is continually growing. SSBSE grew again in terms of the number of submissions obtained this year – our sister event, the Search-Based Software Engineering track at GECCO, also experienced similar growth. SBSE began with the application of metaheuristic search to test data generation in the 1970s. Since then, metaheuristic search has contributed to state of the art results in a plethora of areas that span the entire software engineering lifecycle, including requirements prioritization, automated design, refactoring, bug fixing, reverse engineering and project management.

SSBSE 2011 was the result of the enthusiastic hard work and gracious kind support of several individuals. I have several people to thank. To begin with, I am grateful to Tibor Gyimóthy, General Chair of ESEC/FSE and the ESEC/FSE Steering Committee for allowing us to co-locate with their prestigious event in Szeged, and the support they gave to SSBSE. Thanks in particular are due to László Vidács and Patricia Frittman, who took care of the local arrangements and the interface between FSE and SSBSE.

SSBSE 2011 featured a strong program. It was a great pleasure to work with Mel Ó Cinnéide and Myra Cohen, our Program Chairs. I would like to thank them, too, for their hard work in formulating the Program Committee, managing the review process and putting the program together. Of course, the program could not be formed without the work of the authors themselves, whom we thank for their high-quality work. I would also like to thank the Program Committee for their efforts in reviewing and commenting on the papers, thereby providing the authors with valuable feedback. I am also grateful to Westley Weimer, who not only managed the Graduate Student Track, but worked hard to secure funding from the NSF and CREST to ensure that doctoral students could travel and register for both FSE and SSBSE.

It is my great pleasure that SSBSE hosted two exceptional keynote speakers in Andreas Zeller and Darrell Whitley, both well known for their contributions in software engineering and metaheuristic search, respectively. I would also like to thank Mark Harman and Lionel Briand for providing two tutorials for us on SBSE.

Thanks are also due to the Publicity Chairs, Tanja Vos, Mathew Hall and Gregory Kapfhammer. Tanja was instrumental in securing industrial sponsorship for the symposium, while Mathew managed our various social networks on

Twitter, Facebook and LinkedIn. Gregory helped us further spread the word by means of e-mail campaigns. Further thanks are due to Jon Bradley and his team at Ninefootone Creative for designing our excellent website and a new look that was featured in our promotional material.

I am grateful to Alfred Hofmann at Springer LNCS for managing the production of the proceedings for us, and making the process smooth, efficient and unbureaucratic. Thanks to Gillian Callaghan at the University of Sheffield, who assisted me with managing the finances of this event and setting up the online registration process. Throughout the organization of the symposium Mel, Myra, Westley and I received valuable guidance from the SSBSE Steering Committee, chaired by Mark Harman, to whom we are also grateful.

Thanks are also due to our sponsors. Thanks to Berner & Mattner, IBM, the FITTEST project, Softeam and Sulake for funding the best paper prize. While attracting top-quality submissions was key, it was also one of our aims to provide valuable and useful feedback to the authors of those papers, whether their work was accepted or not. I would like to thank SWELL, the Swedish Research School in Verification and Validation, for funding our prize for best reviewer and thus helping us strive toward this goal. Finally, I am also grateful to Ericsson and Sigrid Eldh, our Industrial Chair, for further valuable support, and the University of Sheffield for supporting the symposium both financially and in kind.

If you were not able to attend in person, I hope that you find these proceedings stimulating and thought-provoking. Either way, do consider submitting a paper next year to SSBSE 2012, when the symposium will be co-located with ICSM in Riva del Garda, Trento, Italy.

June 2011   Phil McMinn

Message from the Program Chairs

On behalf of the SSBSE 2011 Program Committee, it is our pleasure to present the proceedings of the Third International Symposium on Search-Based Software Engineering. It was a privilege to serve on this Organizing Committee and we believe that the quality of the program reflects the excellent efforts of the authors, reviewers, keynote speakers and tutorial presenters.

First and foremost we are grateful for the widespread participation and support from the SBSE community. We received 37 papers in the research track and 6 papers in the graduate student track. The papers emanated from institutions in 21 different countries, namely, Australia, Austria, Brazil, Canada, China, Cyprus, France, Germany, Greece, Hungary, Ireland, Israel, Italy, Norway, Pakistan, Portugal, Russia, Spain, Sweden, Turkey, and the UK, so we can claim to have a truly international authorship.

All submitted papers were reviewed by at least three experts in the field. The review period was followed by a moderated online discussion. In the end, 15 manuscripts were accepted for publication as full papers, and three were accepted in the graduate track. In addition we accepted eight papers for presentation as posters during the symposium.

We particularly wish to thank Westley Weimer for running the graduate student track and taking a very active role in reviewing every paper submitted. Graduate students are a vital part of any research field and we are happy that every paper submitted to this track was good enough to qualify as either a paper or a poster.

The topics covered by the accepted papers at SSBSE 2011 included software testing, software release planning, process reduction, project staff assignments, concept identification, scalability, landscape analysis, parameter tuning, concurrency and model-driven engineering. This broad range illustrates how SBSE continues its expansion into new areas of software engineering. For the first time, there was a full session devoted to Fundamentals of SBSE, which is further evidence that SBSE has become an established discipline.

The SSBSE tradition of inviting keynote speakers from both the search community and from the software engineering community continued and we were delighted to announce our two esteemed keynote speakers: Darrell Whitley (search) and Andreas Zeller (software engineering). The symposium started with a short tutorial introduction to SBSE delivered by Mark Harman, one of the original founders and tireless proselytizers of the field. Lionel Briand presented an valuable tutorial on conducting and analyzing empirical studies in SBSE. We were also very pleased to have a panel of experts from the software engineering community join us for an interactive session where we explored how SBSE can be further applied in software engineering.

We trust that you will enjoy the proceedings of SSBSE 2011 and find them fruitful. We hope to see you at SSBSE 2012 in Trento.

Myra Cohen
Mel Ó Cinnéide

Organization

Organizers

General Chair

Phil McMinn   University of Sheffield, UK

Program Chairs

Mel Ó Cinnéide	University College Dublin, Ireland
Myra Cohen	University of Nebraska-Lincoln, USA

Graduate Student Track Chair

Westley Weimer   University of Virginia, USA

Local Arrangements Chair

László Vidács   University of Szeged, Hungary

Industry Chair

Sigrid Eldh   Ericsson

Publicity Chairs

Mathew Hall	University of Sheffield, UK
Gregory Kapfhammer	Allegheny College, USA
Tanja Vos	Universidad Politécnica de Valencia, Spain

SSBSE Steering Committee

Mark Harman (Chair)	University College London, UK
Giuliano Antoniol	École Polytechnique de Montréal, Canada
Lionel Briand	Simula Research Labs, Norway
Myra Cohen	University of Nebraska-Lincoln, USA
Massimiliano Di Penta	University of Sannio, Italy
Spiros Mancoridis	Drexel University, USA
Phil McMinn	University of Sheffield, UK
Simon Poulding	University of York, UK
Joachim Wegener	Berner & Mattner, Germany

Program Committee

Enrique Alba	University of Málaga, Spain
Giuliano Antoniol	École Polytechnique de Montréal, Canada
Andrea Arcuri	Simula Research Laboratory, Norway
Rami Bahsoon	University of Birmingham, UK
Márcio Barros	Universidade Federal do Estado do Rio de Janeiro, Brazil
Leonardo Bottaci	University of Hull, UK
Jeremy Bradbury	University of Ontario Institute of Technology, Canada
Francisco Chicano	University of Málaga, Spain
Betty Cheng	Michigan State University, USA
John Clark	University of York, UK
Vittorio Cortellessa	University of L'Aquila, Italy
Massimiliano Di Penta	University of Sannio, Italy
Robert Feldt	Chalmers University of Technology, Sweden
Yann-Gaël Guéhéneuc	École Polytechnique de Montréal, Canada
Gregory Kapfhammer	Allegheny College, Pennsylvania, USA
Mark Harman	University College London, UK
Rob Hierons	Brunel University, UK
Colin Johnson	University of Kent, UK
Yvan Labiche	Carleton University, Canada
Spiros Mancoridis	Drexel University, USA
Mark O'Keeffe	Amartus Ltd., Ireland
Simon Poulding	University of York, UK
Xiao Qu	ABB Research, USA
Marek Reformat	University of Alberta, Canada
Marc Roper	University of Strathclyde, UK
Guenther Ruhe	University of Calgary, Canada
Jerffeson Souza	Universidade Estadual do Ceará, Brazil
Paolo Tonella	Fondazione Bruno Kessler - IRST, Italy
Laurence Tratt	Middlesex University, UK
Tanja Vos	Universidad Politecnica de Valencia, Spain
Joachim Wegener	Berner & Mattner, Germany
Tao Xie	North Carolina State University, USA
Shin Yoo	University College London, UK
Yuanyuan Zhang	University College London, UK

External Reviewers

Arthur Baars	Kevin Jalbert	Leandro Minku
Neelesh Bhattacharya	David Kelk	Aminata Sabane
Steven Davies	Segla Kpodjedo	Zohreh Sharafi
Latifa Guerrouj	William Langdon	

Sponsors

Table of Contents

Keynotes

Tutorials

Foundations of SBSE

Graduate Student Track

Concurrency and Models

Requirements and Planning

Software Testing

Comprehension, Transformation and Scalability

Posters

Search-Based Program Analysis

Andreas Zeller

Saarland University, Saarbrücken, Germany
zeller@cs.uni-saarland.de
http://www.st.cs.uni-saarland.de/zeller/

Abstract. Traditionally, program analysis has been divided into two camps: Static techniques analyze code and safely determine what cannot happen; while dynamic techniques analyze executions to determine what actually has happened. While static analysis suffers from overapproximation, erring on whatever could happen, dynamic analysis suffers from underapproximation, ignoring what else could happen. In this talk, I suggest to systematically generate executions to enhance dynamic analysis, exploring and searching the space of software behavior. First results in fault localization and specification mining demonstrate the benefits of search-based analysis.

Keywords: program analysis, test case generation, specifications.

1 The Two Faces of Program Analysis

Program analysis is a problem as old as programming. How can we assert that a program has a specific property? This is *the* central issue in areas like software verification and validation (be it symbolic, concrete, or casual), but also in daily tasks like debugging, program understanding or reengineering. Traditionally, program analysis has been divided into two camps:

Static analysis. infers software properties *symbolically*—that is, just from the code and the code alone. Static analysis requires that all source code be known (or at least accurately be summarized). It is also limited by the halting problem (which states there is no universal method that could predict software behavior), and by the daunting complexity of large systems. As any symbolic method, it must abstract away from details that may compromise the desired property. Still, if all these demands are met, it is a terrific technique: *If* static analysis shows the absence of a property, then this is universally true. On the other hand, static analysis may also err on the positive side and flag the presence of properties which are not true; such false positives are caused by conservative overapproximation.

Dynamic analysis. is different in all central aspects. It is concerned with a finite set of concrete *program runs,* rather than the potentially infinite set of symbolic analysis. It requires that the code in question be executable, but does not require its source. Complexity is not so much an issue, as its runtime

M.B. Cohen and M. Ó Cinnéide (Eds.): SSBSE 2011, LNCS 6956, pp. 1–4, 2011.

is proportional to execution time. It covers all abstraction layers, from the GUI down to the bare circuits. But where static analysis overapproximates, dynamic analysis *underapproximates*: Whatever it finds only applies to the runs observed. If dynamic analysis detects a problem, then this is real; but it may easily miss the one single run with the devastating error.

2 Making Program Analysis More Precise

Increasing the precision of static analysis and the recall of dynamic analysis is a recurrent theme in program analysis:

- The precision of *static analysis* can be improved by adding improved symbolic reasoning tools such as theorem provers or constraint solvers; such tools also benefit from programmer annotations on types or pre- and post-conditions. Likewise, we can make the analysis more control-sensitive, more pointer-sensitive, and in particular more interprocedural.
- The precision of *dynamic analysis* can be improved by adding more executions to investigate. The higher the variance in these executions, the more to learn from. In testing, for instance, the more execution aspects we cover, the higher our chance of triggering a bug; this is why we have so many criteria by which to design tests.

As increases in computational power allow more and more cycle-consuming analyses, we can thus always increase the precision of static analysis. For dynamic analysis, being concrete and therefore precise as can be, we do not have such an option. What we can do, though, is *increase the number of observed runs*. This is where *search-based techniques* come into play.

Traditionally, search-based techniques have been mostly applied to *search-based testing*. Here, the typical aim is to generate an input that would reach a specific point in the program, and thus help to achieve program coverage. The distance between the covered lines and the target point becomes part of a *fitness function* which guides the search towards the covering input. In the past decade, search-based test generation has made tremendous advances; together with its symbolic counterpart, concolic testing, it now allows for obtaining large coverage of real systems automatically.

When we are *generating* runs rather than *observing* runs, we can increase recall of properties (including bugs) at will. However, we also run the risk of generating *nonsensical* executions—and learning from nonsense generates nonsense. If our test generator feeds a NULL pointer into a function that does not expect one, we can make the function crash. Unless that function is visible to third parties, though, this may not be a real problem, as we could easily determine that no caller of that function actually passes NULL. Hence, generated runs may reduce false negatives, but do so by introducing false positives.

Generating nonsensical runs can be avoided by providing a specification of valid inputs; this is the base of *model-driven testing*. But where are we going to get the specifications from? If the tester writes it, how are we going to assess its quality—and find bugs in the model?

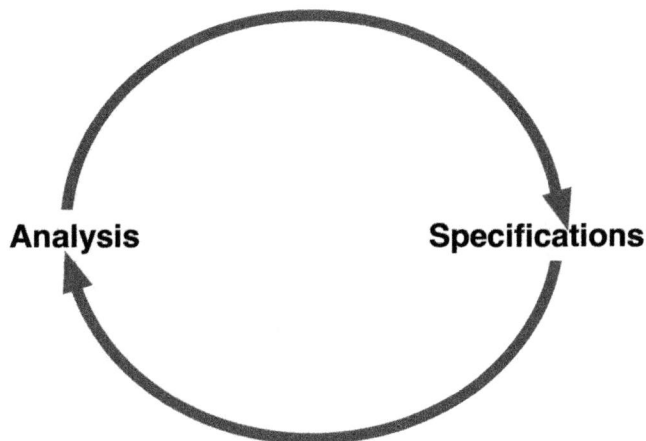

Fig. 1. How Specifications and Analysis depend on each other

3   A Virtuous Cycle

The recent decade has not only made tremendous progress in test case generation, but also in *mining specifications*—that is, extracting models of software behavior from systems that are precise enough to serve as specifications. The precision of specification mining strongly depends on the precision of its underlying analysis—when mining statically, the inferred models will overapproximate behavior; when mining dynamically, the models will underapproximate behavior.

While the models thus depend on the precision of the underlying analysis, the precision of the analysis depends on the presence of precise models. We thus get a circular dependency, sketched in Figure 1.

This cycle is not vicious, it is *virtuous*. We can improve our analysis by mining specifications, and we can improve our specifications by more precise analysis. The analysis would focus on aspects not yet covered by the specification, and the resulting findings (or executions) would then enrich the existing specification. With every iteration, we learn more and more about our system, systematically exploring program behavior by a series of targeted analyses—or, in the case of dynamic analysis, simple executions. This *explorative* way of reasoning about programs is neither inductive nor deductive; its feedback cycle makes it *experimental* instead.

In a way, this cycle is an instance of the *scientific method*[1] where we search for a theory that explains some aspect of the universe. When the theory is sufficiently refined, it becomes a predictive model for software behavior—and hopefully precise enough to overcome both the imprecision of static and the imprecision of dynamic analysis.

---

[1] The term "scientific method" may sound overblown for a basic technique that three-year old children use to explore the world—but it is the term used by sociologists to characterize experimental research, and an experimental approach it certainly is.

4   More on the Topic

In this invited talk, I will be referring to a number of recent research results that implement the above cycle, mining specifications and generating tests at the same time. Most important is the work by Dallmeier et al. [Dal10] which leverages test case generation to systematically enrich specifications; however, Fraser's work on generating oracles [Fra10] uses search-based testing to systematically infer and refine oracles for test cases; in his latest work [Fra11], he even shows how to extend this towards *parameterized* unit tests, going from concrete values to symbolic specifications. None of this works can yet claim to come up with full-fledged specifications that would always be immediately be usable as such. In two position papers [Zel10, Zel11], I have described some of the obstacles that lie ahead of us, and show how to overcome them using a series of real-life examples.

For being in its infancy, the combination of search-based test case generation and program analysis (or in short "search-based analysis") already has produced impressive results. All in all, it would be a mistake to limit search-based approaches to testing alone—there is a whole wide field of hybrid analyses that could benefit from automatic experiments. Let's go and search for them!

References

[Dal10]   Dallmeier, V., Knopp, N., Mallon, C., Hack, S., Zeller, A.: Generating Test Cases for Specification Mining. In: Proc. ISSTA, Trento, Italy (July 2010), http://www.st.cs.uni-saarland.de/publications/details/dallmeier-issta-2010/

[Fra10]   Fraser, G., Zeller, A.: Mutation-driven Generation of Unit Tests and Oracles. In: Proc. ISSTA (2010), http://www.st.cs.uni-saarland.de/publications/details/fraser-issta-2010/

[Fra11]   Fraser, G., Zeller, A.: Generating Parameterized Unit Tests. In: Proc. ISSTA, Toronto, Canada (July 2011), http://www.st.cs.uni-saarland.de/publications/details/fraser-issta-2011/

[Zel10]   Zeller, A.: Mining Specifications: A Roadmap. In: Nanz, S. (ed.) The Future of Software Engineering. Springer, Zurich (2010), http://fose.ethz.ch/proceedings.html

[Zel11]   Zeller, A.: Specifications for free. In: Bobaru, M., Havelund, K., Holzmann, G.J., Joshi, R. (eds.) NFM 2011. LNCS, vol. 6617, pp. 2–12. Springer, Heidelberg (2011), http://dx.doi.org/10.1007/978-3-642-20398-5_2

Exploiting Decomposability Using Recombination in Genetic Algorithms: An Exploratory Discussion

Darrell Whitley

Colorado State University, Fort Collins, CO 80524

Abstract. On certain classes of problems, recombination is more effective if the parents that are being recombined share common subsolutions. These common subsolutions can be used to decompose the recombination space into linearly independent subproblems. If a problem can be decomposed into k subproblems, a single greedy recombination can select the best of 2^k possible offspring. The idea of exploiting decomposability works well for the Traveling Salesman Problem, and appears to be applicable to other problems such as Graph Coloring. For Search Based Software Engineering, these ideas might be useful, for example, when applying Genetic Programming to fix software bugs in large programs. Another way in which we might achieve decomposability is by exploiting program modularity and reoccurring program patterns.

Keywords: Traveling Salesman Problem, Generalized Partition Crossover, Search Based Software Engineering, Graph Coloring, Automatic Bug Repair.

1 Introduction

Historically, genetic algorithms have emphasized recombination as the dominant operator for exploiting structure in the search space, while mutation was thought to be a background operator that helped to maintain diversity. Such a view is, of course, highly simplistic. And these days, such a view is perhaps antiquated. John Holland's original theory used hyperplane sampling to explain how genetic algorithms could yield a robust search [?]. Over the last ten years, both theory and practice has moved away from the idea that genetic algorithms work largely by hyperplane sampling. On the practice side, it is very common to see genetic algorithms that use very small population sizes. This runs counter to the idea that hyperplane sampling is important, because large population are required to sample hyperplanes in any reliable way. Furthermore, the development of

---

⋆ This effort was sponsored by the Air Force Office of Scientific Research, Air Force Materiel Command, USAF, under grant number FA9550-08-1-0422. The U.S. Government is authorized to reproduce and distribute reprints for Governmental purposes notwithstanding any copyright notation thereon.

M.B. Cohen and M. Ó Cinnéide (Eds.): SSBSE 2011, LNCS 6956, pp. 5–15, 2011.

algorithms such as Covariance Matrix Adaptation Evolution Strategies (CMA-ES) have resulted in a new breed of evolutionary algorithms that are far more effective than genetic algorithm on parameter optimization problems [?] [?].

Nevertheless, there are still some areas where genetic algorithms work very well, such as the domain of resource scheduling, and where recombination can greatly accelerate search. Genetic algorithms have also been successfully used to generate new best known solutions to very large Traveling Salesman Problems. But in such domains, it is even harder to put forth an argument that the performance of the genetic algorithm is in any way related to hyperplane sampling. So what is going on? One answer is that genetic algorithms are exploiting decomposability and modularity in the evaluation function.

Assume we have a solution S and a solution Z and we want to build a recombination function R such that $R(S, Z)$ generates a new candidate solution. Further assume that S and Z are *decomposable* relative to each other. This can be meant in a very strong sense, where both the solution and the evaluation function can be decomposed into k parts so that

$$f(S) = f(S_1) + f(S_2) + ... + f(S_k)$$

$$f(Z) = f(Z_1) + f(Z_2) + ... + f(Z_k)$$

and to be decomposable, the parts S_i and Z_i must be interchangeable. Note that if S and Z are decomposable with respect to each other, this need not imply that the overall problem can be decomposed into subproblems. If problems are strongly decomposable in the sense that the problems can be broken into interchangeable, linearly independent subproblems, then $2^k - 2$ new solutions can be generated from the two parent solutions.

We will start by looking at specific results for the Traveling Salesman Problem. We will show that this strong decomposability indeed occurs for instances of the TSP, and that the resulting recombination is extremely powerful. The remainder of this paper is exploratory and speculative. Can this kind of decomposability be found and exploited in other domains? Also, we might be able to define other, weaker kinds of decomposability.

Part of the popularity of the Traveling Salesman Problem (TSP) is that it is easily stated. Given n cities, and a cost matrix that gives the cost of traveling between and city A and B, the goal is to find a circuit that visits all of the cities and which minimizes the combined cost of the circuit. One of the reasons that the TSP is decomposable is that it displays an elementary landscape: for certain local search neighborhoods such as 2-opt and 2-exchange, the evaluation function is an eigenfunction of the graph Laplacian [?] [?] [?]. When we look for other problems that might be decomposable, it is then natural to look at other elementary landscapes for decomposability.

For current purposes, it is enough to note that a key characteristic of elementary landscapes is that the objective function is linear, but with feasibility constraints. The objective function is linear because the cost is just a linear combination of all of the costs associated with traveling from one city to the next.

The feasibility constraints reside in the fact that every city must be visited and visited only once. But is there some way to exploit this linearity?

In a sense, local search methods for the TSP have been exploiting this linearity for decades; one way this is done is by using "partial updates" to the evaluation function when moving from a solution to a neighboring solution. Let X represent the space of possible solutions for a TSP instance, in this case the set of all Hamiltonian circuits that visits all of the cities in a TSP. Let $x \in X$ denote one solution, and let $N(x)$ denote the set of solutions that are reachable in a single move from x using a local search neighborhood operator; thus, $y \in N(x)$ denotes a neighbor of solution x.

Consider the classic 2-opt neighborhood that cuts two edges in solution x, and breaking x into two segments. Then one of the segments is reversed, and the segments are reattached. Clearly, if we have already computed $f(x)$ then this allows for a partial update where

$$f(y) = f(x) - w_{i,j} - w_{q,r} + w_{i,q} + w_{j,r}$$

where $w_{i,j}$ and $w_{q,r}$ are the weights associated with the edges that are cut when a solution is broken into two segments, and $w_{i,q}$ and $w_{j,r}$ are the edges used to reattach the two segments.

So far, this is common knowledge about basic properties of the 2-opt neighborhood operator that is typically used to the define an $O(n^2)$ local search neighborhood for the TSP. But when we exploit this kind of partial evaluation, what we really have done is a linear decomposition of the evaluation function. The two segments are two linearly independent partial solutions, which are then reassembled in a new way.

From this, however, we want to ask three questions:

1) Can recombination also exploit linearly independent partial solutions for the Traveling Salesman Problem? The answer to this question is yes. In this case, the decomposition happens both naturally and easily and the resulting operator is surprisingly powerful. In fact, the resulting operator is able to "tunnel" between local optima and "filter" solutions: recombination can take two locally optimal solutions, decompose them and then reassemble them to generate thousands, even millions of other local optima in $O(n)$ time without doing any additional search.

2) Can similar recombination operators be developed for other problem domains? We will look at Graph Coloring, which also displays an elementary landscape, as well as a neighborhood with a partial update; again we find the problems is decomposable, but the decomposition is (perhaps) not as natural or easy as it is for the TSP. Or perhaps the right way of doing the decomposition has not been found.

3) Can these ideas be exported to the search based software engineering community? At this point, this question is largely unanswered, but we can try to leverage what we know about decomposability and how it can be exploited. We can also draw parallels between the idea of decomposability and modularity and "program patterns". The recent work of Forrest et al. [?,?,?] has

used evolutionary search methods to automatically repair bugs in large programs. These methods work largely by making small "mutations" to search for code changes that repair the software. But in some cases these mutations are not random. In some ways, their "mutation operator" might be seen as another form of modular recombination.

2   Generalized Partition Crossover for the TSP

We first present our recombination operator for the TSP. Let $G' = (V, E')$ represent the graph on which the Traveling Salesman Problem is defined, where V is the set of vertices that correspond to cities, and E' is the set of edges. We will assume G' is fully connected in the sense that there exists an edge for every possible pair of vertices; furthermore, there is an additional cost matrix that defines the cost (i.e., weight) associated with traversing any particular edge.

Assume we have been given two possible solutions, x_1 and x_2, and we want to built a recombination operator that is a function $R(x_1, x_2)$ such that the function returns a new Hamiltonian circuit constructed only using the edges found in solution x_1 and x_2. Furthermore, we will require that if an edge is found in both solution x_1 and x_2, then the new Hamiltonian circuit must also include that edge. If $R(x_1, x_2)$ cannot generate a new Hamiltonian circuit, it returns a flag indicating failure.

We construct a new graph $G = (V, E)$ where V is the (same) set of vertices (i.e., cities) of an instance of a TSP and $E \subset E'$ is the union of the edges found in x_1 and x_2. An edge in E is a *common* edge if it is found in both x_1 and x_2; an edge is an *uncommon* edge if it is in E but not a common edge. Common edges count as a single edge. Next, we partition G into two or more subgraphs; we attempt to find all partitions that cut only 2 edges (such a cut is said to have cost 2). One can easily prove that a cut of cost 2 must cut 2 common edges, otherwise the cost would be greater than 2. Thus a cut of cost 2 divides G into independent subproblems.

Generalized partition crossover (GPX) exploits all partitions of cost 2 in a single recombination in $O(N)$ time [?]. We recombine solutions by creating another subgraph of G, $G_u = (V, E_u)$, where V is the vertex set of the original TSP instance and E_u is the set of *uncommon* edges found in E. If a partition is possible then G_u will be composed of multiple disconnected and independent subgraphs. The topmost graph in figure 1 shows a graph G created from two parents. The edges from one parent are represented by solid lines and those from the other parent by dashed lines. In the bottommost set of subgraphs in figure 1 is the same graph with the common edges deleted (i.e., graph G_u); this breaks the graph into 4 subgraphs. Multiple partitions of this graph have cost 2, as shown by the heavy dark lines.

We use Breadth First Search on G_u to find each connected subgraph of G_u; this has $O(N)$ cost, because the degree of any vertex is at most 4, and each vertex is processed only once. Finding all the cuts of cost 2 breaks the graph G into k pieces which we call *partition components*; not all connected components

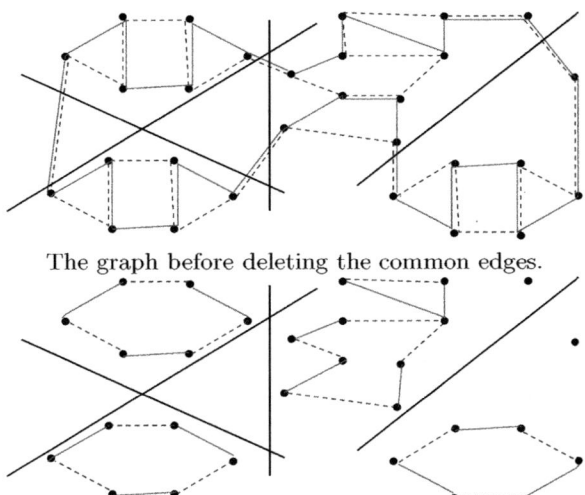

The graph before deleting the common edges.

The graph after deleting the common edges.

Fig. 1. An example of a graph G' created from the union of two parent tours. By deleting common edges, we break this graph into 4 independent subgraphs which are linearly independent.

in G_u yield feasible partition components because they may not yield cuts of cost 2. We then prove the following result [?]:

The GPX Theorem
Let graph G be constructed by unioning the vertices and edges found in two Hamiltonian Circuits for some instance of the TSP. If graph G can be separated into k partition components using only cuts of cost 2, then there are $2^k - 2$ possible distinct offspring. Every potential offspring inherits all the common edges found in the parents, and is composed entirely of edges found in the two parents. If the parents are locally optimal, then every partition component that is inherited is "piecewise" locally optimal.

Because the subpath solutions manipulated by GPX are linearly independent, GPX can be applied in a greedy fashion, selecting the best subsolution from each partition component. Solutions that are "piecewise" locally optimal are usually also true local optima. Therefore, the power of GPX is that it can "filter" large numbers of local optima in a single $O(N)$ recombination step.

GPX is not guaranteed to be feasible. In fact, it is important to realize that GPX almost always fails when it is used to recombine *random* solutions. GPX depends on the two solutions having common subsolutions. On the other hand, GPX is feasible with extremely high frequency when the solutions being recombined are local optima. Locally optima solution have more edges in common.

To ascertain the number of partition components available to GPX, we recombined 50 random local optima generated using 2-opt and 3-opt [?] [?] (see [?] for more details). The results are presented in Table 1. The problems att532,

Table 1. Average number of *partition components* used by GPX in 50 recombinations of random local optima found by 2-opt, 3-opt and LK-search

Instance	att532	nrw1379	u1817
2-opt	3.3 ± 0.2	3.2 ± 0.2	5.0 ± 0.3
3-opt	10.5 ± 0.5	11.3 ± 0.5	26.2 ± 0.7

nrw1379 and u1817 are from the TSPLIB. The number of cities in each instance is indicated by the numerical suffix. GPX was feasible in 100% of the cases when combining these local optima. The majority of offspring produced by GPX are also locally optima.

Clearly, 3-opt induces more partition components than 2-opt because it induces more subtours made up of common edges that can be used to partition the graph. When there are more than 10 partitions, recombination is filtering more than 1000 solutions, most of which are local optima. When there are more than 20 partitions, recombination is filtering more than 1 million solutions, most of which are local optima. GPX also displays excellent scaling: the larger the problem, the larger the number of partitions that are found.

2.1   GPX Experimental Results

We embedded GPX in a very simple genetic algorithm (GA) using a population of only 10. Every solution is improved (when possible) using 1 pass of LK-Search as implemented in the Concord package [?]. Chained Lin-Kernighan (Chained-LK) is one of the better performing local search heuristics for the TSP [?]. We then compared the results to Chained-LK, which also uses exactly the same LK-Search with identical parameter settings. Chained-LK applies LK-search to a single tour, uses a double bridge move [?] to perturb the solution and then reapplies LK-search. Since the population size is 10, the GA+GPX uses 10 applications of LK-search each generation; therefore, Chained LK is allowed to do 10 double-bridge moves and 10 LK-search improvements for every generation executed by the GA+GPX. Both algorithms call LK-search exactly the same number of times. Table 2 lists the average percentage of the cost of the minimum tour found compared to the cost of the global optimum for each problem instance. The GA+GPX was allowed to run for 100 generations in these experiments.

GA+GPX yields better results on all of the problems except nrw1379. This is remarkable because the Hybrid GA must optimize 10 solutions and the best solution must be optimized 10 times faster than Chained-LK to obtain a better result with the same effort. If each algorithm is run longer, the performance of GA+GPX is increasingly better than Chained LK. The last column of Table 2 (SOLVED) shows how many times out of 50 attempts that each method finds the global optimum after 1010 calls to LK-search.

The advantage of this approach is that GPX can be used to recombine solutions generated by any other methods. The disadvantage of GPX is that it never generates new edges, it only exploits the edges found in the current population.

Table 2. Columns marked 10 to 50 show the average percentage of the cost of the minimum tour found above the globally optimal cost averaged over 500 experiments using Chained LK and GA+GPX. SOLVED shows how often each algorithm found an optimal solution.

Generation $\longrightarrow$		10	20	50	100
Instance	Algorithm	110 LK calls	210 LK calls	510 LK calls	SOLVED
att532	GA+GPX	0.18 ± 0	0.12 ± 0	0.07 ± 0	26/50
	Chained-LK	0.21 ± 0.01	0.13 ± 0	0.08 ± 0	16/50
nrw1379	GA+GPX	0.48 ± 0	0.34 ± 0	0.23 ± 0	1/50
	Chained-LK	0.46 ± 0.01	0.32 ± 0	0.19 ± 0	1/50
rand1500	GA+GPX	0.52 ± 0.01	0.36 ± 0	0.22 ± 0	12/50
	Chained-LK	0.54 ± 0.01	0.39 ± 0.01	0.25 ± 0	2/50
u1817	GA+GPX	1.26 ± 0.01	0.95 ± 0.01	0.63 ± 0.01	1/50
	Chained-LK	1.61 ± 0.02	1.19 ± 0.01	0.83 ± 0.01	0/50

So another method is needed to generate high quality solutions that contain edges not found in the current population.

One thing that our experiments have clearly demonstrated is this: random mutations are hopelessly inefficient. We have not been able to accelerate search using random mutations. GPX requires high quality solutions with shared common subsolutions that partition the problem in order to be effective.

3   Graph Coloring and Tunneling

How can we apply the concept of decomposition to graph coloring? Technically we are referring to Graph Vertex Coloring.

In the case of the TSP, the partitions we used were a form of "edge separator" of the graph G created by unioning two solutions. To translate GPX to graph coloring, we are exploring the use of a "vertex separator" of the graph G. We want to retain the exponential leverage from this decomposition: we would like to decompose multiple solutions into k independent subsolutions so we can generate the best of $2^k - 2$ possible solutions.

Assume we can divide the vertices in a graph denoted by G into three mutually exclusive subsets, A, B, and C such that the vertices in A only have edges that connect to vertices in the sets A and C, and the vertices in B only connect to vertices in the sets B and C. If we use C to separate graph G, then the coloring of subgraph A and subgraph B will be independent of each other. Typically, we would like for the size of set C to be minimal. Finding a minimal separator of an arbitrary graph is NP-hard.

Lipton and Tarjan [?] have a constructive method for finding separators in planar graphs. Spectral methods have also been used that extract the second eigenvector from the Laplacian form of the adjacency matrix of the graph. Leighton and Rao used flow-based methods for finding separators [?]. However, we do not require that the separator be minimal or balanced. So clustering methods can also be used to find graph separators. Some types of graphs have good recursive separators (planar graphs, circuit layouts, social networks, and frequency assignment problems). Some types of graphs (e.g., hypercubes) do not have good separators.

Graph separators will clearly give a linear decomposition we are seeking. This decomposition is illustrated in Figure 2. Assume a graph can be broken into subgraphs A, B, C, where C is a separator. If we are given two solutions, and C has a common subsolution, then the solutions for subgraph A and B can be exchanged. The bottom graph in Figure 2 shows the graph broken into subgraph A1, A2, B1 and B2 with the separators being C, D1 and D2. Given two solutions, if subgraphs C, D1 and D2 have a common solution, then subgraphs A1, A2, B1 and B2 can be exchanged, generating up to $2^4 - 2 = 14$ new solutions from the two parents. We can also again be greedy, and only pick the best solution for each subgraph.

Graph Coloring poses several challenges however. For any coloring, we can produce another coloring that is functionally the same by permuting the colors. This means that there is a color matching problem. This is particularly problematic when solutions are only similar, with some common subsolutions, but also subsolutions that are different.

Some preliminary results suggests it might be hard to find common subsolutions that are also graph separators. One solution might be to *force* a common subsolution over a graph separator before recombination. But it is still too soon to say how best to exploit decomposability in Graph Coloring.

4   Questions for Search Based Software Engineering

One of the nice things about problems such as the Traveling Salesman Problem and Graph Coloring is that they have simple but powerful constraints. These are also highly regular problems.

At first glance, there might seem to be little that is simple or regular about problems in search based software engineering. It might also seem futile to hope that a problem might be decomposed in such a way that the evaluation function is a linear combination of subfunctions. But there could be weaker forms of decomposition that are still useful.

On the Traveling Salesman Problems, we have found that random mutations are useless in combination with the GPX operator. This is because GPX can assemble high quality solutions from high quality components. But random mutations cause exactly what one would expect: regression toward the mean, and lower quality solutions. A interesting line of research would be to explore constructive methods that build high quality solutions, but also introduce new diversity that can be exploited by recombination operators such as GPX. This question can also transfer to the field of Search Based Software Engineering.

An interesting example of this occurs in the work of Weimer and Forrest [?,?,?] and colleagues on automatic program repair using a form of genetic programming. The evaluation function takes the form of test cases. Negative test cases that cause the original program to fail are needed. And positive test cases

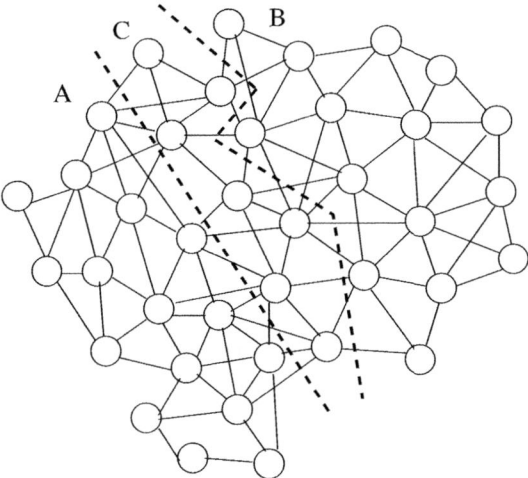

The graph showing a separator C.

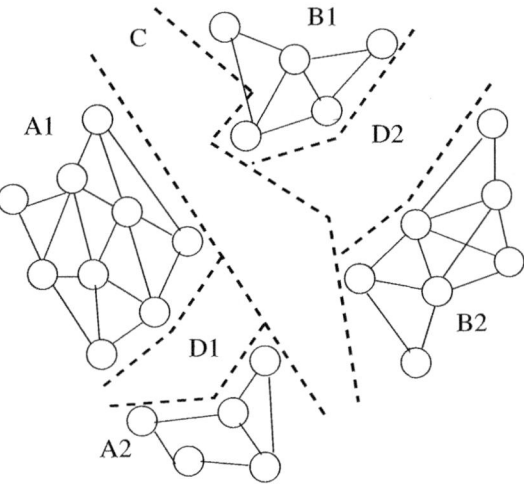

The graph showing another separator that breaks the problem into multiple linearly independent subproblems.

Fig. 2. By exploiting graph separation, we can break this graph into 4 independent subgraphs. From 2 solutions, we can potentially generate up to 16-2, or 14 new solutions.

that can be used to check that other functionality is preserved after the repair are also needed.

What is interesting is how "mutations" are made in the program that is to be repaired. Changes are only made at the statement level, and operators act on Abstract Syntax Trees (AST). The authors then make two key innovations:

First, we restrict the algorithm so that all variations introduced through mutation and crossover reuse structures in other parts of the program. Essentially, we hypothesis that even if a program is missing important functionality (e.g., a null check) in one location, it likely exhibits the correct behavior in another location, which can be copied and adapted to address the error. Second, we constrain the genetic operations of mutation and crossover to operate only on the region of the program that is relevant to the error, specifically the AST nodes on the execution path that produces the faulty behavior. [?]

So the mutations that are being used are not random. And the locations of the mutations are not random. Let statement s represent a statement in the section of program that is to be modified; let s' be a statement from another section of the code. A statement can be deleted ($s \leftarrow \{\}$); a statement can be inserted after another statement ($s \leftarrow \{s; s'\}$); or statements can be swapped ($s \leftarrow s'$ and $s' \leftarrow s$).

An extremely interesting question is how s and s' are selected. The most widely cited publications on this work ([?,?,?]) are relatively short summary papers that do not provide a great deal of detail on the selection of s and s'. Obviously, s and s' must be different. Nevertheless, it seems reasonable that they must also be similar in structure and function if we accept the hypothesis that a program missing functionality in one location exhibits the correct behavior in another location. So a selection progress that allow some randomness, but which is biased toward the selection of statements with similar structure would seem to be useful.

The point is that mutations should not be completely random. One might also argue that the mutations that perform "swaps" are not really mutations at all, but a form of localized recombination that exploits reoccurring patterns in programs. How the operator it is labeled is unimportant, but the idea of reusing patterns in programs is important. Finally, the use of the abstract syntax tree (AST) and the ability to swap statements represents a kind of weak decomposability. This idea might be used further to better exploit decomposability.

5   Conclusions

Generalize Partition Crossover (GPX) is the first operator for the Traveling Salesman Problem that can take two solutions, decompose the two solutions, and reassemble the parts (and use only those partial solutions) to create a new "offspring." It also has the ability to accelerate other heuristic search methods, because good solutions can be collected and mined for their components to more quickly find other high quality solutions. This strategy can be extended to other elementary landscapes, such a graph coloring. Whether the strategy can be executed in other domains in a "computationally competitive" fashion is yet to be determined.

What lessons from there results might be applied to search based software engineering? Certainly the use of decomposition strategies and the use of constructive methods to generate diversity instead of random mutation is one idea that might be borrowed. It might be true that the problems faced by the search based software engineering community might not be regular or decomposable. At the same time, an enormous amount of engineering is built on the use of linear approximations to solve problems that are not strictly linear. So even if we have approximate decomposability, this might be enough.

References

1. Holland, J.: Adaptation in Natural and Artificial Systems. University of Michigan Press (1975)
2. Hansen, N., Kern, S.: Evaluating the CMA evolution strategy on multimodal test functions. In: Proceedings of 8th International Conference on Parallel Problem Solving from Nature, Berlin, Germany, pp. 282–291 (2004)
3. Hansen, N., Ostermeier, A.: Adapting arbitrary normal mutation distributions in evolution strategies: the covariance matrix adaptation. In: Proc. of the 1996 IEEE Int. Conf. on Evolutionary Computation, pp. 312–317. IEEE Service Center, Piscataway (1996)
4. Whitley, D., Sutton, A.: Partial elementary landscapes. In: Proceedings of the Genetic and Evolutionary Computation Conference. ACM Press, New York (2009)
5. Grover, L.K.: Local search and the local structure of NP-complete problems. Operations Research Letters 12, 235–243 (1992)
6. Stadler, P.F.: Spectral landscape theory. In: Crutchfield, J., Schuster, P. (eds.) Evolutionary Dynamics - Exploring the Interplay of Selection, Neutrality, Accident, and Function. Oxford University Press, Oxford (2002)
7. Whitley, D., Hains, D., Howe, A.: A hybrid genetic algorithm for the traveling salesman problem using generalized partition crossover. In: Schaefer, R., Cotta, C., Kołodziej, J., Rudolph, G. (eds.) PPSN XI. LNCS, vol. 6238, pp. 566–575. Springer, Heidelberg (2010)
8. Croes, G.: A method for solving traveling-salesman problems. Operations Research, 791–812 (1958)
9. Lin, S., Kernighan, B.: An effective heuristic algorithm for the traveling-salesman problem. Operations Research, 498–516 (1973)
10. Applegate, D., Cook, W., Rohe, A.: Chained Lin-Kernighan for large traveling salesman problems. INFORMS Journal on Computing 15(1), 82–92 (2003)
11. Johnson, D.S., McGeoch, L.A.: The traveling salesman problem: A case study in local optimization. In: Aarts, E.H.L., Lenstra, J. (eds.) Local Search in Combinatorial Optimization, pp. 215–310. John Wiley and Sons Ltd, Chichester (1997)
12. Lipton, R., Tarjan, R.: A separator theorem for planar graphs. SIAM Journal of Applied Math. 36, 177–189 (1979)
13. Leighton, T., Rao, S.: An approximate max-flow min-cut theorem for uniform multicommodity flow problems with applications to approximation algorithms. In: Proceedings of IEEE Symposium on Foundations of Computer Science, pp. 422–431. IEEE Press, Los Alamitos (1988)
14. Weimer, W., Nguyen, T., Goues, C.L., Forrest, S.: Automatically finding patches using genetic programming. In: International Conference on Software Engineering (ICSE), pp. 364–374 (2009)
15. Forrest, S., Weimer, W., Nguyen, T., Goues, C.L.: A genetic programming approach to automated software repair. In: Genetic and Evolutionary Computation Conference (GECCO), pp. 947–954. ACM Press, New York (2009)
16. Weimer, W., Nguyen, T., Goues, C.L., Forrest, S.: Automatic program repair with evolutionary computation. Communications of the ACM 53(5), 109–116 (2010)

SBSE: Introduction and Motivation

Mark Harman

Software Systems Engineering Group,
Department of Computer Science,
University College London, UK
mark.harman@ucl.ac.uk

Abstract. This tutorial will provide a brief introduction to the field of
Search Based Software Engineering (SBSE) to (re)establish the context
in which we are working in this symposium. There is a paper in the proceedings of the symposium this year, entitled *Ten Years of Search Based
Software Engineering: A Bibliometric Analysis* by Fabrício Freitas and
Jerffeson Souza. This means that there will be no need for me to survey
the history of the subject in this talk. Rather, I will provide a very brief
introduction to the field of SBSE, summarising some of its advantages
and motivations, explaining why software is the ideal engineering material for optimisation algorithms and how SBSE can serve to (re)unify
apparently unconnected areas of Software Engineering.

M.B. Cohen and M. Ó Cinnéide (Eds.): SSBSE 2011, LNCS 6956, p. 16, 2011.
© Springer-Verlag Berlin Heidelberg 2011

Conducting and Analyzing Empirical Studies in Search-Based Software Engineering

Lionel Briand

Simula Research Labs, Norway
briand@simula.no

Abstract. Search-Based Software Engineering (SBSE) has shown itself to be a promising and practical approach to address many long-standing software engineering problems (e.g., test case generation, automatic bug fixing, release planning). They must, however, be carefully evaluated through empirical studies, for example in terms of cost-effectiveness and scalability. Indeed, in most cases, there exist alternatives to solutions based on search, and a careful comparison is typically needed in order to better understand under which conditions each technique can be expected to perform best.

However, because search algorithms are randomized (e.g., metaheuristic search) and many contextual factors can affect their outcome, designing, running, and analyzing such empirical studies is fraught with issues and potential threats to validity. This tutorial aims at providing a number of introductory and fundamental principles to guide the design, execution, and analysis of empirical studies in SBSE. Though such principles will in many cases apply to contexts other than SBSE, the tutorial will target issues that are specific to that realm of research and use representative examples from its literature.

M.B. Cohen and M. Ó Cinnéide (Eds.): SSBSE 2011, LNCS 6956, p. 17, 2011.

Ten Years of Search Based Software Engineering: A Bibliometric Analysis

Fabrício Gomes de Freitas and Jerffeson Teixeira de Souza

Optimization in Software Engineering Group (GOES.UECE)
State University of Ceará, Avenue Paranjana, 1700, Ceará, Brazil
fabriciogf.uece@gmail.com, jeff@larces.uece.br

Abstract. Despite preceding related publications, works dealing with the resolution of software engineering problems by search techniques has especially risen since 2001. By its first decade, the Search Based Software Engineering (SBSE) approach has been successfully employed in several software engineering contexts, using various optimization techniques. Aside the relevance of such applications, knowledge regarding the publication patterns on the field plays an important role to its understanding and identity. Such information may also shed light into SBSE trends and future. This paper presents the first bibliometric analysis to SBSE publications. The study covered 740 publications of the SBSE community from 2001 through 2010. The performed bibliometric analysis concerned mainly in four categories: Publication, Sources, Authorship, and Collaboration. Additionally, estimates for the next years of several publication metrics are given. The study also analyzed the applicability of bibliometric laws in SBSE, such as Bradfords and Lotka.

Keywords: sbse research analysis, bibliometric, authorship pattern.

1 Introduction

Optimization approaches have been applied to solve software engineering problems since the 1970s [1]. The early works were mostly concerned of solving software testing problems, and, in particular, test data generation. Until the 1990s, some sporadic works also used search techniques in software estimations and software management.

In 2001, the SEMINAL (Software Engineering using Metaheuristic INnovative ALgorithms) workshop was organized to discuss the wider use of optimization methods in the software engineering context [2]. Also in 2001, a special issue of the Information and Software Technology journal was devoted to the application of search methods in software engineering. A paper [3] stated the validity of the approach in the software engineering context and the term "Search Based Software Engineering" (SBSE) was coined to identify such approach. Since then, the SBSE approach has received increasing attention. The frequency and diversity of SBSE applications has increased significantly, and it is now considered a consolidated research field [4].

M.B. Cohen and M. Ó Cinnéide (Eds.): SSBSE 2011, LNCS 6956, pp. 18–32, 2011.

From 2001 to 2010, the number of works relating to the field has increased considerably. As an attempt to cover the state-of-the-art status of the field, survey papers on SBSE have been presented [4][5]. Beyond the information summarized in such works, mainly concerned on the applications and problems tackled, publication patterns of the field should also be analyzed. This sort of information may be used as a way to improve the understanding of the field, recognize its research community, and identify its trends, among others.

Given the importance of such aspects for the development of the SBSE field, this work presents the first bibliometric analysis of the area. The main contributions of this paper are to:

1. Provide facts about the growth of the field, regarding both publications and authors. For completeness' sake, the analysis is performed in a year-on-year basis, and includes the discussion of several related metrics.
2. Indicate rankings of the SBSE literature. This aspect includes the most cited papers, the most prolific authors, and the journal with most SBSE papers.
3. Show the distribution of the SBSE publications among the available sources. Additionally, an analysis of the number of publications in conference proceedings against the number of journal articles is performed.
4. Present and discuss the level of collaboration among researchers in the SBSE literature. The collaboration is analysed regarding the amount the authors in the papers, and also as in relation to the cooperation among different universities and countries. The level of participation of researches institute and companies is also analysed.
5. Verify the application of two bibliometric laws in SBSE: Bradford's and Lotka's laws.
6. Compare the behaviour of the field in its first official decade against the previous period (since 1970 until 2000), and supply estimates for the next years regarding some bibliometric metrics, based on the previous behavior.

The paper is organized as follows. Section 2 describes the methodology used in this study, including the definition of the categories analysed, as well as the data used. Section 3 shows the bibliometric analysis for the four categories analysed (Publications, Sources, Authorship, and Collaboration) in the 2001-2010 period. Section 4 presents and discusses the estimates for the next years of the area. Section 5 briefly compares the metrics for the decade 2001-2010 with publication patterns of the period before 2001. Finally, Section 6 discusses conclusions and states future works.

2   Methodology

The bibliometric analysis presented in this study is divided on four main segments. Each segment represents a group of statistics related to a bibliometric aspect. The segments are described on Section 2.1.

In Section 2.2, the data used for the study is explained, together with its source.

2.1   Segments

Publications. This category covers information about the SBSE published works. The number of publications of a research field is an important indicative of its development. The evolution of this amount through the years is also a significant figure. The most cited works are also presented and discussed.

Sources. One aspect related to the publications is the type of venue where the works are published. In this context, the distribution of the SBSE publications among sources such as conference proceedings, journals, books, etc., is analyzed. In addition, this category also examines the core journals of the field, i.e., the venues that published the most amounts of SBSE articles. This data is used to verify the Lotka's bibliometric law [6] of scientific productivity.

Authorship. Aside the works of a field, the researchers authoring these works should also be studied. In order to do this, the year by year amount of active, new and cumulative authors on SBSE is presented. The distribution of the number of works published by authors is used to evaluate the validity of the Bradford's bibliometric law [7] in the SBSE field. A ranking of the most prolific authors is also discussed.

Collaboration. The level of collaboration among SBSE authors is covered in this category. The analysis comprises two aspects: the number of authors per paper, and collaboration among groups. The cooperation among groups includes internal collaboration, when two or more groups in the same country collaborate in the paper, and external collaboration, when there are authors from more than one country.

2.2 Data Source

The source of the publications is one important aspect for a bibliometric analysis. One alternative is to use academic databases, but them may not include all the works from a field. For the SBSE field, this problem can be avoided by the use of the SBSE Repository from SEBASE [8], which is a tool that provides a comprehensive list of SBSE publications. Indeed, by covering works from different sources, it includes papers that may not appear in a particular database. The list is actively updated, including updates suggested by the SBSE community. Such repository is appropriate as source of information for this study, since it portrays the wider status of the field.

The inclusion of a work may take time. Then, more recent works may not appearr in the database. The publication data online in late 2010 covered 667 publications in 2001-2010. Those data were used for all the segments, but "Publications". For such segment, we were able to get an ongoing updated list in June 2011 with 740 works.

The repository is formed by a list of publications, and tools for search and ordering. For our analysis, scripts were used in order to extract the required information. Some information necessary for the study were not available in the repository. The citations data were collected for each work in Scopus and Google Scholar. Authors' affiliations were obtained by the related information in each work.

3 SBSE Bibliometric Analysis

3.1 Publications

The number of publications in a field is a central information of its development. Table 1 presents, on a year-on-year basis, the evolution of the number of SBSE publications. The cumulative amount by each year is also presented. The contribution of a year on the total amount and the growth of the quantity against the previous year are also indicated.

Table 1. Number of works in each year between 2001 and 2010, including cumulative amount

Year	Quantity	%	Growth	Cumulative	%	Growth
2001	24	3.24%	-	24	3.24%	-
2002	30	4.05%	25.00%	54	7.30%	125.00%
2003	37	5.00%	23.33%	91	12.30%	68.52%
2004	45	6.08%	21.62%	136	18.38%	49.45%
2005	54	7.30%	20.00%	190	25.68%	39.71%
2006	61	8.24%	12.96%	251	33.92%	32.11%
2007	83	11.22%	36.07%	334	45.14%	33.07%
2008	127	17.16%	53.01%	461	62.30%	38.02%
2009	126	17.03%	-0.79%	587	79.32%	27.33%
2010	153	20.68%	21.43%	740	100.00%	26.06%
2001-2010	740	100.00%	-	740	100.00%	-

As shown in Table 1, the quantity of works by year was continuously increasing since 2001. Indeed, in the first three years after 2001, for example, the growth rate between sequential years was higher than 20%. Also, significant growth rates of 36.07% and 53.01% are found in 2007 and 2008, respectively. In 2009 there was a negativegrowth of 0.79%. In 2010, the number of works published was 21.43% higher than the previous year (153 against 126). In addition, the works published in 2010 correspond to 20.68 of all works, being the first year in number of publications. This shows that the field progress was still in considerable development in 2010.

The cumulative amounts on the first years indicate that the SBSE community achieved the first hundred publications in 2004, i.e., three years after its formal creation. The next hundred publications level was reached only two years after 2004, in 2006. Then, the next hundred publications were achieved in 2007, i.e., only one year after the previous landmark. These findings are a way to indicate the acceleration on the number of SBSE publications in the period.

Table 1 indicates that the cumulative number of publications in 2007 was equivalent to 45.14% of the total. This means that more than half (54.86%) of the SBSE publications were published through 2008 and 2010. Therefore, more than 50% of the SBSE works were published in the last 30% years of the considered period, which indicates the concentration of the most advances in recent years.

A final analysis in Table 1 regards the cumulative growth acquired in 2010, which was of 26.06%. This figure is an additional indication that the SBSE field is still expanding at significant rates, even after 10 years.

Table 2 below presents a ranking of the most cited publications of the decade. The order in the list is set according to the citation count in Scopus. Additionally, the citations given by Google Scholar are also shown, in order to present a more complete citation scenario, given that Google Scholar cover publications such as books, chapters, thesis, technical reports, and other types of publication that are not present in academic databases. Since this bibliometric analysis is concerned with the time period until 2010, the data shown in Table 2 the citation statics until December 31th, 2010.

Table 2. The 15 most cited SBSE works, ordered by Scopus

Ref.	Authors	Work	Scopus	GS
[9]	McMinn, Phil	Search-based software test data generation: a survey	209	382
[10]	Wegner, J., Baresel, A. and Sthamer, H.	Evolutionary test environment for automatic structural testing	162	282
[11]	Michael, C., McGraw, G. and Schatz, M.	Generating software test data by evolution	158	298
[12]	Clarke, J. et al.	Reformulating software engineering as a search problem	90	149
[3]	Harman, M. and Jones, B.	Search-based software engineering	82	163
[13]	Harman, M. et al.	Testability transformation	77	122
[14]	Li. Z., Harman, M. and Hierons, R.	Search algorithms for regression test case prioritization	75	126
[4]	Harman, M.	The current state and future of search based software engineering	72	171
[15]	Mitchell, B. and Mancondris, S.	On the automatic modularization of software systems using the bunch tool	71	105
[16]	Dolado, J.	On the problem of the software cost function	71	128
[17]	Cohen, M. et al.	Constructing test suites for interaction testing	69	120
[18]	Tonella, P.	Evolutionary testing of classes	67	138
[19]	Greer, D. and Ruhe, G.	Software release planning: An evolutionary and iterative approach	65	119
[20]	Bagnall, A., Rayward-Smith, V. and Whittley, I.	The next release problem	63	91
[21]	Canfora, G. et al.	QoS-aware replanning of composite Web services	54	137

From the 15 works presented in Table 2, 7 are related to software testing, including the 3 most cited works. Among these 7 publications, the test data generation issue is covered in 4, including the most cited work [9]. This observation may be related to the higher amount of software testing works in the SBSE publications. Nonetheless, the fact represents the high force and impact of the software testing area in SBSE in general, and of test data generation inside software testing.

General works also occurs vastly among the most cited publications [10][4]. Additionally, the most cited work is a survey [9]. Another main publication area on Table 2 is requirement engineering [19][20].

3.2   Source

As cited in Section 22, the data of 2010 for the following segments is not complete. Nevetheless, the analysis represents the state of SBSE up to 2010 with some works of the year. In order to further improve the publication analysis presented in Section 3.1, this section shows the distribution of the works among different sources. Table 3 presents the amount of 2001-2010 works in five main publications types, and it also shows the percentage contribution of each type in relation to all publications. In Table 4, the two main sources are examined yearly.

Table 3. Number of works from 2001 through 2010 by publication type

Type	Proceeding	Journal	Book/Chapter	Tech Report	Thesis	Other
Amount	469	140	6	23	26	3
%	70.32%	20.99%	0.89%	3.45%	3.90%	0.45%

Table 4. Works in proceedings and journal, and its relation (2001-2010)

Year	2001	2002	2003	2004	2005	2006	2007	2008	2009	2010	01-10
Proceeding	8	24	33	30	38	33	63	80	89	71	469
Journal	16	3	2	7	11	18	16	32	22	13	140
Proceeding/ Journal	0.50	3.00	16.50	4.29	3.46	1.83	3.94	3.64	4.05	5.46	3.35

From Table 3, the source with more works published in the decade is conference proceedings (70.32%), followed by journals (20.99%). This preponderance of proceeding publications compared to journal articles is also observed in the Computer Science field as a whole [22]. The SBSE publication in books, including chapters, achieved only 6 works, which represents less than 1% (0.89%). This overall behavior is also in general consonant with the one presented in the overall Computer Science field [22]. The number of of works for technical reports and thesis, in the time span analyzed, were similar (3.45% and 3.90%, respectively).

The relation between the number of works published in conference proceedings and journals is a measure to be studied. In the decade under analysis, 2001 was the only year with this figure below 1.00, i.e., with more journal articles than proceedings papers. This result reflects the publication of the special issue of Information and Software Technology, in December 2001. In the subsequent years, the relation reached levels that, in general, were more than 2.00, with the exception of 2006 (1.83). In 2003, this measure got abruptly to more than 16.00. This observation was caused by the significantly increase of publication in conference in 2003 against 2002, which was not followed by articles in journals. From 2008 onwards, the values are increasing: 3.64, 4.05, 5.46; from 2008 to 2010, respectively. This trend is partially explained by the foundation of conferences dedicated to the area, which added a large number of papers. The specialized venues include the International Workshop on Search-Based Software Testing (SBST) in 2008, and the International Symposium on Search Based Software Engineering (SSBSE) in 2009.

Despite this predominance of proceedings publications, journal articles are generally taken as fundamental contributions to a field [22]. Thus, special attention to this publication type should be given. In Table 5, the top 11 journals with the most amounts of SBSE publications are presented.

As shown in Table 3, the top 3 journals are software engineering focused. Beyond that, the majority of the 11 journals are of software engineering. Aside general software engineering venues, as the top 3, journals of specific areas are also present, including software testing and requirements engineering. As a sign of the cross-disciplinarily of SBSE, journals of Operational Research and Soft Computing are also present. Among the venues on the ranking, three journals dedicated special issues to SBSE: Information and Software Technology (2001), Computers and Operations Research (2008), and Journal of Software Maintenance and Evolution (2008).

Table 5. Ranking of journals with the most number of SBSE publications

Journal	#	%
Information and Software Technology	23	16.43%
Journal of Systems and Software	12	8.57%
IEEE Transactions on Software Engineering	10	7.14%
Computers and Operations Research	7	5.00%
Software Testing, Verification and Reliability	5	3.57%
Applied Soft Computing	4	2.86%
IEEE Transactions on Reliability	4	2.86%
Information Sciences	4	2.86%
Journal of Software Maintenance and Evolution	3	2.14%
Requirements Engineering	3	2.14%
Soft Computing	3	2.14%

Table 6 shows the distribution of SBSE articles among journals. In this case, the data shows how many journals have published each number of papers.

Table 6. Number of journals that published each article amount

Article amount	23	12	10	7	5	4	3	2	1
Journals	1	1	1	1	1	3	3	14	34

By examining the data in Table 6, the Bradford's Law [7] is applied. This bibliometric law states that the journals that publish works from a field may be grouped in three categories, each with roughly a third of the publications. The relation among the number of journals in each group is estimated to be of $1:n:n^2$, which means that among groups it is necessary to look into exponentially more journals to find the same number of articles. The first group is composed by the core journals, i.e., the main venues for the field. The next group has journals with average number of papers. The last category, the long tail, is formed by several journals, each with few publications. From Table 6, the top three journals play as core journals, since they correspond to 45 articles, which is 32.14% of all. The next group is found in the next 12 journals (41 articles, or 29.28%). In order to represent the last articles, the 43 remaining journal are necessary. Then, the Bradford relation in SBSE is 3:12:43.

3.3 Authorship

Table 7 shows statistics regarding the number of publishing authors in the SBSE field. The "New" column shows the number of authors publishing for the first time in each year, considering the time span from 2001 to 2010. The percentage participation and growth of this aspect are also presented. The "Active" column refers to the amount of different authors publishing in a given year. Finally, the numerical relation between new and active authors is indicated.

The number of authors joining the SBSE community has significantly increased each year since 2001. Therefore, beyond the strong increase in the number of publications (as shown in Table 1), the number of new authors also firmly increased. The increase in the number of publications could be merely because of regular authors. Alternatively, in fact, more authors continue to publish SBSE works for the first time each year. Indeed, 2010 alone was responsible for more than 10% (12.32%) of the new authors in the decade. The renewing factor was even higher since 2008, with 17.25% in 2008 and 17.63% in 2009.

Table 7. Statistics for new and active authors per year (2001-2010)

Year	New	%	Growth	New/Works	Active	Growth	New/Active
2001	49	6.36%	-	2.04	49	-	1.00
2002	43	5.58%	-12.24%	1.43	60	22.45%	0.72
2003	54	7.00%	25.58%	1.46	83	38.33%	0.65
2004	48	6.23%	-11.11%	1.07	87	4.82%	0.55
2005	51	6.62%	6.25%	0.98	100	14.94%	0.51
2006	67	8.69%	31.37%	1.12	116	16.00%	0.58
2007	95	12.32%	41.79%	1.14	162	39.66%	0.59
2008	133	17.25%	40.00%	1.08	230	41.98%	0.58
2009	136	17.63%	2.26%	1.10	236	2.61%	0.58
2010	95	12.32%	-30.15%	1.07	168	-28.81%	0.57
2001-2010	771	100%	-	-	-	-	-

An additional study concerning the new authors is to analyze this aspect taking into account the number of works in each year. As expected, the highest value is found in 2001, since all authors, in the time span, are considered new in that year. The amount in general reduces through the years. An observation that must be highlighted is that in 2010, despite the fewer new authors, the average amount of new authors per works is similar to the presented in previous years. This also occurs in the relation between new and active authors: in 2010 there were less new authors, but they corresponded to 57% of the authors in that year, indicating the dynamism of the SBSE community.

In addition to the new authors, the number of active authors is also an aspect of interest. From Table 7, one can observe that this number has increased since 2001, with exception to 2010, when the number of active authors was 28.81% lower than in 2009. However, 2010 stands as the third year with most active authors, which is a sign of the yet strong recent activity of the SBSE field.

Using the information of new authors in each year given in Table 7, the cumulative amount per year can be calculated. The evolution of such statistic is presented in Figure 1. Until 2005, the cumulative amount achieved 245 (31.78%). This means that the last half of the decade was responsible for about 70% of the authors.

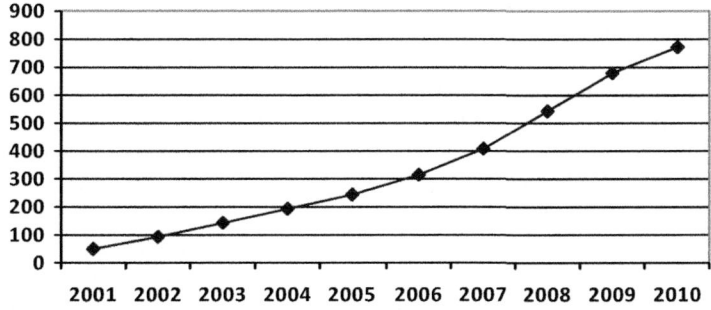

Fig. 1. Cumulative evolution of number of authors, between 2001 and 2010

In Table 8 below, the distribution of publications among authors is presented.

Table 8. Number of authors that published each number of works

Works	1	2	3	4	5	6	7	8	9	10	11	12	14	16	18	19	20	24	27	86
Authors	477	126	58	27	27	12	9	6	8	4	1	4	2	1	1	1	3	2	1	1

Authors who published only one work represent the larger group, formed of 477 researches (61.87% of the SBSE community). Researchers that published two works also add up to more than a hundred, being in total 126, or 16.34%. As the number of publication increases, in general the number of authors with that amount reduces. In fact, there is a bibliometric law to study this phenomenon. The Lotka's law indicates that the number of authors publishing n works is roughly $1/n^2$ of the amount that published one work. In fact, the exponent in the fraction is specific for each field, and also may vary over time, but number 2 is generally used. It should be highlighted that the law is only an estimate and its accuracy may depend on the scientific field under analysis and the considered time span.

As a result from Lotka's law, the expected number of authors with one publication is 60%. By the previous analysis, it can be observed that this roughly occurs in the SBSE field (61.87%). In addition, the number of authors with two publications is expected to be $(1/2^2)*60\%$, equals to 15%, which also can be considered valid for the SBSE community (16.34%). For three publications, the number of authors, according to Lotka's law, should be $(1/3^2)*60\%$, about 6.67%. In SBSE, there are 8.69% in this group. The number of authors with 4 publications, 27, is also cosistent to the expected value from Lotka's law (25). For 10 publications, the amount also nearly conforms to the law, with 4 authors ($1/10^2*60\%$ from 771). For authors with more publications, however, the Lotka's law does not apply. For 20 publications, for instance, the expected number of authors is 1, while there are 3 authors in SBSE.

Among the authors, a ranking of the most prolific ones can be formed. Table 10 indicates a list ordered with regard to the total number of publications, including conference works, journal articles, books chapters, etc. The percentage participation in relation to all SBSE publications is also given. In order to present more complete information, the amount and position of each author concerning only publications in conference proceedings and journal articles is also presented.

From Table 10, the most prolific author has participated in more than 10% (11.15%) of the SBSE publications. For the 2nd position, the percentage participation is of 3.50%, indicating a large gap between the 1st position and this one. On the other hand, from the 2nd spot onwards, the difference among the sequential positions is not so large, which indicates a smooth distribution among the authors. The first and second authors with most publications appear alone in their positions. That also happens with positions 5, 6, 7, and 10. In the other positions, some authors share the same spot: there are two authors in 3rd, three in 4th, two in 8th, and three in 9th.

Given the information in Table 10, it is possible to compare the main order, that takes into account all publications, with the specific ranking for conferences and journals. Aside from authors in 1st, 5th, and one in 9th, the spots of the authors differs among the different rankings. For instance, authors in 9th place in the total ordering appear in 3rd in journal articles.

A final analysis of Table 10 can be performed by taking information from Table 2, that concerns on the most cited publications. Among the 15 most cited publications, 10 have at least one of the most prolific authors shown in Table 9. If we consider the top 10 most cited publications, the participation of one of the most prolific authors achieves 8. This indicates that in SBSE there is a correlation between the groups of authors from the most cited publications and the most prolific authors group

Table 9. The ranking of SBSE authors with more than 10 publications in 2001-2010

Rank	Author	Works	%	Conference Proceedings (rank)	Journal Articles (rank)
1	Mark Harman	86	11.15%	61 (1)	20 (1)
2	Xin Yao	27	3.50%	19 (2)	4 (5)
3	John Clark	24	3.11%	15 (5)	7 (2)
3	Robert Mark Hierons	24	3.11%	16 (4)	7 (2)
5	Andrea Arcuri	20	2.59%	15 (5)	1 (8)
5	Joachim Wegener	20	2.59%	15 (5)	5 (4)
5	Massimiliano Di Penta	20	2.59%	17 (3)	3 (6)
8	Phil McMinn	19	2.46%	15 (5)	4 (5)
9	Giuliano Antoniol	18	2.33%	16 (4)	2 (7)
10	Enrique Alba	16	2.08%	13 (6)	3 (6)
11	Andre Baresel	14	1.82%	11 (7)	3 (6)
11	Francisco Chicano	14	1.82%	11 (7)	3 (6)
13	Günther Ruhe	12	1.56%	5 (12)	6 (3)
13	Shin Yoo	12	1.56%	7 (10)	2 (7)
13	Spiros Mancoridis	12	1.56%	9 (8)	3 (6)
13	Stefan Wappler	12	1.56%	9 (8)	1 (8)
17	Per Kristian Lehre	11	1.43%	7 (10)	1 (8)

3.4 Collaboration

After the previous study regarding the authorship in SBSE, the cooperation among the authors is discussed in this section. Firstly, Table 10 shows statistics about the number of authors per paper. Papers with more than five authors were grouped together with the ones with five authors. The yearly evolution of the percentage participation of each group is shown in Figure 2.

Table 10. Authorship pattern in the period 2001-2010

Authors	1	2	3	4	5+
# Works	87	230	209	101	40
%	13.04%	34.48%	31.33%	15.14%	6.00%

Considering the decade 2001-2010, the predominant group of collaboration is the one with 2 authors (34.48%). The next group, with 3 authors, has a similar rate (31.33%). The number of publications with one author, 87, corresponds to 13.04%,

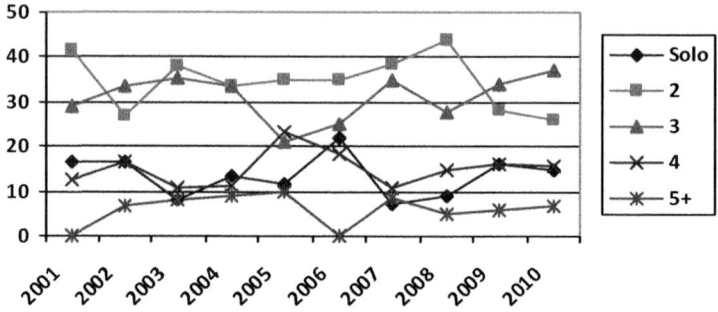

Fig. 2. Authorship percentage evolution per year

which indicates a collaboration rate of 86.96%, i.e., nearly 87% of SBSE publications have more than one author. In Computer Science, this collaboration rate reached 86% [23]. From Figure 2, the predominance of papers with 2 authors is observed through the years. Indeed, it happened in seven of the ten years. However, since 2008 the group with 2 authors is in a trend of reduction, while, simultaneously, the group with 3 authors is increasing. With the exception of 2007, the group with 5 or more author is the small one in the years.

Table 11 shows the collaborative level, i.e., the average of authors per paper, in each year, including the average for the decade. For better visualization of the evolution, the data are also presented in Figure 3.

Table 11. Collaborative level (CL) of SBSE, i.e., the average amount of authors per paper

Year	2001	2002	2003	2004	2005	2006	2007	2008	2009	2010	01-10
CL	2.37	2.80	2.89	2.73	2.86	2.40	2.78	2.64	2.71	2.75	2.70

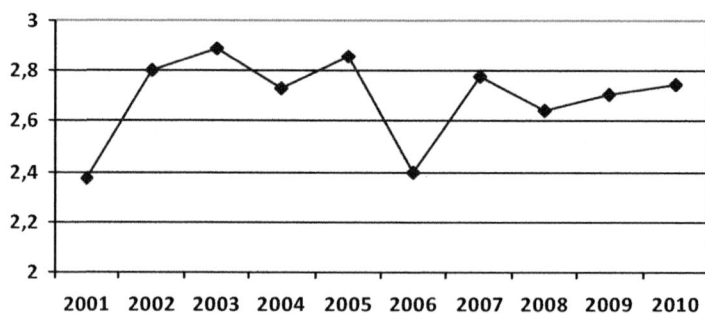

Fig. 3. Evolution of SBSE collaborative level by year (2001-2010)

As show in Table 11 and Figure 3, the average number of authors per paper strongly increases between 2001 and 2002. Until 2005, the value remained near 2.8, and in 2006 reduced to about the same level of 2001. Given the increase trend of papers with 3 authors alongside the decrease of papers with 2 authors since 2008, the average amount shows an increase trend since 2008.

Table 12. Collaboration aspect regarding authors' affiliation

Year	External	% year	Internal	% year	Out Univ.	% year
2001	1	4.17%	6	25.00%	6	25.00%
2002	3	10.00%	7	23.33%	7	23.33%
2003	4	10.81%	9	24.32%	6	16.22%
2004	8	17.78%	13	28.89%	8	17.78%
2005	6	11.54%	8	15.38%	3	5.77%
2006	7	11.67%	15	25.00%	8	13.33%
2007	12	14.46%	20	24.10%	9	10.84%
2008	22	17.89%	28	22.76%	16	13.01%
2009	20	15.38%	25	19.23%	17	13.46%
2010	6	6.82%	16	18.18%	6	6.82%
2001-2010	89	11.54%	147	19.02%	86	11.10%

The Table 12 above shows statistics about collaboration concerning authors' affiliations. The cooperation among countries occurred in more than 10% of the papers, with exception for 2001. In 2004 and 2008, the rate achieved more than 17%. Aside the percentage participation, it is important to highlight the increase in the amount of such collaboration throughout the years. The internal cooperation, i.e., with authors in different institutions of the same country, has achieved, except in 2005, more than 20%, which shows a strong internal collaboration. The other aspect counts the participation of research institutes outside universities and software companies. From Table 13, the percentage evolution of this cooperation shows that in general the rates in the last five years are lower than in the previous years: in 2001-2005, the value range from 5% to 25%; among 2006 and 2010 the rate varies from 6% to 13%. In the decade as a whole, the percentage is more than 10% (11.10%).

4 Further Analysis

In Section 4.1, we compare measures from SBSE between the period pre-2001 (1976-2000) with the 2001-2010 decade. In 4.2 estimates for the next five years are given. Due to size constraints, only some statistics are covered in this section.

4.1 SBSE Pre-2001

Table 13 regards authorship in SBSE pre-2001. During the 25 years on that period, the number of SBSE authors reached 122 against the 771 authors in the 2001-2010 decade (Table 7). The CL column indicates the collaborative level, i.e., the average number of authors per paper. The value for the pre-2001 period, 2.52, is similar to 2.70 for 2001-2010 (Table 11). In the number of authors per paper, an interesting change can be observed. Before 2001, the predominance was of 1 author (27.91%), followed by 2 authors per paper (26.74%). In the 2001-2010 time span (Table 10), the most predominant groups are "2 authors" (34.48%), and "3 authors" (31.33%).

Table 13. Authorship measures for SBSE pre-2001 (1976-2000)

Ative Authors	CL	Amount of authors per paper				
		1	2	3	4	5+
122	2.52	27.91%	26.74%	22.09%	17.44%	5.81%

4.1 Estimates

The estimation used the linear trend approach, since it was successful to estimate the values for 2010 based on the data from the previous years. Projections for the next 5 years of the number of active authors, number of works, and relation between conference proceeding papers and journal articles (C/J) are given in Table 14.

Table 14. Estimates of number of works and active authors for 2011-2015

Year	2011	2012	2013	2014	2015
Authors	179	191.9	204.8	217.7	230.6
Works	94.4	101.5	108.6	115.7	122.8
C/J	4,17	4,08	3,99	3,89	3,80

As shown in Table 14, the number of active authors is expected to achieve 200 by 2013. Such landmark occurred in 2008 and 2009 (Table 7), but the decreased observed in 2010 (168) reflects on the trend. Based on the estimations, 2011 is to have less than 100 publications. The low behavior in 2010 also explains this landmark in 2011. The relation between conference and journal publications has a decreasing trend. This indicates that the field is expected to have relatively more publications in journals.

5 Conclusions

SBSE publications have, in general, continuously increased since 2001. In 2009 however, there was a negative growth compared to 2008. In relation to all works published in 2001-2009, 2010 had a cumulative growth of 26.06%, which indicates the recent development on the field. Other sign of that expansion is that more than 50% of the publications in the decade were from the last three years. Among the most cited works, software testing is the predominant area. Among software testing works, the data generation problem stands as the most cited issue in SBSE.

Conference proceedings are the most common type of publication in SBSE. In the decade 2001-2010, the rate achieved 70.32%. Publication in books and chapters are weakly represented. The relation between conference proceeding and journal articles was 3.35 in the decade, i.e., in average 3.35 conference works for each journal article. The relation increased in the last three years of the decade. In journals that most published SBSE papers, there is a predominance of software engineering venues, but journals of operational research and soft computing are also present. The Bradford's Law seems to apply to SBSE, and the core journals for SBSE was identified as the top three venues.

The joining of new authors in SBSE is still significant. The year 2010 was responsible for 12% of the total in the decade. In the last five years of the decade, a rate of about 0.58 was observed in the participation of new authors in each year. The Lotka's Law was found to be applicable to the SBSE field in most cases. A correlation between the most prolific authors and authors with the most cited papers was also found.

The predominant number of author per paper in 2001-2010 is two. However, the evolution through the years indicates the reduction of that group and the ascending of papers with 3 authors. The collaboration among countries was observed in 11.54% of the papers. Cooperation among affiliations inside countries reached 19%, indicating the high level of cooperation in the SBSE field. The presence of authors from research institutes and software companies achieved 11.10% of publications in 2001-2010.

The comparison of the decade against the pre-2001 period shows that the predominant group of authors per paper went from 1 to 2. The collaboration level increased from 2.52 to 2.70, indicating more collaboration in 2001-2010. Estimates for the next 5 years using the linear trend show the expected continuous expansion of the field. Additionally, relatively, more journal articles are expected to be published.

Future works regard the coverage of more recent works uncovered in the last three segments, mainly from 2010. Further research includes bibliometric analysis specific on SBSE areas, such as software testing or requirements engineering. The identification of the most collaborative authors and countries may also be addressed.

Acknowledgments. The authors would like to thank Mark Harman for directing the SEBASE Project, and Yuanyuan Zhang for the organization of the SEBASE SBSE Repository.

References

1. Miller, W., Spooner, D.L.: Automatic Generation of Floating-Point Test Data. IEEE Transactions on Software Engineering 2(3), 223–226 (1976)
2. Harman, M., Jones, B.F.: The SEMINAL Workshop: Reformulating Software Engineering as a Metaheuristic Search Problem. ACM SIGSOFT Software Engineering Notes 26(6), 62–66 (2001)
3. Harman, M., Jones, B.F.: Search-based Software Engineering. Information & Software Technology 43(14), 833–839 (2001)
4. Harman, M.: The Current State and Future of Search Based Software Engineering. In: Proceedings of International Conference on Software Engineering/Future of Software Engineering 2007, Minneapolis, pp. 342–357 (2007)
5. Harman, M., Mansouri, S., Zhang, Y.: Search Based Software Engineering: A Comprehensive Analysis and Review of Trends Techniques and Applications. Technical report (2007)
6. Lotka, A.: The frequency distribution of scientific productivity. Journal of the Washington Academy of Sciences 16(12), 317–323 (1926)
7. Bradford, S.: Sources of information on specific subjects. Journal of Information Science 10(4), 173–180 (1985)
8. SEBASE SBSE Repository,
   http://www.sebase.org/sbse/publications/repository.html

9. McMinn, P.: Search-based software test data generation: a survey. Software Testing, Verification and Reliability 14(2), 105–156 (2004)
10. Wegener, J., Baresel, A., Sthamer, H.: Evolutionary Test Environment for Automatic Structural Testing. Information and Software Technology - Special Issue on Software Engineering using Metaheuristic Innovative Algorithms 43(14), 841–854 (2001)
11. Michael, C.C., McGraw, G., Schatz, M.A.: Generating Software Test Data by Evolution. IEEE Transactions on Software Engineering 27(12), 1085–1110 (2001)
12. Clarke, J., Dolado, J.J., Harman, M., Hierons, R.M., Jones, B., Lumkin, M., Mitchell, B., Mancoridis, S., Rees, K., Roper, M., Shepperd, M.J.: Reformulating Software Engineering as a Search Problem. IEE Proceedings Software 150(3), 161–175 (2003)
13. Harman, M., Hu, L., Hierons, R., Wegener, J., Sthamer, H., Baresel, A., Roper, M.: Testability Transformation. IEEE Transaction on Software Engineering 30(1), 3–16 (2004)
14. Li, Z., Harman, M., Hierons, R.M.: Search Algorithms for Regression Test Case Prioritization. IEEE Transactions on Software Engineering 33(4), 225–237 (2007)
15. Mitchell, B., Mancoridis, S.: On the Automatic Modularization of Software Systems using the Bunch Tool. IEEE Transactions on Software Engineering 32(3), 193–208 (2006)
16. Dolado, J.J.: On the Problem of the Software Cost Function. Information and Software Technology 43(1), 61–72 (2001)
17. Cohen, M.B., Gibbons, P.B., Mugridge, W.B., Colbourn, C.J.: Constructing Test Suites for Interaction Testing. In: Proceedings of the 25th International Conference on Software Engineering, Portland, pp. 38–48 (2003)
18. Tonella, P.: Evolutionary Testing of Classes. In: Proceedings of the 2004 ACM SIGSOFT International Symposium on Software Testing and Analysis, Boston, pp. 119–128 (2004)
19. Greer, D., Ruhe, G.: Software Release Planning: An Evolutionary and Iterative Approach. Information & Software Technology 46(4), 243–253 (2004)
20. Bagnall, A.J., Rayward-Smith, V.J., Whittley, I.M.: The Next Release Problem. Information and Software Technology 43(14), 883–890 (2001)
21. Canfora, G., Di Penta, M., Esposito, R., Villani, M.L.: QoS-Aware Replanning of Composite Web Services. In: Proceedings of 2005 IEEE International Conference on Web Services, Orlando, pp. 121–129 (2005)
22. Franceschet, M.: The role of conference publications in CS. Communications of the ACM 53(12) (2010)
23. Franceschet, M., Constantine, A.: The effect of scholar collaboration on impact and quality of academic papers. Journal of Informetrics 4(4) (2010)

On Parameter Tuning in
Search Based Software Engineering

Andrea Arcuri[1] and Gordon Fraser[2]

[1] Simula Research Laboratory
P.O. Box 134, 1325 Lysaker, Norway
arcuri@simula.no
[2] Saarland University – Computer Science
Saarbrücken, Germany
fraser@cs.uni-saarland.de

Abstract. When applying search-based software engineering (SBSE) techniques one is confronted with a multitude of different parameters that need to be chosen: Which population size for a genetic algorithm? Which selection mechanism to use? What settings to use for dozens of other parameters? This problem not only troubles users who want to apply SBSE tools in practice, but also researchers performing experimentation – how to compare algorithms that can have different parameter settings? To shed light on the problem of parameters, we performed the largest empirical analysis on parameter tuning in SBSE to date, collecting and statistically analysing data from more than a million experiments. As case study, we chose test data generation, one of the most popular problems in SBSE. Our data confirm that tuning does have a critical impact on algorithmic performance, and over-fitting of parameter tuning is a dire threat to external validity of empirical analyses in SBSE. Based on this large empirical evidence, we give guidelines on how to handle parameter tuning.

Keywords: Search based software engineering, test data generation, object-oriented, unit testing.

1 Introduction

Recent years have brought a large growth of interest in search based software engineering (SBSE) [1], especially in software testing [2]. The field has even matured to a stage where industrial applications have started to appear [3,4]. One of the key strengths of SBSE leading to this success is its ability of automatically solving very complex problems where exact solutions cannot be deterministically found in reasonable time. However, to make SBSE really usable in practice, no knowledge of search algorithms should be required from practitioners who want to use it, as such knowledge is highly specialized and might not be widespread. In other words, SBSE tools should be treated as "black boxes" where the internal details are hidden, otherwise technology transfer to industrial practice will hardly be feasible.

One of the main barriers to the use of a search algorithm in SBSE is *tuning*. A search algorithm can have many parameters that need to be set. For example, to use a genetic

M.B. Cohen and M. Ó Cinnéide (Eds.): SSBSE 2011, LNCS 6956, pp. 33–47, 2011.

algorithm, one has to specify the population size, type of selection mechanism (roulette wheel, tournament, rank-based, etc.), type of crossover (single point, multi-point, etc.), crossover probability, type and probability of mutation, type and rate of elitism, etc. The choice of all these parameters might have a large impact on the performance of a search algorithm. In the worst case, an "unfortunate" parameter setting might make it impossible to solve the problem at hand.

Is it possible to find an *optimal* parameter setting, to solve this problem once and for all? Unfortunately, this is not possible, and this has been formally proven in the *No Free Lunch* (NFL) theorem [5]: All algorithms perform on average equally on *all* possible problems. For any problem an algorithm is good at solving, you can always find another problem for which that algorithm has worse performance than other algorithms. Because the same algorithm with different parameter settings can be considered as a family of different algorithms, the NFL theorem applies to tuning as well. However, the NFL is valid only when *all* possible search problems are considered. SBSE only represents a subset of all possible problems, so it could be possible to find "good" parameter settings that work well for this subset. Such a known good configuration is important when handing tools over to practitioners, as it is not reasonable to expect them to tune such tools as that would require deep knowledge of the tools and of search algorithms in general. Similarly, it is also important from a research perspective to avoid skewing results with improper parameter settings.

In this paper, we present the results of the largest empirical analysis of tuning in SBSE to date to address the question of parameter tuning. We chose the scenario of test data generation at unit test level because it is one of the most studied problems in SBSE [1]. In particular, we consider test data generation for object-oriented software using the EVOSUITE tool [6], where the goal is to find the minimal test suite that maximizes branch coverage (having a small test suite is important when no automated oracles are available and results need to be manually checked by software testers). We chose to consider five parameter settings (e.g., population size and crossover rate). To make the experiments finish in feasible time, we only considered 20 software classes as case study (previous empirical analyses of EVOSUITE were based on thousands of different classes [6]). Still, this led to more than *one million* experiments that took weeks to run even on a cluster of computers.

Although it is well known that parameter tuning has impact on the performance of search algorithms, there is little empirical evidence in the literature of SBSE that tries to quantify its effects. The results of the large empirical analysis presented in this paper provide compelling evidence that parameter tuning is indeed critical, and unfortunately *very* sensitive to the chosen case study. This brings to a compulsory use of *machine learning* techniques [7] if one wants to evaluate tuning in a sound scientific way. Furthermore, a problem related to tuning that is often ignored is the *search budget*. A practitioner might not want to deal with the choice of a genetic algorithm population size, but the choice of the computational time (i.e., how long she/he is willing to wait before the tool gives an output) is something that has a strong impact on tuning. To improve performance, tuning should be a function of the search budget, as we will discuss in more details in the paper.

This paper is organized as follows. Section 2 discusses related work on tuning. The analyzed search algorithm (a genetic algorithm used in EVOSUITE) is presented in Section 3 with a description of the parameters we investigate with respect to tuning. Section 4 presents the case study and the empirical analysis. Guidelines on how to handle parameter tuning are discussed in Section 5. Threats to validity are discussed in Section 6. Finally, Section 7 concludes the paper.

2   Related Work

Eiben *et al.* [8] presented a survey on how to control and set parameter values of evolutionary algorithms. In their survey, several techniques are discussed. Of particular interest is the distinction between *parameter tuning* and *parameter control*: The former deals with how to choose parameter values *before* running a search algorithm. For example, should we use a population size of 50 or 100? On the other hand, parameter control deals with how to change parameter values *during* the run of a search algorithm. A particular value that is good at the beginning of the search might become sub-optimal in the later stages. For example, in a genetic algorithm one might want to have a high mutation rate (or large population size) at the beginning of the search, and then decrease it in the course of the evolution; this would be conceptually similar to temperature cooling in simulated annealing. In this paper we only deal with parameter tuning. Parameter control is a promising area of research, but mainly unexplored in SBSE.

Recently, Smit and Eiben [9] carried out a series of experiments on parameter tuning. They consider the tuning of six parameters of a genetic algorithm applied to five numerical functions, comparing three settings: a default setting based on "common wisdom", the best tuning averaged on the five functions (which they call *generalist*), and the best tuning for each function independently (*specialist*). Only one fixed search budget (i.e., maximum number of fitness evaluations as stopping criterion) was considered. Our work shares some commonalities with these experiments, but more research questions and larger empirical analysis are presented in this paper (details will be given in Section 4).

In order to find the best parameter configuration for a given case study, one can run experiments with different configurations, and then the configuration that gives highest results on average can be identified as best for that case study. However, evaluating all possible parameter combinations is infeasible in practice. Techniques to select only a subset of configurations to test that have high probability of being optimal exist, for example regression trees (e.g., used in [10]) and response surface methodology (e.g., used in [11]). The goal of this paper is to study the effects of parameter tuning, which includes also the cases of sub-optimal choices. Such type of analysis requires an exhaustive evaluation. This is done only for the sake of answering research questions (as for example to study the effects of a sub-optimal tuning). In general, a practitioner would be interested only in the best configuration.

If a practitioner wants to use a search algorithm on an industrial problem (not necessarily in software engineering) that has not been studied in the literature, then she would need to tune the algorithm by herself, as default settings are likely to bring to poor performance. To help practitioners in making such tuning, there exist frameworks such as GUIDE [12]. The scope of this paper is different: we tackle *known* SBSE problems (e.g., test data generation for object-oriented software). For known problems, it is possible to carry out large empirical analyses in laboratory settings.

There might be cases in which, even on known problems, it might be useful to let the practitioners perform/improve tuning (if they have enough knowledge about search algorithms), and tools like EvoTest support this [3]. As an example, a SBSE problem instance type might need to be solved several times (e.g., a software system that is slightly modified during time). Another example could be to do tuning on a sub-system before tackling the entire system (which for example could be millions of lines of code). Whether such cases occur in practice, and whether the tuning can be safely left to practitioners, would require controlled empirical studies in industrial contexts. As such empirical evidence is currently lacking in the literature of SBSE, we are in the conditions to claim that parameter tuning is needed before releasing SBSE tool prototypes.

3   Search Algorithm Setting

We performed our experiments in a domain of test generation for object-oriented software. In this domain, the objective is to derive test suites (sets of test cases) for a given class, such that the test suite maximizes a chosen coverage criterion while minimizing the number of tests and their length. A test case in this domain is a sequence of method calls that constructs objects and calls methods on them. The resulting test suite is presented to the user, who usually has to add test oracles that check for correctness when executing the test cases.

The test cases may have variable length [13], and so earlier approaches to testing object-oriented software made use of method sequences [14,15] or strongly typed genetic programming [16,17]. In our experiments, we used the EVOSUITE [6] tool, in which one individual is an entire test suite of variable size. The entire search space of test suites is composed of all possible test suites of sizes from 1 to a predefined maximum N. Each test case can have a size (i.e., number of statements) from 1 to L. For each position in the sequence of statements of a test case, there can be up to I_{max} possible statements, depending on the SUT and the position within the test case (later statements can reuse objects instantiated in previous statements). The search space is hence extremely large, although finite because N, L and I_{max} are finite.

Crossover between test suites generates two offspring O_1 and O_2 from two parent test suites P_1 and P_2. A random value α is chosen from [0,1], and the first offspring O_1 contains the first $\alpha|P_1|$ test cases from the first parent, followed by the last $(1 - \alpha)|P_2|$ test cases from the second parent. The second offspring O_2 contains the first $\alpha|P_2|$ test cases from the second parent, followed by the last $(1 - \alpha)|P_1|$ test cases from the first parent.

The mutation operator for test suites works both at test suite and test case levels: When a test suite $\mathcal{T}$ is mutated, each of its test cases is mutated with probability $1/|\mathcal{T}|$. Then, with probability $\sigma = 0.1$, a new test case is added to the test suite. If it is added, then a second test case is added with probability σ^2, and so on until the ith test case is not added (which happens with probability $1 - \sigma^i$). Test cases are added only if the limit N has not been reached.

If a test case is mutated, then three types of operations are applied with probability $1/3$ in order: remove, change and insert. When removing statements out of a test case of length l, each statement is removed with probability $1/l$. Removing a statement might invalidate dependencies within the test case, which we attempt to repair; if this repair fails, then dependent statements are also deleted. When applying the change mutation, each statement is changed with probability $1/l$. A change means it is replaced with a different statement that retains the validity of the test case; e.g., a different method call with the same return type. When inserting statements, we first insert a new statement with probability $\sigma' = 0.5$ at a random position. If it is added, then a second statement is added with probability σ'^2, and so on until the ith statement is not inserted. If after applying these mutation operators a test case t has no statement left (i.e., all have been removed), then t is removed from $\mathcal{T}$. The initial population of test cases is generated randomly, by repeatedly performing the insertion operator also used to mutate test cases.

The search objective we chose is branch coverage, which requires that a test suite exercises a program in such a way that every condition (if, while, etc.) evaluates to true and to false. The fitness function is based on the well-established branch distance [18], which estimates the distance towards a particular evaluation of a branch predicate. The overall fitness of a test suite with respect to all branches is measured as the sum of the normalized branch distancesof all branches in the program under test. Using a fitness function that considers all the testing targets at the same time has been shown to lead to better results than the common strategy of considering each target individually [6]. Such an approach is particularly useful to reduce the negative effects of infeasible targets for the search.

We applied several bloat control techniques [19] to avoid that the size of individuals becomes bloated during the search.

In the experiments presented in this paper, we investigated five parameters of the search, which are not specific to this application domain. The first parameter is the *crossover rate*: Whenever two individuals are selected from the parent generation, this parameter specifies the probability with which they are crossed over. If they are not crossed over, then the parents are passed on to the next stage (mutation), else the offspring resulting from the crossover are used at the mutation stage.

The second parameter is the *population size*, which determines how many individuals are created for the initial population. The population size does not change in the course of the evolution, i.e., reproduction ensures that the next generation has the same size as the initial generation.

The third parameter is the *elitism rate*: Elitism describes the process that the best individuals of a population (its elite) automatically survive evolution. The elitism rate is sometimes specified as a percentage of the population that survives, or as the number of individuals that are copied to the next generation. For example, with an elitism rate set to 1 individual, the best individual of the current population is automatically copied to the next generation. In addition, it is still available for reproduction during the normal selection/crossover/mutation process.

In a standard genetic algorithm, elitism, selection and reproduction is performed until the next population has reached the desired population size. A common variant is *steady state* genetic algorithms, in which after the reproduction the offspring replace their parents in the current population. As the concept of elitism does not apply to steady state genetic algorithms, we treat the steady state genetic algorithm as a special parameter setting of the elitism rate.

The fourth parameter is the *selection mechanism*, which describes the algorithm used to select individuals from the current population for reproduction. In roulette wheel selection, each individual is selected with a probability that is proportionate to its fitness (hence it is also known as fitness proportionate selection). In tournament selection, a number of individuals are uniformly selected out of the current population, and the one with the best fitness value is chosen as one parent for reproduction. The *tournament size* denotes how many individuals are considered for the "tournament". Finally, rank selection is similar to roulette wheel selection, except that the probability of an individual being selected is not proportionate to its fitness but to its rank when ranking individuals according to their fitness. The advantage of this approach over roulette wheel selection is that the selection is not easily dominated by individuals that are fitter than others, which would lead to premature convergence. The probability of a ranking position can be weighted using the *rank bias* parameter.

Finally, the fifth parameter we consider is whether or not to apply a *parent replacement check*. When two offspring have been evolved through crossover and mutation, checking against the parents means that the offspring survive only if at least one of the two offspring has a better fitness than their parents. If this is not the case, the parents are used in the next generation instead of the offspring.

In addition to these parameters, another important decision in a genetic algorithm is when to stop the search, as it cannot be assumed that an optimal solution is always found. The search budget can be expressed in many different formats, for example, in terms of the time that the search may execute. A common format, often used in the literature to allow better and less biased comparisons, is to limit the number of fitness evaluations. In our setting, the variable size of individuals means that comparing fitness evaluations can be meaningless, as one individual can be very short and another one can be very long. Therefore, in this setting (i.e., test data generation for object-oriented software) we rather count the number of statements executed.

4   Experiments

In this paper, we use as case study a subset of 20 Java classes out of those previously used to evaluate EVOSUITE [6]. In choosing the case study, we tried to balance the different types of classes: historical benchmarks, data structures, numerical functions, string manipulations, classes coming from open source applications and industrial software. Apart from historical benchmarks, our criterion when selecting individual classes was that classes are non-trivial, but on which EVOSUITE may still achieve high coverage to allow for variation in the results. We therefore selected classes where EVO-SUITE used up its entire search budget without achieving 100% branch coverage, but still achieved more than 80% coverage.

We investigated five parameters:

- Crossover rate: $\{0, .2, .5, .8, 1\}$.
- Population size: $\{4, 10, 50, 100, 200\}$.

- Elitism rate: $\{0, 1, 10\%, 50\%\}$ or steady state.
- Selection: roulette wheel, tournament with size either 2 or 7, and rank selection with bias either 1.2 or 1.7.
- Parent replacement check (activated or not).

Notice that the search algorithm used in EVOSUITE has many other parameters to tune. Because the possible number of parameter combinations is exponential in the number of parameters, only a limited number of parameters and values could be used. For the evaluation we chose parameters that are common to most genetic algorithms, and avoided parameters that are specific in EVOSUITE to handle object-oriented software. Furthermore, because the goal of this paper is to study the effects of tuning, we analyzed all the possible combinations of the selected parameters. On the other hand, if one is only interested in finding the "best" tuning for the case study at hand, techniques such as the response surface methodology could be used to reduce the number of configurations to evaluate.

Another important factor is the *search budget*. A search algorithm can be run for any arbitrary amount of time – for example, a practitioner could run a search algorithm for one second only, or for one hour. However, the search budget has a strong effect on parameter tuning, and it is directly connected to the concept of *exploration* and *exploitation* of the search landscape. For example, the choice of a large population size puts more emphasis on the exploration of the search landscape, which could lead to a better escape from local optima. On the other hand, a large population can slow down the convergence to global optima when not so many local optima are present. If one has a small search budget, it would be advisable to use a small population size because with a large population only few generations would be possible. Therefore, parameter tuning is strongly correlated to the search budget. In fact, the search budget is perhaps the only parameter a practitioner should set. A realistic scenario might be the following: During working hours and development, a software engineer would have a small budget (in the order of seconds/minutes) for search, as coding and debugging would take place at the same time. On the other hand, a search could then be left running overnight, and results collected the morning after. In these two situations, the parameter settings (e.g. population size) should be different. In this paper, we consider a budget of 100,000 function call executions (considering the number of fitness function evaluations would not be fair due to the variable length of the evolved solutions). We also consider the cases of a budget that is a tenth (10,000) and ten times bigger (1,000,000).

For each class in the case study, we run each combination of parameter settings and search budget. All experiments were repeated 15 times to take the random nature of these algorithms into account. Therefore, in total we had $20 \times 5^4 \times 2 \times 3 \times 15 = 1,125,000$ experiments. Parameter settings were compared based on the achieved coverage. Notice that, in testing object-oriented software, it is also very important to take the size of the generated test suites into account. However, for reasons of space, in this paper we only consider coverage, in particular branch coverage.

Using the raw coverage values for parameter setting comparisons would be too noisy. Most branches are always covered regardless of the chosen parameter setting, while many others are simply infeasible. Given b the number of covered branches in a run for a class c, we used the following normalization to define a *relative coverage r*:

$$r(b,c) = \frac{b - min_c}{max_c - min_c},$$

where min_c is the worst coverage obtain in *all* the 56,250 experiments for that class c, and max_c is the maximum obtained coverage. If $min_c == max_c$, then $r = 1$.

To analyze all these data in a sound manner, we followed the guidelines in [20]. Statistical difference is measured with the Mann-Whitney U-test, whereas effect sizes are measured with the Vargha-Delaney $\hat{A}_{12}$ statistics. The $\hat{A}_{12}$ statistics measures the probability that a run with a particular parameter setting yields better coverage than a run of the other compared setting. If there is no difference between two parameter setting performances, then $\hat{A}_{12} = 0.5$. For reasons of space it is not possible to show all the details of the data and analyses. For example, instead of reporting all the p-values, we only state when those are lower than 0.05.

In the analyses in this paper, we focus on four specific settings: worst (W), best (B), default (D) and tuned (T). The worst combination W is the one that gives the worst coverage out of the $5^4 \times 2 = 1,250$ combinations, and can be different depending on the class under test and chosen search budget. Similarly, B represents the best configuration out of 1,250. The "default" combination D is arbitrarily set to population size 100, crossover rate 0.8, rank selection with 1.7 bias, 10% of elitism rate and no parent replacement check. These values are *in line* with common suggestions in the literature, and that we used in previous work. In particular, this default setting was chosen *before* running any of the experiments. Finally, given a set of classes, the tuned configuration T represents the configuration that has the highest average relative coverage on all that set of classes. When we write for example $\hat{A}_{DW} = 0.8$, this means that, for the addressed class and search budget, a run of the default configuration D has 0.8 probability of yielding a coverage that is higher than the one obtained by a run of the worst configuration W.

The data collected from this large empirical study could be used to address *several* research questions. Unfortunately, for reasons of space we only focus on the four that we believe are most important.

RQ1: How Large is the Potential Impact of a Wrong Choice of Parameter Settings?

In Table 1, for each class in the case study and test budget 100,000, we report the relative coverage (averaged out of 15 runs) of the worst and best configurations. There are cases in which the class under test is trivial for EVOSUITE (e.g., DateParse), in which tuning is not really important. But, in most cases, there is a very large difference between the worst and best configuration (e.g., BellmanFordIterator). A wrong parameter tuning can make it hard (on average) to solve problems that could be easy otherwise.

> *Different parameter settings cause*
> *very large variance in the performance.*

Table 1. Relative coverage averaged out of 15 runs for default, worst and best configuration. Effect sizes for default compared to worst ($\hat{A}_{DW}$) and and compared to best configuration ($\hat{A}_{DB}$). Statistically significant effect sizes are in bold.

Class	Default	Worst	Best	$\hat{A}_{DW}$	$\hat{A}_{DB}$
Cookie	0.49	0.33	0.86	**0.93**	**0.00**
DateParse	1.00	1.00	1.00	0.50	0.50
Triangle	1.00	0.60	1.00	**0.70**	0.50
XMLElement	0.90	0.43	0.97	**1.00**	**0.10**
ZipOutputStream	1.00	0.47	1.00	**0.77**	0.50
CommandLine	0.41	0.11	0.59	**0.98**	0.34
Remainder	0.82	0.30	0.98	**0.98**	**0.13**
Industry1	0.95	0.53	0.98	**1.00**	**0.18**
Industry2	0.90	0.42	0.95	**1.00**	**0.11**
Attribute	0.47	0.21	0.90	**1.00**	**0.00**
DoubleMetaphone	0.63	0.22	0.96	**1.00**	**0.00**
Chronology	0.77	0.43	0.94	**1.00**	**0.00**
ArrayList	1.00	0.67	1.00	**0.67**	0.50
DateTime	0.60	0.21	0.95	**1.00**	**0.00**
TreeMap	0.65	0.00	0.78	**0.93**	**0.27**
Bessj	0.65	0.42	0.95	**1.00**	**0.00**
BellmanFordIterator	0.13	0.00	1.00	0.57	**0.07**
TTestImpl	0.55	0.21	1.00	**0.88**	**0.00**
LinkedListMultimap	0.81	0.18	1.00	**1.00**	**0.03**
FastFourierTransformer	1.00	0.29	1.00	**0.98**	0.47

RQ2: How Does a "Default" Setting Compare to the Best and Worst Achievable Performance?

Table 1 also reports the relative coverage for the default setting, with effect sizes of the comparisons with the worst and best configuration. As one would expect, a default configuration has to be better than the worst, and worse/equal to the best configuration. However, for most problems, although the default setting is *much better* than the worst setting (i.e., $\hat{A}_{DW}$ values close to 1), it is unfortunately *much worse* than the best setting (i.e., $\hat{A}_{DB}$ values are close to 0). When one uses randomized algorithms, it is reasonable to expect variance in the performance when they are run twice with a different seed. However, consider the example of Bessj in Table 1, where $\hat{A}_{DW} = 1$ and $\hat{A}_{DB} = 0$. In that case, the coverage values achieved by the default setting in 15 runs are always better than any of the 15 coverage values obtained with the worst configuration, but also always worse than any of the 15 runs obtained with best configuration. These data suggest that, if one does not have the possibility of tuning, then the use of a default setting is not particularly inefficient. However, there is large space for performance improvement if tuning is done.

> *Default parameter settings perform relatively well, but are far from optimal on individual problem instances.*

RQ3: If we Tune a Search Algorithm Based On a Set of Classes, How Will Its Performance Be On Other New Classes?

To answer this research question, for each class, we tuned the algorithm on the *other* 19 classes, and then compared this tuned version with the default and best configuration for the class under test. Table 2 reports the data of this analysis. If one makes tuning on a sample of problem instances, then we would expect a relatively good performance on new instances. But the $\hat{A}_{TB}$ values in Table 2 are in most of the cases low and statistically significant. This means that parameter settings that should work well on average can be particularly inefficient on new instances compared to the best tuning for those instances. In other words, there is a very high variance in the performance of parameter settings.

Of particular interest are the $\hat{A}_{TD}$ values. In three cases they are equal to 0.5 (so no difference between tuned and default settings), in seven cases they are higher than 0.5 (so tuning helps), but then in 10 cases they are lower than 0.5 (but only in four cases there is statistically significant difference). This means that, on the case study used in this paper, doing tuning is even *worse* than just using some arbitrary settings coming from the literature! This might be explained with the concept of *over-fitting* in machine learning [7]. A too intensive tuning on a set of problem instances can result in parameter settings that are too specific for that set. Even the case of 19 problem instances, as done in this paper, is too small to avoid such type of over-fitting.

> Tuning should be done on a very large sample of problem instances. Otherwise, the obtained parameter settings are likely to be worse than arbitrary default values.

RQ4: What are the Effects of the Search Budget On Parameter Tuning?

For each class and the three search budgets, we compared the performance of the default setting against the worst and the best; Table 3 shows the data of this analysis. For a very large search budget one would expect not much difference between parameter settings, as all achievable coverage would be reached with high probability. Recall that it is not possible to stop the search before because, apart from trivial cases, there are always infeasible testing targets (e.g., branches) whose number is unknown. The data in Table 3 show that trend for many of the used programs (e.g., see LinkedListMultimap) regarding the default and best settings, but the worst setting is still much worse than the others (i.e., $\hat{A}_{DW}$ close to 1) even with a search budget of one million function calls. What is a "large" search budget depends of course on the case study. For example, for DateParse, already a budget of 100,000 is enough to get no difference between best, worst and default configuration. On the other hand, with a search budget of 1,000,000, for example for CommandLine there is still a statistically strong difference.

As said, a very large search budget might reduce the importance of tuning. However, when we increase the search budget, that does not always mean that tuning becomes less important. Consider again the case of CommandLine: At budget 10,000, the $\hat{A}_{DW}$ is not statistically significant (i.e., close to 0.5 and Mann-Whitney U-test has p-value greater than 0.05), whereas it gets higher (close to 1) for 100,000 and then for

Table 2. Relative coverage averaged out of 15 runs for tuned configuration. Effect sizes for tuned compared to default ($\hat{A}_{TD}$) and and compared to best configuration ($\hat{A}_{TB}$). Statistically significant effect sizes are in bold.

Class	Tuned	$\hat{A}_{TD}$	$\hat{A}_{TB}$
Cookie	0.78	**0.98**	**0.27**
DateParse	1.00	0.50	0.50
Triangle	1.00	0.50	0.50
XMLElement	0.81	0.40	**0.11**
ZipOutputStream	0.93	0.47	0.47
CommandLine	0.38	0.32	**0.22**
Remainder	0.62	**0.23**	**0.05**
Industry1	0.90	**0.24**	**0.08**
Industry2	0.84	0.30	**0.17**
Attribute	0.52	**0.75**	**0.00**
DoubleMetaphone	0.57	**0.08**	**0.00**
Chronology	0.87	**0.76**	**0.28**
ArrayList	1.00	0.50	0.50
DateTime	0.93	**1.00**	0.30
TreeMap	0.32	0.33	**0.26**
Bessj	0.81	**0.92**	**0.18**
BellmanFordIterator	0.00	0.43	**0.00**
TTestImpl	0.68	**0.93**	**0.03**
LinkedListMultimap	0.98	**0.96**	**0.33**
FastFourierTransformer	0.97	**0.28**	**0.25**

1,000,000. For $\hat{A}_{DB}$, it is statistically significant when budget is 10,000, but not when we increase the budget to 100,000. Interestingly, it comes back to be statistically significant at 1,000,000, with an effect size that is even stronger than in the case of budget 10,000. How come? The reason is that the testing targets have different difficulty to be covered. Even with an appropriate tuning, for some targets we would still need a minimum amount of search budget. If the search budget is lower than that threshold, then we would not cover (with high probability) those targets even with the best tuning. Therefore, tuning might not be so important if either the search budget is too "large", or if it is too "small", where "large" and "small" depend on the case study. But such an information is usually not known before doing tuning.

> *Available search budget has strong impact on the parameter settings that should be used.*

5   Guidelines

The empirical analysis carried out in this paper clearly shows that tuning has a strong impact on search algorithm performance, and if it is not done properly, there are dire risks in ending up with tuned configurations that are worse than suggested values in the

Table 3. For each test budget, effect sizes of default configuration compared to the worst ($\hat{A}_{DW}$) and best configuration ($\hat{A}_{DB}$). Statistically significant effect sizes are in bold. Some data are missing (-) due to the testing tool running out of memory.

Class	Test Budget					
	10,000		100,000		1,000,000	
	$\hat{A}_{DW}$	$\hat{A}_{DB}$	$\hat{A}_{DW}$	$\hat{A}_{DB}$	$\hat{A}_{DW}$	$\hat{A}_{DB}$
Cookie	**0.77**	**0.07**	**0.93**	**0.00**	**0.82**	**0.11**
DateParse	**0.63**	0.50	0.50	0.50	0.50	0.50
Triangle	**0.67**	0.50	**0.70**	0.50	**0.69**	0.50
XMLElement	**0.81**	**0.07**	**1.00**	**0.10**	**1.00**	0.50
ZipOutputStream	**0.87**	0.43	**0.77**	0.50	**0.71**	0.50
CommandLine	0.54	**0.23**	**0.98**	0.34	**1.00**	**0.00**
Remainder	**0.72**	**0.21**	**0.98**	**0.13**	**1.00**	0.46
Industry1	0.63	**0.00**	**1.00**	**0.18**	-	-
Industry2	**0.82**	**0.06**	**1.00**	**0.11**	**1.00**	0.42
Attribute	**0.80**	**0.06**	**1.00**	**0.00**	**1.00**	**0.15**
DoubleMetaphone	**0.87**	**0.06**	**1.00**	**0.00**	**0.92**	**0.14**
Chronology	**0.90**	**0.08**	**1.00**	**0.00**	**1.00**	**0.17**
ArrayList	**0.70**	0.43	**0.67**	0.50	**1.00**	0.50
DateTime	0.69	**0.06**	**1.00**	**0.00**	**0.88**	0.45
TreeMap	0.60	**0.24**	**0.93**	**0.27**	**1.00**	**0.27**
Bessj	**0.83**	**0.10**	**1.00**	**0.00**	**1.00**	0.33
BellmanFordIterator	0.50	**0.00**	0.57	**0.07**	-	-
TTestImpl	**0.88**	**0.21**	**0.88**	**0.00**	**0.95**	**0.31**
LinkedListMultimap	0.60	**0.05**	**1.00**	**0.03**	**0.96**	0.50
FastFourierTransformer	**0.83**	**0.00**	**0.98**	0.47	-	-

literature. To avoid these problems, it would hence be important to use machine learning techniques [7] when tuning parameters. Which ones to use is context dependent, and a detailed discussion is beyond the scope of this paper. Instead, we discuss some basic scenarios here, aiming at developers who want to tune parameters before releasing SBSE tool prototypes, or researchers who want to tune tools for scientific experiments. Further details can be found for example in [7].

Given a case study composed of a number of problem instances, randomly partition it in two non-overlapping subsets: the *training* and the *test* set. A common rule of thumb is to use 90% of instances for the training set, and the remaining 10% for the test set. Do the tuning using only the problem instances in the training set. Instead of considering all possible parameter combinations (which is not feasible), use techniques such as the response surface methodology (e.g., used in [11]). Given a parameter setting that performs best on this training set, then evaluate its performance on the test set. Draw conclusions on the algorithm performance only based on the results on this test set.

If the case study is "small" (e.g., because composed of industrial systems and not open-source software that can be downloaded in large quantities), and/or if the cost of running the experiment is relatively low, use k-fold cross validation [7]. In other words, randomly partition the case study in k non-overlapping subsets (a common value is $k = 10$). Use one of these as test set, and merge the other $k - 1$ subsets to use them as training set. Do the tuning on the training set, and evaluate the performance on the test set. Repeat this process k times, every time with a different subset for the test set, and remaining $k - 1$ for the training set. Average the performance on all the results obtained from all the k test sets, which will give some value v describing the performance of the algorithm. Finally, apply tuning on *all* the case study (do not use any test set), and keep the resulting parameter setting as the final one to use. The validity of this parameter setting would be estimated by the value v calculated during the cross validation.

Comparisons among algorithms should never be done on their performance on the training set — only use the results on validation sets. As a rule of thumb, if one compares different "tools" (e.g., prototypes released in the public domain), then no tuning should be done on released tools, because parameter settings are an essential component that *define* a tool. On the other hand, if the focus is on evaluating algorithms at a high level (e.g., on a specific class of problems, is it better to use population based search algorithms such as genetic algorithms or single individual algorithms such as simulated annealing?), then each compared algorithm should receive the same amount of tuning.

6   Threats to Validity

Threats to *internal validity* might come from how the empirical study was carried out. To reduce the probability of having faults in our experiment framework, it has been carefully tested. But it is well known that testing alone cannot prove the absence of defects. Furthermore, randomized algorithms are affected by chance. To cope with this problem, we repeated each experiment 15 times with different random seeds, and we followed rigorous statistical procedures to evaluate their results.

Threats to *construct validity* come from the fact that we evaluated parameter settings only based on structural coverage of the resulting test suites generated by EVOSUITE . Other factors that are important for practitioners and that should be considered as well are the size of the test suites and their readability (e.g., important in case of no formal specifications when assert statements need to be manually added). Whether these factors are negatively correlated with structural coverage is a matter of further investigation.

Threats to *external validity* come from the fact that, due to the very large number of experiments, we only used 20 classes as case study, which still took weeks even when using a computer cluster. Furthermore, we manually selected those 20 classes, in which we tried to have a balance of different kinds of software. A different selection for the case study might result in different conclusions. However, to the best of our knowledge, there is no standard benchmark in test data generation for object-oriented software that we could have rather used.

The results presented in this paper might not be valid on all software engineering problems that are commonly addressed in the literature of SBSE. Based on the fact that parameter tuning has large impact on search algorithm performances, we hence strongly encourage the repetition of such empirical analysis on other SBSE problems.

7   Conclusion

In this paper, we have reported the results of the largest empirical study in parameter tuning in search based software engineering to date. In particular, we focus on test data generation for object-oriented software using the EVOSUITE tool [6].

It is well known that parameter tuning has effects on the performance of search algorithms. However, this paper is the first that quantifies these effects for a search based software engineering problem. The results of this empirical analysis clearly show that arbitrary parameter settings can lead to sub-optimal search performance. Even if one does a first phase of parameter tuning on some problem instances, the results on new problem instances can be very poor, even worse than arbitrary settings. Hence, tuning should be done on (very) large samples of problem instances. The main contribution of this paper is that it provides compelling empirical evidence to support these claims based on rigorous statistical methods.

To entail technology transfer to industrial practice, parameter tuning is a task of responsibility of who develops and releases search based tools. It is hence important to have *large* tuning phases on which *several* problem instances are employed. Unfortunately, parameter tuning phases can result in over-fitting issues. To validate whether a search based tool can be effective in practice once delivered to software engineers that will use it on their problem instances, it is important to use machine learning techniques [7] to achieve sound scientific conclusions. For example, tuning can be done on a subset of the case study (i.e., the so called *training set*), whereas performance evaluation would be done a on a separate and independent set (i.e., the so called *test set*). This would reduce the dire threats to external validity coming from over-fitting the parameter tuning. To the best of our knowledge, in the literature of search based software engineering, in most of the cases parameter tuning is either not done, done on the *entire* case study at hand, or its details are simply omitted.

Another issue that is often neglected is the relation between tuning and search budget. The final user (e.g., software engineers) in some cases would run the search for some seconds/minutes, in other cases they could afford to run it for hours/days (e.g., weekends and night hours). In these cases, to improve search performance, the parameter settings should be different. For example, the population size in a genetic algorithm could be set based on a linear function of the search budget. However, that is a little investigated topic, and further research is needed.

Acknowledgements. Andrea Arcuri is supported by the Norwegian Research Council. Gordon Fraser is funded by the Cluster of Excellence on Multimodal Computing and Interaction at Saarland University, Germany.

References

1. Harman, M., Mansouri, S.A., Zhang, Y.: Search based software engineering: A comprehensive analysis and review of trends techniques and applications. Technical Report TR-09-03, King's College (2009)
2. Ali, S., Briand, L., Hemmati, H., Panesar-Walawege, R.: A systematic review of the application and empirical investigation of search-based test-case generation. IEEE Transactions on Software Engineering 36(6), 742–762 (2010)

3. Vos, T., Baars, A., Lindlar, F., Kruse, P., Windisch, A., Wegener, J.: Industrial Scaled Automated Structural Testing with the Evolutionary Testing Tool. In: IEEE International Conference on Software Testing, Verification and Validation (ICST), pp. 175–184 (2010)
4. Arcuri, A., Iqbal, M.Z., Briand, L.: Black-box system testing of real-time embedded systems using random and search-based testing. In: Petrenko, A., Simão, A., Maldonado, J.C. (eds.) ICTSS 2010. LNCS, vol. 6435, pp. 95–110. Springer, Heidelberg (2010)
5. Wolpert, D.H., Macready, W.G.: No free lunch theorems for optimization. IEEE Transactions on Evolutionary Computation 1(1), 67–82 (1997)
6. Fraser, G., Arcuri, A.: Evolutionary generation of whole test suites. In: International Conference On Quality Software, QSIC (2011)
7. Mitchell, T.: Machine Learning. McGraw Hill, New York (1997)
8. Eiben, A., Michalewicz, Z., Schoenauer, M., Smith, J.: Parameter control in evolutionary algorithms. Parameter Setting in Evolutionary Algorithms, 19–46 (2007)
9. Smit, S., Eiben, A.: Parameter tuning of evolutionary algorithms: Generalist vs. specialist. Applications of Evolutionary Computation, 542–551 (2010)
10. Bartz-Beielstein, T., Markon, S.: Tuning search algorithms for real-world applications: A regression tree based approach. In: IEEE Congress on Evolutionary Computation (CEC), pp. 1111–1118 (2004)
11. Poulding, S., Clark, J., Waeselynck, H.: A principled evaluation of the effect of directed mutation on search-based statistical testing. In: International Workshop on Search-Based Software Testing, SBST (2011)
12. Da Costa, L., Schoenauer, M.: Bringing evolutionary computation to industrial applications with GUIDE. In: Genetic and Evolutionary Computation Conference (GECCO), pp. 1467–1474 (2009)
13. Arcuri, A.: A theoretical and empirical analysis of the role of test sequence length in software testing for structural coverage. IEEE Transactions on Software Engineering (2011), http://doi.ieeecomputersociety.org/10.1109/TSE.2011.44
14. Tonella, P.: Evolutionary testing of classes. In: ISSTA 2004: Proceedings of the ACM International Symposium on Software Testing and Analysis, pp. 119–128. ACM, New York (2004)
15. Fraser, G., Zeller, A.: Mutation-driven generation of unit tests and oracles. In: ISSTA 2010: Proceedings of the ACM International Symposium on Software Testing and Analysis, pp. 147–158. ACM, New York (2010)
16. Wappler, S., Lammermann, F.: Using evolutionary algorithms for the unit testing of object-oriented software. In: GECCO 2005: Proceedings of the 2005 Conference on Genetic and Evolutionary Computation, pp. 1053–1060. ACM, New York (2005)
17. Ribeiro, J.C.B.: Search-based test case generation for object-oriented Java software using strongly-typed genetic programming. In: GECCO 2008: Proceedings of the 2008 GECCO Conference Companion on Genetic and Evolutionary Computation, pp. 1819–1822. ACM, New York (2008)
18. McMinn, P.: Search-based software test data generation: A survey. Software Testing, Verification and Reliability 14(2), 105–156 (2004)
19. Fraser, G., Arcuri, A.: It is not the length that matters, it is how you control it. In: IEEE International Conference on Software Testing, Verification and Validation, ICST (2011)
20. Arcuri, A., Briand, L.: A practical guide for using statistical tests to assess randomized algorithms in software engineering. In: IEEE International Conference on Software Engineering, ICSE (2011)

Elementary Landscape Decomposition of the Test Suite Minimization Problem

Francisco Chicano, Javier Ferrer, and Enrique Alba

University of Málaga, Spain
{chicano,ferrer,alba}@lcc.uma.es

Abstract. Landscape theory provides a formal framework in which combinatorial optimization problems can be theoretically characterized as a sum of a special kind of landscape called elementary landscape. The decomposition of the objective function of a problem into its elementary components provides additional knowledge on the problem that can be exploited to create new search methods for the problem. We analyze the Test Suite Minimization problem in Regression Testing from the point of view of landscape theory. We find the elementary landscape decomposition of the problem and propose a practical application of such decomposition for the search.

Keywords: Fitness landscapes, test suite minimization, regression testing, elementary landscapes.

1   Introduction

The theory of landscapes focuses on the analysis of the structure of the search space that is induced by the combined influences of the objective function of the optimization problem and the choice neighborhood operator [8]. In the field of combinatorial optimization, this theory has been used to characterize optimization problems and to obtain global statistics of the problems [11]. However, in recent years, researchers have been interested in the applications of landscape theory to improve the search algorithms [5].

A *landscape* for a combinatorial optimization problem is a triple (X, N, f), where $f : X \mapsto \mathbb{R}$ defines the objective function and the *neighborhood operator* function $N(x)$ generates the set of points reachable from $x \in X$ in a single application of the neighborhood operator. If $y \in N(x)$ then y is a neighbor of x.

There exists a special kind of landscapes, called *elementary landscapes*, which are of particular interest due to their properties [12]. We define and analyze the elementary landscapes in Section 2, but we can advance that they are characterized by the *Grover's wave equation*:

$$\underset{y \in N(x)}{\text{avg}}\{f(y)\} = f(x) + \frac{\lambda}{d}\left(\bar{f} - f(x)\right)$$

where d is the size of the neighborhood, $|N(x)|$, which we assume is the same for all the solutions in the search space, $\bar{f}$ is the average solution evaluation over

M.B. Cohen and M. Ó Cinnéide (Eds.): SSBSE 2011, LNCS 6956, pp. 48–63, 2011.
© Springer-Verlag Berlin Heidelberg 2011

the entire search space, λ is a characteristic constant and $\text{avg}\{f(y)\}_{y \in N(x)}$ is the average of the objective function f computed in its neighborhood:

$$\text{avg}_{y \in N(x)}\{f(y)\} = \frac{1}{|N(x)|} \sum_{y \in N(x)} f(y) \tag{1}$$

For a given problem instance whose objective function is elementary, the values $\bar{f}$ and λ can be easily computed in an efficient way, usually from the problem data. Thus, the wave equation makes it possible to compute the average value of the fitness function f evaluated over all of the neighbors of x using only the value $f(x)$, without evaluating any of the neighbors. This means that in elementary landscapes we get additional information from a single solution evaluation. We get an idea of what is the quality of the solutions around the current one. This information can be used to design more clever search strategies and operators which effectively use the information.

Lu *et al.* [5] provide a nice example of the application of the landscape analysis to improve the performance of a search method. In their work, the performance of the Sampling Hill Climbing is improved by avoiding the evaluation of non-promising solutions. The average fitness value in the neighborhood of the solutions computed with (1) is at the core of their proposal.

When the landscape is not elementary it is always possible to write the objective function as a sum of elementary components, called *elementary landscape decomposition* of a problem [1]. Then, Grover's wave equation can be applied to each elementary component and all the results are summed to give the average fitness in the neighborhood of a solution. Furthermore, for some problems the average cannot be limited to the neighborhood of a solution, but it can be extended to the second-order neighrbors (neighbors of neighbors), third-order neighbors, and, in general, to any arbitrary region around a given solution, including the whole search space. Sutton *et al.* [10] show how to compute the averages over *spheres* and *balls* of arbitrary radius around a given solution in polynomial time using the elementary landscape decomposition of real-valued functions over binary strings. In [9] they propose a method that uses these averages over the balls around a solution to escape from plateaus in the MAX-k-SAT problem. The empirical results noticed an improvement when the method was applied. Langdon [4] also analyzed the spheres of arbitrary radius from the point of view of landscape theory, highlighting that the Walsh functions are eigenvectors of the spheres and the mutation matrix in GAs.

If we extend the landscape analysis of the objective function f to their powers (f^2, f^3, etc.), Grover's wave equation allows one to compute higher-order moments of the fitness distribution around a solution and, with them, the variance, the skewness and the kurtosis of this distribution. Sutton *et al.* [10] provide an algorithm for this computation.

We analyze here the Test Suite Minimization problem in regression testing from the point of view of landscape theory. This software engineering problem consists in selecting a set of test cases from a large test suite that satisfies a given condition, like maximizing the coverage and minimizing the oracle cost [13].

The remainder of the paper is organized as follows. In Section 2 we present the mathematical tools required to understand the rest of the paper and Section 3 formally defines the Test Suite Minimization problem. Section 4 presents the two main contributions: the elementary landscape decomposition of the objective function of the problem and its square. We provide closed-form formulas for both f and f^2. In the mathematical development we include a novel application of the Krawtchouk matrices to the landscape analysis. Section 5 proposes an application of the decompositions of f and f^2 and presents a short experimental study showing the benefits (and drawbacks) of the proposal. Finally, with Section 6 we conclude the paper.

2   Background

In this section we present some fundamental results of landscape theory. We will only focus on the relevant information required to understand the rest of the paper. The interested reader can deepen on this topic in [7].

Let (X, N, f) be a landscape, where X is a finite set of solutions, $f : X \to \mathbb{R}$ is a real-valued function defined on X and $N : X \to \mathcal{P}(X)$ is the neighborhood operator. The adjacency and degree matrices of the neighborhood N are defined as:

$$A_{xy} = \begin{cases} 1 \text{ if } y \in N(x) \\ 0 \text{ otherwise} \end{cases} ; \quad D_{xy} = \begin{cases} |N(x)| \text{ if } x = y \\ 0 \qquad \text{otherwise} \end{cases} \tag{2}$$

We restrict our attention to regular neighborhoods, where $|N(x)| = d > 0$ for a constant d, for all $x \in X$. Then, the degree matrix is $D = dI$, where I is the identity matrix. The Laplacian matrix Δ associated to the neighborhood is defined by $\Delta = A - D$. In the case of regular neighborhoods it is $\Delta = A - dI$. Any discrete function, f, defined over the set of candidate solutions can be characterized as a vector in $\mathbb{R}^{|X|}$. Any $|X| \times |X|$ matrix can be interpreted as a linear map that acts on vectors in $\mathbb{R}^{|X|}$. For example, the adjacency matrix A acts on function f as follows

$$A f = \begin{pmatrix} \sum_{y \in N(x_1)} f(y) \\ \sum_{y \in N(x_2)} f(y) \\ \vdots \\ \sum_{y \in N(x_{|X|})} f(y) \end{pmatrix} ; \quad (A f)(x) = \sum_{y \in N(x)} f(y) \tag{3}$$

Thus, the component x of $(A f)$ is the sum of the function value of all the neighbors of x. Stadler defines the class of *elementary landscapes* where the function f is an eigenvector (or eigenfunction) of the Laplacian up to an additive constant [8]. Formally, we have the following

Definition 1. *Let (X, N, f) be a landscape and Δ the Laplacian matrix of the configuration space. The function f is said to be elementary if there exists a constant b, which we call* offset, *and an eigenvalue λ of $-\Delta$ such that $(-\Delta)(f - b) = \lambda(f - b)$. The landscape itself is elementary if f is elementary.*

We use $-\Delta$ instead of Δ in the definition to avoid negative eigenvalues. In connected neighborhoods (the ones we consider here) the offset b is the average value of the function over the whole search space: $b = \bar{f}$. Taking into account basic results of linear algebra, it can be proved that if f is elementary with eigenvalue λ, $af + b$ is also elementary with the same eigenvalue λ. Furthermore, in regular neighborhoods, if g is an eigenfunction of $-\Delta$ with eigenvalue λ then g is also an eigenvalue of A, the adjacency matrix, with eigenvalue $d - \lambda$. The average value of the fitness function in the neighborhood of a solution can be computed using the expression $\text{avg}\{f(y)\}_{y \in N(x)} = \frac{1}{d}(A\ f)(x)$. If f is an elementary function with eigenvalue λ, then the average is computed as:

$$\text{avg}_{y \in N(x)}\{f(y)\} = \text{avg}_{y \in N(x)}\{f(y) - \bar{f}\} + \bar{f} = \frac{1}{d}(A\ (f - \bar{f}))(x) + \bar{f}$$

$$= \frac{d - \lambda}{d}(f(x) - \bar{f}) + \bar{f} = f(x) + \frac{\lambda}{d}(\bar{f} - f(x))$$

and we get Grover's wave equation. In the previous expression we used the fact that $f - \bar{f}$ is an eigenfunction of A with eigenvalue $d - \lambda$.

The previous definitions are general concepts of landscape theory. Let us focus now on the binary strings with the one-change neighborhood, which is the representation and the neighborhood we use in the test suite minimization problem. In this case the solution set X is the set of all binary strings of size n. Two solutions x and y are neighboring if one can be obtained from the other by flipping a bit, that is, if the Hamming distance between the solutions, denoted with $\mathcal{H}(x, y)$, is 1. We define the sphere of radius k around a solution x as the set of all solutions lying at Hamming distance k from x [10]. A *ball* of radius k is the set of all the solutions lying at Hamming distance lower or equal to k. In analogy to the adjacency matrix we define the sphere and ball matrices of radius k as:

$$S_{xy}^{(k)} = \begin{cases} 1 \text{ if } \mathcal{H}(x, y) = k \\ 0 \text{ otherwise} \end{cases} ; \quad B_{xy}^{(k)} = \sum_{\rho=0}^{k} S_{xy}^{(\rho)} = \begin{cases} 1 \text{ if } \mathcal{H}(x, y) \leq k \\ 0 \text{ otherwise} \end{cases} \quad (4)$$

Since the ball matrices are based on the sphere matrices we can focus on the latter. The sphere matrix of radius one is the adjacency matrix of the one-change neighborhood, A, and the sphere matrix of radius zero is the identity matrix, I. Following [10], the matrices $S^{(k)}$ can be defined using the recurrence:

$$S^{(0)} = I; \quad S^{(1)} = A; \quad S^{(k+1)} = \frac{1}{k + 1}\left(A \cdot S^{(k)} - (n - k + 1)S^{(k-1)}\right) \quad (5)$$

With the help of the recurrence we can write all the matrices $S^{(k)}$ as polynomials in A, the adjacency matrix. For example, $S^{(2)} = \frac{1}{2}\left(A^2 - nI\right)$. As we previously noted, the eigenvectors of the Laplacian matrix Δ are eigenvectors of the adjacency matrix A. On the other hand, if f is eigenvector of A, then it is also an eigenvector of any polynomial in A. As a consequence, all the functions that are elementary are eigenvectors (up to an additive constant) of $S^{(k)}$ and their eigenvalues can be computed using the same polynomial in A that gives the expression for $S^{(k)}$. The same is true for the ball matrices $B^{(k)}$, since they are a sum of sphere matrices. Let us define the following series of polynomials:

$$S^{(0)}(x) = 1 \tag{6}$$

$$S^{(1)}(x) = x \tag{7}$$

$$S^{(k+1)}(x) = \frac{1}{k+1}\left(x \cdot S^{(k)}(x) - (n - k + 1)S^{(k-1)}(x)\right) \tag{8}$$

We use the same name for the polynomials and the matrices related to the spheres. The reader should notice, however, that the polynomials will be always presented with their argument and the matrices have no argument. That is, $S^{(k)}$ is the matrix and $S^{(k)}(x)$ is the polynomial. Using the previous polynomials, the matrix $S^{(k)}$ can be written as $S^{(k)}(A)$ (the polynomial $S^{(k)}(x)$ evaluated in the matrix A) and any eigenvector g of A with eigenvalue λ is also an eigenvector of $S^{(k)}(A)$ with eigenvalue $S^{(k)}(\lambda)$.

One relevant set of eigenvectors of the Laplacian in the binary representation is that of Walsh functions [11]. Furthermore, the Walsh functions form an orthogonal basis of eigenvectors in the configuration space. Thus, they have been used to find the elementary landscape decomposition of problems with a binary representation like the SAT [6]. We will use these functions to provide the landscape decomposition of the objective function of the test suite minimization problem. Given the space of binary strings of length n, $\mathbb{B}^n$, a (non-normalized) Walsh function with parameter $w \in \mathbb{B}^n$ is defined as:

$$\psi_w(x) = \prod_{i=1}^{n}(-1)^{w_i x_i} = (-1)^{\sum_{i=1}^{n} w_i x_i} \tag{9}$$

Two useful properties of Walsh functions are $\psi_w \cdot \psi_v = \psi_{w+v}$ where $w + v$ is the bitwise sum in $\mathbb{Z}_2$ of w and v; and $\psi_w^2 = \psi_w \cdot \psi_w = \psi_{2w} = \psi_0 = 1$. We define the *order* of a Walsh function ψ_w as the value $\langle w|w \rangle = \sum_{i=1}^{n} w_i$, that is, the number of ones in w. A Walsh function with order p is elementary with eigenvalue $\lambda = 2p$ [8]. The average value of a Walsh function of order $p > 0$ is zero, that is, $\overline{\psi_w} = 0$ if w has at least one 1. The only Walsh function of order $p = 0$ is $\psi_0 = 1$, which is a constant.

In the mathematical development of Section 4 we will use, among others, Walsh functions of order 1 and 2. Thus, we present here a special compact notation for those binary strings having only one or two bits set to 1. We will denote with $\underline{i}$ the binary string with position i set to 1 and the rest set to 0. We also denote with $\underline{i,j}$ ($i \neq j$) the binary string with positions i and j set to 1 and the rest to 0. We omit the length of the string n, but it will be clear from the context. For example, if we are considering binary strings in $\mathbb{B}^4$ we have $\underline{1} = 1000$ and $\underline{2,3} = 0110$. Using this notation we can write

$$\psi_{\underline{i}}(x) = (-1)^{x_i} = 1 - 2x_i \tag{10}$$

Given a set of binary strings W and a binary string u we denote with $W \wedge u$ the set of binary strings that can be computed as the bitwise AND of a string in W and u, that is, $W \wedge u = \{w \wedge u | w \in W\}$. For example, $\mathbb{B}^4 \wedge 0101 = \{0000, 0001, 0100, 0101\}$.

Since the Walsh functions form an orthogonal basis of $\mathbb{R}^{2^n}$, any arbitrary pseudoboolean function can be written as a weighted sum of Walsh functions in the following way:

$$f = \sum_{w \in \mathbb{B}^n} a_w \psi_w \tag{11}$$

where the values a_w are called Walsh coefficients. We can group together the Walsh functions having the same order to find the elementary landscape decomposition of the function. That is:

$$f^{(p)} = \sum_{\substack{w \in \mathbb{B}^n \\ \langle w | w \rangle = p}} a_w \psi_w \tag{12}$$

where each $f^{(p)}$ is an elementary function with eigenvalue $2p$. The function f can be written as a sum of the $n+1$ elementary components, that is: $f = \sum_{p=0}^{n} f^{(p)}$. Thus, any function can be decomposed in a sum of at most n elementary landscapes, since we can add the constant value $f^{(0)}$ to any of the other elementary components.

Once we know that the possible eigenvalues of the elementary components of any function f are $2p$ with $0 \leq p \leq n$, we can compute the possible eigenvalues of the sphere matrices. Since the size of the neighborhood is $d = n$, we conclude that the only possible eigenvalues for the spheres are $S^{(k)}(n - 2p)$ with $p \in \{0, 1, \ldots, n\}$. With the help of Eqs. (6) to (8) we can write a recurrence formula for the eigenvalues of the sphere matrices whose solution is $S^{(k)}(n - 2p) = \mathcal{K}_{k,p}^{(n)}$, where $\mathcal{K}_{k,p}^{(n)}$ is the (k, p) element of the n-th Krawtchouk matrix [10], which is an $(n + 1) \times (n + 1)$ integer matrix. We will use Krawtchouk matrices to simplify the expressions and reduce the computation of the elementary components of the test suite minimization. The interested reader can deepen on Krawtchouk matrices in [3]. One important property of the Krawtchouk matrices that will be useful in Section 4 is:

$$(1 + x)^{n-p}(1 - x)^p = \sum_{k=0}^{n} x^k \mathcal{K}_{k,p}^{(n)} \tag{13}$$

Each component $f^{(p)}$ of the elementary landscape decomposition of f is an eigenfunction of the sphere matrix of radius r with eigenvalue $S^{(r)}(n - 2p) = \mathcal{K}_{r,p}^{(n)}$. Thus, we can compute the average fitness value in a sphere of radius r around a solution x as:

$$\text{avg}_{y | \mathcal{H}(y,x)=r} \{f(y)\} = \binom{n}{r}^{-1} \sum_{p=0}^{n} \mathcal{K}_{r,p}^{(n)} f^{(p)}(x) \tag{14}$$

We can also compute the c-th moment of the function f in a sphere of radius r if we know the elementary landscape decomposition of f^c:

$$\mu_c = \operatorname*{avg}_{y|\mathcal{H}(y,x)=r}\{f^c(y)\} = \binom{n}{r}^{-1} \sum_{p=0}^{n} \mathcal{K}_{r,p}^{(n)} \left(f^c\right)^{(p)} (x) \tag{15}$$

3   Test Suite Minimization Problem

When a piece of software is modified, the new software is tested using some previous test cases in order to check if new errors were introduced. This check is known as *regression testing*. In [14] Yoo and Harman provide a very complete survey on search-based techniques for regression testing. They distinguish three different related problems: test suite minimization, test case selection and test case prioritization. The problem we face here is the test suite minimization [13]. We define the problem as follows. Let $\mathcal{T} = \{t_1, t_2, \ldots, t_n\}$ be a set of tests for a program and let $\mathcal{M} = \{m_1, m_2, \ldots, m_k\}$ be a set of elements of the program that we want to cover with the tests. After running all the tests $\mathcal{T}$ we find that each test can cover several program elements. This information is stored in a matrix T that is defined as:

$$T_{ij} = \begin{cases} 1 \text{ if node } m_i \text{ is covered by test } t_j \\ 0 \text{ otherwise} \end{cases} \tag{16}$$

We define the coverage of a subset of tests $X \subseteq \mathcal{T}$ as:

$$coverage(X) = |\{i|\exists j \in X, T_{ij} = 1\}| \tag{17}$$

The problem consists in finding a subset $X \subseteq \mathcal{T}$ such that the coverage is maximized while the number of tests cases in the set $|X|$ is minimized. We can define the objective function of the problem as the weighted sum of the coverage and the number of tests. Thus, the objective function can be written as:

$$f(X) = coverage(X) - c \cdot |X| \tag{18}$$

where c is a constant that set the relative importance of the cost and coverage. It can be interpreted as the cost of a test measured in the same units as the benefit of a new covered element in the software. We assume here that all the elements in $\mathcal{M}$ to be covered have the same value for the user and the cost of testing one test in $\mathcal{T}$ is the same for all of them. We defer to future work the analysis of the objective function when this assumption is not true. Although the function proposed is a weighted sum, which simplifies the landscape analysis, non-linear functions can be also used and analyzed.

In the following we will use binary strings to represent the solutions of the problem. Thus, we introduce the decision variables $x_j \in \mathbb{B}$ for $1 \leq j \leq n$. The variable x_j is 1 if test t_j is included in the solution and 0 otherwise. With this binary representation the coverage, the number of ones of a string and the objective function f can be written as:

$$coverage(x) = \sum_{i=1}^{k} \max_{j=1}^{n}\{T_{ij}x_j\}; \quad ones(x) = \sum_{j=1}^{n} x_j \tag{19}$$

$$f(x) = \sum_{i=1}^{k} \max_{j=1}^{n}\{T_{ij}x_j\} - c \cdot ones(x) \tag{20}$$

4   Elementary Landscape Decomposition

In this section we present two of the main contributions of this work: the elementary landscape decomposition of f and f^2. In order to simplify the equations let us introduce some notation. Let us define the sets $V_i = \{j | T_{ij} = 1\}$. V_i contains the indices of the tests which cover the element m_i. We also use in the following the term T_i to refer to the binary string composed of the elements of the i-th row of matrix T. T_i is a binary mask with 1s in the positions that appear in V_i.

4.1   Decomposition of f

The goal of this section is to find the Walsh decomposition of f. We first decompose the functions $coverage(x)$ and $ones(x)$ into elementary landscapes and then we combine the results. Let us start by analyzing the $coverage$ function and, in particular, let us write the maximum in its definition as a weighted sum of Walsh functions with the help of (10).

$$\max_{j=1}^{n}\{T_{ij}x_j\} = 1 - \prod_{j=1}^{n}(1 - T_{ij}x_j) = 1 - \prod_{j \in V_i}(1 - x_j)$$

$$= 1 - \prod_{j \in V_i} \frac{1 + \psi_j(x)}{2} = 1 - 2^{-|V_i|} \prod_{j \in V_i}(1 + \psi_j(x)) \tag{21}$$

We can expand the product of Walsh functions in (21) using $\psi_u \psi_v = \psi_{u+v}$ to get the Walsh decomposition of $\max_{j=1}^{n}$.

$$\max_{j=1}^{n}\{T_{ij}x_j\} = 1 - 2^{-|V_i|} \prod_{j \in V_i}(1 + \psi_j(x)) = 1 - 2^{-|V_i|} \sum_{W \in \mathcal{P}(V_i)} \prod_{j \in W} \psi_j(x) \tag{22}$$

$$= 1 - 2^{-|V_i|} \sum_{w \in \mathbb{B}^n \wedge T_i} \psi_w(x)$$

Using the Walsh decomposition we can obtain that elementary landscape decomposition. The elementary components are the sums of weighted Walsh functions having the same order (number of ones in the string w). We can distinguish two cases: the constant elementary component (with order 0) and the non-constant components. Then, the elementary landscape decomposition of $\max_{j=1}^{n}$ is:

$$\max_{j=1}^{n} \{T_{ij}x_j\}^{(0)} = 1 - \frac{1}{2^{|V_i|}} \tag{23}$$

$$\max_{j=1}^{n} \{T_{ij}x_j\}^{(p)} = -\frac{1}{2^{|V_i|}} \sum_{\substack{w \,\in\, \mathbb{B}^n \,\wedge\, T_i \\ \langle w, w \rangle = p}} \psi_w(x) \quad \text{where } p > 0 \tag{24}$$

Eqs. (23) and (24) are the elementary landscape decomposition of the coverage of one single software element. We just have to add all the components of all the k elements to get the elementary landscape decomposition of $coverage(x)$. However, we should highlight that the previous expression is not very efficient to compute the components of the maximum. We can observe that it requires to compute a sum of $\binom{|V_i|}{p}$ Walsh functions. Before combining all the pieces to get the elementary landscape decomposition of the objective function of the problem, we need first to find a simpler and more efficient expression for the elementary components of the coverage of one single element.

Up to the best of our knowledge, this is the first time that the following mathematical development is performed in the literature. The essence of the development, however, is useful by itself and can be applied to other problems with binary representation in which the Walsh analysis can be applied (like the Max-SAT problem). We will focus on the summation of (24). Let us rewrite this expression again as:

$$\sum_{\substack{w \,\in\, \mathbb{B}^n \,\wedge\, T_i \\ \langle w, w \rangle = p}} \psi_w(x) = \sum_{\substack{W \,\in\, \mathcal{P}(V_i) \\ |W| = p}} \prod_{j \in W} \psi_{\underline{j}}(x) \tag{25}$$

Now we can identify the second member of the previous expression with the coefficient of a polynomial. Let us consider the polynomial $Q_x^{(i)}(z)$ defined as:

$$Q_x^{(i)}(z) = \prod_{j \in V_i} (z + \psi_{\underline{j}}(x)) = \sum_{l=0}^{|V_i|} z^l \left(\sum_{\substack{W \,\in\, \mathcal{P}(V_i) \\ |W| = |V_i| - l}} \prod_{j \in W} \psi_{\underline{j}}(x) \right) = \sum_{l=0}^{|V_i|} q_l z^l \tag{26}$$

From (26) we conclude that the summation in (25) is the coefficient of $z^{|V_i|-p}$ in the polynomial $Q_x^{(i)}(z)$, that is, $q_{|V_i|-p}$. According to (10) and (26) we can write $Q_x^{(i)}(z) = (z+1)^{n_0^{(i)}} (z-1)^{n_1^{(i)}}$ where $n_0^{(i)}$ and $n_1^{(i)}$ are the number of zeros and ones, respectively, in the positions x_j of the solution with $j \in V_i$. It should be clear that $n_0^{(i)} + n_1^{(i)} = |V_i|$. Now we can profit from the fact that, according to (13), the polynomials $Q_x^{(i)}(z)$ are related to the Krawtchouk matrices by $Q_x^{(i)}(z) = (-1)^{n_1^{(i)}} \sum_{l=0}^{|V_i|} \mathcal{K}_{l,n_1^{(i)}}^{|V_i|} z^l$ and we can write $q_l = (-1)^{n_1^{(i)}} \mathcal{K}_{l,n_1^{(i)}}^{|V_i|}$. Finally we obtain:

$$\sum_{\substack{w \in \mathbb{B}^n \wedge T_i \\ \langle w, w \rangle = p}} \psi_w(x) = \sum_{\substack{W \in \mathcal{P}(V_i) \\ |W| = p}} \prod_{j \in W} \psi_j(x) = q_{|V_i|-p} = (-1)^{n_1^{(i)}} \mathcal{K}_{|V_i|-p,n_1^{(i)}}^{|V_i|} \quad (27)$$

The first N Krawtchouk matrices can be computed in $O(N^3)$. Furthermore, they can be computed once and stored in a file for future use. Thus, we transform the summation over a large number of Walsh functions into a count of the number of ones in a bit string and a read of a value stored in memory, which has complexity $O(n)$. Eq. (27) is an important result that allows us to provide an algorithm for evaluating the elementary landscape decomposition of our objective function. This algorithm is more efficient than the one proposed by Sutton *et al.* in [10]. We can now extend the elementary landscape decomposition to the complete coverage of all the elements. That is:

$$coverage^{(0)}(x) = \sum_{i=1}^{k} \max_{j=1}^{n} \{T_{ij}x_j\}^{(0)} = \sum_{i=1}^{k} \left(1 - \frac{1}{2^{|V_i|}}\right) \quad (28)$$

$$coverage^{(p)}(x) = \sum_{i=1}^{k} \max_{j=1}^{n} \{T_{ij}x_j\}^{(p)} = -\sum_{i=1}^{k} \frac{1}{2^{|V_i|}} (-1)^{n_1^{(i)}} \mathcal{K}_{|V_i|-p,n_1^{(i)}}^{|V_i|} \quad (29)$$

where $p > 0$. The previous expressions can be computed in $O(nk)$.

We now need the decomposition of the function $ones(x)$:

$$ones(x) = \sum_{j=1}^{n} x_j = \sum_{j=1}^{n} \frac{1 - \psi_j(x)}{2} = \frac{n}{2} - \frac{1}{2} \sum_{j=1}^{n} \psi_j(x) \quad (30)$$

Then, we can write:

$$ones^{(0)}(x) = \frac{n}{2}; \quad ones^{(1)}(x) = \frac{-1}{2} \sum_{j=1}^{n} \psi_j(x) = ones(x) - \frac{n}{2} \quad (31)$$

which is the elementary landscape decomposition of $ones(x)$. Finally, we combine this result with the decomposition of $coverage(x)$ to obtain the decomposition of f:

$$f^{(0)}(x) = \sum_{i=1}^{k} \left(1 - \frac{1}{2^{|V_i|}}\right) - c \cdot \frac{n}{2} \quad (32)$$

$$f^{(1)}(x) = -\sum_{i=1}^{k} \frac{1}{2^{|V_i|}} (-1)^{n_1^{(i)}} \mathcal{K}_{|V_i|-1,n_1^{(i)}}^{|V_i|} - c \cdot \left(ones(x) - \frac{n}{2}\right) \quad (33)$$

$$f^{(p)}(x) = -\sum_{i=1}^{k} \frac{1}{2^{|V_i|}} (-1)^{n_1^{(i)}} \mathcal{K}_{|V_i|-p,n_1^{(i)}}^{|V_i|} \quad \text{where } 1 < p \le n \quad (34)$$

All of the previous expressions can be computed in $O(nk)$. Since the maximum number of elementary components is equal to n, we can obtain the evaluation of all the elementary components of an arbitrary solution x in $O(n^2 k)$. We found an algorithm with complexity $O(nk)$ to compute all the elementary components of f. This complexity is lower than the $O(n^n)$ complexity of the algorithm proposed in [10].

4.2   Decomposition of f^2

In the previous section we found the elementary landscape decomposition of f. In this section we are interested in the elementary landscape decomposition of f^2, since it allows to compute the variance in any region (sphere or ball) around any arbitrary solution x. The derivation of the elementary landscape decomposition of f^2 is based again in the Walsh analysis of the function. Combining the Walsh decomposition in (22) with the one of (30) and the definition of f in (20), the function f^2 can be written as:

$$f^2(x) = \left[\left(k - \frac{cn}{2} \right) - \sum_{i=1}^{k} \left(\frac{1}{2|V_i|} \sum_{w \in \mathbb{B}^n \wedge T_i} \psi_w(x) \right) + \frac{c}{2} \sum_{j=1}^{n} \psi_j(x) \right]^2$$

We need to expand the expression in order to find the elementary landscape decomposition. Due to space constraints we omit the intermediate steps and present the final expressions of the elementary components of f^2:

$$\left(f^2\right)^{(0)}(x) = \beta^2 + \frac{c^2}{4} n - \sum_{i=1}^{k} \frac{c|V_i| + 2\beta}{2|V_i|} + \sum_{i,i'=1}^{k} \frac{1}{2|V_i \cup V_{i'}|} \tag{35}$$

$$\left(f^2\right)^{(1)}(x) = c\beta(n - 2ones(x)) - \sum_{i=1}^{k} \left(\frac{(c|V_i| + 2\beta)(-1)^{n_1^{(i)}}}{2|V_i|} \mathcal{K}^{|V_i|}_{|V_i|-1,n_1^{(i)}} \right)$$
$$+ \sum_{i,i'=1}^{k} \left(\frac{(-1)^{n_1^{(i \vee i')}}}{2|V_i \cup V_{i'}|} \mathcal{K}^{|V_i \cup V_{i'}|}_{|V_i \cup V_{i'}|-1,n_1^{(i \vee i')}} \right)$$
$$- c \sum_{i=1}^{k} \frac{n - 2ones(x) - |V_i| + 2n_1^{(i)}}{2|V_i|} \tag{36}$$

$$\left(f^2\right)^{(2)}(x) = \frac{c^2}{2}(-1)^{ones(x)} \mathcal{K}^n_{n-2,ones(x)} - \sum_{i=1}^{k} \left(\frac{(c|V_i| + 2\beta)(-1)^{n_1^{(i)}}}{2|V_i|} \mathcal{K}^{|V_i|}_{|V_i|-2,n_1^{(i)}} \right)$$
$$+ \sum_{i,i'=1}^{k} \left(\frac{(-1)^{n_1^{(i \vee i')}}}{2|V_i \cup V_{i'}|} \mathcal{K}^{|V_i \cup V_{i'}|}_{|V_i \cup V_{i'}|-2,n_1^{(i \vee i')}} \right)$$
$$- c \sum_{i=1}^{k} \frac{(-1)^{n_1^{(i)}}}{2|V_i|} \mathcal{K}^{|V_i|}_{|V_i|-1,n_1^{(i)}} \left(n - 2ones(x) - |V_i| + 2n_1^{(i)} \right) \tag{37}$$

$$\left(f^2\right)^{(p)}(x) = -\sum_{i=1}^{k}\left(\frac{(c|V_i|+2\beta)(-1)^{n_1^{(i)}}}{2^{|V_i|}}\mathcal{K}_{|V_i|-p,n_1^{(i)}}^{|V_i|}\right)$$

$$+\sum_{i,i'=1}^{k}\left(\frac{(-1)^{n_1^{(i\vee i')}}}{2^{|V_i\cup V_{i'}|}}\mathcal{K}_{|V_i\cup V_{i'}|-p,n_1^{(i\vee i')}}^{|V_i\cup V_{i'}|}\right)$$

$$-c\sum_{i=1}^{k}\frac{(-1)^{n_1^{(i)}}}{2^{|V_i|}}\mathcal{K}_{|V_i|-p+1,n_1^{(i)}}^{|V_i|}\left(n-2ones(x)-|V_i|+2n_1^{(i)}\right)\quad(38)$$

where $\beta = k - cn/2$, $n_1^{(i\vee i')}$ are the number of ones in the positions x_j of the solution with $j \in V_i \cup V_{i'}$ and $p > 2$. The elementary components (36), (37) and (38) can be computed in $O(nk^2)$. Furthermore, we found an algorithm which computes all (not only one) the components in $O(nk^2)$.

5   Application of the Decomposition

In Section 4 we have derived closed-form formulas for each elementary component of f and f^2. Using this decompositions we can compute the average μ_1 and the standard deviation σ of the fitness distribution in the spheres and balls of arbitrary radius around a given solution x. Once we have the evaluation of the elementary components, the first and second order moments of f, μ_1 and μ_2, can be computed from Eqs. (32)-(34) and (35)-(38) in $O(n)$ for any ball or sphere around the solution using (15). The standard deviation can be computed from the two first moments using the equation $\sigma = \sqrt{\mu_2 - \mu_1^2}$.

How can we use this information? We propose here the following operator. Given a solution x compute the μ_1 and σ of the fitness distribution around the solution in all the spheres and balls up to a maximum radius r. We can do this in $O(nk^2)$, assuming that r is fixed. Using the averages and the standard deviations computed, we check if there is a high probability of finding a solution in a region around x that is better than the best so far solution. This check is based on the expression $\mu_1 + d \cdot \sigma - best$, where d is parameter and $best$ is the fitness value of the best so far solution. The higher the value of the previous expression, the higher the probability of finding a solution in the corresponding region that is better than the best solution. The previous expression is based on the idea that most of the samples of a distribution can be found around the average at a distance that is a few times the standard deviation. For example, at least 75% of the samples can be found in the interval $[\mu_1 - 2\sigma, \mu_1 + 2\sigma]$. In the case of the normal distribution, the percentage is 95%. In our operator, if $\mu_1 + d \cdot \sigma > best$, then it is likely that a solution better than the best found can be inside the considered region. If that happens, then a local search is performed in the region. This local search evaluates all the solutions in that region and replaces the current one by the best solution found. The pseudocode of the operator is in Algorithm 1.

We call this operator Guarded Local Search (GLS) because it applies the local search only in the case that there exists some evidence for the success. In addition, the local search is performed in the region in which most probably a

Algorithm 1. Pseudocode of the GLS operator

```
1: best = best so far solution;
2: bestRegion = none;
3: quality = −∞;
4: for r ∈ all the considered regions do
5:    (μ₁,σ) = computeAvgStdDev(x,r);
6:    if μ₁ + d · σ − best > quality then
7:       quality = μ₁ + d · σ − best;
8:       bestRegion = r;
9:    end if
10: end for
11: y=x;
12: if quality > 0 then
13:    y = applyLocalSearchInRegion (x,bestRegion)
14: end if
15: return y
```

better solution would be found, thus minimizing the computation cost of a local
search in a larger region. We expect our proposed operator to have an important
intensification component. Thus, a population-based metaheuristic would be a
good complement to increase the diversification of the combined algorithm. The
operator can improve the quality of solutions of the algorithm it is included in,
but it also will increase the runtime. However, this runtime should be quite lower
than the one obtained if the local search would be applied at every step of the
algorithm.

5.1 Experimental Study

As a proof of concept, we analyze the performance of the proposed operator in
this section. For this experimental study we use a steady-state Genetic Algorithm (GA) with 10 individuals in the population, binary tournament selection,
bit-flip mutation with probability $p = 0.01$ of flipping a bit, one-point crossover
and elitist replacement. The stopping condition is to create 100 individuals (110
fitness evaluations). We compare three variants of the GA that differ in how the
local search is applied. The first variant does not include any local search operator. In the second variant, denoted with GLSr, the GLS operator of Algorithm 1
is applied to the offspring after the mutation. The regions considered are all the
spheres and balls up to radius r. The third variant, LSr, always applies the local
search after the mutation in a ball of radius r.

For the experiments we selected six programs from the Siemens suite. The
programs are `printtokens`, `printtokens2`, `schedule`, `schedule2`, `totinfo` and
`replace`. They are available from the Software-artifact Infrastructure Repository [2]. Each program has a large number of available test suites, from which
we select the first 100 tests covering different nodes. Thus, in our experiments
$n = 100$. The constant tuning the oracle cost was set to $c = 1$. We used three
values for the radius r: from 2 to 4. In the GLS the parameter d was set to $d = 2$.

Since we are dealing with stochastic algorithms we performed 30 independent executions and we show in Table 1 the average values obtained for the fitness of the best solution found and the execution time of the algorithms, respectively.

Table 1. Fitness of the best solution found and computation time (in seconds) of the algorithms (averages over 30 independent runs)

Alg.	printtokens		printtokens2		schedule		schedule2		totinfo		replace	
	Fit.	Secs.	Fit.	Secs.	Fit.	Secs.	Fit.	Secs.	Fit.	Secs.	Fit.	Secs.
GA	89.20	0.03	103.13	0.10	84.57	0.07	78.70	0.10	86.87	0.03	71.90	0.03
GLS2	105.17	37.93	119.63	69.73	101.60	21.10	93.60	52.63	102.30	39.07	88.13	37.30
LS2	113.27	10.67	129.00	20.73	111.07	3.80	103.10	3.17	110.00	3.03	97.67	5.53
GLS3	106.33	136.97	120.87	84.10	103.40	31.80	95.30	29.90	103.03	33.40	90.73	60.73
LS3	113.63	159.30	129.80	141.33	111.80	298.07	103.97	90.67	110.00	88.13	98.00	141.37
GLS4	105.27	390.03	121.47	363.53	103.40	237.17	96.37	212.70	104.33	206.50	91.13	368.97
LS4	114.00	3107.47	129.97	2943.03	112.00	2098.00	104.00	1875.67	110.00	1823.80	98.00	3602.47

We can observe in Table 1 that the ordering of the algorithms according to the solutions quality is LSr > GLSr > GA. This is the expected result, since LSr always applies a depth local search while GLSr applies the local search only in some favorable circumstances. An analysis of the evolution of the best fitness value reveals that this ordering is kept during the search process.

If we focus on the computation time required by the algorithms, we observe that GA is always the fastest algorithm. When $r \geq 3$, GLSr is faster than LSr. However, if $r = 2$ then LSr is faster than GLSr. This means that the complete exploration of a ball of radius $r = 2$ is faster than determining if a local search should be applied in the GLS operator. Although we show here the computation times, it should be noted that this depends on the implementation details and the machines used. For this reason the stopping condition is the number of evaluations. The great amount of time required to compute the elementary components is the main drawback of the GLS operator. However, this computation can be parallelized, as well as the application of the local search. In particular, Graphic Processing Units (GPUs) can be used to compute the elementary components in parallel.

6   Conclusion

We have applied landscape theory to find the elementary landscape decomposition of the Test Suite Minimization problem in regression testing. We have also decomposed the squared objective function. Using the closed-form formulas of the decomposition we can compute the average and the standard deviation of the fitness values around a given solution x in an efficient way. With these tools we proposed an operator to improve the quality of the solutions. This operator applies a local search around the solution only if the probability of finding a best solution is high. The results of an experimental study confirms that the operator improves the solutions requiring a moderate amount of computation. A blind local search outperforms the results of our proposed operator but requires a large amount of computation as the size of the explored region increases.

The future work should focus on new applications of the theory but also on new theoretical implications of the elementary landscape decomposition, such as determining the difficulty of a problem instance by observing its elementary components or predicting the behaviour of a search algorithm when applied to a problem.

Acknowledgements. We thank the anonymous reviewers for their interesting and fruitful comments. This research has been partially funded by the Spanish Ministry of Science and Innovation and FEDER under contract TIN2008-06491-C04-01 (the M* project) and the Andalusian Government under contract P07-TIC-03044 (DIRICOM project).

References

1. Chicano, F., Whitley, L.D., Alba, E.: A methodology to find the elementary landscape decomposition of combinatorial optimization problems. Evolutionary Computation (in Press) doi: 10.1162/EVCO_a_00039
2. Do, H., Elbaum, S., Rothermel, G.: Supporting controlled experimentation with testing techniques: An infrastructure and its potential impact. Empirical Softw. Engg. 10, 405–435 (2005),
   http://portal.acm.org/citation.cfm?id=1089922.1089928
3. Feinsilver, P., Kocik, J.: Krawtchouk polynomials and krawtchouk matrices. In: Baeza-Yates, R., Glaz, J., Gzyl, H. (eds.) Recent Advances in Applied Probability, pp. 115–141. Springer, US (2005)
4. Langdon, W.B.: Elementary bit string mutation landscapes. In: Beyer, H.-G., Langdon, W.B. (eds.) Foundations of Genetic Algorithms, January 5-9, 2011, pp. 25–41. ACM Press, Schwarzenberg (2011)
5. Lu, G., Bahsoon, R., Yao, X.: Applying elementary landscape analysis to search-based software engineering. In: Proceedings of the 2nd International Symposium on Search Based Software Engineering (2010)
6. Rana, S., Heckendorn, R.B., Whitley, D.: A tractable walsh analysis of SAT and its implications for genetic algorithms. In: Proceedings of AAAI, pp. 392–397. AAAI Press, Menlo Park (1998)
7. Reidys, C.M., Stadler, P.F.: Combinatorial landscapes. SIAM Review 44(1), 3–54 (2002)
8. Stadler, P.F.: Toward a theory of landscapes. In: López-Peña, R., Capovilla, R., García-Pelayo, R., Waelbroeck, H., Zertruche, F. (eds.) Complex Systems and Binary Networks, pp. 77–163. Springer, Heidelberg (1995)
9. Sutton, A.M., Howe, A.E., Whitley, L.D.: Directed plateau search for MAX-k-SAT. In: Proceedings of SoCS, Atlanta, GA, USA (July 2010)
10. Sutton, A.M., Whitley, L.D., Howe, A.E.: Computing the moments of k-bounded pseudo-boolean functions over Hamming spheres of arbitrary radius in polynomial time. Theoretical Computer Science (in press) doi:10.1016/j.tcs.2011.02.006
11. Sutton, A.M., Whitley, L.D., Howe, A.E.: A polynomial time computation of the exact correlation structure of k-satisfiability landscapes. In: Proceedings of GECCO, pp. 365–372. ACM, New York (2009)

12. Whitley, D., Sutton, A.M., Howe, A.E.: Understanding elementary landscapes. In: Proceedings of GECCO, pp. 585–592. ACM, New York (2008)
13. Yoo, S., Harman, M.: Pareto efficient multi-objective test case selection. In: Proceedings of the 2007 International Symposium on Software Testing and Analysis (ISSTA 2007), July 9-12, 2007, pp. 140–150. ACM, London (2007)
14. Yoo, S., Harman, M.: Regression testing minimisation, selection and prioritisation: A survey. Journal of Software Testing, Verification and Reliability (2010)

A Fuzzy Approach to Requirements Prioritization

Dayvison Chaves Lima, Fabrício Freitas, Gutavo Campos, and Jerffeson Souza

Optimization in Software Engineering Group (GOES.UECE), State University of Ceará,
Avenue Paranjana, 1700, Ceará, Brazil
{dayvison,fabriciogf.uece}@gmail.com,
{gustavo,jeff}@larces.uece.br

Abstract. One of the most important issues in a software development project is the requirements prioritization. This task is used to indicate an order for the implementation of the requirements. This problem has uncertain aspects, therefore Fuzzy Logic concepts can be used to properly represent and tackle the task. The objective of this work is to present a formal framework to aid the decision making in prioritizing requirements in a software development process, including ambiguous and vague data.

Keywords: Requirements Prioritization, SBSE Applications, Fuzzy Logic.

1 Introduction

Search Based Software Engineering (SBSE) is a field that proposes to modeling and solve complex software engineering problems by using search techniques, such as metaheuristics. Among the problems already tackled, the requirements prioritization problem has received special attention recently.

In [1], approaches to deal with the requirement prioritization problem are presented, where genetic algorithm is employed. Such optimization approach does not consider the fuzzy and vagueness human goals, such as linguistics evaluations of stakeholders.

Examples of goals that may be measured in a fuzzy linguist approach are stakeholders' satisfaction, deliver on time, deliver on budget, deliver all planned scope, meet quality requirements, team satisfaction, and deliver all high-priority functionalities in the first release.

An approach to prioritize requirements using fuzzy decision making was proposed in [2]. The proposed algorithm assists stakeholders in analyzing conflicting requirements in terms of goals and constraints of reaching to a crisp optimal decision value against which an appropriate priority can be assigned to the conflicting requirement. The influence of requirements prioritization on goals was not considered.

Therefore, the objective of this work is to present a formal framework guided by fuzzy goals to be used in the requirements prioritization task.

Section 2 presents the proposed formal framework. Section 3 shows some initial results with the requirement prioritization problem. Section 4 outlines conclusions and future works.

M.B. Cohen and M. Ó Cinnéide (Eds.): SSBSE 2011, LNCS 6956, pp. 64–69, 2011.

2 Formal Framework

In this framework, capital letters denote sets, fuzzy sets and fuzzy relations, $U = 0.0 + 0.1 + ... + 1.0$ is the discourse universe for the definition of fuzzy sets and $L = [0,1]$ is the interval for defining the participation values, $F(U)$ denotes the family of fuzzy sets defined in U. Section 2.1 formalizes the information regarding the Software Fuzzy Goals. Section 2.2 formalizes an evaluation function for this approach.

2.1 Definitions

This first part of the framework allows the representation of fuzzy software goals, fuzzy desired situations and fuzzy requirements for the stakeholder. Each attribute of a goal is represented by a linguistic variable (X) [3] [4]. The values of these variables are sentences in the language formed by terms that are aspiration level values, e. g., $T("Aspiration") = ... + low + medium + ... + high + ...$ The meaning of these levels corresponds to fuzzy subsets of U, e. g., $low = [1.0, 1.0, 0.9, 0.7, 0.5, 0.2, 0.0, 0.0, 0.0, 0.0, 0.0]$ and $high = [0.0, 0.0, 0.0, 0.0, 0.0, 0.0, 0.3, 0.5, 1.0, 1.0, 1.0])$. Where the "+" sign represents the union of the elements of set.

A pair (variable, aspiration level) defines a fuzzy software goal. In general, more than one fuzzy software goal is used in the specifications of a desired fuzzy situation. Each goal contributes to a different degree to the meaning of the situation. The next three definitions formalize software goal, desired situation and requirement.

Definition 1. A software goal Gm is fuzzy if the aspiration level Am, assigned to attribute Xm of a desired situation, is described in terms of a fuzzy subset of U:

$$G_m = \left(X_{m,}, A_m = \sum_{i=1}^{L} A_m(u_i)/u_i \right), \tag{1}$$

where X_m is the name of the m-th linguistic variable that represents the m-th attribute of a desired situation; L is the limit of elements in U; A_m is a particular linguistic value of X_m belonging to $T("Aspiration")$ and represents the aspiration level assigned to X_m; and $A_m(u_i)$ is the participation degree of $u_i \in U$ in the fuzzy set that defines $A_m \in F(U)$.

Definition 2. A situation is denominated fuzzy if its concept is a fuzzy set described in terms of fuzzy goals Gm and the degrees of participation μm (m = 1, ..., M), subjectively indicating how much these goals are important in a fuzzy desired situation DS,

$$DS = \sum_{m=1}^{M} \mu_m/G_m \tag{2}$$

Definition 3. A requirement Rer is denominated fuzzy if its concept is a fuzzy set described in terms of pairs (Xm, Rmr) and degrees of participation μm (m = 1, ..., M),

$$Re_r = \sum_{m=1}^{M} \mu_m/(X_m, R_{mr}) \qquad (3)$$

where X_m is the name of the m-th linguistic variable employed for the representation of the m-th attribute in a desired fuzzy situation; and $R_{mr} \in F(U)$ are particular linguistic values of X_m belonging to $T("Aspiration")$ and represents the achieved level assigned to the attribute X_m due the implementation of the requirement r.

2.2 Evaluation Function

The evaluation function for fuzzy requirements considers similarity measurements between the fuzzy sets that express the achieved and the aspired levels in each one of the attributes, and their respective values of importance within the context of the fuzzy requirements and fuzzy desired situations [5]:

$$f_{eval(Re_r, DS)} = \sum_{m=1}^{M} \mu_m \alpha(R_{mr}, A_m) / \sum_{m=1}^{M} \mu_m \qquad (4)$$

Where α is a similarity measurement between fuzzy sets and assumes, in this article, the form:

$$\alpha(R_{mr}, A_m) = 1 - \left(\sum_{i=1}^{L} |R_{mr}(u_i) - A_m u_i| / L^{1/2} \right) \qquad (5)$$

where $u_i \in U$ and L is the limit of elements in U.

The second term of the difference in (5) is the Euclidean distance between fuzzy sets [6]. It is worth noting that: $\alpha: F(U)xF(U) \rightarrow [0, 1]$. Therefore, as the similarity values between the levels in Re_r and DS increase, f_eval increases. In this case, for each m = 1, ..., M, if $R_{mr} = A_m$ then f_eval is 1 maximum and equal to 1. As the similarity values decrease, f_eval decreases, reaching a minimum equal to 0. These properties allow the stakeholder to obtain measurements as promising as the fuzzy requirements are in the design of a satisfactory prioritization.

3 Evaluation

This section presents some tests performed with the prioritization mechanism, programmed from the formal framework proposed in the last section. It was divided into two subsections. Section 3.1 presents information on the evaluation instance. Section 3.2 presents a specific prioritization problem, the solution produced by the proposed prioritization mechanism, and a brief analysis of these initial results.

3.1 Evaluation Instance

The evaluation instance used for testing the framework for requirements prioritization in a fuzzy linguistic approach is composed of seven goals and nine requirements.

These goals are frequently used in [7] to help stakeholders to reflect the dimensions of the success of a software development project. The objective is to verify the capability of the proposed framework over the prioritization task and its level of responsiveness in requirements evaluation changes.

Table 1 describes some aspired levels and their representation in terms of fuzzy sets. Table 2, according to Definition 1, describes the scenario with seven attributes (X_m) that define seven fuzzy software goals (G_m). According to Definition 2, it presents a description of the fuzzy aspired level and the importance degree (μ_m) of the goals that define the fuzzy desired situation (DS). According to Definition 3, it also presents the achieved fuzzy levels (R_{mr}) of the fuzzy requirements (Re_{mr}) in the attributes that define the desired situation. Fuzzy aspired levels in the seven fuzzy software goals that define the desired situation were represented by [m, h, l, h, l, h, m].

Consider, as an example, the development of an ATM system. The attribute X_1 may represent "Deliver all high-priority functionalities in the first release" and has an aspired level medium (m) in the software goal G_1, that defines the fuzzy desired situation. The requirements Re_4 and Re_7 are, for example, "Withdrawal Transaction" and "Show Welcome Message" respectively. In this example, the first transaction contributes in high degree (h) to the level of attribute X_1, while the second influences at low level (l) to X_1, as can be seen in table 2.

Table 1. Description of each priority in linguistic terms and their representation in terms of fuzzy sets

Linguistic Term	Fuzzy Set Representation
low (l)	[1.0, 1.0, 0.9, 0.7, 0.5, 0.2, 0.0, 0.0, 0.0, 0.0, 0.0]
medium (m)	[0.0, 0.0, 0.0, 0.8, 0.9, 1.0, 0.7, 0.0, 0.0, 0.0, 0.0]
high (h)	[0.0, 0.0, 0.0, 0.0, 0.0, 0.0, 0.3, 0.5, 1.0, 1.0, 1.0]

Table 2. Description of each fuzzy requirement, contribution level to achievement of goals and desired state of each goal

Attributes (X_m)	X_1	X_2	X_3	X_4	X_5	X_6	X_7
Importance (μ_m)	0.6	1.0	0.4	0.2	0.4	0.8	0.6
Desired Situation (DS)	m	h	l	h	l	h	m
Re_1	m	h	l	h	l	h	m
Re_2	h	m	h	m	h	l	l
Re_3	h	h	m	h	l	m	h
Re_4	h	l	m	h	l	l	h
Re_5	m	l	l	m	h	h	m
Re_6	h	l	m	h	l	m	h
Re_7	l	m	m	h	l	h	h
Re_8	m	m	m	h	l	h	h
Re_9	h	m	m	h	l	h	h

3.2 Prioritization Results

Table 3 describes the results of the execution of three tests. At each column, there is a requirement description and a real number representing the level of similarity of that requirement to goals. For each test, one variable was changed to alter the generated prioritized list obtained with the application of the evaluation function in Expressions (4) and (5). Test 1 was the control test where requirement Re_1 was left purposely equal to the desired state. In Test 2, the desired fuzzy situation DS was changed to [m, l, l, h, l, h, m], where just the aspired level in X_2 was changed from high to low. In Test 3 the importance of G_4 was changed from 0.2 to 0.8. In the fourth test the values of representation of linguistic variables "low", "medium" and "high" were all changed to 0.1.

Table 3. Prioritized lists generated form each test. First value is the requirement number and second is the level of importance to goals

Test 1	Test 2	Test 3	Test 4
Re_1,1.00	Re_5,0.88	Re_1,1.00	Re_1,1.00
Re_5,0.68	Re_1,0.80	Re_8,0.69	Re_2,1.00
Re_8,0.64	Re_8,0.67	Re_5,0.63	Re_3,1.00
Re_3,0.57	Re_7,0.58	Re_3,0.62	Re_4,1.00
Re_7,0.55	Re_6,0.57	Re_7,0.61	Re_5,1.00
Re_9,0.53	Re_9,0.56	Re_9,0.59	Re_6,1.00
Re_6,0.37	Re_4,0.56	Re_6,0.45	Re_7,1.00
Re_4,0.36	Re_3,0.37	Re_4,0.44	Re_8,1.00
Re_2,0.26	Re_2,0.29	Re_2,0.26	Re_9,1.00

As expected, in Test 1 Re_1 achieved 100% of similarity with goals since it has exactly the same definition of the desired fuzzy situation [m, h, l, h, l, h, m], this is also seen in Test 3. There was a reordering in Tests 2 an 3 influenced by the changes in the aspiration and importance levels. For Test 2, for example, there is no requirement whit 100% of similarity, since all of them are different from the desired situation. For Test 3, as expected, Re_1 was still at the top of the list, and the reduction on importance of G_4 motived the new requirements' order. For Test 4, we find that by using the same value to represent the linguistic variables, there is no improvement proved unexpectedly strong, given that all requirements are evaluated the same way.

4 Conclusion and Future Works

Requirements prioritization is a hard task to be performed. Previous works tackled the problem without bearing in mind the uncertainty present in a software development process. This paper proposed a formal framework guided by fuzzy goals to be applied to solve the requirements prioritization problem.

Besides presenting the formal framework, a sample application to evaluate the effectiveness of the proposed approach was described. The results demonstrated the ability of the approach in relation to the flexibility that may occurs in the task. For the tests, the variation of a configuration leads to a new solution by the proposed framework.

Future studies include interdependency between goals, also included the prioritization taking into account the evaluation of the stakeholders involved and changing the value of the contribution of goals for the use of fuzzy terms instead of real numbers, and application of the framework to a real world project.

References

1. Brasil, M., Freitas, F., Silva, T., Souza, J., Cortés, M.: A New Multiobjective Optimization Approach for Release Planning in Iterative and Incremental Software Development. In: Proceedings of the Brazilian Workshop on Optimization in Software Engineering (WOES 2010), pp. 30–37 (2010) (in Portuguese)
2. Gaur, V., Soni, A.: An Integrated Approach to Prioritize Requirements using Fuzzy Decision Making. IACSIT International Journal of Engineering and Technology 2(4), 320–328 (2010)
3. Wilhelm, M., Parsaei, H.: A Fuzzy Linguistic Approach to Implementing a Strategy for Computer Integrated Manufacturing. Fuzzy Sets and Systems 42(2), 191–204 (1991)
4. Zadeh, L.: Fuzzy Sets. Information and Control, 338–353 (1965)
5. Driankov, D.: An outline of a fuzzy sets approach to decision making with interdependent goals. Fuzzy Sets and Systems 21(3), 275–288 (1987)
6. Lazim, M., Abu Osman, M.: Measuring Teachers' Beliefs about Mathematics: A fuzzy Set. International Journal of Social Sciences 4(1), 39–43 (2009)
7. Cohn, M.: Project Sucess Sliders. In: Mountain Goat Software, http://www.mountaingoatsoftware.com/tools/project-success

Multi-level Automated Refactoring Using Design Exploration

Iman Hemati Moghadam*

School of Computer Science and Informatics
University College Dublin, Ireland
Iman.Hemati-Moghadam@ucdconnect.ie

Abstract. In the past few years, there has been a growing interest in automating refactoring activities using metaheuristic approaches. These current refactoring approaches involve source-to-source transformation. However, detailed information at source-code level makes precondition checking and source-level refactorings hard to perform. It also severely limits how extensively a program can be refactored. While design improvement tools can be used for a deep and fast design exploration, it is left to the programmer to manually apply the required refactorings to the source code, which is a burdensome task.

To tackle the above problems, our proposal is based on a multi-level refactoring approach that involves both design and source code in the refactoring process. Initially, the program design is extracted from the source code. Then, in a design exploration phase, using a metaheuristic approach, the design is transformed to a better one in terms of a metrics suite as well as the user perspective. The source code is then refactored based on both the improved design and the metrics suite. Using this approach, we expect a deeper and faster exploration of the program design space, that may result more opportunities for design improvement.

Keywords: Multi-level refactoring, search-based refactoring, design exploration.

1   Introduction and Problem Description

A software system must constantly change to cope with new requirements or to adjust to a new environment. As it evolves, very often, its design erodes unless it is regularly refactored to ensure that it is kept appropriate for its functionality. In fact, the design should be simultaneously updated to accommodate new requirements. However, manual refactoring is a tedious, complicated, and error-prone activity [11], so it is natural to automate this process as much as possible.

Over the past few years, there has been a growing interest in automating refactoring activities based on metaheuristic approaches. These approaches are attractive because they propose a simple solution to the complex process of

---

* Under supervision of Dr. Mel Ó Cinnéide.

M.B. Cohen and M. Ó Cinnéide (Eds.): SSBSE 2011, LNCS 6956, pp. 70–75, 2011.
© Springer-Verlag Berlin Heidelberg 2011

refactoring, which is usually characterized by several competing and conflicting objectives [4].

A search-based refactoring approach uses metaheuristic approaches to guide the refactoring process, and software metrics to direct the process towards higher quality designs. In this approach, a refactoring is acceptable if it, apart from preserving the behavior of the system, improves the merit of the design based on a metrics suite.

Using a search-based refactoring approach, it is possible to apply many refactorings without programmer intervention and hence improve automatically the design to an acceptable level of quality. However, it may cause difficulties in preserving programmer understandability. In fact, in this process, the programmer only sees the end result of the refactoring process and is liable to find it hard to understand especially when a large number of refactorings are applied to the system.

The current code improvement approaches, including metaheuristic ones, involve source-to-source transformation that leads to another drawback. The source code contains low-level detailed information and this makes computing preconditions on source code and performing source-level refactorings complicated and time-consuming. Furthermore, strong static code dependence between source code entities such as relationships between methods and attributes disallow many refactorings. It limits how fundamentally the design of a program can be changed.

Metaheuristic approaches have been used to perform design-level refactoring to UML-like design models [2], [10], [13]. While these approaches can indeed be used for deep design exploration, it is left to the programmer to manually apply the refactorings to the source code, which can be a burdensome task. Furthermore, in an agile context where source code is the only documentation of the system and UML models are not maintained, this approach cannot be used.

The research described in this paper presents a new approach to cope with the above-mentioned problems, one that also provides the benefits of both code and design improvement approaches. It is based on a combination of code and design improvement tools and addresses existing problems with programmer comprehension of the refactored program. It also enables a deeper exploration of the program design space than has been possible up until now.

The remainder of this article is structured as follows: The key idea of this research project is described in Section 2. Our progress to date is presented in Section 3. In Section 4, we survey related work and conclude in Section 5.

2   Proposed Solution

The main goal of this research project is to investigate how a refactoring approach can be extended to perform radical, rather than surface, design exploration, and to address the problem of comprehension of the refactored program. To achieve these goals, our proposal is to involve design and source code as well as the user in the refactoring process.

The proposed solution is based on a multi-level refactoring approach as illustrated in Fig. 1. In this approach the refactoring process is divided into two steps namely *Design Exploration* and *Full Refactoring* as follows:

1. **Design Exploration:** Initially, a UML-like design model is extracted from the source code using extract model process. Then, in a design exploration phase, using metaheuristic approaches, the design is transformed to a better design in terms of a metrics suite. As most of the program detail, especially in method bodies, has been abstracted away, precondition checking and refactoring execution become much faster. This will also enable a more extensive search of the design space than has been hitherto possible. At the end of the design exploration phase, a number of possible best (Pareto optimal) designs are presented to the user who selects one design as desirable design they wish to use.
2. **Full Refactoring:** In this detailed refactoring phase, the source code is refactored under the general guidance of the metrics suite, but crucially using the design selected in stage (1) as the ultimate goal. When this process completes, the resulting program will have the same functional behaviour as the original, and a design close to the one chosen by the user in stage (1).

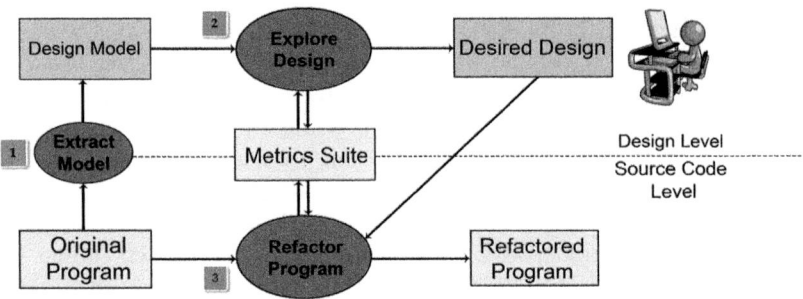

Fig. 1. Multi-level refactoring using a search-based refactoring approach

2.1 Key Research Questions

The main research questions involved in this research project are as follows:

RQ 1: Does the proposed approach produce programs of higher quality than a source-to-source refactoring approach in terms of *metrics values*?

RQ 2: Does the approach lead to a better understanding of refactoring process as well as the refactored program in terms of *the user perspective*?

RQ 3: Does the approach produce programs that are a *greater design distance* from the original than those produced by the source-to-source refactoring approach?

RQ 4: The refactoring process is informed not only by the metrics suite, but also by the user-selected design and the series of transformations that led to this program design. How this combination is best used to guide the search is an open question.

RQ 5: The refactoring process is guided by a metrics suite. Which metrics should be in this suite to achieve the best design improvement is an open question. While a number of "off-the-shelf" suites are available (QMOOD [3], MOOD [1], etc.), we expect the answer to lie in a tailored metrics suite.

RQ 6: Can the same (or similar) metrics suite be used for the design exploration process as for the refactoring process?

2.2 Plan for Evaluation

The value of multi-level automated refactoring will be assessed by building a search-based refactoring tool that implements the concept and then evaluates it.

Concerning RQ1, empirical experiments will be carried out where a software system that has some design problems will be refactored using both the multilevel refactoring approach as well as the non-interactive source-to-source refactoring approach. The two refactored programs will then be compared. The hypothesis that multi-level refactoring is valuable will be proven if the proposed approach can produce better programs in terms of metrics values including in metrics suite.

Regarding RQ2, a user study will be conducted with experienced, industry-based software engineers to ascertain whether the proposed approach can improve the user understandability of refactoring process as well as the refactored program. Experiments will be conducted, similar to those used to evaluate RQ1, where the effectiveness of proposed approach is measured based on user perspective which is evaluated using questionnaires. In this experiment, it is assumed that the users are familiar with the systems under investigation and know the existing design problems in these systems.

3 Progress to Date

To validate the proposed approach, an automated refactoring tool called Code-Imp[1] has been implemented [6]. It takes Java 6 source code as input, extracts design metric information, calculates quality values according to an evaluation function, and applies refactorings to the source code. Its output consists of the refactored input code as well as detailed refactorings and metrics information.

Code-Imp supports different combinations (weighted-sum and Pareto optimality) of over 30 software quality metrics and uses various search techniques including different hill climbing techniques to guide the refactoring process. The tool focuses on design-level refactorings that have a significant impact on program design. Currently, it supports 14 refactorings such as moving methods and fields around the class hierarchy, splitting and merging classes, and also changing inheritance relationship to delegation relationship and vice versa.

Currently, we are extending Code-Imp to direct the process of refactoring not only using the metrics suite, but also based on the user-selected design. The design is expressed as a UML model and we are investigating how this combination can achieve the best trade-off between metrics and the desired design.

---

[1] Combinatorial Optimisation for Design Improvement.

4   Related Work

Related work is discussed along two dimensions: *search-based refactoring tools* and *search-based design tools*. They differ from each other in that search-based design happens during the design of a software system (before implementing it in source code), while search-based refactoring occurs after a software system is designed and implemented [13].

Search-based refactoring: The idea of considering object-oriented design improvement as a combinatorial optimization problem was initially investigated by O'Keeffe and Ó Cinnéide [8], [9]. They showed how a search-based refactoring approach can be used to improve the quality of a program in terms of *Flexibility*, *Understandability*, and *Reusability* based on the QMOOD metrics suite. Seng et al. [12] proposed a similar approach based on a genetic algorithm to optimize the program by moving methods between classes in program. Similar work was done by Harman and Tratt [5] except that they introduced the idea of using a Pareto optimal approach to make the combination of metrics easier. Jensen and Cheng [7] used genetic programming to drive a search-based refactoring process that aims to introduce design patterns.

Search-based design: Simons et. al [13] showed how an interactive, evolutionary search technique can improve activities in upstream software design. They used a multi-objective GA to design a class structure from a design problem derived from use cases. In this approach, a designer and software agents cooperate together to guide the search towards a better class design. Raiha et. al [10] extracted initial design from a responsibility dependence graph and proposed a GA-based approach to automatically produce software architectures containing some design patterns. Amoui et al. [2] investigated how introducing architecture design patterns to a UML design model using GA can improve reusability of software architecture.

5   Conclusion

In recent years, there has been an amount of work done in using search-based techniques to improve the design of existing code by means of refactoring. However, attention to the source code alone during the refactoring process has made previous approaches not as effective as they could be. To improve the approach, what really is needed is a design-level search that is unhindered by source code detail and can therefore traverse the design space fluidly.

As a solution, we proposed a multi-level refactoring approach as a combination of code and design improvement tools to refactor a program based on both its design and source code. We anticipate the proposed approach, apart from improving the quality of the design with respect to metrics and user perspective, is capable of expanding the search space that were not previously possible. To validate the approach, we presented Code-Imp as an infrastructure that has been implemented to facilitate experiments based on this proposed solution.

References

1. Brito e Abreu, F., Carapuça, R.: Candidate metrics for object-oriented software within a taxonomy framework. Journal of Systems and Software 26, 87–96 (1994)
2. Amoui, M., Mirarab, S., Ansari, S., Lucas, C.: A genetic algorithm approach to design evolution using design pattern transformation. International Journal of Information Technology and Intelligent Computing 1(2), 235–244 (2006)
3. Bansiya, J., Davis, C.: A hierarchical model for object-oriented design quality assessment. IEEE Transactions on Software Engineering 28, 4–17 (2002)
4. Harman, M., Mansouri, S.A., Zhang, Y.: Search based software engineering: A comprehensive analysis and review of trends techniques and applications. Tech. Rep. TR-09-03 (April 2009)
5. Harman, M., Tratt, L.: Pareto optimal search based refactoring at the design level. In: Proceedings of the 9th Annual Conference on Genetic and Evolutionary Computation, GECCO 2007, pp. 1106–1113. ACM, New York (2007)
6. Hemati Moghadam, I., Ó Cinnéide, M.: Code-imp: a tool for automated search-based refactoring. In: Proceeding of the 4th Workshop on Refactoring Tools, WRT 2011, pp. 41–44. ACM, New York (2011)
7. Jensen, A.C., Cheng, B.H.: On the use of genetic programming for automated refactoring and the introduction of design patterns. In: Proceedings of the 12th Annual Conference on Genetic and Evolutionary Computation, pp. 1341–1348 (2010)
8. O'Keeffe, M., Ó Cinnéide, M.: Search-based software maintenance. In: Proceedings of the 10th Conference on Software Maintenance and Reengineering (CSMR 2006), pp. 249–260. IEEE, Italy (2006)
9. O'Keeffe, M., Ó Cinnéide, M.: Search-based refactoring for software maintenance. Journal of Systems and Software 81(4), 502–516 (2008)
10. Raiha, O., Koskimies, K., Mkinen, E.: Genetic Synthesis of Software Architecture. In: Li, X., et al. (eds.) SEAL 2008. LNCS, vol. 5361, pp. 565–574. Springer, Heidelberg (2008)
11. Roberts, D.B.: Practical Analysis for Refactoring. Ph.D. thesis, Department of Computer Science, Champaign, IL, USA (1999)
12. Seng, O., Stammel, J., Burkhart, D.: Search-based determination of refactorings for improving the class structure of object-oriented systems. In: Proceedings of the 8th Annual Conference on Genetic and Evolutionary Computation, GECCO 2006, pp. 1909–1916. ACM, New York (2006)
13. Simons, C., Parmee, I., Gwynllyw, R.: Interactive, evolutionary search in upstream object-oriented class design. IEEE Transactions on Software Engineering 36(6), 798–816 (2010)

Complexity Metrics for Hierarchical State Machines

Mathew Hall*

Department of Computer Science, University of Sheffield, UK
m.hall@dcs.shef.ac.uk

Abstract. Automatically generated state machines are constrained by their complexity, which can be reduced via hierarchy generation. A technique has been demonstrated for hierarchy generation, although evaluation of this technique has proved difficult.

There are a variety of metrics that can be used to provide indicators of how complicated a state machine or statechart is, one such example is cyclomatic complexity (the number of edges - the number of states + 2). Despite this, the existing complexity metric for statecharts does not operate on the hierarchy, instead providing an equivalent cyclomatic complexity for statecharts by ignoring it.

This paper defines two new metrics; Top Level Cyclomatic Complexity and Hierarchical Cyclomatic Complexity. These metrics assess the complexity of a hierarchical machine directly, as well as allowing for comparison between the original, flat state machine and its hierarchical counterpart.

1   Introduction

One of the problems that precludes the widespread use of state machines is their inefficient growth of complexity with size; as the number of states increase, the likelihood of duplication of parts of the machine increases. Complexity impacts understandability [1], meaning state machines get less understandable as they grow, jeopardising their utility in reverse engineering scenarios.

Adding a hierarchy to a machine reduces its complexity by providing abstraction, breaking the machine into multiple levels of behavioural detail. State hierarchies were originally proposed by Harel in statecharts [4] which add "superstates", which contain more superstates or simple states to represent a hierarchy.

Search-based hierarchy generation has been used to generate groupings for software module dependency graphs based on the number of edges between groups of modules [9]. An information-theoretic method has also been used [6] to accomplish the same goal. The former method has also been used to produce hierarchies for state machines [3].

Published results of these techniques both exhibit a common flaw; in the absence of an expert, evaluation of results is difficult. Metrics allow results to

---

* Supported by EPSRC grant EP/F065825/1 REGI: Reverse Engineering State Machine Hierarchies by Grammar Inference.

M.B. Cohen and M. Ó Cinnéide (Eds.): SSBSE 2011, LNCS 6956, pp. 76–81, 2011.

be compared and ranked without the requirement of a pre-determined solution to compare them to (or human participation to provide ranking). Structural properties affect the cognitive complexity of software [10]; therefore metrics that express these properties numerically express the complexity of the artefact under investigation.

Statechart specific metrics have been defined, although none take into account the hierarchy of the states, but simply the connectivity between them. This work proposes two metrics for this purpose; principally to facilitate evaluation of automatic hierarchy generation techniques. In addition to these metrics, this work also formally defines a hierarchical state machine as an extension of a labeled transition system.

2   Background

One oft-used metric is McCabe Cyclomatic Complexity (CC) [8]. Defined as $E - N + 2$, where E is the number of edges in a graph, and N is the number of nodes, it offers an estimate of how complex an artefact is. Originally applied to software systems (where the graph is the control-flow graph) it gives an approximate indicator of the difficulty developers will have when maintaining a module.

CC has been applied to statecharts in two ways. One such way is to calculate the sum of the CC of the code that implements each state [11]. Another is to perform the normal CC calculation, ignoring superstates, operating only on simple states, known as structural cyclomatic complexity (SCC) [2].

The value of the latter, if applied in the context of reverse engineering hierarchies would rarely change, as the number of simple states is constant. The number of transitions, however may reduce complexity [5]. The transition count is reduced whenever every state in a superstate has one or more transitions in common. These common transitions are replaced by a single transition from the superstate, resulting in fewer overall edges.

Despite this reduction of cyclomatic complexity, this metric is reduced to counting the number of edges in the machine when comparing results; rather than analysing the abstraction in the form of redistribution of complexity.

This work is applied to hierarchical state machines (HSMs). These can be viewed as an extension of a labeled transition system (LTS), a generalisation of a state machine, consisting of only states and transitions with an associated label. These extensions are defined below.

3   Hierarchical State Machines

A hierarchical machine adds a structure to the states, encoded in sets, to the machine. States represent superstates, which may contain superstates themselves, as well as zero or more simple states (a superstate must never be empty).

The standard used in this work also takes superstate transitions from the similar statechart formalism. It is possible for a transition to occur from not

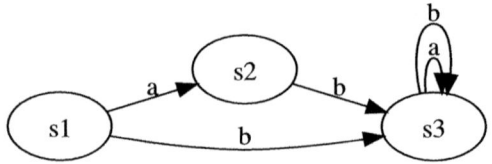

Fig. 1. The example state machine L

only a single state, but also a superstate. These transitions are shorthand for a transition occurring from every state in a superstate.

An example LTS L, given by $L = (Q, T) = (\{s_1, s_2, s_3\}, T\})$ where $T = \{(s_1, a, s_2), (s_1, b, s_3), (s_2, b, s_3), (s_3, a, s_3), (s_3, b, s_3)\}$ is shown in figure 1. Q encodes the states in the machine, while T encodes the transitions. T is a set of transitions, each $t \in T$ is a tuple - (s, l, d) where s is the source of the transition (any element of Q), l is the label for the transition and d is the destination (again, $d \in Q$).

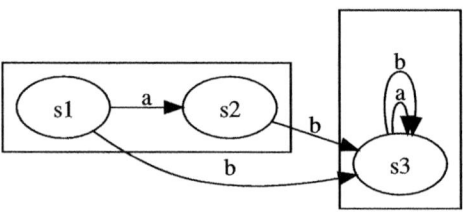

Fig. 2. One possible HSM for L

An HSM is defined as (H, T); figure 2 gives an example hierarchy for L. In an HFSM the set of states is expanded to the set of superstates and basic states, which encodes the hierarchy in nested sets. In the example $H = \{\{s_1, s_2\}, \{s_3\}\}$.

The set of transitions T is also modified, such that the source of any transition s may be any element of one of the sets in H, although the destination d must still be a basic state (i.e. any element of Q).

Not shown in this example, there is a common transition that could be replaced by a single superstate transition,$(\{s_1, s_2\}, b, s_3)$.

4   Metrics for HFSMs

Two metrics are defined, $TLCC$, which provides an overview of the abstracted machine, and HCC which conveys the complexity of the whole hierarchy. These metrics are defined for HSMs as defined in section 3.

4.1   Top-Level Cyclomatic Complexity

Top-level cyclomatic complexity is the result of viewing the HFSM at the maximum level of abstraction. It is equivalent to the CC of the result of transforming every top-level superstate into a single state, its edges being those that left the superstate it is made from.

Abstracting this to an HSM, E is taken to be the size of the number of inter-edges of a machine and N is taken to be the number of top-level superstates of the machine, $|H|$. As will be shown in section 4.2, it can also be used to operate on superstates themselves; in this case the immediate superstates become the top-level states used in the calculation.

This results in the definition:

$$TLCC(H) = \sum_{c \in H} |inter(c)| - |H| + 2$$

Where:

$$inter(c) = \{(s, l, d) \in edges(c) : !in(c, d)\}$$

$inter(c)$ gives all the edges that leave a given state or superstate, that is, their destination is not within c or its substates. Conversely, the edges that do not leave a superstate can be obtained by $edges(c) \setminus inter(c)$.

$edges(c)$ is all the edges of a superstate or state c, as well as the edges of the states that make up a superstate (and so on). It is given by

$$edges(c) = \{(s, l, d) \in T : in(c, s)\}$$

in is a recursive predicate that indicates membership of a state or superstate in another superstate:

$$in(c, s) = \begin{cases} true, & \text{if } c = s \\ true, & \text{if } \exists a.(in(a, s)) : a \in c \\ false, & \text{otherwise} \end{cases}$$

Figure 4 shows the effective graph $TLCC$ operates on when calculating for figure 3. In this example $TLCC = 20 - 3 + 2 = 19$. This illustrates the loss of

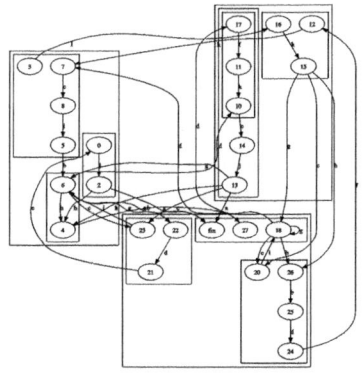

Fig. 3. An example HSM

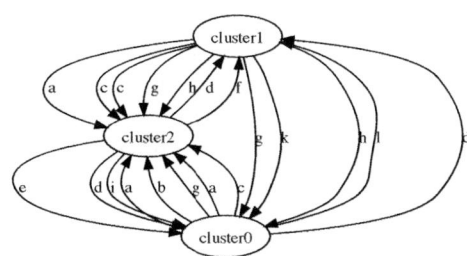

Fig. 4. The effective HSM $TLCC$ operates on

abstraction and also highlights a possible source of complexity; repeated edges. It may be that the overall CC for a machine is less than the $TLCC$ for it purely because the number of nodes (states) to be considered is reduced, but the number of edges only reduces when a transition can be formed from a superstate, which may not arise in some cases.

This metric effectively quantifies the cyclomatic complexity of the top level of abstraction; capturing the "first look" complexity a human perceives when starting to work with the hierarchical machine. This metric still does not attain the goal of quantifying the overall complexity, however.

4.2   Hierarchical Complexity

To combat the shortcomings of TLCC as well as the lack of hierarchy consideration of SCC a metric is proposed; this metric captures the complexity of the whole hierarchy, applying a reduced weight to nodes appearing lower in the hierarchy. Although they contribute less to the complexity, they are still counted; additionally, different lower-level hierarchy arrangements result in different values, which is not the case for the metrics discussed in sections 2 and 4.1

This metric is given by:

$$HCC(S, T, d) = \frac{TLCC(H, T)}{d} + \sum_{c \in H} HCC(c, T, d + 1)$$

As it is recursive, HCC is calculated with an initial depth 1, to apply it to a HSM $X = (H, T)$ the calculation starts with $HCC(H, T, 1)$. The final parameter is the depth of the current superstate. The example given in figure 4 has a HCC of $19 + (2 + 1 + 0)/2 + (0 + 1 + 1)/3 + (0 + 0 + 0)/3 + (1 + 0)/3 + 1/4 = 21.75$. This contrasts to its lower SCC of 14.

5   Conclusions and Future Work

This paper presents two novel metrics designed specifically for statecharts. The first, $TLCC$ provides an estimate of the complexity the abstraction at its most simple level. The second, HCC, allows a single metric to capture the quality of abstraction offered by a particular hierarchy for a state machine.

Both metrics produce higher values than SCC, although this is because they compare different things. SCC is lower as the number of states is always higher, whereas for $TLCC$ the number of nodes often drops, resulting in a higher overall value.

Although the metrics are now defined, they still need to undergo validation; a method for validation of similar metrics exists proposed [7], this could easily be applied to these metrics.

This work is similar to fitness functions for search-based clustering algorithms (as mentioned in section 2); where the goal is to provide an objective value of a candidate solution to direct a search. The difference between the two techniques is the goal; fitness functions seek to approximate an absolute measure of quality, whereas metrics are often used for relative comparison. These goals are similar, however and these proposed metrics could also be used to optimise a clustering, or the fitness functions used as metrics.

References

1. Cruz-Lemus, J.A., Maes, A., Genero, M., Poels, G., Piattini, M.: The impact of structural complexity on the understandability of UML statechart diagrams. Information Sciences 180(11), 2209–2220 (2010)
2. Genero, M., Miranda, D., Piattini, M.: Defining metrics for UML statechart diagrams in a methodological way. In: Jeusfeld, M.A., Pastor, Ó. (eds.) ER Workshops 2003. LNCS, vol. 2814, pp. 118–128. Springer, Heidelberg (2003)
3. Hall, M., McMinn, P., Walkinshaw, N.: Superstate identification for state machines using search-based clustering. In: Proceedings of the 12th Annual Conference on Genetic and Evolutionary Computation, pp. 1381–1388 (July 2010)
4. Harel, D.: Statecharts: A visual formalism for complex systems. Science of Computer Programming 8, 231–274 (1987)
5. Kumar, A.: Schaem: A method to extract statechart representation of FSMs. In: IEE International Advance Computing Conference 2009 (January 2009)
6. Lutz, R.: Evolving good hierarchical decompositions of complex systems. Journal of systems architecture 47(7), 613–634 (2001)
7. Genero, M., David Mir, M.P.: Empirical validation of metrics for UML statechart diagrams.... Quantitative Approaches in Object-oriented... (January 2002)
8. McCabe, T.: A complexity measure. IEEE Transactions on Software Engineering 2(4), 308–320 (1976)
9. Mitchell, B.S., Mancoridis, S.: On the automatic modularization of software systems using the bunch tool, vol. 32, pp. 193–208 (2006)
10. Poels, G., Dedene, G.: Measures for assessing dynamic complexity aspects of object-oriented conceptual schemes. In: Laender, A.H.F., Liddle, S.W., Storey, V.C. (eds.) ER 2000. LNCS, vol. 1920, pp. 499–512. Springer, Heidelberg (2000)
11. Yacoub, S., Ammar, H., Robinson, T.: Dynamic metrics for object oriented designs. In: Proceedings of Sixth International Software Metrics Symposium 1999, pp. 50–61 (1999)

Comparing Metaheuristic Algorithms for Error Detection in Java Programs

Francisco Chicano[1], Marco Ferreira[2], and Enrique Alba[1]

[1] University of Málaga, Spain
{chicano,eat}@lcc.uma.es
[2] Instituto Politécnico de Leiria, Portugal
mpmf@estg.ipleiria.pt

Abstract. Model checking is a fully automatic technique for checking concurrent software properties in which the states of a concurrent system are explored in an explicit or implicit way. The main drawback of this technique is the high memory consumption, which limits the size of the programs that can be checked. In the last years, some researchers have focused on the application of guided non-complete stochastic techniques to the search of the state space of such concurrent programs. In this paper, we compare five metaheuristic algorithms for this problem. The algorithms are Simulated Annealing, Ant Colony Optimization, Particle Swarm Optimization and two variants of Genetic Algorithm. To the best of our knowledge, it is the first time that Simulated Annealing has been applied to the problem. We use in the comparison a benchmark composed of 17 Java concurrent programs. We also compare the results of these algorithms with the ones of deterministic algorithms.

Keywords: Model checking, Java PathFinder, simulated annealing, particle swarm optimization, ant colony optimization, genetic algorithm.

1 Introduction

Software is becoming more and more complex. That complexity is growing for a variety of reasons, not the least of them is the need of concurrent and distributed systems. Recent programming languages and frameworks, such as Java and .NET, directly support concurrency mechanisms, making them an usual choice when developing concurrent and/or distributed systems. However, since these systems introduce interactions between a large number of components, they also introduce a larger number of points of failure. And this possible errors are not discoverable by the common testing mechanisms that are used in software testing. This creates a new need: to find software errors that may arise from the components communication, resource access and process interleaving. These are subtle errors that are very difficult to detect as they may depend on the order the environment chooses to execute the different threads, or components of the system. Some examples of this kind of errors are deadlocks, livelocks and starvation.

M.B. Cohen and M. Ó Cinnéide (Eds.): SSBSE 2011, LNCS 6956, pp. 82–96, 2011.
© Springer-Verlag Berlin Heidelberg 2011

One technique used to validate and verify programs against several properties like the ones mentioned is *model checking* [1]. Basically, a model checker uses a simplified implementation of the program, that is, a *model*, creating and traversing the graph of all the possible states of that model to find a path starting in the initial state that violates the given properties. If such a path is found it is a counterexample of the property that can be used to correct the program. Otherwise, if the algorithm used for the search of the counterexample is complete, the model is proven to be correct regarding the given properties.

The amount of states of a given concurrent system is very high even in the case of small systems, and it usually increases in a exponential way with the size of the model. This fact is known as *the state explosion problem* and limits the size of the model that a model checker can verify. Several techniques exist to alleviate this problem, such as partial order reduction [2], symmetry reduction [3], bitstate hashing [4] and symbolic model checking [5]. However, exhaustive search techniques are always handicapped in real concurrent programs because most of these programs are too complex even for the most advanced techniques.

When, even after state or memory reduction is somehow performed, the number of states becomes too big, two problems appear: the memory required to search for all states is too large and/or the time required to process those states is extremely long for practical purposes. That means that either the model checker will not be able to find an error nor prove the correctness of the model or, if it does find an error or prove the correctness of the model, it will not be in a practical run time. In those cases, the classical search algorithms like Depth First Search (DFS) or Breadth First Search (BFS), which are the most commonly used in model checking, are not suited.

However, using the old software engineering adage: "a test is only successful if it finds an error", we can think of model checking not as a way to prove correctness, but rather as a technique to locate errors and help in the testing phase of the software life cycle [6]. In this situation, we can stop thinking in complete search algorithms and start to think in not complete, but possibly guided search algorithms that lead to an error (if it exists) faster. That way, at least one of the objectives of model checking is accomplished. Therefore, techniques of bounded (low) complexity as those based on heuristics will be needed for medium/large size programs working in real world scenarios.

In this article we will study the behavior of several algorithms, including deterministic complete, deterministic non-complete, and stochastic non-complete search algorithms. In particular, the contributions of this work are:

- We analyze, compare and discuss the results of applying ten algorithms for searching errors in 17 Java programs.
- We include in the comparison algorithms from four different families of meta-heuristics: evolutionary algorithms (two variants), particle swarm optimization, simulated annealing, and ant colony optimization.
- We use a simulated annealing algorithm (SA) for the first time in the domain of model checking.

– We use large Java models that actually pose a challenge for traditional model
checking techniques and thus expand the spectrum of checkable programs.

The paper is organized as follows. In the next section we introduce some background information on heuristic model checking and Java PathFinder, which is
the model checker used in this work. Section 3 presents a formal definition of
the problem at hands. In Section 4 we briefly present the algorithms used in the
experimental study and their parameters. Then, we describe the experiments
performed and discuss the obtained results in Section 5. We conclude the paper
in Section 6.

2   Heuristic Model Checking

The search for errors in a model can be transformed in the search for one objective node (a program state that violates a given condition) in a graph, the
transition graph of the program, which contains all the possible states of the
program. For example, if we want to check the absence of deadlocks in a Java
program we have to search for states with no successors that are not end states.

Once we have transformed the search for errors in a search in a graph, we can
use classical algorithms for graph exploration to find the errors. Some classical
algorithms used in the literature with this aim are depth first search (DFS)
or breadth first search (BFS). It is also possible to apply graph exploration
algorithms that takes into account heuristic information, like A*, *Weighted* A*,
Iterative Deeping A*, and *Best First Search*. When heuristic information is used
in the search, we need a map from the states to the heuristic values. In the
general case, this maps depends on the property to check and the heuristic value
represents a preference to explore the corresponding state. The map is usually
called *heuristic function*, that we denote here with h. The lower the value of h
the higher the preference to explore the state, since it can be near an objective
node.

The utilization of heuristic information to guide the search for errors in model
checking is called *heuristic* (or *guided*) *model checking*. The heuristic functions
are designed to guide the search first to the regions of the transition graph in
which the probability of finding an error state is higher. This way, the time
and memory required to search an error in a program is decreased on average.
However, the utilization of heuristic information has no advantage when the
program has no error. In this case, the whole transition graph must be explored.

A well-known class of non-exhaustive algorithms for solving complex problems
is the class of metaheuristic algorithms [7]. They are search algorithms used in
optimization problems that can find good quality solutions in a reasonable time.
Metaheuristic algorithms have been previously applied to the search of errors in
concurrent programs. In [8], Godefroid and Khurshid applied Genetic Algorithms
in one of the first work on this topic. More recently, Alba and Chicano used
Ant Colony Optimization [9] and Staunton and Clark applied Estimation of
Distribution Algorithms [10].

2.1   Verification in Java PathFinder

There are different ways of specifying the model and the desired properties. Each model checker has its own way of doing it. For example, in SPIN [4] the model is specified in the Promela language and the properties are specified using Linear Temporal Logic (LTL). It is usual to provide the model checker with the properties specified using temporal logic formulas, either in LTL or CTL. It is also usual to find specific modelling languages for different model checkers. Promela, DVE, and SMV are just some examples. However, model checkers exist that deal with models written in popular programming languages, like C or Java. This is the case of Java PathFinder (JPF) [11], which is able to verify models implemented in JVM[1] bytecodes (the source code of the models is not required). The properties are also specified in a different way in JPF. Instead of using temporal logic formulas, the JPF user has to implement a class that tells the verifier algorithm if the property holds or not after querying the JVM internal state. Out of the box, JPF is able to check the absence of deadlocks and unhandled exceptions (this includes assertion violations). Both kind of properties belong to the class of *safety properties* [12].

In order to search for errors, JPF takes the `.class` files (containing the JVM bytecodes) and use its own Java virtual machine implementation (JPF-JVM in the following) to advance the program instruction by instruction. When two or more instructions can be executed, one of them is selected by the search algorithm and the other ones are saved for future exploration. The search algorithm can query the JVM internal state at any moment of the search as well as store a given state of the JVM and restore a previously stored state. From the point of view of the Java model being verified, the JPF-JVM is not different from any other JVM: the execution of the instructions have the same behaviour. The JPF-JVM is controlled by the search algorithm, which is an instance of a subclass of the `Search` class. In order to include a new search algorithm in JPF, the developer has to create a new class and implement the corresponding methods. This way, JPF can be easily extended; one aspect that is missing in other model checkers like SPIN. The role of the search algorithm is to control the order in which the states are explored according to the search strategy and to detect the presence of property violations in the explored states.

In JPF, it is possible to use search algorithms guided by heuristic information. To this aim, JPF provides some classes that ease the implementation of heuristic functions and heuristically-guided search algorithms.

3   Problem Formalization

In this paper we tackle the problem of searching for safety property violations in concurrent systems. As we previously mentioned, this problem can be translated into the search of a walk in a graph (the transition graph of the program) starting

---

[1] JVM stands for Java Virtual Machine.

in the initial state and ending in an objective node (error state). We formalize here the problem as follows.

Let $G = (S, T)$ be a directed graph where S is the set of nodes and $T \subseteq S \times S$ is the set of arcs. Let $q \in S$ be the *initial node* of the graph, $F \subseteq S$ a set of distinguished nodes that we call *objective nodes*. We denote with $T(s)$ the set of successors of node s. A finite walk over the graph is a sequence of nodes $\pi = \pi_1 \pi_2 \ldots \pi_n$ where $\pi_i \in S$ for $i = 1, 2, \ldots, n$ and $\pi_i \in T(\pi_{i-1})$ for $i = 2, \ldots, n$. We denote with π_i the ith node of the sequence and we use $|\pi|$ to refer to the length of the walk, that is, the number of nodes of π. We say that a walk π is a *starting walk* if the first node of the walk is the initial node of the graph, that is, $\pi_1 = q$.

Given a directed graph G, the problem at hand consists in finding a starting walk π ($\pi_1 = q$) that ends in an objective node, that is, $\pi_* \in F$. The graph G used in the problem is the transition graph of the program. The set of nodes S in G is the set of states in of the program, the set of arcs T in G is the set of transitions between states in the program, the initial node q in G is the initial state of the program, the set of objective nodes F in G is the set of error states in the program. In the following, we will also use the words *state*, *transition* and *error state* to refer to the elements in S, T and F, respectively. The transition graph of the program is usually so large that it cannot be completely stored in the memory of a computer. Thus, the graph is build as the search progresses. When we compute the states that are successors in the transition graph of a given state s we say that we have *expanded* the state.

4   Algorithms

In this section we will present the details and configurations of the ten algorithms we use in the experimental section. In Table 1 we show the ten algorithms classified according two three criteria: completeness, determinism and guidance. We say that an algorithm is *complete* if the algorithm ensures the exploration of the whole transition graph when no error exists. For example, DFS and BFS are complete algorithms, but Beam Search and all the metaheuristic algorithms used here are non-complete algorithms. One algorithm is *deterministic* if the states are explored in the same order each time the algorithms is run. DFS and Beam Search are examples of deterministic algorithms, while Random Search and all the metaheuristics are non-deterministic algorithms. *Guidance* refers to the use of heuristic information. We say that an algorithm is *guided* when it uses heuristic information. A* and Beam Search are guided algorithms while Random Search and BFS are unguided algorithms.

For the evaluation of the tentative solutions (walks in the transition graph) we use the same objective function (also called *fitness* function) in all the algorithms. Our objective is to find deadlocks in the programs and we prefer short walks. As such, our fitness function f is defined as follows:

$$f(x) = deadlock + numblocked + \frac{1}{1 + pathlen} \qquad (1)$$

Table 1. Algorithms used in the experimental section

Algorihm	Acronym	Complete?	Deterministic?	Guided?
Depth First Search [11]	DFS	yes	yes	no
Breadth First Search [11]	BFS	yes	yes	no
A* [11]	A*	yes	yes	yes
Genetic Algorithm [13]	GA	no	no	yes
Genetic Algorithm [13] with Memory Operator	GAMO	no	no	yes
Particle Swarm Optimization [14]	PSO	no	no	yes
Ant Colony Optimization [9]	ACOhg	no	no	yes
Simulated Annealing	SA	no	no	yes
Random Search	RS	no	no	no
Beam Search [11]	BS	no	yes	yes

where *numblocked* is the number of blocked threads generated by the walk while *pathlen* represents the number of transitions in the walk and *deadlock* is a constant which takes a high value if a deadlock was found and 0 otherwise. The high value that *deadlock* can take should be larger than the maximum number of threads in the program. This way we can ensure that any walk leading to a deadlock has better fitness than any walk without deadlock. All the metaheuristic algorithms try to maximize f.

The random search is a really simple algorithm that works by building limited-length random paths from the initial node of the graph. Then, it checks if an error was found in the path.

In the following we describe the SA algorithm, since it is the first time that this algorithm is applied to this problem (up to the best of our knowledge). We omit the details of the remaining algorithms due to space constraints. The interested reader should refer to the corresponding reference (shown in Table 1).

4.1 Simulated Annealing

Simulated annealing (SA) is a trajectory-based metaheuristic introduced by Kirkpatrick *et al.* in 1983 [15]. It is based on the statistical mechanics of annealing in solids. Just like in the physical annealing, SA allows the solution to vary significantly while the virtual temperature is high and stabilizes the changes as the temperature lows, freezing it when the temperature reaches 0. We show the pseudocode of SA in Algorithm 1.

SA works by generating an initial solution S, usually in some random form, and setting the temperature T to an initial (high) temperature. Then, while some stopping criteria is not met, SA randomly selects a neighbor solution N of S and compares its energy (or fitness) against the current solution's energy, getting the difference ΔE in temperature between them. The neighbor solution is accepted as the new solution if it is better than the current one or, in case it is worse, with a probability that is dependent on both ΔE and temperature T. SA then updates the temperature using some sort of decaying method. When the stopping criteria is met, the algorithm returns the current solution S.

Algorithm 1. Pseudo code of Simulated Annealing

1: S = generateInitialSolution();
2: T = initialTemperature;
3: **while** not stoppingCondition() **do**
4:     N = getRandomNeighbor(S);
5:     ΔE = energy(N) - energy(S);
6:     **if** $\Delta E > 0$ OR random(0,1) < probabilityAcceptance($\Delta E, T$) **then**
7:         $S = N$
8:     **end if**
9:     T = updateTemperature(T);
10: **end while**
11: **return** S

The energy function in this case is the objective function f defined in Equation (1). Since we want to maximize this function (the energy), given an energy increase ΔE and a temperature T, the probability of acceptance is computed using the following expression:

$$probabilityAcceptance(\Delta E, T) = e^{\frac{\Delta E}{T}} \tag{2}$$

One critical function of the Simulated Annealing is the `updateTemperature` function. There are several different ways to implement this method. In our implementation we used a simple, yet commonly used technique: multiplying the temperature by a number α between 0 and 1 (exclusive). The smaller that number is, the faster the temperature will drop. However, if we detect a local maxima (if the solution isn't improved for a number of iterations) we reset the temperature to its initial value to explore new regions.

4.2   Parameter Settings

In a comparison of different kinds of algorithms one problem always poses: how to compare them in a fair way? This problem is aggravated by the fact that the algorithms work in fundamentally different ways: some algorithms search only one state at a time, some search for paths. Some check only one state per iteration, others check many more states per iteration, etc. This large diversification makes it very hard to select the parameters that make the comparison fair. The fairest comparison criterion seems to be the computational time available to each algorithm. However, this criterion would make it impossible to use the results in a future comparison because the execution environment can, and probably will, change. Furthermore, the implementation details also affect the execution time and we cannot guarantee that the implementations used in the experiments are the most effective ones. For this reason, we decided to established a common limit for the number of states each algorithm may expand. After a defined number of states have been expanded the search is stopped and the results can be compared.

In order to maintain the parameterization simple, we used the same maximum number of expanded states for every model even though the size of each model is considerably different. We defined that maximum number of states to be 200 000, as it was empirically verified to be large enough to allow the algorithms to find errors even on the largest models. Having established a common value for the effort each algorithm may use, the parameterization of each individual algorithm can be substantially different from each other. For instance, we don't have to define the same number of individuals in the GA as the same number of particles in the PSO or as the same number of ants in the ACO. This gives us the freedom to choose the best set of parameters for each algorithm. However, in the case of the stochastic algorithms, and since this is a parameter that largely affects their execution, we have used the same heuristic function for all of them.

DFS, BFS and A* do not require any parameter to be set as they are generic, complete and deterministic search algorithms. For the metaheuristic algorithms, on the other hand, there are a variety of parameters to be set and although they could be optimized for each individual experiment, we have opted to use the same set of parameters for every experiment. These parameters were obtained after some preliminary experiments trying to get the best results for each particular algorithm. The parameters are summarized, together with the ones of RS and BS, in Table 2.

5   Experimental Section

In our experiments we want to verify the applicability of metaheuristic algorithms to model checking. We performed several experiments using the algorithms of the previous section and different Java implemented models. In order to determine the behavior of each search algorithm we have selected several types of models, including the classical Dining Philosophers toy model (both in a cyclic and a non-cyclic version), the more complex Stable Marriage Problem and two different communication protocols: GIOP and GARP. The Dining Philosopher models illustrate the common deadlock that can appear on multi-threaded algorithms. The difference of the cyclic and non-cyclic version is that while in the first one, called phi, each philosopher cycles through the pick forks, eat, drop forks and think states, in the non-cyclic version, called din, each philosopher only picks the forks, eats and drops the forks once, thus limiting the number of possible deadlocks. The Stable Marriage Problem (mar) has more interactions between threads and its implementation leads to a dynamic number of threads during executions. It contains both a deadlock and an assertion violation. Both the Dining Philosophers problem and the Stable Marriage Problem can be instantiated in any size (scalable), which makes them good choices to study the behavior of the search algorithms as the model grows. Finally, the communication protocols represent another typical class of distributed systems prone to errors. Both of these protocol implementations have known deadlocks which makes them suitable for non-complete search algorithms, because although they cannot prove correctness of a model, they can be used to prove the incorrectness and help the programmer to understand and fix the properties violations.

The results obtained from the experiments can be analyzed in several ways. We will discuss the results on the success of each algorithm in finding the errors,

Table 2. Parameters of the algorithms

Beam Search		Random Search	
Parameter	Value	Parameter	Value
Queue limit (k)	10	Path length	350

GeGA algorithm	
Parameter	Value
Minimum path size	10
Maximum path size	350
Population size	50
Selection operator	Tournament (5 individuals)
Crossover probability	0.7
Mutation probability	0.01
Elitism	true (5 individuals)
Respawn	after 5 generations with same population average fitness or 50 generations without improvement in best fitness

GeGAMO algorithm	
Parameter	Value
Minimum path size	10
Maximum path size	50
Population size	50
Selection operator	Tournament (3 individuals)
Crossover probability	0.7
Mutation probability	0.01
Elitism	true (3 individuals)
Memory operator frequency	10
Memory operator size	25
Respawn	after 5 generations with same population average fitness or 60 generations without improvement in best fitness

PSO algorithm		ACOhg algorithm	
Parameter	Value	Parameter	Value
Number of Particles	10	Length of ant paths	300
Minimum path size	10	Colony size	5
Maximum path size	350	Pheromone power (α)	1
Iterations Until Perturbation	5	Heuristic power (β)	2
Initial inertia	1.2	Evaporation rate (ρ)	0.2
Final inertia	0.6	Stored solutions (ι)	10
Inertia change factor	0.99	Stage length (σ_s)	3

SA algorithm	
Parameter	Value
Path size	350
Initial temperature	10
Temperature decay rate (α)	0.9
Iterations without improvement	50

measured as the hit rate, and the length of the error trail leading to the error. Deterministic algorithms always explore the states in the same order, which means that only one execution per problem instance is needed. The results of stochastic search algorithms, however, could change at each execution. For this reason, each stochastic algorithm was executed 100 times per problem instance.

5.1   Hit Rate

We show the results of hit rate in Table 3. Regarding the Dining Philosophers cyclic problem (phi), we can observe that none of the exact search algorithms could find an error in the larger instances. In fact, all of them (DFS, BFS and A*) exhausted the available memory starting with 12 philosophers, while all of the stochastic search algorithms (GA, GAMO, PSO, SA, ACOhg and even RS) and BS had a high hit rate in all of the instances. To better understand the reason for this, Figure 1(a) shows the distribution of the explored states after 200 000 states had been observed by two exact algorithms (DFS and BFS) and two stochastic algorithms (GA and RS). The remaining search algorithms were removed from the figure in order to have an uncluttered graphic. Figure 1(a) shows that DFS searched only one state per depth level (states explored in depths superior to 350 are not shown to maintain the graphic readability). That is coherent with the search algorithm which searches first in depth. However, this makes it difficult to find the error if it is not on the first transitions of each state. BFS, on the other hand, tried to fully explore each depth level before advancing to the next one. However, since the `phi` problem is a very wide problem (meaning that at each state there is a large number of possible outgoing transitions), the 200 000 states limit was reached quite fast. We can see a large difference in the behavior of the stochastic search algorithms. Both explore the search space both widely and in depth, simultaneously. This means that they avoid using all the resources in the few first depth levels, but also do not try to search too deep. Although they only visit the same number of states as their exact counterparts, they are spreader than the exact algorithms, which helps them find the error state. Considering that there are paths leading to errors in depths around 60, it is easy to see in Figure 1(a) why the stochastic algorithms found at least one of them while the exact algorithms missed them.

On the non-cyclic version of Dining Philosophers (`din`), DFS was able to detect errors in larger instances than the other exact algorithms. Figure 1(b) shows the reason why: since this problem is not cyclic, it ends after all the philosophers have had their dinner. Considering 12 philosophers, this happens, invariably, after 50 transitions. Since DFS has no more states to follow it starts to backtrack and check other transitions at the previous states. DFS concentrates its search at the end of the search space, and since the error state is at depth 36 (which is near the end), it is able to backtrack and explore other states at that depth level before consuming all the available memory. Figure 1(b) shows how

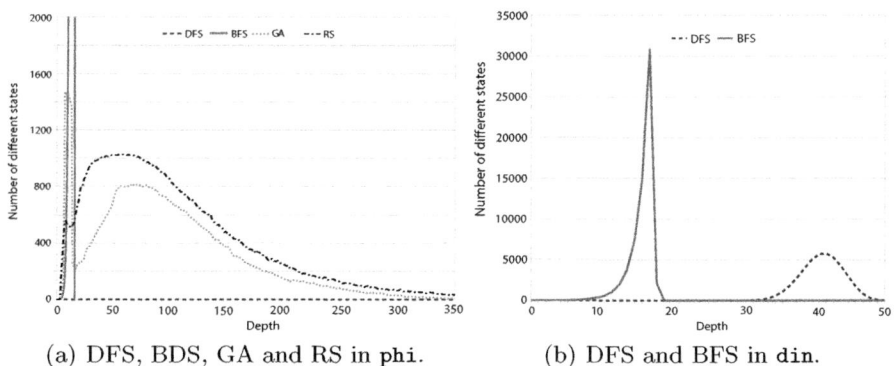

(a) DFS, BDS, GA and RS in `phi`.   (b) DFS and BFS in `din`.

Fig. 1. Search behavior of algorithms. The X axis is the depth in the graph and the Y axis is the number of expanded states.

Table 3. Hit rate of the algorithms

Problem	DFS	BFS	A*	GA	GAMO	PSO	SA	ACOhg	RS	BS
phi 4	100	100	100	100	100	100	100	100	100	100
phi 12	0	0	0	100	100	100	100	100	100	100
phi 20	0	0	0	100	100	100	100	100	100	100
phi 28	0	0	0	100	100	100	100	100	100	100
phi 36	0	0	0	82	100	53	79	100	100	100
din 4	100	100	100	100	100	100	100	100	100	100
din 8	100	0	0	100	100	100	76	100	96	100
din 12	100	0	0	100	96	85	13	68	0	100
din 16	0	0	0	91	58	20	0	2	0	100
din 20	0	0	0	52	24	0	0	0	0	100
mar 2	100	100	100	100	100	100	100	100	100	100
mar 4	100	100	100	100	100	100	96	100	100	100
mar 6	100	0	0	100	100	100	100	100	100	100
mar 8	100	0	0	100	95	100	100	100	100	100
mar 10	100	0	0	100	25	100	100	100	100	100
giop	100	0	0	100	68	100	100	100	100	100
garp	0	0	0	100	2	80	87	87	100	0

many different states per depth level the DFS and BFS algorithms had checked after 200 000 expanded states. Although 200 000 were not enough for BFS to find the error, we can see that DFS was already exploring in the error state neighborhood. BFS, on the other hand, concentrates the search in the beginning of the search space and, after visiting 200 000 states, it is still far from the neighborhood of the error state. The din problem is much less forgiving than phi. There is only one error state, and one chance to find it. This creates an interesting problem: the probability that a random walk through the search space would find the error decreases substantially. In fact, our results show exactly that: RS starts to miss the error as the number of philosophers grow (and search space increases, therefore). All the metaheuristic search algorithms found the error in larger instances, but they too started to struggle to find it. Only the genetic algorithms found the error in all instances. Since these are the only algorithms in the set that mixes paths from different individuals to create new ones, it seems that they were able to find a pattern to reach the error, while the other stochastic algorithms have not. Finally, BS finds the error in all the cases.

Like the din problem, mar is also finite. This means that there is a (relatively small) limit on the maximum depth the search algorithm may look into. This knowledge, and the fact that DFS successfully found an error in all the problem instances may lead us to think that the problem is small and, therefore, simple. That is not, however, the case: the size of the search space grows exponentially with the size of couples. An interesting observation is that shape of the search space remains mainly unaffected with the growth of the number of couples, as seen in Figure 2. Considering the size of the search space, the good results of RS and the observations we made on the Dining Philosophers problems, it seems that the mar problem have many different paths leading to an error state. To

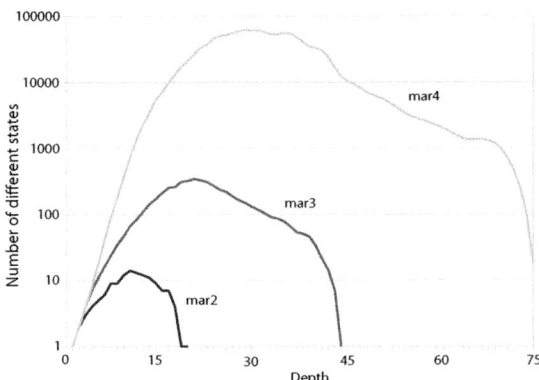

Fig. 2. Search space for the `mar` problem as seen by DFS for instances of 2, 3 and 4 couples. Note that the Y axis is logarithmic.

check this hypothesis we have checked all of the search space for the `mar` problem with 3 couples and found that with only 5156 different states in the search space, there are 30 error states and 216 different paths leading to those error states. This is indeed a large number of paths for the search space size and supports our hypothesis.

In general, when searching for errors, we have observed that non-complete algorithms have a higher success rate than the tested complete algorithms. From figures 1(b) and 2 we can observe that one reason seems to be the concentration of the search in either the beginning of it (BFS) or the end of it (DFS). Pure stochastic algorithms, like random search, explores a wider portion of the space at all the allowed depths (our random implementation is depth bounded). The metaheuristic algorithms tend to explore more through the search space and exploit areas that seem interesting, which typically are neither at the beginning or at the end of the search space. Complete search algorithms start to fail to search the whole search space very soon. Are they really applicable for software model checking? If some form of abstraction can be used, then maybe. However they still require large amount of memory and they are not checking the final implementation, so specific implementation details could still violate the properties checked before. However, failing to prove the model correctness does not mean they cannot be used to find errors. The `mar` problem is a good example of that. The search space could not be completely verified after using only 4 couples, but DFS was able to find errors even with 10 couples. The ability of DFS and BFS to find errors in large search spaces depends not so much on the size of the search space but more on its shape, as shown in the `din` and `mar` tests.

5.2   Length of the Error Trails

The length of the error trail for each algorithm is also an important result that must be compared. Since the error trail is the information the developers have to debug the application, the more concise it is, the better. So, shorter error trails means that less irrelevant states exists in the trail, making it easier for the developer to focus on what leads to the errors As with the hit rate, exact algorithms always return the same error trail for each problem. Stochastic algorithms do not, so we present in Table 4 both the averages of the length of the first error trail found and of the shortest error trail length found in the 100 executions. We include both of these values because the stochastic algorithms do not stop after an error has been found, but only after 200 000 states have been expanded, which means that more than one path to an error may be found during the search.

Table 4. Length of the error trails (first/shortest)

Prob.	DFS	BFS	A*	GA	GAMO	PSO	SA	ACOhg	RS	BS
phi 4	169	16	16	48/16	28/16	52/16	47/16	71/16	50/16	22
phi 12	–	–	–	149/52	78/58	173/55	178/70	175/72	193/62	74
phi 20	–	–	–	220/116	131/114	248/126	251/140	244/163	319/135	224
phi 28	–	–	–	267/192	188/174	275/210	278/216	351/268	504/227	393
phi 36	–	–	–	283/269	248/232	282/278	290/274	495/381	616/324	753
din 4	12	12	12	12/12	12/12	12/12	12/12	12/12	12/12	12
din 8	24	–	–	24/24	24/24	24/24	24/24	24/24	24/24	24
din 12	36	–	–	36/36	36/36	36/36	36/36	36/36	–	36
din 16	–	–	–	48/48	48/48	48/48	–	48/48	–	48
din 20	–	–	–	60/60	60/60	–	–	–	–	60
mar 2	14	12	12	13/12	13/12		13/12	12/12	13/12	12
mar 4	63	26	28	42/27	39/27	43/27	45/29	42/28	44/29	36
mar 6	140	–	–	91/48	75/56	94/51	93/57	93/56	92/55	59
mar 8	245	–	–	148/77	108/94	154/79	149/91	152/92	151/88	172
mar 10	378	–	–	199/109	154/142	215/114	207/127	214/130	223/125	260
giop	232	–	–	251/238	252/247	263/236	264/243	256/242	284/239	355
garp	–	–	–	184/115	123/121	184/128	204/147	305/278	245/111	–

In all the problems, BFS shows the shortest possible error trail. However, as we have seen in the previous section, it starts to fail to find the error very quickly, so it cannot be used as a base comparison value for all the problem instances. DFS, on the other hand, finds the error in larger instances but the error trails provided by this algorithm are the largest of all the algorithms, with one exception: the `giop` problem. In this problem, the shortest error trail consists on always choosing the left-most transition available in each state, which is exactly the behavior DFS always present. The A* behaves mostly like BFS, again with one strange exception: in the `mar4` problem, the error trail is not the smallest one possible. This means that the heuristic we used is not very good for this problem, as it slightly misleads A*. This is also the reason for the low hit rate of A*. BS is very effective at finding the error but the length of the tail is usually far from the optimum, except for some small instances.

Among the stochastic algorithms, the genetic algorithms seem to be the ones that provide the shortest error trails. There is a difference in behavior between the GA using the memory operator (GAMO) and not using it. While the GA usually finds the shortest error trail, the length of the error trail for the first error found is usually smaller using the memory operator, and is not too far from the shortest error trail. This means that if we change the stopping criteria of the algorithms in order to stop as soon as an error is found, then using the memory operator seems to be a better choice. All the guided stochastic algorithms show good results both on the first error trail and the shortest error trail. RS, which is not guided, also shows good results in these problems when we consider the shortest error trails only. However, the length of the first error trail found by RS is usually much larger than the ones found by the other algorithms.

6   Conclusion and Future Work

In this work we presented a comparison of five metaheuristic algorithms and five other classical search algorithms to solve the problem of finding property violations in concurrent Java programs using a model checking approach. We used a benchmark of 17 Java programs composed of three scalable programs with different sizes and two non-scalable programs. We analyzed the results of the algorithms in terms of efficacy: the ability of a search algorithm to find the property violation and the length of the error trail. The experiments suggests that metaheuristic algorithms are more effective to find safety property violations than classical deterministic and complete search algorithms that are commonly used in the explicit-state model checking domain. They also suggest that non-complete guided search algorithms, such as Beam Search, have some advantages against both guided and non-guided complete search algorithms such as A^* and DFS. Finally, these experiments also suggest that distributing the search effort in different depths of the search space tends to raise the efficacy of the search algorithm.

As future work we can explore the possibility of designing hybrid algorithms that can more efficiently explore the search space by combining the best ideas of the state-of-the-art algorithms. We can also design stochastic complete algorithms that are able to find short error trails in case error exist in the software and can also verify the program in case no error exists.

Acknowledgements. This research has been partially funded by the Spanish Ministry of Science and Innovation and FEDER under contract TIN2008-06491-C04-01 (the M* project) and the Andalusian Government under contract P07-TIC-03044 (DIRICOM project).

References

1. Clarke, E.M., Grumberg, O., Peled, D.A.: Model Checking. MIT Press, Cambridge (2000)
2. Clarke, E.M., Grumberg, O., Minea, M., Peled, D.: State space reduction using partial order techniques. International Journal on Software Tools for Technology Transfer (STTT) 2(3), 279–287 (1999)

3. Lafuente, A.L.: Symmetry reduction and heuristic search for error detection in model checking. In: Workshop on Model Checking and Artificial Intelligence (2003)
4. Holzmann, G.J.: The SPIN Model Checker. Addison-Wesley, Reading (2004)
5. Burch, J., Clarke, E., Long, D., McMillan, K., Dill, D.: Symbolic model checking for sequential circuit verification. IEEE Transactions on Computer-Aided Design of Integrated Circuits and Systems 13(4), 401–424 (1994)
6. Bradbury, J.S., Cordy, J.R., Dingel, J.: Comparative assessment of testing and model checking using program mutation. In: Proceedings of the 3rd Workshop on Mutation Analysis (MUTATION 2007), Windsor, UK, pp. 210–222 (2007)
7. Blum, C., Roli, A.: Metaheuristics in combinatorial optimization: Overview and conceptual comparison. ACM Comput. Surv. 35(3), 268–308 (2003)
8. Godefroid, P., Khurshid, S.: Exploring very large state spaces using genetic algorithms. International Journal on Software Tools for Technology Transfer 6(2), 117–127 (2004)
9. Alba, E., Chicano, F.: Finding safety errors with ACO. In: Proceedings of the Genetic and Evolutionary Computation Conference, pp. 1066–1073. ACM Press, London (2007)
10. Staunton, J., Clark, J.A.: Searching for safety violations using estimation of distribution algorithms. In: International Workshop on Search-Based Software Testing, pp. 212–221. IEEE Computer Society, Los Alamitos (2010)
11. Groce, A., Visser, W.: Heuristics for model checking java programs. International Journal on Software Tools for Technology Transfer (STTT) 6(4), 260–276 (2004)
12. Manna, Z., Pnueli, A.: The temporal logic of reactive and concurrent systems. Springer-Verlag New York, Inc., New York (1992)
13. Alba, E., Chicano, F., Ferreira, M., Gomez-Pulido, J.: Finding deadlocks in large concurrent java programs using genetic algorithms. In: Proceedings of Genetic and Evolutionary Computation Conference, pp. 1735–1742. ACM, New York (2008)
14. Ferreira, M., Chicano, F., Alba, E., Gómez-Pulido, J.A.: Detecting protocol errors using particle swarm optimization with java pathfinder. In: Smari, W.W. (ed.) ISHPC 2000, pp. 319–325 (2008)
15. Kirkpatrick, S., Gelatt, C.D., Vecchi, M.P.: Optimization by simulated annealing. Science 220(4598), 671–680 (1983)

Applications of Model Reuse When Using Estimation of Distribution Algorithms to Test Concurrent Software

Jan Staunton and John A. Clark

Department of Computer Science, University of York, UK
{jps,jac}@cs.york.ac.uk

Abstract. Previous work has shown the efficacy of using Estimation of Distribution Algorithms (EDAs) to detect faults in concurrent software/systems. A promising feature of EDAs is the ability to analyse the information or model learned from any particular execution. The analysis performed can yield insights into the target problem allowing practitioners to adjust parameters of the algorithm or indeed the algorithm itself. This can lead to a saving in the effort required to perform future executions, which is particularly important when targeting expensive fitness functions such as searching concurrent software state spaces. In this work, we describe practical scenarios related to detecting concurrent faults in which reusing information discovered in EDA runs can save effort in future runs, and prove the potential of such reuse using an example scenario. The example scenario consists of examining problem families, and we provide empirical evidence showing real effort saving properties for three such families.

1 Introduction

Estimation of Distribution Algorithms (EDAs) have been established as a strong competitor to Evolutionary Algorithms (EAs) and other bio-inspired techniques for solving complex combinatorial problems [8]. EDAs are similar to Genetic Algorithms (GAs), but replace the combination and mutation phases with a probabilistic model building and sampling phase. It has been shown that EDAs can outperform GAs on a range of problems. In addition to strong performance, another advantage of EDAs is the potential for the analysis of the probabilistic models constructed at each generation. Model analysis can yield insights into a target problem allowing for tuning of EDA parameters, or indeed the algorithm itself, potentially saving computation effort in future instances.

Recently, we have shown the potential for EDAs, combined with aspects of model checking, to detect faults in concurrent software by sampling the state-space of the program intelligently [11,12]. Using a customised version of N-gram GP [9], we have achieved greater performance than a number of traditional algorithms, GAs and Ant Colony Optimisation (ACO) on a wide range of problems, including programs expressed in industrial languages such as Java. For

M.B. Cohen and M. Ó Cinnéide (Eds.): SSBSE 2011, LNCS 6956, pp. 97–111, 2011.
© Springer-Verlag Berlin Heidelberg 2011

large problems, exploring the state-space can become expensive, leading to a longer runtime and the potential exhaustion of resources. In order to combat this effect, we propose using information, specifically information from the models constructed, from earlier executions of the EDA in future executions in an attempt to save computational effort. We term this approach "model reuse".

In this work, we outline practical scenarios related to detecting faults in concurrent software in which model reuse could potentially save computation effort. These scenarios could potentially be extended to scenarios involving sequential software, and even hardware systems. We then provide empirical evidence showing the potential of model reuse with regards to detecting faults in problem families. A problem family is a program or system that can be scaled up or down with respect to some parameter, typically the number of processes within the system. Our system is implemented using the ECJ evolutionary framework [7] and the HSF-SPIN model checker [5]. To our knowledge, this is the first instance of model analysis being used to save computational effort, and therefore lower cost, in the Search-Based Software Engineering (SBSE) domain.

This paper is structured as follows: Section 2 gives a brief overview of how EDAs and the EDA-based model checking technique work. Section 3 describes the concept of model reuse, along with a number of practical scenarios in which model reuse could reduce computational effort. Section 4 describes empirical work showing the potential for model reuse in practical scenarios. We conclude the paper with a summary and outline future work in Section 5.

2   EDA-Based Model Checking

2.1   EDAs

Estimation of Distribution Algorithms (EDAs) are population-based probabilistic search techniques that search solution spaces by learning and sampling probabilistic models [8]. EDAs iterate over successive populations or bags of candidate solutions to a problem. Each population is sometimes referred to as a generation. To construct a successor population, EDAs build a probabilistic model of promising solutions from the current population and then sample that model to generate new individuals. The newly generated individuals replace individuals in the current population to create the new population according to some replacement policy. An example replacement policy is to replace half of the old population with new individuals. The initial population can be generated randomly, or seeded with previously best known solutions. The algorithm terminates when a termination criterion is met, typically when a certain number of generations are reached or a good enough solution has been found.

The pseudocode of a basic EDA algorithm is shown in Algorithm 1. Readers who are familiar with Genetic Algorithm (GA) literature can view EDAs as similar to a GA with the crossover and mutation operators replaced with the model building and sampling steps. EDAs can be seen as strategically sampling the solution space in an attempt to find a "good" solution whilst learning a model of "good" solutions along the way. EDAs are sometimes referred to as

Algorithm 1. Pseudocode for basic EDA

```
P = InitialPopulation();
evaluate(P);
while not(termination_criterion) do
    S = SelectPromisingSolutions(P);
    M = UpdateModelUsingSolutions(S);
    N = SampleFromModel(M);
    P = ReplaceIndividuals(N);
    evaluate(P);
end while
```

Probabilistic Model-Building Genetic Algorithms (PMBGAs), a full overview of which can be found in [8].

2.2 Searching State-Spaces with EDAs

To search for concurrent faults using EDAs, we use aspects of model checking. Model Checking is a technique for analysing reactive concurrent systems [4]. A model checking tool can automatically verify that a given specification is satisfied by a model of a system. A model checking tool achieves this by taking a description of a system and a specification, and then exhaustively checks all possible behaviours of that system to determine if the specification is violated. The description of the system can be in a number of formats, including being expressed in industrial languages such as Java. Specifications are given as a set of properties and are typically expressed in a formal language such as Linear Temporal Logic (LTL). Example specifications include "The system must not deadlock" and "The server must respond once a request has been made by a client".

A possible behaviour of a system is typically referred to as a path. A path p is a sequence of states which begins in an initial state of the system/program, and ends in either a terminal state (a state from which no transition can occur) or a state previously encountered on p. A path can also be seen as a sequence of actions causing transitions between states. A transition system/state space is shown in Figure 1, showing all of the main features pertinent to this work. The goal of a model checking tool is to find a path that violates a given specification, known as a "counterexample". This goal is typically achieved using a Depth-first Search. If no such path exists in the system after an exhaustive check, then the system is said to satisfy the specification. For large systems, however, it is often impossible to check all possible paths due to a lack of time and memory. This is known as the state-space explosion problem [4]. In these situations, it may suffice to detect a counterexample rather than check the system exhaustively. For this purpose, a number of heuristic mechanisms exist. Best-first Search for instance expands states during the search in an order determined by a heuristic [5]. Heuristics exist for searching for a variety of faults [6,5], including deadlock and violations of LTL formulae. Counterexamples with fewer states are often preferred for debugging purposes, as superfluous transitions are eliminated. To this end techniques including A* search can be used that penalise longer paths [10].

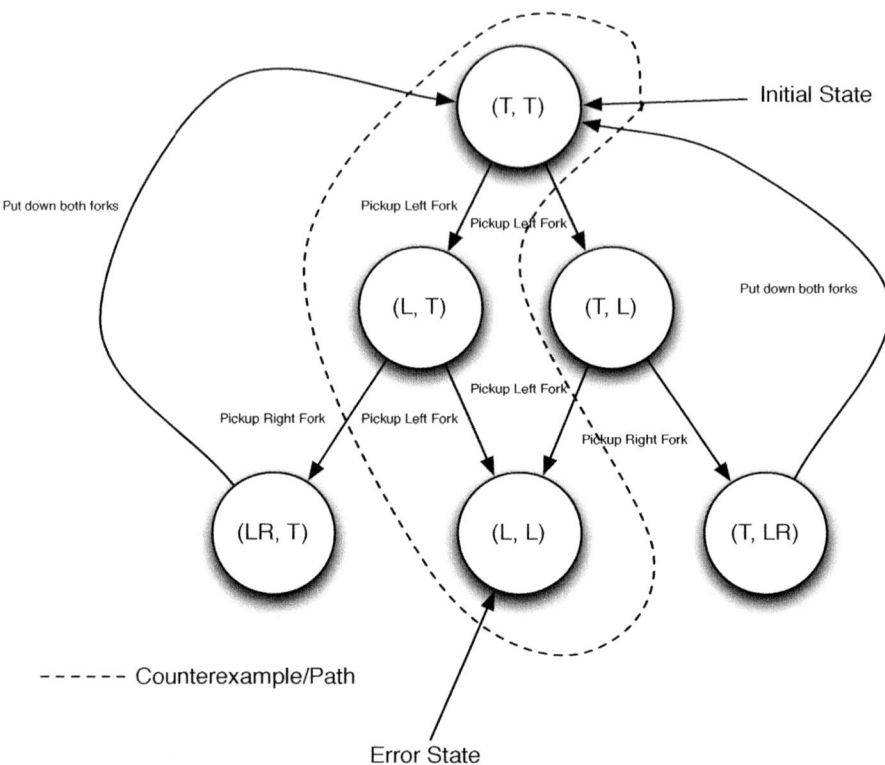

Fig. 1. Figure of a Dining Philosopher transition system/state space visualised as a digraph. States are shown as circles, with edges between them labelled with actions on the left. The path highlighted is a counterexample that leads to a deadlock state.

Metaheuristic mechanisms have been shown to be promising when used to detect faults in concurrent software/systems. Genetic Algorithms have been shown to be effective at detecting deadlock in Java programs [3]. Ant Colony Optimisation has also been shown to be effective at detecting a variety of different errors types, including deadlock and LTL formulae violations [1,2], in Promela models. Recently, we have shown how an EDA-based model checking algorithm based upon N-gram GP can be used to discover short errors in concurrent systems [11,12]. Using this work, we show how the algorithm described in [11,12] can be modified to allow for information in previous runs to save computational effort in later runs. Our system is implemented using ECJ [7] and HSF-SPIN [5]. HSF-SPIN is a model checking framework that analyses Promela specifications, and implements a variety of heuristics for checking a range of properties.

2.3   Brief Overview of EDA-Based Model Checking

Before a description of the technique is given, it helps to summarise the overall theme. The goal of the EDA is to detect a path in the transition system which leads to a fault. To this end, the EDA samples a set of paths from the transition system (referred to as a population) and selects a subset of "fit" paths determined by a fitness function. Using the individuals in the fit subset, a probabilistic model is constructed. The model is then sampled in order to construct new paths which replace current members of the population. In order to generate new paths, the model is built so that it can answer the following the question. Given the n most recent actions that have occurred on the path currently under construction, by what distribution should the next action be selected? The model can be thought of as a strategy for navigating a transition system.

Solution Space. In order to encode paths in the transition system, we use a simple string representation. Paths in a transition system can be seen as a sequence of actions causing transitions between states. The alphabet of the strings used in this work is the set of all actions possible in the transition system. In this work, the alphabet consists of information gathered by HSF-SPIN whilst constructing the transition system. Examples of the alphabet members used in this work can be found in Figure 2, which shows a typical path through a Dining Philosophers transition system. The alphabet members do not refer to specific philosophers, but instead refer to actions that can be performed by any one of the philosophers in the system. By modelling paths through a transition system without referring to specific processes, sequences of actions regardless of which processes executed them are modelled. This represents a minor abstraction from modelling actions performed by specific processes, reducing the size of the alphabet and therefore reducing the solution space searched by the EDA.

```
1.  (NULL TRANSITION)
2.  ( models/deadlock . philosophers . noloop . prm : 3 2 ) ( break )
3.  ( models/deadlock . philosophers . noloop . prm : 1 2 ) ( left ? fork )
4.  ( models/deadlock . philosophers . noloop . prm : 1 2 ) ( left ? fork )
```

Fig. 2. A typical trace/string/path from HSF-SPIN on the Dining Philosopher problem with 2 philosophers. This trace ends in a deadlocked state, because all the philosophers have picked up their left fork.

Modelling Paths. In order to model paths in the transition system, we use a customised version of N-gram GP [9]. An n-gram is a subsequence of length n from a longer sequence. N-gram GP learns the joint probabilities of fit string subsequences of length n. The rationale is that N-gram GP is modelling a strategy to use whilst exploring a transition system. The n-grams are seen as a recent history of actions on a particular path. The distribution associated with the n-gram in the probabilistic model describes the actions that are most likely to minimise a fitness function, hopefully leading to a counterexample. The model is "queried" with n-grams during the sampling phase in order to probabilistically choose actions that are more likely to lead to a fault.

For each generation a set of "fit" paths is selected using truncation selection and the fitness function described later in this work. In order the learn the model or strategy from a set of fit paths, a simple sliding window frequency count algorithm is used. Once the paths are selected, a frequency count of actions occurring after each unique n-gram in the paths is performed. The frequency count is then normalised to obtain distributions for each n-gram observed. A simple illustration of this process can be seen in Figure 3. In addition to learning n-gram distributions, in this work the distributions for (n-1)-grams and (n-2)-grams etc. down to 1-grams are also constructed and these additional distributions are used during the sampling phase.

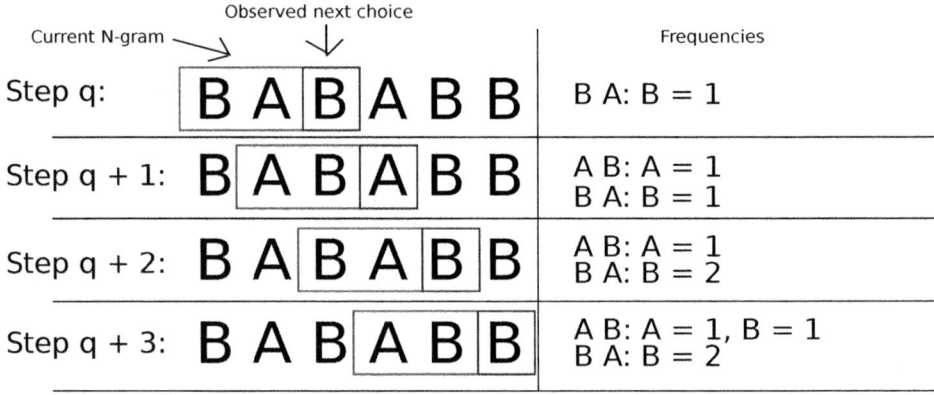

Fig. 3. Illustration of the N-gram learning process (2-grams in this case). A frequency count is performed for each unique N-gram in selected set of strings (only one string is shown). The boxes represent a basic sliding window algorithm, with frequency counts display on the right.

Sampling the Model. Once a set of individuals are selected and a model created, the model is then sampled to create the next generation. A number of paths are generated from the model to replace individuals in the current generation according to some policy. In this work, we generate the entire new generation using newly sampled individuals. To generate a path in the transition system, the algorithm starts with the initial state of the transition system and an empty path. Then, the algorithm must choose an action to execute from the available actions in the current state. To do this, the model is queried with the most recent n moves from the path, in this case an empty string, and a distribution is returned. From the initial state, a set of actions are possible, each of which leads to a potentially new state. Using the distribution obtained from the model for the current n-gram, an action is probabilistically chosen and executed. If more than one process is in a position to execute the chosen action, then a single process is selected at random from those that can execute the chosen action at random to progress. This leads to a new state s. The action chosen is appended to the current path, and the process is repeated using the new state and the new path. This process repeats until either an error is found, a terminal state is reached or a state is reached that has been previously encountered on the current path.

N-gram GP was initially used to evolve programs, allowing any sequence of alphabet members to constitute a program. However, in this work we must generate valid paths in the transition system. If we used the process described above without modification, it is entirely possible to generate invalid paths in the transition system. There are a number of special cases when generating a path, and these are described and handled in [11]. Mutation is implemented by taking an arbitrary choice every m transitions according to some parameter.

3   Model Reuse

A typical GA run will produce a sequence of bags of solutions to a target problem. In the case of detecting concurrent faults, this will amount to sets of paths within the transition system which may or may not lead to an error. Whilst it is possible to use some of these solutions to seed future runs, even a small change to the target problem could destroy the applicability of these solutions. Similarly, Ant Colony Optimisation constructs pheromone trails that may lose relevance once the target problem has been changed. The EDA-based model checking technique, on the other hand, produces a strategy for navigating a transition system in addition to structures that represent solutions. We believe that with some simple steps the models can be used to reduce computational effort on future instances of similar problems. Outlined below are a number of potential practical scenarios for model reuse that could greatly reduce computational effort.

3.1   Reuse during Debugging

The first proposed scenario for model reuse is during the testing/debugging phases of the development life cycle. It is plausible that during any execution of the EDA a constructed model can represent a strategy for finding not just a single error but multiple errors, as well as "problem areas" of the state space. If a single error has been found in an execution e on the ith revision of the system, e could be halted in order to fix the bug. This would create the $i + 1$th revision. Once the error has been corrected, execution can continue using the model constructed in the last generation of e, labelled m. It is also plausible that erroneous actions from the ith revision of the system in m can be mapped to the corrected actions in the revised system, allowing for the EDA to focus on these areas initially. This may potentially eliminate computation if errors still exist in the area of the state space where the initial error was found. Equally, if a practitioner is confident that the error has been corrected, the area of the state space can be added to a tabu list, allowing the EDA to focus effort elsewhere.

3.2   Reuse during Refinement

Another potential scenario for reusing models is during refinement. During implementation, versions of the system are refined to meet various ends, including performance improvements and bug fixing. Refinements may increase the size of the transition system enormously. In order to combat this, it is plausible that the EDA can be executed on the more abstract version of the system/software in order to determine potential problem areas that rank highly with the fitness function. The models constructed during these initial explorations can then potentially be used to explore future refinements of the system. If refining the system increases the state space size significantly, then significant computational effort could be spared. There is also the potential to map actions from the abstract system to actions in the refined system, potentially increasing the saving of computational effort.

3.3   Reuse When Tackling Problem Families

We have speculated in previous papers [11,12] that the EDA-based technique is learning effective strategies for navigating the state spaces of problem families, rather than just the problem instance itself. A problem family is simply a system which can be scaled up and down respective to some parameter, typically the number of processes/threads in the system/software. This opens up the possibility of models learned whilst tackling small instances of a problem family can be used to save effort whilst finding errors in larger instances. Finding the same error in a number of instances of a problem family can provide additional debugging information, potentially shortening the debugging life cycle. Problem families arise frequently in practical situations [4], in both hardware and software systems.

In this work, we provide empirical evidence showing how computational effort can be saved when detecting errors in problem families. Extra information can be gained from detecting faults in varying instances of a problem family, and this can save time and ultimately lower costs when building and debugging practical systems.

4   Experimentation with Problem Families

4.1   Sample Models

In order to demonstrate the ability for model reuse, we aim to show that the EDA can learn structures in three problem families. The three test cases used in this work are listed in Table 1. The test cases are diverse in the system description as well as the property under test. The dining philosophers model is a classic problem in which n philosophers contend over forks in order to eat from a shared meal in the middle. n philosophers are sat around a circular table with n forks, one between each adjacent pair of philosophers. Each philosopher requires two forks in order to eat. Each philosopher picks up the fork to the left of them, then the fork to the right, eats some food, then releases the right and left fork in that order. With this behaviour, there is the possibility of deadlock as all philosophers can pick up the left fork denying access to the right fork for every philosopher. The EDA will be aiming to find deadlocked states within the dining philosopher model.

Table 1. Models and the respective properties violated

Model	Processes	LoC	Property
Dining Philosopher No Loop n	$n+1$	35	Deadlock
Leader n	$n+1$	117	Assertion
GIOP n	$n+6$	740	$\Box(p \rightarrow \Diamond q)$

For the second test case, a leader election system is modelled by the Leader model. In this model, n processes must agree on a common leader process in a unidirectional ring configuration. The faulty protocol used to establish a leader allows members of the ring to disagree on a leader. An assertion represents this specification, and the EDA algorithm will be aiming to find violations of this assertion. The final test case implements the CORBA Global Inter-ORB protocol (GIOP) with n clients using a single server configuration. The system violates a property specified in LTL. This model is particularly large, and is reported as difficult to find errors in for large n (large n being $n >= 10$) [2,12].

In this set of examples, we have a deadlock, an assertion and an LTL violation in order to show the applicability of the technique to errors other than deadlock. Whilst the Dining Philosophers problem is a well studied toy problem, the GIOP model is derived from an industrial source, adding credibility to using this approach in industrial scenarios. Finally, whilst the Dining Philosophers model is symmetrical in nature (all the processes have the same description), the GIOP model is asymmetric, adding further weight to the empirical argument that the technique could be effective in industrial scenarios.

4.2 Heuristics

The fitness function detailed in Algorithm 2 is used to rank solutions and makes use of heuristic information implemented in the HSF-SPIN framework [5]. The heuristics implemented in HSF-SPIN give information about a single state only. Algorithm 3 combines the information from the individual states in a path to give a heuristic measure for the entire path. This is done by simply summing the heuristic information of all the states along the path. The algorithm aims to minimise this cumulative total, whilst favouring shorter paths and paths with errors. The same heuristic is used on all of the runs in this work.

HSF-SPIN implements a variety of heuristics which can be used on various types of properties. In Algorithm 3, the *s.HSFSPINMetric* is calculated using the following heuristics. We use the active processes heuristic for finding deadlock in the Dining Philosophers model [6,5]. The active processes heuristic, when given a state, returns the number of processes that can progress in that state.

Algorithm 2. Fitness function used to rank individuals. Individuals that are "closer" to violating a property are favoured.

Require: A, B are Individuals;
  if *A.error_found* ≠ *B.error_found* **then**
    return IndividualWithErrorFound(A,B);
  else if *A.error_found* **and** *B.error_found* **then**
    return IndividualWithShortestPath(A,B);
  else
    return IndividualWithLowestHSFSPINMetric(A,B);
  end if

Algorithm 3. HSF-SPIN heuristic metric algorithm.

Require: I is an Individual;
  aggregateMetric = 0;
  for all *States s* ∈ *I.Path* **do**
    aggregateMetric += s.HSFSPINMetric;
  end for
  return aggregateMetric;

When looking for assertion violations in the Leader model, the formula-based heuristic is used [6,5]. The formula-based heuristic estimates how close a state is to violating a formula by examining the satisfaction of constituent sub-formulae in that state. And finally, when searching for LTL formulae violations, we use the HSF-SPIN distance-to-endstate heuristic [6,5]. The distance-to-endstate heuristic estimates how many transitions a state is away from the end state of a product Büchi automaton, a structure used when verifying LTL properties and implemented in HSF-SPIN. Put simply, the distance-to-endstate heuristic estimates how far a state is away from violating the LTL specification.

4.3   Parameters

The parameters for all of the executions are derived from small scale empirical work, as well as experimental results from our previous publications [11,12]. We expect that these parameters may work well on a wide variety of problems, but some problems may need extra tuning. An n-gram length of 3 was used, meaning models for 3-grams, 2-grams and 1-grams are constructed from each generation. The model is completely destroyed and rebuilt from the selected individuals at each generation. This also means that the reused model is essentially a seed model for the runs on larger instances. The population size for each generation was set to 150. This means that 150 paths are sampled from the model to build each generation. The mutation parameter for these experiments is set to 0.001, meaning that on average 1 in 1000 transition choices are made randomly, disregarding the model. The elitism parameter was set to 1, meaning that the top individual from the population is copied to the next generation. In order to build the model from which the next generation is sampled, truncation selection selects the top 20% of individuals from the population. This means that the top

30 individuals from the current population are used to build the EDA/N-gram model. All individuals in the population are replaced at each generation with individuals sampled from the model. The algorithm terminates once it reaches 200 generations, allowing for the potential optimisation of counterexamples. Initially, the model is a blank model meaning that all the paths evaluated during the first generation are completely random.

4.4   Smaller Instances

In order to learn strategies that can be used on any instance of a particular problem family, we ran the EDA algorithm on a small instance of each problem family. For the Dining Philosophers problem family, a small instance is a system with 32 philosophers. For the Leader model, we use a unidirectional ring with 3 members. And finally, for the GIOP model, we use a single server 2 client configuration. For each model, we allow the algorithm to run for a fixed number of generations, allowing execution to continue if an error is found in order to optimise the model and find shorter counterexamples. The model constructed from the final generation of a single execution is the model used in the subsequent executions on the larger instances. The model is simply serialised out to a file to be used as input to a future run. At this stage, there is the possibility of inspecting the model in order to make improvements. In this work however, the model is used verbatim in the execution on the larger model. Models from various runs can potentially be archived for use in future work. Some measurements from these initial runs can be found in Table 2. We have proven empirically in earlier papers [11,12] that the EDA is capable of consistently finding good strategies in the time scales shown in Table 2. The numbers below the First Error header are numbers relating to the first error found during the execution. The best error table shows the numbers related to the shortest error found.

Table 2. Measurements from the initial runs

Measurement	Dining Philosophers	Leader	GIOP
First error:			
Generations	3	0	0
Path Length	34	35	59
States	73,058	35	729
Time	27.45s	0.3s	0.3s
Best error:			
Generations	3	0	17
Path Length	34	32	21
States	73,058	2,080	80,478
Time	27.45s	0.63s	3m8s
Total for run:			
Generations	50	200	200
States	1,150,400	1,040,495	931,691
Time	13m30s	19m47s	37m33s

4.5   Larger Instances

The larger instances of the problem families consist of the following. For the Dining Philosopher problem family, we used a 128 philosopher system. For the Leader system, we used a unidirectional ring with 10 voters. Unfortunately it is not possible to scale this model further due to implementation limitations on the part of the system, not the EDA. And finally, for the GIOP system, an instance with a single server and 20 clients is used. The sizes of both the Dining Philosopher system and the GIOP system were chosen due to the availability of measurements on those systems without model reuse. We are confident that the technique will scale beyond these numbers, but due to time contraints we could not explore larger instances.

The statistics shown in Tables 3, 4 and 5 are taken from 100 executions on the Dining Philosopher, Leader and GIOP systems respectively. Each of the 100 runs used the single model constructed in the initial run stage described in Section 4.4. Any statistics in the "n/m" format are stating the "median/mean". In order to compare total amounts of computation, the "With Model Reuse" column in the tables includes the computation up to the best error found in the initial runs. We argue that this is a fair definition of the computation involved in building a model initially because practitioners are likely to limit the number of generations to find a good enough error, especially if the EDA-based technique is used regularly during a development life cycle. The "Without Initial Run" column shows the numbers of the reuse run only, without the computation of the strategy on the smaller instance. Statistical comparisons with the results obtained without model reuse are indicated with plus (significant difference) and minus (insignificant difference) symbols. In order to compare the model reuse runs against the non-reuse runs, we use the Wilcoxon rank-sum test with a significance level of $\alpha = 0.05$.

Table 3. Measurements from the model reuse runs on the Dining Philosophers 128 system

Measurement	Without Model Reuse	With Model Reuse	Without Initial Run
First error:			
Generations	19/19.4(+)	3/3	0/0
Path Length	130/130(-)	130/130	130/130
States	1,831.394/1,898,568.21(+)	73,831/74,281.1	773/1,223.1
Time	47m24s/1h14m32s(+)	29.572s/30.057s	2.122s/2.606s
Best error:			
Generations	19/19.4(+)	3/3	0/0
Path Length	130/130(-)	130/130	130/130
States	1,831.394/1,898,568.21(+)	73,831/74,281.1	773/1,223.1
Time	47m24s/1h14m32s(+)	29.572s/30.057s	2.122s/2.606s

The results in Table 3 show statistics for the Dining Philosopher problem family. In the Dining Philosopher system, there is a single error. The error can be reached in multiple ways but is always at the same depth/path length. This explains the similarity between the first and best results. From the numbers achieved, it is clear that model reuse can have a huge impact on the amount of computational effort required to find errors in the larger instance. The mean time

Table 4. Measurements from the model reuse runs on the Leader 10 system

Measurement	Without Model Reuse	With Model Reuse	Without Initial Run
First error:			
Generations	0/0(-)	0/0	0/0
Path Length	84/82.75(+)	71/71.21	71/71.21
States	84/82.75(+)	2,151/2,151.21	71/71.21
Time	0.239s/0.622s(+)	1.127s/1.606s	0.497s/0.976s
Best error:			
Generations	17/20.26(-)	15/19.23	15/19.23
Path Length	36/35.45(-)	36/35.47	36/35.47
States	193,616/225,050.01(-)	163,429/209,150.82	161,349/207,070.82
Time	22m51s/25m57s(+)	4m7s/5m19s	4m6s/5m18s

Table 5. Measurements from the model reuse runs on the GIOP 20 system

Measurement	Without Model Reuse	With Model Reuse	Without Initial Run
First error:			
Generations	0/0.01(+)	17/17	0/0
Path Length	132/150.09(+)	61/73.37	61/73.37
States	40,421/60,681.01(+)	90,773/98,194.14	10,295/17,716.14
Time	1m26s/2m1s(+)	3m28s/3m46s	19.56s/38.017s
Best error:			
Generations	30/28.71(+)	20/28.21	3/11.21
Path Length	31/31.21(+)	26/25.6	26/25.6
States	13,068,139/12,337,306(+)	1,495,644/4,942,260.07	1,415,166/4,861,782.07
Time	6h47m16s/8h13m24s(+)	57m34s/3h12m14s	54m26s/3h9m6s

to discover an error is reduced by over 99%. This means that rather than wait an hour for additional information regarding the error, information can be obtained in a mere 30 seconds, potentially reducing time spent in the debugging cycle substantially in this case. We expected a large gain on the Dining Philosopher family as it is a symmetrical problem. The strategy to finding an error in the Dining Philosopher is trivial, "Always choose the action that is Pickup the Left Fork".

The results in Table 4 show statistics for the Leader election problem family. In this problem family, the results are less impressive than that of the Dining Philosopher family. We attribute this to the fact that the EDA can find a short counterexample with little computation, often in the first generation before any strategy building has taken place. This suggests that the model is trivial and does not require mechanisms to reduce computational effort. However, we still obtain a significant speed increase in terms of time spent searching the transition system. We attribute this to the EDA exploring a narrower area of the state space on the larger instance due to the initial strategy constructed from the smaller instance. This may avoid expanding useless parts of the search space, resulting in a reduction in CPU and memory usage.

The most impressive results are listed in Table 5 for the GIOP problem family. We expected poorer results on this model due to the description of the system being asymmetric. However, not only is a 62% reduction of mean time in finding a best error achieved (86% reduction in the median time), the quality of the solutions discovered are also improved. The improvement in the path length of the solutions found allow a practitioner to instantly assess the properties of the error. In this instance, the paths are of a similar length meaning it is highly likely that only a subset of the processes in the system are required to cause the error. If all 20 clients were involved, you can expect a substantial increase in the path length over the 2 client model. The Dining Philosopher system, for instance, requires that all processes perform actions to cause a deadlock, and this is reflected by the increase in path length from the 32 philosopher system to the 128 philosopher system. Model reuse and the ability of the EDA to find and optimise counterexamples efficiently [11,12] could make the EDA-based technique a valuable tool for practitioners, as useful information such as this could be revealed along with other insights. Furthermore, the practitioner could gain this information with zero effort, as there is the potential for this approach to be automated.

5 Conclusion

To summarise, we have presented an approach for saving computational and manual effort when building and debugging concurrent systems using the EDA-based technique described in [11,12]. This is achieved by reusing information, specifically information from the models constructed, from an earlier execution to aid the search in a future execution. The analysis and reuse of modelling information learned by EDAs is an often cited advantage [8], and we have used this advantage in a practical scenario. Using this new approach, we have shown that it is possible to save computational effort when analysing problem families, and described other scenarios where effort could potentially be saved. Our results show that information can been gained using an insignificant amount of additional computational resources. This information can yield insights that can save time in the debugging phase, which could ultimately lower development costs. The scenario we have tested in this paper could potentially be automated, meaning no manual effort would be required to gain additional information. At the time of writing, we believe that this is the first application of EDA model analysis/reuse in the SBSE domain.

We believe that there is ample scope for further work in this area. The scenarios for model reuse described and tested in this work are likely a subset of what is possible. There may well be other scenarios in which this work could be beneficial, and not just in the concurrent software testing domain. N-gram GP is essentially a sequence modelling algorithm, and approaches like this could be used wherever the solution space can be represented as a sequence. This could include problems that can be couched as graph search. We feel that the EDA described in [11,12] can be applied to stress testing. In this application domain, the EDA could be used to learn problematic sequences that cause the performance of systems to degrade or indeed completely fail. Augmenting the sequence modelling used in our work is another potential avenue of future research. We have previously outlined a number of ways in which N-gram GP can be improved to further increase efficiency when tackling large problems [11]. Using an entirely different sequence modelling approach may also increase the efficacy of the EDA in the concurrent software testing domain.

Acknowledgments. This work is supported by an EPSRC grant (EP/D050618/1), SEBASE: Software Engineering By Automated SEarch.

References

1. Alba, E., Chicano, F.: Finding safety errors with ACO. In: Proceedings of the 9th Annual Conference on Genetic and Evolutionary Computation, pp. 1066–1073. ACM Press, New York (2007)
2. Alba, E., Chicano, F.: Searching for liveness property violations in concurrent systems with ACO. In: Proceedings of the 10th Annual Conference on Genetic and Evolutionary Computation, pp. 1727–1734. ACM, New York (2008)
3. Alba, E., Chicano, F., Ferreira, M., Gomez-Pulido, J.: Finding deadlocks in large concurrent java programs using genetic algorithms. In: Proceedings of the 10th Annual Conference on Genetic and Evolutionary Computation, pp. 1735–1742. ACM, New York (2008)
4. Clarke, E.M., Grumberg, O., Peled, D.A.: Model Checking. The MIT Press, Cambridge (2000)
5. Edelkamp, S., Lafuente, A.L., Leue, S.: Directed explicit model checking with HSF-SPIN. In: Proceedings of the 8th International SPIN Workshop on Model Checking of Software, pp. 57–79. Springer-Verlag New York, Inc., New York (2001)
6. Edelkamp, S., Leue, S., Lluch-Lafuente, A.: Protocol verification with heuristic search. In: AAAI-Spring Symposium on Model-based Validation Intelligence, pp. 75–83 (2001)
7. Luke, S., Panait, L., Balan, G., et al.: Ecj 16: A java-based evolutionary computation research system (2007)
8. Pelikan, M., Goldberg, D.E., Lobo, F.G.: A survey of optimization by building and using probabilistic models. Computational Optimization and Applications 21(1), 5–20 (2002)
9. Poli, R., McPhee, N.F.: A linear estimation-of-distribution GP system. In: O'Neill, M., Vanneschi, L., Gustafson, S., Esparcia Alcázar, A.I., De Falco, I., Della Cioppa, A., Tarantino, E. (eds.) EuroGP 2008. LNCS, vol. 4971, pp. 206–217. Springer, Heidelberg (2008)
10. Russell, S.J., Norvig, P., Canny, J.F., Malik, J., Edwards, D.D.: Artificial intelligence: a modern approach. Prentice hall, Englewood Cliffs (1995)
11. Staunton, J., Clark, J.A.: Searching for safety violations using estimation of distribution algorithms. In: IEEE International Conference on Software Testing, Verification, and Validation Workshop, pp. 212–221 (2010)
12. Staunton, S., Clark, J.A.: Finding short counterexamples in promela models using estimation of distribution algorithms. To appear: Search-based Software Engineering Track, Genetic and Evolutionary Computation Conference (2011)

Identifying Desirable Game Character Behaviours through the Application of Evolutionary Algorithms to Model-Driven Engineering Metamodels

James R. Williams, Simon Poulding,
Louis M. Rose, Richard F. Paige, and Fiona A.C. Polack

Department of Computer Science,
University of York, UK
{jw,smp,louis,paige,fiona}@cs.york.ac.uk

Abstract. This paper describes a novel approach to the derivation of model-driven engineering (MDE) models using metaheuristic search, and illustrates it using a specific engineering problem: that of deriving computer game characters with desirable properties. The character behaviour is defined using a human-readable domain-specific language (DSL) that is interpreted using MDE techniques. We apply the search to the underlying MDE metamodels, rather than the DSL directly, and as a result our approach is applicable to a wide range of MDE models. An implementation developed using the Eclipse Modeling Framework, the most widely-used toolset for MDE, is evaluated. The results demonstrate not only the derivation of characters with the desired properties, but also the identification of unexpected features of the behavioural description language and the game itself.

1 Introduction

The search-based approach to deriving Model Driven Engineering (MDE) models described in this paper is generic, but was motivated by a specific engineering challenge encountered by the authors: that of deriving suitable game player characters in a computer game called 'Super Awesome Fighter' (SAF).

The SAF game was developed to illustrate MDE concepts to high-school students and is played between two human-specified fighters, or a human-specified fighter and a pre-defined (or 'non-player') opponent. A human player specifies their fighter's behaviour using a bespoke Fighter Description Language (FDL) which covers aspects such as the power of the fighter's kick, the reach of its punch, and whether the fighter punches, kicks, walks towards its opponent, or runs away in particular situations. The description of both fighters is provided to the game engine at the beginning of the game and interpreted using MDE tools. Play then proceeds automatically, and at each stage of the game, the game engine decides on the appropriate action for the fighters according to their FDL

M.B. Cohen and M. Ó Cinnéide (Eds.): SSBSE 2011, LNCS 6956, pp. 112–126, 2011.

descriptions. The winner is the fighter with the best 'health' at the end of the game.

For the game to be interesting, it should be challenging – but not impossible – for a human player to specify a winning fighter. For example, it should not be too easy for a human player to describe a fighter that beats all other opponents, both human and non-player. Similarly, the pre-defined non-player fighter should consistently win against the poorest human-specified fighters, but nonetheless should be beatable by the best fighters. We found that checking these requirements for the game play was difficult and time-consuming when fighters descriptions were investigated manually, and so were motivated to consider an automated search-based approach.

The paper makes two major contributions. Firstly, we demonstrate the use of Search-Based Software Engineering techniques in deriving fighters with particular properties, such as consistently beating all opponents. The search algorithm is a form of Grammatical Evolution (GE), which is a natural choice for this application since the FDL is an example of a context-free grammar to which GE is normally applied. The fighters derived by the search algorithm provide useful information for the software engineer in modifying the game play or the Fighter Description Language to ensure a suitable challenge for human players.

The second contribution is an implementation of the genotype-to-phenotype mapping process that is central to GE using the Eclipse Modeling Framework (EMF), a widely-used MDE toolset. Since the fighter description is implemented as a model using EMF, and the FDL is a concrete syntax for this model, the use of EMF model transformation technologies is a very convenient method of performing the mapping for this particular application. Moreover, we have implemented the mapping process in an automated and generic manner, enabling its use with other optimisation problems where solutions are expressed in terms of MDE models.

Related work that applies metaheuristic search to MDE models includes the use of particle swarm optimisation and simulated annealing in model transformation [7]; the evolutionary generation of behavioural models [4]; and the analysis of non-functional properties of architectures described using MDE [11]. However, such combinations of Search-Based Software Engineering and MDE are relatively rare, and our intention is that our generic implementation of GE using an appropriate toolset will facilitate further research in this area[1].

The paper is structured as follows. Section 2 describes relevant background material: Grammatical Evolution, MDE concepts and terminology, and details of the Fighter Description Language. The generic genotype-to-phenotype mapping process using EMF model transformation is explained in section 3. An empirical evaluation of the approach is described in section 4. Section 5 concludes the paper and outlines future work.

---

[1] The code for the GE implementation, the SAF game, and the results of the empirical work, are available from: http://www-users.cs.york.ac.uk/jw/saf

2 Background

This section explains the main features of Grammatical Evolution, relevant Model-Driven Engineering concepts and terminology, and the Fighter Description Language.

2.1 Grammatical Evolution

The technique of Grammatical Evolution (GE) was first described Ryan and O'Neill [15,14] as a mechanism for automatically deriving 'programs' in languages defined by a context-free grammar where the definition is expressed using Backus-Naur form (BNF). Applications of GE include symbolic regression [15], deriving rules for foreign exchange trading [1], and the interactive composition of music [17].

The central process in GE is the mapping from a linear genotype, such as a bit or integer string, to a phenotype that is an instance of a valid program in the language according to the BNF definition. Figure 1 illustrates the process using a simple grammar for naming pubs (bars).

The pub naming grammar is defined in BNF at the top of figure 1 and consists a series of production rules that specify how non-terminal symbols (the left-hand sides of the rule, such as <noun-phrase>) may be constructed from other non-terminals symbols and from terminal symbols (constant values that have no

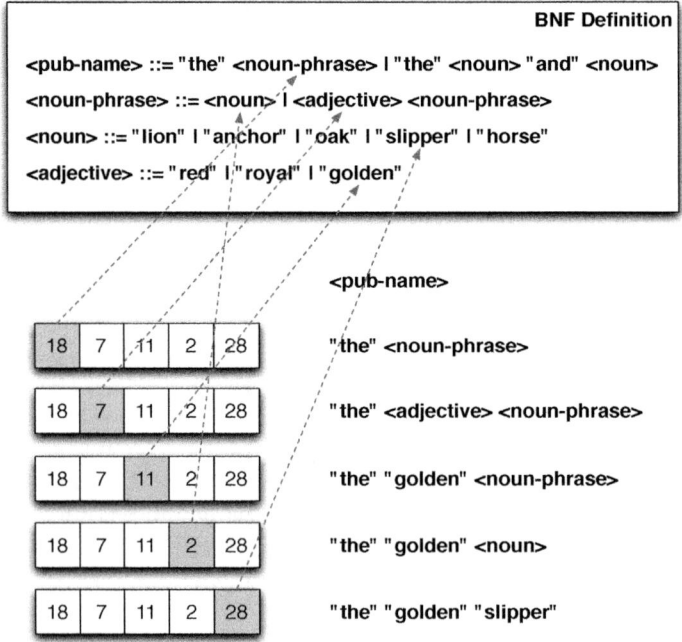

Fig. 1. An example of genotype-to-phenotype mapping in Grammatical Evolution

production rule, such as "red"). Vertical bars separate a series of choices as to how to construct the non-terminal symbols.

At the left of figure is the genotype that will be mapped to the phenotype, in this case, a pub name valid according to the naming grammar. The genotype consists of a sequence of integer values, each of which is termed a *codon*. The mapping process starts with the first production rule in the grammar, that for the non-terminal <pub-name>. There are three options as to how to produce this non-terminal, and the value of the first codon determines which choice to use by taking the value modulo the number of choices. In this case the codon value is 18, there are 2 choices, 18 mod 2 = 0, and so the first choice of the two, "the" <noun-phrase>, is used. The next construction decision is for the non-terminal <noun-phrase> and it uses the value of the second codon. The codon has a value of 7, there are 2 choices, 7 mod 2 = 1, and so the second choice is used. Production continues in this way until there are no more non-terminals to produce.

Should the mapping process require more codon values than are present in the genotype, codon values are re-used starting at the first codon. This process is known as *wrapping*. It is possible for the mapping process to enter an endless loop as a result of wrapping. Therefore, a sensible upper limit is placed on the number of wrappings that may occur, and any genotype which causes this limit to be reached is assigned the worst possible fitness.

Ryan and O'Neill's original work on Grammatical Evolution used a specific genetic algorithm, with a variable length genotype and specialist genetic operators. More recent work makes a distinction between the genotype-to-phenotype mapping process, and the underlying search algorithm, using, for example, differential evolution [12] and particle swarm optimisation [13], in place of the genetic algorithm. We take a similar approach in the work described in this paper by designing a genotype-to-phenotype mapping process that is independent of the underlying search algorithm.

2.2 Model-Driven Engineering

A *model* can be thought of as an *abstraction* of a problem under scrutiny; the abstraction is typically created for a specific purpose. Models have been used in many engineering disciplines for years, yet in software engineering models have often played a secondary role – as documentation or a means of problem exploration [16]. *Model-driven engineering* (MDE) is a software development practice that treats models as first-class artefacts in the development process. MDE focuses on modelling the system at the level of the application domain, and via a series of automatic transformations, generating code.

Models in MDE are defined and constrained by their *metamodel* – another model that establishes the form a model can take; a metamodel can be thought of as the *abstract syntax* of the model [8]. A model that adheres to the concepts and rules specified in a metamodel is said to *conform* to that metamodel.

An important concept in MDE is model transformation [2]. Examples of common transformations are generating code from a model (a *model-to-text* transformation), generating a model from code (a *text-to-model* transformation), and transforming a model into one that conforms to a different metamodel (a *model-to-model* transformation). Other model management activities include validating models, migrating models to newer versions of their metamodel, merging models, and comparing models.

One of the most widely used modelling frameworks is the Eclipse Modeling Framework (EMF) [18], part of the Eclipse IDE[2]. EMF provides mechanisms for creating, editing and validating models and metamodels, as well as for generating code from models. EMF generates a Java implementation of metamodels where each of the metamodel's classes (called meta-classes) corresponds to a single Java class. This means that these classes can be instantiated to create models conforming to the metamodel. EMF can also create (tree-based or graphical) editors for models conforming to metamodels [18].

2.3   The Fighter Description Language

The fighting game, SAF, introduced in section 1 allows the behaviour of fighter characters to be defined in a bespoke domain-specific language, the *fighter description language* (FDL). Fighters in SAF are MDE models, which are described by the FDL. Figure 2 shows a simplified version of the metamodel for a SAF fighter.

A fighter (`Bot`) in SAF has two features - a `Personality` and a `Behaviour`. A fighter's `Personality` is defined by a set of `Characteristics` – defining the power and reach of the fighter (values range between 0 and 9). These characteristics represent trade-offs: a more powerful strength characteristic limits the speed with which the fighter can move. If one of the characteristics is not specified by the user, its value defaults to 5. The `Behaviour` of a fighter is made up of a set of `BehaviourRules`. `BehaviourRules` specify how the fighter should behave in certain `Conditions`. A rule is composed of a `MoveAction` and a `FightAction`. FDL offers the ability to specify a *choice* of move and fight actions using the keyword `choose`. For example, a rule can define that they want to either block high or block low, and the game will pick one of these at random.

We have defined FDL using Xtext [3], a tool and language that enables the creation of custom languages based upon metamodels. Xtext generates a text-to-model parser for languages, meaning that the concrete syntax of FDL can automatically be parsed into a model and used with the SAF game. Furthermore, the Xtext grammar definition language also conforms to a metamodel and it is this metamodel that allows us to perform grammatical evolution over FDL (and other languages defined using Xtext). Listing 1 illustrates the syntax of FDL using an example fighter[3].

---

[2] Eclipse website: http://www.eclipse.org
[3] The FDL grammar is available from: http://www-users.cs.york.ac.uk/jw/saf.

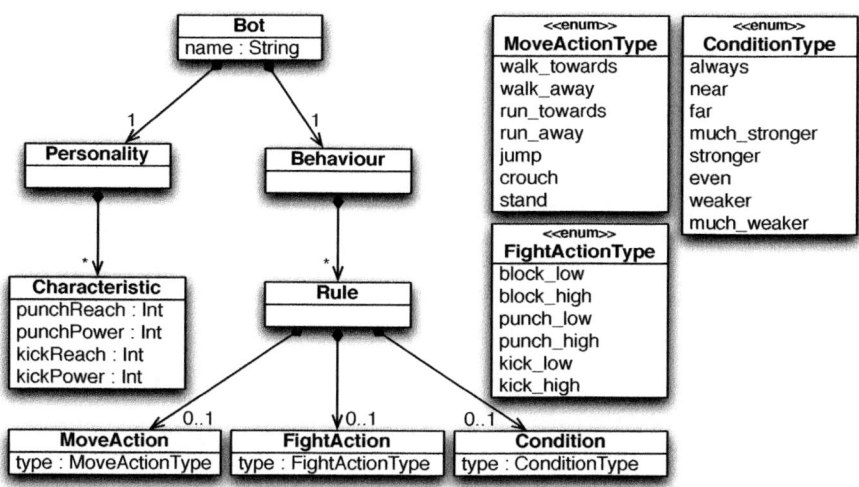

Fig. 2. The simplified metamodel for the character behaviour language used in SAF

```
1  JackieChan{
2    kickPower = 7
3    punchPower = 5
4    kickReach = 3
5    punchReach = 9
6    far[run_towards punch_high]
7    near[choose(stand crouch) kick_high]
8    much_stronger[walk_towards punch_low]
9    weaker[run_away choose(block_high block_low)]
10   always[walk_towards block_high]
11 }
```

Listing 1. An example character defined using FDL

Our choice of using Xtext was due to our familiarity with it, and our approach can be implemented for any equivalent grammar definition language that has a metamodel, such as EMFText [5].

The next section shows how the Xtext grammar defined for FDL can be used with metaheuristic search in order to discover the set of behaviours that define a good fighter.

3   Genotype to Phenotype Transformation

In this section we explain the process of mapping the genotype (integer string) to the phenotype (fighter) using model transformations. The inputs to the process are the genotype and the definition of the Fighter Description Language grammar. The latter is initially defined as a text file, but the mapping utilises a more convenient form of the grammar expressed as a model that conforms to the Xtext metamodel.

3.1   Creating the Genotype Model

The first step in the process is to turn the genotype into a model representation in order to perform the model transformation. Figure 3 illustrates the metamodel of our genotype. A `Genotype` is composed on a number of `Codons`. A `Codon` has one attribute – its `value`, and one reference – a pointer to the `next` codon in the chromosome.

The integer string from the search algorithm is used to create a model that conforms to this metamodel. A `Codon` class is created for each codon, and its `value` attribute is set to the value of the codon. Each `Codon`'s `next` reference is set to the successive codon, with the final codon in the chromosome pointing back to the first. This creates a cycle, meaning that genotype wrapping is handled automatically by traversing the references. An example model that conforms to this metamodel is shown as part of figure 4.

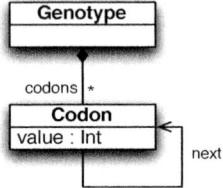

Fig. 3. The metamodel for a Genotype

3.2   Transliterating the Phenotype

The next step is to transform this model of the genotype into a model of the phenotype (the Fighter Description Language). The transformation is written in the Epsilon Object Language (EOL) [10], a general purpose model management language that is part of the Epsilon model management platform [9]. Figure 4 is an overview of this transformation process.

As grammar definitions written in Xtext conform to a metamodel, we can define the transformation at the metamodel level, enabling the mapping process to be applied to any Xtext grammar. The Xtext metamodel contains metaclasses for all aspects of the grammar, including production rules, choices, and terminals. Each production rule in a grammar model is represented as an object conforming to a class in the Xtext metamodel and contains references to other objects in the model that represent its non-terminals and terminals. This representation facilitates the mapping process: where there is a choice in a production rule, codons from the genotype model are used to select which reference to use and therefore which path to travel through the model. When the path reaches a terminal string, it is added to the output string.

To illustrate this approach, consider the rule in the fragment of the FDL grammar shown in listing 2. This rule specifies the characteristics of a fighter, and contains four choices. When parsed into a model conforming to the Xtext metamodel, it takes the shape of figure 5.

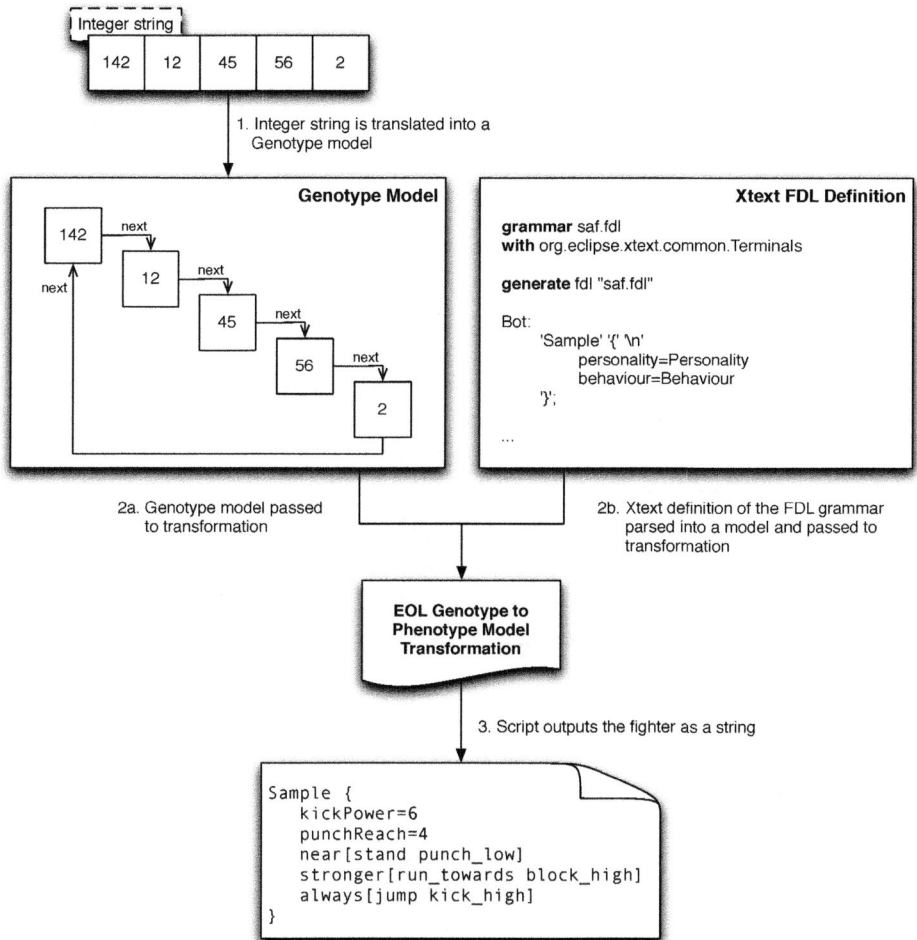

Fig. 4. The process followed in order to transform the genotype into the phenotype

When this rule is reached during the transformation, the current codon's value identifies which alternative to execute by taking the codon's value modulo the number of choices. If the first alternative is chosen, the keywords punchReach and = will be added to the output string, and the next codon in the genotype model will select the NUMBER to assign to the selected characteristic. The execution can then traverse back up the reference chain and execute the next production rule in sequence, or terminate. If the user-defined number of genotype wrappings is reached during the execution, the transformation aborts. Otherwise, the transformation results in a string that conforms to the grammar of interest – in our case, a fighter.

```
1  Characteristic:
2    'punchReach' '=' value=NUMBER '\n' | 'punchPower' '=' value=
3      NUMBER '\n' |
4    'kickReach' '=' value=NUMBER '\n'  |'kickPower' '=' value=
5      NUMBER '\n' ;
```

Listing 2. The Xtext grammar rule for defining characteristics of a fighter

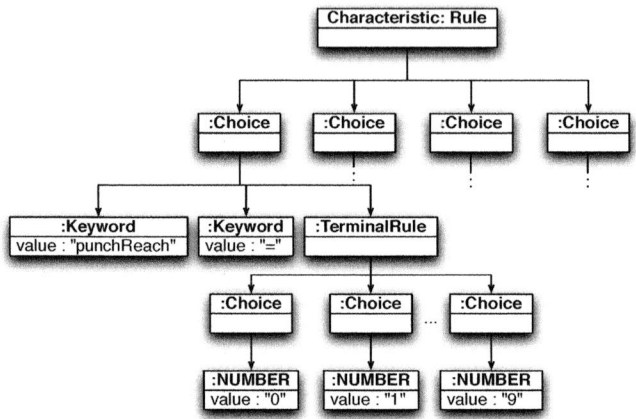

Fig. 5. A section of the FDL grammar model demonstrating how choices are made during the transformation process

4   Evaluation and Results

The previous section described a generic process for mapping an integer string genotype to a phenotype using EMF model transformation technologies. To illustrate and evaluate the approach, we return to the specific application described in the introduction where the phenotype is the SAF game Fighter Description Language (FDL), a concrete syntax for model of the fighter's capabilities and behaviour.

The objective of this evaluation is to understand the feasibility of the proposed search-based approach in the context of the original motivating problem: that of investigating the requirements for interesting and challenging SAF game play. These requirements are expressed as two experimental questions:

EQ1. Is it possible to specify unbeatable fighters? If so, it may be necessary to amend either the game play or restrict the fighter description language to limit the possibility of a human player specifying such a fighter.

EQ2. Is it possible to derive a fighter that wins 80% of its fights against a range of other fighters? Such a fighter could be used as the pre-defined non-player opponent since it would provide an interesting, but not impossible, challenge for human players. The figure of 80% is an arbitrary choice that we believe represents a reasonably challenging opponent for human players.

Since this is an initial evaluation of feasibility, no explicit consideration of efficiency (speed and resource usage) of the approach is made. We plan to make a detailed evaluation of efficiency as part of our future work.

4.1   Empirical Method

To answer these two questions, our GE implementation is applied to the problem by pairing the genotype-to-phenotype mapping described above with a suitable metaheuristic search algorithm. The primary experiments use a genetic algorithm as the search algorithm, and in addition we perform secondary experiments using random search in order to assess whether the problem is sufficiently trivial that solutions can be found by random sampling of the search space.

Fitness Metric. An assessment of the properties of "unbeatable" (EQ1) and "wins 80% of its fights" (EQ2) requires a set of opponents to be defined. It is not practical to test how the a candidate fighter performs against *all* possible opponents, and so we created a 'panel' of representative opponents by asking our colleagues to specify what they believed would be winning fighters. (Note that our colleagues are acting simply as examples of typical human game players: they are *not* attempting to perform manually the equivalent of our proposed automated search-based approach in exploring the capabilities of the FDL.) The fitness of a candidate fighter is then assessed by having it play the SAF game against each opponent in the panel. The game play is stochastic owing to the choose construct in the DSL, and so each candidate fighter fights each opponent a number of times so that a more accurate fitness can be estimated.

The fitness of a candidate fighter is based on the difference between the number of fights won by the candidate fighter against the panel, and a target number of winning fights. It is calculated as:

$$f = \left| \rho\, n_{\text{opps}}\, n_{\text{fights}} - \sum_{o=1}^{n_{\text{opps}}} \sum_{i=1}^{n_{\text{fights}}} w_{o,i} \right| \tag{1}$$

where n_{opps} is the number of opponents in the panel; n_{fights} the number of fights with each opponent; ρ the proportion of fights that the fighter should win, and $w_{o,i}$ an indicator variable set to 1 if the fighter wins the ith fight against the oth opponent, and 0 otherwise. The proportion of fights to win, ρ, is set to 1 for experiments on EQ1, indicating an optimal fighter must win all fights against all opponents in the panel, and is set to 0.8 for experiments on EQ2. Fighters with lower fitnesses are therefore better since they are closer to winning the desired proportion of fights.

Algorithm Settings and Implementation. The algorithm settings, including the parameters used in the genotype-to-phenotype mapping and in the fitness calculation, are listed in table 1. Since the efficiency of the algorithms is not being explicitly evaluated in this work, no substantial effort was made to tune the parameters to this particular problem, and the choice of some parameter

Table 1. Parameter settings for the genetic algorithm, genotype-to-phenotype mapping, and fitness metric

parameter	setting
number of codons	20
codon value range	0–32767
population size	20
maximum number of generations	50
initialisation method	random codon values
selection method (for reproduction)	tournament, size 2
reproduction method	single point crossover
mutation method	integer mutation (random value)
mutation probability (per codon)	0.1
number of elite individuals	2
maximum wrappings (during mapping)	10
number of opponents (n_{opps})	7
number of fights (n_{fights})	5

settings, for example the use of integer mutation, was made with reference to existing GE studies, such as [6].

The genetic algorithm was a bespoke implementation in Java since this is the language used in the interface to the genotype-and-phenotype mapping. A bespoke implementation was chosen as this was throught to provide a more flexible basis for proposed future work on co-evolutionary strategies. However, other evolutionary computation libraries written in Java, such as ECJ[4], could have been used in conjunction with our genotype-to-phenotype mapping process.

For random search, the bespoke genetic algorithm implementation was used but with the mutation probability set to 1.0. This has the effect of selecting a entirely new random population at each generation (apart from the elite individuals which are retained unchanged in the next generation).

Response. Four experiments were performed: one for each combination of question (EQ1 or EQ2) and algorithm (genetic algorithm or random search). Within each experiment, the algorithm was run 30 times, each run with a different seed to the pseudo-random number generator. Our chosen response metric is a measure of the effectiveness of the approach: the proportion of runs resulting in an 'optimal' (as defined by EQ1 or EQ2) fighter. Since the fitness metric is noisy as a result of the stochastic choose construct in the FDL, the condition for optimality is slightly relaxed to allow candidate fighters with a fitness of 1.0 or less; in other words, an optimal fighter may differ by at most one from the desired number of winning fights rather than requiring an exact match. This condition also accommodates the situation where the choice of ρ causes the term $\rho\, n_{\mathrm{opps}}\, n_{\mathrm{fights}}$ in the fitness function to be non-integer.

---

[4] ECJ website: http://cs.gmu.edu/eclab/projects/ecj/

Table 2. The proportion of successful runs (those that find an 'optimal' fighter) for the four experiments. The ranges in parentheses are the 95% confidence intervals. Values are rounded to 2 significant figures.

experimental question	search algorithm	proportion successful
EQ1 ($\rho = 1.0$)	genetic algorithm	0.67 (0.50 – 0.83)
EQ1 ($\rho = 1.0$)	random search	0 (0 – 0.12)
EQ2 ($\rho = 0.8$)	genetic algorithm	0.97 (0.88 – 1.0)
EQ2 ($\rho = 0.8$)	random search	0.47 (0.31 – 0.66)

```
1 fighter{
2   punchReach=9
3   even[choose(crouch walk_towards) choose(block_high
        punch_low)]
4   always[crouch block_low]
5 }
```

Listing 3. Example of an 'unbeatable' fighter description found by the genetic algorithm

4.2   Results and Analysis

Table 2 summarises the results of the four experiments[5]. The 'proportion successful' column is the fraction of algorithm runs in which an 'optimal' fighter was found. The 95% confidence intervals are shown in parentheses after the observed value, and are calculated using the Clopper-Pearson method (chosen since it is typically a conservative estimate of the interval).

For EQ1, the objective was to derive unbeatable fighters. The results show that unbeatable fighters can be derived: the genetic algorithm found such examples in approximately 67% of the algorithm runs. Listing 3 shows a particularly simple example of an optimal 'unbeatable' fighter derived during one algorithm run. The ease of derivation using a genetic algorithm is not necessarily an indication of the ease with which a human player may construct an unbeatable fighter. Nevertheless, it is plausible that a human player could derive unbeatable fighters with descriptions as simple as that in listing 3, and therefore the game play or the FDL may need to be re-engineered to avoid such fighters.

For EQ2, the objective was to derive challenging fighters that won approximately 80% of the fights against the panel of opponents. The results show that it was easy for the genetic algorithm and possible, but not as easy, for random search to derive descriptions for such fighters, such as the example shown in listing 4.

---

[5] Detailed results are available from: `http://www-users.cs.york.ac.uk/jw/saf`.

```
1  fighter{
2    kickReach=9
3    stronger[choose(jump run_away) choose(kick_low block_low)]
4    far or much_weaker[choose(crouch run_towards) choose(
          punch_low punch_high)]
5    always[crouch kick_low]
6  }
```

Listing 4. Example of an 'challenging' fighter description found by the genetic algorithm

An unintended, but very useful, outcome of these experiments was that search process exposed some shortcomings in the Fighter Description Language that were not discovered by human players. One example was that the game engine requires that the fighter description specify a behaviour for every situation (whether weaker or stronger than the opponent fighter, or near or far from it), but the language grammar does not enforce this requirement. This was resolved by ensuring that all descriptions contained an always clause.

```
1  fighter{
2    punchPower=9
3    punchPower=7
4    punchPower=2
5    kickPower=7
6    punchPower=2
7    kickPower=2
8    near[crouch punch_low]
9    stronger or far[choose(run_towards run_towards) kick_high]
10   much_weaker and weaker[walk_away block_low]
11   always[crouch kick_high]
12 }
```

Listing 5. Example of an 'unbeatable' fighter description that illustrates language shortcomings

Further examples of language shortcomings are illustrated in the description shown in listing 5: characteristics of punchPower and kickPower are specified multiple times (lines 2 to 7); the condition much_weaker and weaker can never be satisfied (line 10); and both choices in the choose clause are the same (line 9). Although none of these issues prevent game play – only one of the repeated characteristics is used; the condition is never considered; and the choose clause is equivalent to simply run_towards – they are not intended (and, moreover, unnecessarily increase the size of the search space). The language might be modified to avoid these shortcomings.

Finally, we compare the efficacy of the genetic algorithm and random search on the two experimental questions. The results for EQ1 in table 2 suggest that random search cannot find an 'unbeatable' fighter (at least in the same upper limit on the number of fitness evaluations as the genetic algorithm), and that the problem is non-trivial. For EQ2, random search does succeed in the easier problem of finding 'challenging' fighters, but with less consistency than the genetic algorithm. The non-overlapping confidence intervals indicate that the differences between random search and the genetic algorithm are statistically significant for both questions.

5   Conclusions and Future Work

In this paper we have presented a novel application of Grammatical Evolution to the derivation of fighting game characters that possess desirable properties. The genotype-to-phenotype mapping process uses model transformation technologies from the Eclipse Modeling Framework, facilitating the implementation for this specific application, as well as enabling the same approach to be used on other optimisation problems where the solutions are expressed as MDE models. The range of potential applications include not only other domain specific languages that conform to a metamodel, but also more general models.

We intend to continue this work in a number of directions. Firstly, in the context of this specific application, the opponents against which the fighter's fitness metric is assessed could be derived using co-evolutionary methods rather than a human-derived panel. We speculate that currently the fighter properties of 'unbeatable' and 'challenging' may not be applicable beyond the panel of human-derived opponents, and that by co-evolving a larger, diverse panel of opponents, fighters with more robust properties may be derived. Secondly, non-player fighters could be dynamically evolved during the game play: each time a human player finds a winning fighter, a more challenging non-player opponent could be evolved, thus ensuring the human player's continued interest.

More generally, we aim to improve the generality of the genotype-to-phenotype mapping process. A first step is to accommodate cross-referencing, whereby multiple parts of the phenotype must refer to the same instantiated element; this feature was not required for the SAF Fighter Definition Language. This enhancement would permit the mapping to be used with any Xtext grammar definition to generate concrete instances. We also intend to investigate the use of *bi-directional* model transformation, enabling a reverse phenotype-to-genotype mapping in addition to current genotype-to-phenotype: this would be useful for search problems in which an additional local search is performed on the phenotype as part of a hybrid search algorithm, or an invalid phenotype is repaired, and such changes need to be brought back in to the genotype.

References

1. Brabazon, A., O'Neill, M.: Evolving technical trading rules for spot foreign-exchange markets using grammatical evolution. Computational Management Science 1, 311–327 (2004)

2. Czarnecki, K., Helsen, S.: Feature-based survey of model transformation approaches. IBM Systems Journal 45(3), 621–645 (2006)
3. Efftinge, S., Voelter, M.: oAW xText: A framework for textual DSLs. In: Proc. Workshop on Modelling, Eclipse Con. (2006)
4. Goldsby, H.J., Cheng, B.H.C.: Avida-MDE: a digital evolution approach to generating models of adaptive software behavior. In: Proc. Genetic and Evolutionary Computation Conf., GECCO 2008, pp. 1751–1758 (2008)
5. Heidenreich, F., Johannes, J., Karol, S., Seifert, M., Wende, C.: Derivation and Refinement of Textual Syntax for Models. In: Paige, R.F., Hartman, A., Rensink, A. (eds.) ECMDA-FA 2009. LNCS, vol. 5562, pp. 114–129. Springer, Heidelberg (2009)
6. Hugosson, J., Hemberg, E., Brabazon, A., O'Neill, M.: Genotype representations in grammatical evolution. Applied Soft. Computing 10, 36–43 (2010)
7. Kessentini, M., Sahraoui, H., Boukadoum, M.: Model Transformation as an Optimization Problem. In: Busch, C., Ober, I., Bruel, J.-M., Uhl, A., Völter, M. (eds.) MODELS 2008. LNCS, vol. 5301, pp. 159–173. Springer, Heidelberg (2008)
8. Kleppe, A.: A language description is more than a metamodel. In: Fourth Int'l Workshop on Software Language Eng. (October 2007)
9. Kolovos, D.S., Rose, L.M., Paige, R.F.: The Epsilon book (2010) (unpublished)
10. Kolovos, D.S., Paige, R.F., Polack, F.A.C.: The Epsilon Object Language (EOL). In: Rensink, A., Warmer, J. (eds.) ECMDA-FA 2006. LNCS, vol. 4066, pp. 128–142. Springer, Heidelberg (2006)
11. Li, R., Chaudron, M.R.V., Ladan, R.C.: Towards automated software architectures design using model transformations and evolutionary algorithms. In: Proc. Genetic and Evolutionary Computation Conf (GECCO 2010), pp. 1333–1340 (2010)
12. O'Neill, M., Brabazon, A.: Grammatical differential evolution. In: Proc. 2006 Int'l Conf. Artificial Intelligence (ICAI 2006), pp. 231–236 (2006)
13. O'Neill, M., Brabazon, A.: Grammatical swarm: The generation of programs by social programming. Natural Computing 5, 443–462 (2006)
14. O'Neill, M., Ryan, C.: Grammatical evolution. IEEE Trans. Evol. Comput. 5(4), 349–358 (2001)
15. Ryan, C., Collins, J.J., Neill, M.O.: Grammatical Evolution: Evolving Programs for an Arbitrary Language. In: Banzhaf, W., Poli, R., Schoenauer, M., Fogarty, T.C. (eds.) EuroGP 1998. LNCS, vol. 1391, pp. 83–96. Springer, Heidelberg (1998)
16. Selic, B.: The pragmatics of model-driven development. IEEE Software 20(5), 19–25 (2003)
17. Shao, J., McDermott, J., O'Neill, M., Brabazon, A.: Jive: A Generative, Interactive, Virtual, Evolutionary Music System. In: Di Chio, C., Brabazon, A., Di Caro, G.A., Ebner, M., Farooq, M., Fink, A., Grahl, J., Greenfield, G., Machado, P., O'Neill, M., Tarantino, E., Urquhart, N. (eds.) EvoApplications 2010. LNCS, vol. 6025, pp. 341–350. Springer, Heidelberg (2010)
18. Steinberg, D., Budinsky, F., Paternostro, M., Merks, E.: EMF Eclipse Modeling Framework. The Eclipse Series, 2nd edn., Addison-Wesley, Reading (2009)

Cooperative Co-evolutionary Optimization of Software Project Staff Assignments and Job Scheduling

Jian Ren[1], Mark Harman[1], and Massimiliano Di Penta[2]

[1] Department of Computer Science, University College London, UK
[2] Department of Engineering, University of Sannio, Italy

Abstract. This paper presents an approach to Search Based Software Project Management based on Cooperative Co-evolution. Our approach aims to optimize both developers' team staffing and work package scheduling through cooperative co-evolution to achieve early overall completion time. To evaluate our approach, we conducted an empirical study, using data from four real-world software projects. Results indicate that the Co-evolutionary approach significantly outperforms a single population evolutionary algorithm. Cooperative co-evolution has not previously been applied to any problem in Search Based Software Engineering (SBSE), so this paper reports the first application of cooperative co-evolution in the SBSE literature. We believe that co-evolutionary optimization may fit many applications in other SBSE problem domains, since software systems often have complex inter-related subsystems and are typically characterized by problems that need to be co-evolved to improve results.

Keywords: Cooperative Co-Evolutionary Algorithm, Staff Assignments, Work Package Scheduling, Software Project Planning, Search Based Software Engineering.

1   Introduction

Software project management has been the subject of much recent work in the SBSE literature. Previous work has investigated the project staffing and planning problem either as a single-objective problem, or as a multi-objective problem in which the multiple objectives are, to some degree, conflicting objectives [3,4,13]. In this paper we introduce an alternative approach based on the use of a Cooperative Co-Evolutionary Algorithm (CCEA). We believe that a Cooperative Co-Evolutionary approach to project management is attractive because it allows us to model a problem in terms of sub problems (e.g., in project scheduling and staffing, the allocation of work packages to teams and allocation of staff to teams). These sub problems can be inter-related, but separate problems, for which the overall solution depends on the identification of suitable sympathetic sub-solutions to each of the subproblems.

We show how the two primary features of a project plan—i.e., the allocation of staff to teams and the allocation of teams to work packages—can be formulated as two populations in a Cooperative Co-evolutionary search. Co-evolution has been previously used in SBSE work [1,6,7], but all previous approaches have used *competing* subpopulations; the so-called predator–prey model of Co-evolution. In this paper, we adopt the alternative approach to co-evolution; Cooperative Co-evolution, in which the subpopulations

M.B. Cohen and M. Ó Cinnéide (Eds.): SSBSE 2011, LNCS 6956, pp. 127–141, 2011.

work symbiotically rather than in conflict with one another. We believe that this form of co-evolution may also find many other applications in SBSE work, since many Software Engineering problems are characterized by a need to find cooperating subsystems that are evolved specifically to work together symbiotically.

We implemented our approach and evaluated it on data from four real world software projects from four different companies, ranging in size form 60 to 253 individual work packages. We report the results on the efficiency and effectiveness of our approach, compared to a random search and to a single population approach. Our results indicate that the co-evolutionary approach has great promise; over 30 runs for each approach, co-evolution significantly outperforms both random and single population approaches for the effectiveness of the project plans found, while it also appears to be at least as efficient as a single population approach.

The paper makes two primary contributions: (1) The paper introduces a novel formulation of the Software Project Planning Problem using Cooperative Co-evolution and, to the best of our knowledge, this is the first paper in the SBSE literature to use cooperative co-evolution. (2) The paper reports the results of an empirical study with an implementation of our co-evolutionary approach, compared to random and single population evolution. The obtained results provide evince to support the claim that cooperative co-evolution is more efficient and effective than single population evolution and random search.

2   Problem Statement and Definitions

This section describes the problem model for the work packages scheduling and staff assignment problem in detail and addresses the use of the CCEA.

Finding an optimal work package scheduling for a large project is difficult due to the large search space and many different considerations that need to be balanced. Also, finding an optimal way to construct its project teams is crucial as well. In this paper, we focus on team construction with regard to team size.

In order to formulate this problem into a model, we make the following assumptions to simplify the problem: (1) staff members are identical in terms of skills and expertise, and staff only work on one team during the whole project, (2) WPs are sequentially distributed to teams, but they may still be processed at the same time, and (3) only one kind of dependency is considered: Finish-to-Start (FS). All three assumptions were found to be applicable to the four projects studied in this paper, all of which are real world software projects and therefore, though limiting, our assumptions do not preclude real world application.

2.1   Ordering/Sequence of Work Packages

To model the work needed to complete a project, we decompose the project according to its Work Breakdown Structure (WBS). WBS is widely used as a method of project decomposition. In a given WBS, the whole project is divided into a number of l small Work Packages (WPs): $\mathbf{WP} = \{wp_1, wp_2, \cdots, wp_l\}$. Two attributes of a WP, wp_i, are considered in this paper: (1) the estimated effort, e_i, required to complete wp_i, and (2) the WP predecessor(s), dep_i, which need to be completed before wp_i can start to be processed. The estimated efforts for all WPs are represented as a vector: $\mathbf{E} = \{e_1, e_2, \cdots, e_l\}$, e.g.: wp_i requires e_i person-days to complete; and dependence information is represented as a two-dimensional vector as: $\mathbf{Dep} = \{dep_1, dep_2, \cdots, dep_l\}$ where $dep_i = \{wp_j, \cdots, wp_k\}$ if the predecessors of wp_i are $wp_j, \cdots,$ and wp_k.

The order in which the WPs are considered is represented as a string, shown in Figure 1, where the WP ordering in the string indicates a specific sequence for distributing the WPs to project teams. Constraints of precedence relationships are satisfied as each is processed, with the effect that a project cannot start until its dependent WPs have been completed.

Distributing Order:	$1st$	$2nd$	$3rd$	$\cdots$	$(l-1)th$	l-th
Work Package ID:	3	2	6	$\cdots$	l	$l-4$

Fig. 1. WPO Chromosome: The gray area is the representation of the solutions for the ordering for distributing a set of l work packages. A solution is represented by a string of length l, each gene corresponding to the distributing order of the WPs and the alleles, drawn from $\{1, ..., l\}$, representing an individual WP.

2.2 Staff Assignments to Teams

A total of n staff are assigned to m teams to execute the WPs. The size of each team (their 'capacity') is denoted by a sequence $\mathbf{C} = \{c_1, c_2, \cdots, c_m\}$.

Staff:	S_1	S_2	S_3	$\cdots$	S_{n-1}	S_n
Assigned To Team No.:	2	4	3	$\cdots$	m	3

Fig. 2. TC Chromosome: The gray area is the representation of the solutions for Team Construction or the assignments of a set of n staff to a set of m teams. A solution is represented by a string of length n, with each gene corresponding to a staff and the alleles, drawn from $\{1, ..., m\}$, representing assignment of the staff.

2.3 Scheduling Simulation

We use a single objective fitness evaluation for both populations in our co-evolutionary approach, i.e., the project completion time. The processing of the WPs by the teams is simulated by a simple queuing simulation as described in previous work [13,20]. In this approach, the WP dependence constraints are satisfied by arranging the order in which WPs are assigned to teams. However, we want to avoid the order in which the successor wp_i is right after its predecessor wp_j. In such a case, wp_i has to wait until wp_j is finished before it can be distributed to an available team. There are two ways for the managers to minimize the team's unused available time: 1) interlacing: managers can choose to insert one or more WPs between wp_i and wp_j so when wp_i is waiting for wp_j those inserted WPs can keep all the teams functioning, or 2) using mitigation: distribute the predecessor wp_j to a team with the highest possible capacity, so that the completion time of the predecessor is the shortest, and therefore, the wait time of wp_i is mitigated to be the shortest one. In our case, we simply rely on the search based algorithm that, by producing different WP orderings, can enact both interlacing or mitigation. Further details about the simulation of WP scheduling can be found in a previous work [13].

3 Optimization Method: Cooperative Co-evolutionary Algorithm

The Cooperative Co-Evolution Algorithm (CCEA) [21] was proposed to solve large and complex problems by implementing a divide-and-conquer strategy. CCEA was originally designed to decompose a high-dimensional problem into smaller sub-problems that could be handled by conventional evolutionary algorithms [24]. Using CCEA, the individuals from each population represent a sub-solution to the given problem. To search for a solution, the members of each population are evolved independently, and interactions between populations only occur to obtain fitness.

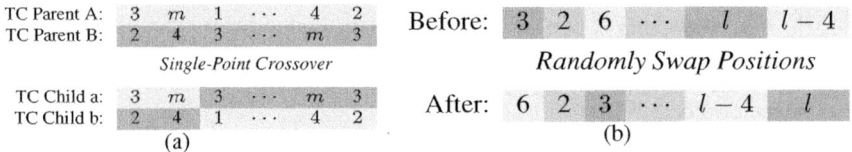

Fig. 3. (a) TC Single Point Crossover and (b) WPO Mutation

3.1 Solution Representations and Genetic Operators

There are two species of solutions in this evolutionary process: One (WPO) contains solutions representing the ordering in which WPs are distributed to teams, and the other (TC) represents the Team Constructions, i.e., the number of staffing persons for each team.

For solutions representing staff assignments or TC, as shown in Figure 2, we encoded the solutions in the following format. The assignment of a set of n staff to a set of m teams is represented as a string of length n. Each gene of the chromosome corresponds to a staff member. The alleles ranging from 1 to m represent the team that the staff is assigned to. A single-point crossover is performed for the TC specie. Basically, the child takes half of chromosome from each of both parents. The mutation operator is thus set to assign each staff randomly to another team.

To achieve a fair comparison between projects, we chose the number of staff $n = 50$ and the number of working teams $m = 5$. Also, we verify every new generated solution of TCs before evaluating it with the fitness function, to ensure in each solutions every team has at least one staff member. This "no empty team" check is required because a team can be empty during the evolutionary process if all staff members are assigned to other teams. The representation of WP ordering is shown in Figure 1. The crossover operator for such a representation is explained in [13], while the mutation operator randomly swaps a WP to another position in the queue, with a mutation rate of 0.2 per gene, calibrated after trying other (higher and lower) rates.

To satisfy the dependency constraints among WPs, a dependency check is required. Solutions that violate the dependency constraints are "repaired" as explained in Section 2.3.

3.2 Initial Populations

The initial populations are randomly generated and subject to satisfy the of "no empty team" rule and dependency constraints among WPs. The population size is set to 50 for both species.

3.3 Termination Condition

We experimented with 3 sets of configurations formed of the Internal (I) and External (E) number of generations for CCEA. The number of internal generations relates to the evolution of each sub-population, while the number of external generations represents how many times each population provides an updated reference to help the other population co-evolve. As shown in Table 1, these 3 configurations are all allowed the same budget of fitness evaluations. Although all these three configurations evolve solutions in both TC and WPO populations for the same number of generations, the level of communication between the two populations varies.

Table 1. Three sets of configurations for CCEA each of which requires the same total number of evaluations before it is terminated

Config.	Int_Gen	Ext_Gen
I	1	100
II	10	10
III	100	1

For instance, with Config. I, CCEA evolves solutions in both populations for a single generation only (internal generation) and then provides the updated individuals for fitness evaluations of the other population. Finally, before the evolution process terminates, the TC population provides an updated reference for the WPO population for a total of 100 iterations (external generation), and vice versa. Config. III is not a CCEA by definition because during the whole period of the cooperative co-evolutionary process, the communication only happens only once. Therefore Config. III is a 'non-co-evolutionary' approach, against which we compare the other (co-evolutionary) approaches. By implementing the non co-evolutionary approach as a 'special case' (by suitable choice of parameters) we remove one source of possible bias that would otherwise result from experimenting with two totally different implementations: one co-evolutionary and the other not.

4 Empirical Study

The goal of this empirical study is to compare our new CCEA approach with a non-co-evolutionary genetic algorithm and a random search. We study the effectiveness and efficiency of our approach, alternatives and (for purely 'sanity check' purposes) random search on four industrial projects, named *Projects A, B, C and D*, described below and for which quantitative data are summarized in Table 2.

Table 2. Characteristics of the four industrial projects

Projects	#WPs	#Dependencies	Total Effort
A	84	0	4287 (person-hours[1])
B	120	102	594 (person-days)
C	253	226	833 (person-days)
D	60	57	68 (person-days)

Project A is a massive maintenance project for fixing the Y2K problem in a large financial computing system from a European organization. According to its WBS, the application was decomposed into WPs, i.e., loosely coupled, elementary units subject to maintenance activities. Each WP was managed by a WP leader and assigned to a maintenance team. No WP dependency was documented, and thus, no constraint had to be satisfied in *Project A* scheduling. *Project A* can be considered as representative of massive maintenance projects related to highly-standardized tasks such as currency conversion, change of social security numbering, etc. *Project B* aimed at delivering the next release of a large data-intensive, multi-platform software system, written in several languages, including DB II, SQL, and .NET. *Project C* aimed at delivering an online selling system to provide North American businesses of all sizes with a fast and flexible way to select, acquire and manage all their hardware and software needs. The system includes the development and testing of website, search engine, and order management, etc. *Project D* is a medium-sized project implemented in a large Canadian sales company. This project aims to add new enhancement to the supply chain of the company by allowing instant and on-demand conversion of quotes to orders. This change is both internal and customer facing and ultimately affects every level of the organization (Web, internal development, database, sales, and customers).

The empirical study addresses the following research questions:

RQ1: (Sanity Check) Do the CCEA approach and the single population alternative significantly outperform random search?

RQ1.1: Does the single population GA outperform random search?

RQ1.2: Do the CCEAs outperform random search?

RQ2: (Effectiveness) How effective is the CCEA approach compared to the alternatives in terms of finding an earlier completion time?

RQ3: (Efficiency) Given the same number of evaluations, which algorithm finds the best-so-far solution soonest?

The population size in our implementation was set to 100 and the number of generations is listed in Table 1 for the three different configurations. For the CCEA, the fitness of an individual in either species depends on the results of its simulations with 6 individuals from the other species. Children compete with their parents, and, to select parents for reproduction, the algorithm randomly picks a number of parents and performs a tournament selection to identify parents for breeding. The pool of children is half the population size, i.e., 25. That is, the best 25 children had the chance to compete with their parents.

---

[1] The raw information of required effort for Project A was documented in 'person-hours' by the team that produced it. Since we do not know their mapping from hours to days, we leave the data in its raw form.

5   Empirical Study Results

In this section, we report results of the study described in Section 4.

5.1   Analysis of the Cooperative Co-evolutionary Progress

Results for all four projects and for the 3 CCEA configurations are plotted on Figures 4 and 5. In each sub-figure, the tick labels on the horizontal axis indicate the total number of internal generations that have been carried out, and also indicates the point at which the algorithm updated the population used for fitness computation. At each point on the horizontal axis, the entire population is depicted using a boxplot to give both a sense of the values obtained for completion time as the evolution progresses and the distribution of the fitness values in the population.

The fitness values of the entire population during the whole CCEA process are represented as boxplots. We can observe that the number of internal generations is the same for both populations within a specific sub-figure, as they fill equally spread vertical bands on the sub-figures. As can be seen from the sub-figures in the top rows in Figures 4 and 5, Config. I tends to find better solutions sooner than the other two configurations. On the second rows we can observe an noticeable interlacing of the co-evolutions between the two populations. For instance, as in Figure 4(c), the evolutionary process on each population takes 10 internal generations. The first 10 internal generations—plotted within the interval [1, 10] on the horizontal axis—record the evolutionary progress of TC. After the first round of evolution on TC, the solutions on WPO start evolving during the interval [11, 20]. On the third row of the sub-figures, it can be seen that the optimization of WPO produced more benefit—in terms of project completion time—than what done for TC. This can be noticed in Figure 4(e), where both species evolved for only one round (i.e., one external generation) and, in each round, they evolved for 100 generations (i.e., 100 internal generations). As indicated by the generation number on the horizontal axis, results from the TC species are plotted on the interval [1, 100], while results from the WPO species are plotted on the interval [101, 200]. As we can see from the completion time (vertical axis) the optimization of WPO leads to a noticeable improvement in the fitness function values obtained.

5.2   Results on Effectiveness

In this section we report the comparison of the effectiveness of three sets of CCEA configuration and the random search. Each algorithm was run 30 times on each of the 4 sets of project data to allow for statistical evaluation and comparison of the results.

Figure 6 reports—for the various configurations—fitness values for the best individual solutions found by CCEA in the 30 runs.

As shown in the figures for Projects B, C, and D, in terms of the ability to effectively find the best solutions, CCEA performs better with Config. I and worse with Config. III. As explained in Section 3.3, Config. III is the single population evolutionary algorithm, while Config. I and II are bona fidè CCEAs. Therefore, our results provide evidence to support the claim that CCEAs outperform the single population evolutionary algorithm.

The random search generates twice the number of solutions of the CCEAs during the evolutionary process, and despite that, is clearly outperformed by the CCEAs in terms

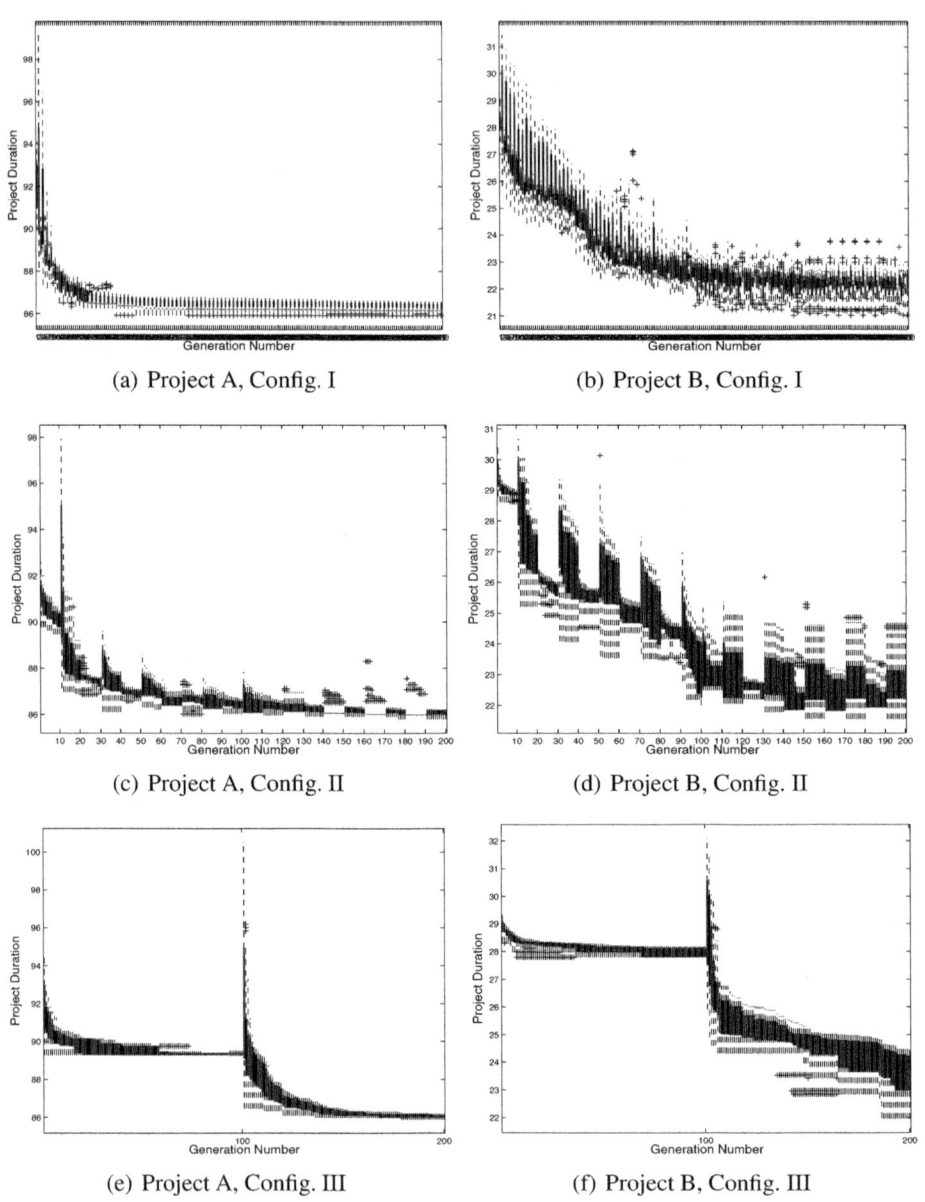

(a) Project A, Config. I

(b) Project B, Config. I

(c) Project A, Config. II

(d) Project B, Config. II

(e) Project A, Config. III

(f) Project B, Config. III

Fig. 4. Projects A and B: Boxplots of completion times for all solutions found by different CCEAs configurations

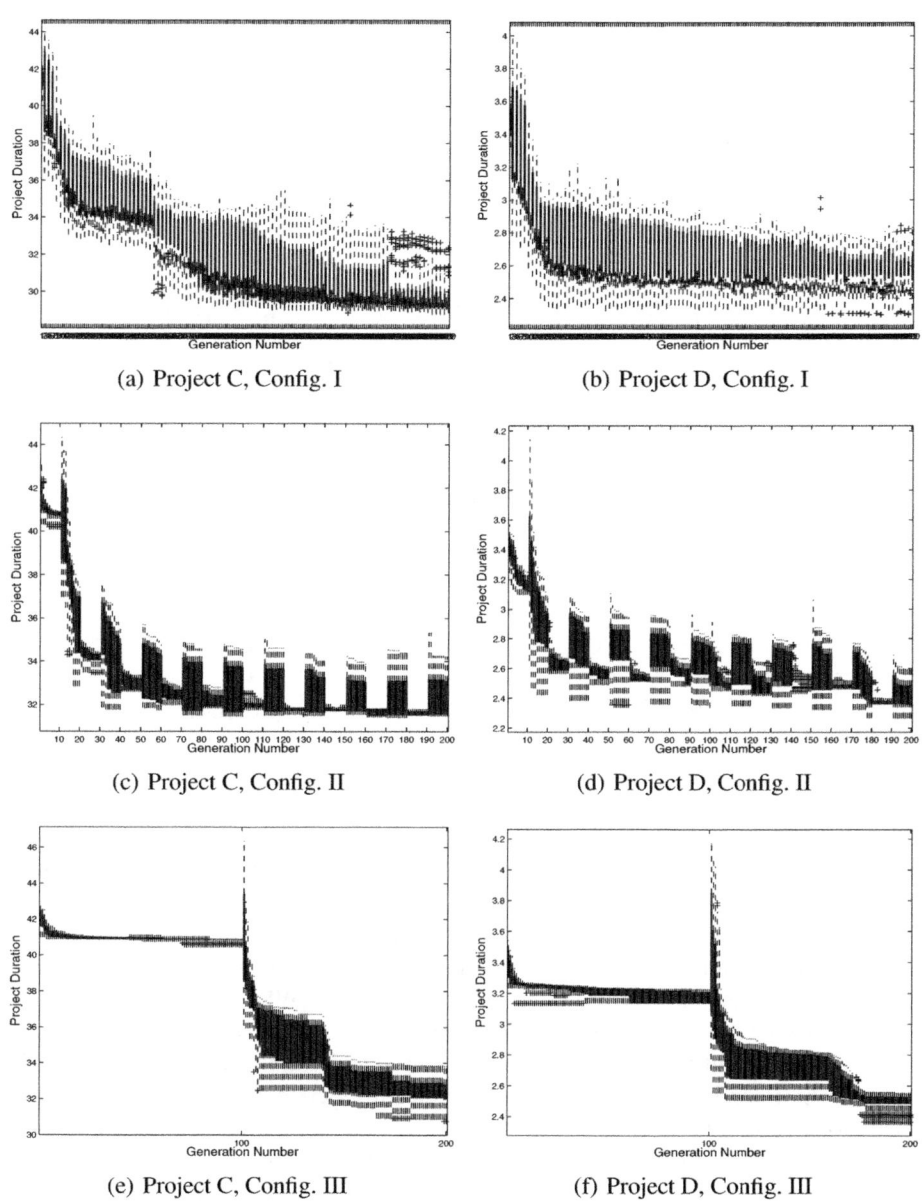

(a) Project C, Config. I

(b) Project D, Config. I

(c) Project C, Config. II

(d) Project D, Config. II

(e) Project C, Config. III

(f) Project D, Config. III

Fig. 5. Projects C and D: Boxplots of completion times for all solutions found by different CCEAs configurations

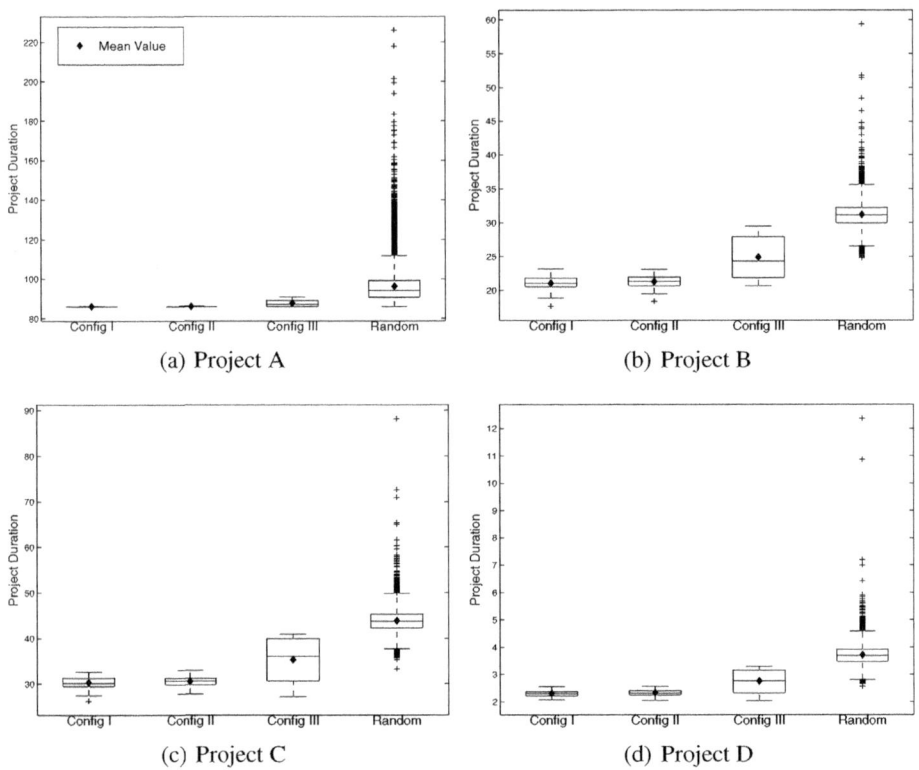

Fig. 6. Boxplots of all the best solutions found in 30 runs of the three CCEA configurations, and in random search runs

of fitness function quality. This observation is supported by a Wilcoxon Rank Sum Test (WRST) performed to calculate the statistical significance of the difference between the solutions produced by the different CCEAs configurations and Random. Since we are performing multiple comparisons on the same data set, *p-values* are corrected using the Holm's correction. The Wilcoxon Rank Sum Test (WRST) *p-values* reported in Table 3, as well as boxplots shown in Figure 6, indicate that all evolutionary algorithms perform significantly better than a random search, and that the best solutions found by the CCEAs (Config. I and II) perform significantly better than the single population evolutionary algorithm (Config. III).

For Project A, while all CCEAs perform significantly better than random search, the practical benefit in terms of lower project completion time achieved is not as evident as for the other projects. This is because in Project A there are no dependencies between WPs; the project is a conceptually simple, multiple application of a massive mainte-nance task (fixing Y2K problem repeatedly using a windowing approach). Since there are no dependencies, there is no delay introduced by the need for waiting on dependent WPs. For this reason, the WP scheduling and team construction have little impact on the overall completion time.

Table 3. Wilcoxon Rank Sum Test (unpaired) test adjusted p-values for the pairwise comparison of the three configurations

p-*values* for WRST	Projects			
	A	B	C	D
Config. I vs II	0.7229	0.1885	0.4481	0.2449
Config. I vs III	5.04E-08	3.00E-11	2.78E-07	2.19E-07
Config. II vs III	1.47E-07	8.86E-10	2.08E-06	1.28E-06
Config. I vs Random	3.97E-40	3.82E-40	3.83E-40	3.83E-40
Config. II vs Random	3.97E-40	3.82E-40	3.83E-40	3.83E-40
Config. III vs Random	2.70E-30	6.04E-37	3.13E-36	3.66E-36

In conclusion, the obtained results support the following two claims: (1) all three CCEAs were found to perform better than the random search, which means the CCEAs passed the 'sanity check' set by **RQ1**, and (2) **RQ2** is answered as the result of the WRST test that indicated the best solutions found by Config. I and II are significantly better than those found by Config. III. We conclude that there is evidence to suggest that co-evolution is effective to deal with software project staffing and scheduling.

5.3 Results on Efficiency

To answer **RQ3**, we extended the experiments with 30 runs of 3 CCEAs configurations until the solutions produced by all algorithms became stable, and, to allow a fair comparison, the random search was set to have the same number of fitness evaluations. The progress of the CCEAs and the random search in finding better solutions are plotted in Figure 7. The fitness values are averaged over 30 runs for CCEAs, while for the random search, the figure shows the best solutions found for the number of evaluations indicated on the horizontal axis.

As shown in Figures 7(b), 7(c), and 7(d), respectively for Projects B, C and D, in most cases, the CCEAs find better solutions than the non-cooperative algorithm. However, there is an exception found for Project A as shown in Figure 7(a), for which the CCEA does not outperform its rivals. We believe that this is due to the dependence-free nature of Project A (as mentioned before, it has no dependencies).

In conclusion, with regard to the efficiency of finding better solutions (**RQ3**), we find evidence that CCEAs outperform random search in general, and that the CCEA with more frequent communication between two populations (Config. I) performs better than the others (Config. II, III, and Random).

5.4 Threats to Validity

Construct validity threats may be due to the simplifications made when modeling the development/maintenance process through a simulation. In particular (i) we assumed communication overhead negligible and (ii) we did not consider developers' expertise. However, accounting for these variables was out of scope for this paper, as here the intent was to compare CCEA with non-co-evolutionary genetic algorithms.

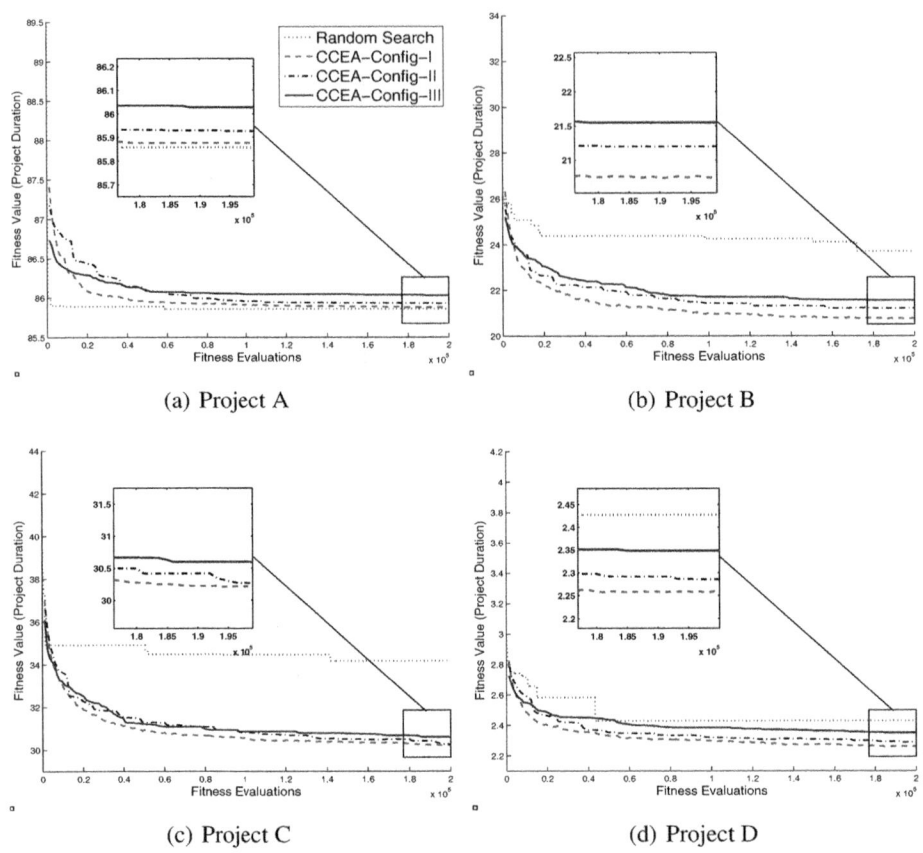

(a) Project A

(b) Project B

(c) Project C

(d) Project D

Fig. 7. Efficiency Comparison of the Random Search and CCEAs

Threats to *internal validity* can be due, in this study, to the bias introduced in our results by the intrinsic randomness of GA and, of course, of the random approach. We mitigate such a threat by performing statistical tests on the results.

Threats to *conclusion validity* concern the relationship between treatment and outcome. Wherever possible, we use appropriate statistics—Wilcoxon test with Holm's correction in particular—to robustly test our conclusions.

Threats to *external validity* concern the generalization of our findings. We performed experiments on data from four industrial projects having different characteristics in terms of size, domain, and relationships among WPs. However, further studies are desirable to corroborate the obtained results.

6   Related Work

This section provides a brief overview of related work on search-based project planning.

Chang *et al.* were the first to publish on search-based project planning [10], with their introduction of the Software Project Management Net (SPMNet) approach for project scheduling and resource allocation, which was evaluated on simulated project data. Aguilar-Ruiz *et al.* [2] also presented early results on evolutionary optimization for search-based project planning, once again evaluated on synthetically created software project data. Chicano and Alba [3,4] applied search algorithms to software projects to seek to find allocations that achieve earliest completion time. Alvarez-Valdes *et al.* [5] applied a scatter search approach to the problem of minimizing project completion duration.

Project management has recently [12] been the subject of a study of the human-competitiveness of SBSE, which found that optimization techniques are able to produce effective results in a shorter time than human decision makers. This work demonstrates that SBSE is a suitable approach to consider for project planning activities since it can find solutions that the human decision maker may otherwise miss. While the ultimate decision is likely to rest with the human decision maker, it is therefore important to find suitable SBSE techniques that can support this decision making activity.

Other authors have also worked on SBSE as a means of decision support for software engineering managers and decision makers in the planning stages of software engineering projects focusing on early lifecycle planning [8,11,18,19,23] as we do in the present paper, but also reaching forward to subsequent aspects of the software engineering lifecycle that also require planning, such as scheduling of bug fixing tasks [14,22]. Like our present work, some of this work has considered multiple objectives [4,15]. This is very natural in software project planning which is typified by many different concerns, each of which must be balanced against the others; and issue that is reported to be inherently as part of much work on SBSE [16]. However, no previous work has used co-evolution for project planning to blanch these different objectives.

SBSE can also be used as a way to analyze and understand Software Project Planning, yielding insight into planning issues, rather than seeking to necessarily provide a specific 'best' project plan [17]. For example SBSE has been used to study the effect of Brooks law [9] on project planning [20]. It has also been used to balance the competing concerns of risk and completion time [15]. Our work may be used in this way, since we can study the way the two populations evolve with respect to one another and the ways in which they are symbiotic. A thorough exploration of this possibility remains a topic for future work.

Di Penta *et al.* [13] compared the performance of different search-based optimization techniques, namely Genetic Algorithms, Simulated Annealing, and Hill Climbing to perform project planning on data from two industrial projects (Projects A and B also used in this study). The present paper can be thought of as an extension of the previous work of Di Penta *et al.*, because it uses the same representation and fitness function, while proposing and evaluating the use of completely unexplored optimization approach: co-evolutionary optimization.

7   Conclusions and Future Work

This paper proposes the use of Cooperative Co-Evolutionary Algorithms (CCEA) to solve software project planning and staffing problems. The co-evolutionary algorithm evolves two populations, one representing WP ordering in a queue (which determines their assignment to teams), and the other representing developers distribution among teams.

We conducted an empirical study using data from four industrial software projects, aimed at comparing CCEA project planning and staffing with (i) random search and (ii) single population optimization using genetic algorithms, as previously proposed by Di Penta *et al.* [13]. Results of the empirical study show that CCEA is able to outperform random search and single population GA, in terms of effectiveness (i.e., best solutions proposed in terms of project completion time) and efficiency (i.e., a smaller number of evaluations required).

Future work aims at extending the study reported in this paper with further data sets and, above all, at considering a more sophisticated project model, which accounts for further factors not considered in this study, such as developers' skills and expertise, communication overhead models, and schedule robustness.

References

1. Adamopoulos, K., Harman, M., Hierons, R.M.: How to Overcome the Equivalent Mutant Problem and Achieve Tailored Selective Mutation Using Co-evolution. In: Deb, K., et al. (eds.) GECCO 2004. LNCS, vol. 3103, pp. 1338–1349. Springer, Heidelberg (2004)
2. Aguilar-Ruiz, J.S., Santos, J.C.R., Ramos, I.: Natural Evolutionary Coding: An Application to Estimating Software Development Projects. In: Proceedings of the 2002 Conference on Genetic and Evolutionary Computation (GECCO 2002), New York, USA, pp. 1–8 (2002)
3. Alba, E., Chicano, F.: Management of Software Projects with GAs. In: Proceedings of the 6th Metaheuristics International Conference (MIC 2005), pp. 13–18. Elsevier Science Inc., Austria (2005)
4. Alba, E., Chicano, F.: Software Project Management with GAs. Information Sciences 177(11), 2380–2401 (2007)
5. Alvarez-Valdes, R., Crespo, E., Tamarit, J.M., Villa, F.: A Scatter Search Algorithm for Project Scheduling under Partially Renewable Resources. Journal of Heuristics 12(1-2), 95–113 (2006)
6. Arcuri, A., Yao, X.: A Novel Co-evolutionary Approach to Automatic Software Bug Fixing. In: Proceedings of the IEEE Congress on Evolutionary Computation (CEC 2008), pp. 162–168. IEEE Computer Society, Hongkong (2008)
7. Arcuri, A., Yao, X.: Co-Evolutionary Automatic Programming for Software Development. Information Sciences (2010)
8. Barreto, A., de O. Barros, M., Werner, C.M.L.: Staffing a Software Project: a Constraint Satisfaction and Optimization-based Approach. Computers & Operations Research 35(10), 3073–3089 (2008)
9. Brooks Jr., F.P.: The Mythical Man Month: Essays on Software Engineering. Addison-Wesley Publishing Company, Reading (1975)
10. Chao, C., Komada, J., Liu, Q., Muteja, M., Alsalqan, Y., Chang, C.: An Application of Genetic Algorithms to Software Project Management. In: Proceedings of the 9th International Advanced Science and Technology, Chicago, Illinois, USA, pp. 247–252 (March 1993)
11. Cortellessa, V., Marinelli, F., Potena, P.: An Optimization Framework for Build-or-Buy Decisions in Software Architecture. Computers & Operations Research 35(10), 3090–3106 (2008)
12. de Souza, J.T., Maia, C.L., de Freitas, F.G., Coutinho, D.P.: The Human Competitiveness of Search Based Software Engineering. In: Second International Symposium on Search Based Software Engineering (SSBSE 2010), pp. 143–152 (2010)

13. Di Penta, M., Harman, M., Antoniol, G.: The Use of Search-Based Optimization Techniques to Schedule and Staff Software Projects: An Approach and An Empirical Study. Softw., Pract. Exper. 41(5), 495–519 (2011)
14. Fernando Netto, M.B., Alvim, A.: A Hybrid Heuristic Approach for Scheduling Bug Fix Tasks to Software. In: Proceedings of the 1st International Symposium on Search Based Software Engineering (SSBSE 2009). IEEE, UK (2009)
15. Gueorguiev, S., Harman, M., Antoniol, G.: Software Project Planning for Robustness and Completion Time in the Presence of Uncertainty using Multi Objective Search Based Software Engineering. In: Proceedings of the 11th Annual Conference on Genetic and Evolutionary Computation (GECCO 2009), pp. 1673–1680. ACM, Canada (2009)
16. Harman, M.: The Current State and Future of Search Based Software Engineering. In: Briand, L., Wolf, A. (eds.) Future of Software Engineering 2007, Los Alamitos, California, USA, pp. 342–357 (2007)
17. Harman, M.: The Relationship between Search Based Software Engineering and Predictive Modeling. In: 6th International Conference on Predictive Models in Software Engineering, Timisoara, Romania (2010)
18. Kapur, P., Ngo-The, A., Ruhe, G., Smith, A.: Optimized Staffing for Product Releases and Its Application at Chartwell Technology. Journal of Software Maintenance and Evolution: Research and Practice (Special Issue Search Based Software Engineering) 20(5), 365–386 (2008)
19. Kremmel, T., Kubalík, J., Biffl, S.: Software Project Portfolio Optimization with Advanced Multiobjective Evolutionary Algorithms. Applied Soft Computing 11(1), 1416–1426 (2011)
20. Penta, M.D., Harman, M., Antoniol, G., Qureshi, F.: The Effect of Communication Overhead on Software Maintenance Project Staffing: a Search-Based Approach. In: Proceedings of the 23rd IEEE International Conference on Software Maintenance (ICSM 2007), pp. 315–324. IEEE, France (2007)
21. Potter, M.A., Couldrey, C.: A cooperative coevolutionary approach to partitional clustering. In: Schaefer, R., Cotta, C., Kołodziej, J., Rudolph, G. (eds.) PPSN XI. LNCS, vol. 6238, pp. 374–383. Springer, Heidelberg (2010)
22. Xiao, J., Afzal, W.: Search-based Resource Scheduling for Bug Fixing Tasks. In: Proceedings of the 2nd International Symposium on Search Based Software Engineering (SSBSE 2010), pp. 133–142. IEEE, Italy (2010)
23. Xiao, J., Osterweil, L.J., Wang, Q., Li, M.: Dynamic Resource Scheduling in Disruption-Prone Software Development Environments. In: Rosenblum, D.S., Taentzer, G. (eds.) FASE 2010. LNCS, vol. 6013, pp. 107–122. Springer, Heidelberg (2010)
24. Yang, Z., Tang, K., Yao, X.: Large Scale Evolutionary Optimization Using Cooperative Coevolution. Information Sciences 178(15), 2985–2999 (2008)

An Ant Colony Optimization Approach to the Software Release Planning with Dependent Requirements

Jerffeson Teixeira de Souza, Camila Loiola Brito Maia,
Thiago do Nascimento Ferreira, Rafael Augusto Ferreira do Carmo,
and Márcia Maria Albuquerque Brasil

Optimization in Software Engineering Group (GOES.UECE),
State University of Ceará (UECE)
60740-903 Fortaleza, Brazil
jeff@larces.uece.br,
{camila.maia,thiagonascimento.uece@,carmorafael}@gmail.com,
marcia.abrasil@gmail.com

Abstract. Ant Colony Optimization (ACO) has been successfully employed to tackle a variety of hard combinatorial optimization problems, including the traveling salesman problem, vehicle routing, sequential ordering and timetabling. ACO, as a swarm intelligence framework, mimics the indirect communication strategy employed by real ants mediated by pheromone trails. Among the several algorithms following the ACO general framework, the Ant Colony System (ACS) has obtained convincing results in a range of problems. In Software Engineering, the effective application of ACO has been very narrow, being restricted to a few sparse problems. This paper expands this applicability, by adapting the ACS algorithm to solve the well-known Software Release Planning problem in the presence of dependent requirements. The evaluation of the proposed approach is performed over 72 synthetic datasets and considered, besides ACO, the Genetic Algorithm and Simulated Annealing. Results are consistent to show the ability of the proposed ACO algorithm to generate more accurate solutions to the Software Release Planning problem when compared to Genetic Algorithm and Simulated Annealing.

Keywords: Ant Colony Optimization, Search Based Software Engineering, Software Release Planning.

1 Introduction

The Search Based Software Engineering (SBSE) field [1] has been benefiting from a number of general search methods, including, but not limited to, Genetic Algorithms, Simulated Annealing, Greedy Search, GRASP and Tabu Search. Surprisingly, even with the large applicability and the significant results obtained by the Ant Colony Optimization (ACO) metaheuristic, very little has been done regarding the employment of this strategy to tackle software engineering problems modeled as optimization problems.

Ant Colony Optimization [2] is a swarm intelligence framework, inspired by the behavior of ants during food search in nature. ACO mimics the indirect communication strategy employed by real ants mediated by pheromone trails, allowing individual ants to

M.B. Cohen and M. Ó Cinnéide (Eds.): SSBSE 2011, LNCS 6956, pp. 142–157, 2011.

adapt their behavior to reflect the colony's search experience. Ant System (AS) [3] was the first algorithm to follow the ACO general framework. First applied to tackle small instances of the Traveling Salesman Problem (TSP), AS was not able to compete with state-of-the-art algorithms specifically designed for this traditional optimization problem, which stimulated the development of significant extensions to this algorithm. In particular, the Ant Colony System (ACS) algorithm [4] improved AS by incorporating an elitist strategy to update pheromone trails and by changing the rule used by ants to select the next movement. These enhancements considerably increased the ability of the algorithm to generate precise solutions to hard and different combinatorial problems, including the TSP [4], vehicle routing [5], sequential ordering [6] and timetabling [7].

The application of ACO to address software engineering problems has been very narrow, but relevant. To this date, as detailed in the next section of this paper, the literature has reported works using ACO on software testing [8], model checking [9] and requirement engineering [10,11]. Thus, it seems that the full potential of the ACO algorithm is far from being completely explored by the SBSE research community.

In Requirement Engineering, some important problems have been shaped and addressed as optimization problems, including the Software Requirement Prioritization problem [12], the Next Release problem (NRP) [13] and a multi-objective version of the NRP [14], to mention some. Finally, a search based representation of the Software Release Planning problem (SRP) was formulated in [15], dealing with the allocation of requirements to software releases, or increments, by considering the importance of the requirements as specified by the stockholders, and respecting dependency and effort constraints.

As an important Requirement Engineering problem, several strategies have been applied in the attempt to solve the Software Release Planning problem, including Genetic Algorithms and Simulated Annealing. However, no attempt has been made, thus far, to adapt and apply the Ant Colony Optimization metaheuristic to this problem, even though such an application seems reasonably justified, given the nature of the Software Release Planning problem which can be interpreted as a Multiple Knapsack Problem and the fact that ACO has been reported to perform significantly well in solving such problem [18,19,20].

Therefore, this paper will report the results of a work aimed at answering the following research questions:

> RQ1. – *ACO for the Software Release Planning problem*: how can the ACO algorithm be adapted to solve the Software Release Planning problem in the presence of dependent requirements?
>
> RQ2. – *ACO versus Other Metaheuristics*: how does the proposed ACO adaptation compare to other metaheuristics in solving the Software Release Planning problem in the presence of dependent requirements?

The remaining of the paper is organized as follows: Section 2 summarizes prior works on the application of ACO to solve software engineering problems. Section 3 formally defines the Software Release Planning problem. Next, in Section 4, the proposed ACO algorithm for the Software Release Planning problem is presented, starting with the encoding of the problem, followed by a detailed description of the algorithm. Section 5 discusses, initially, the design of the experiments aimed at answering our second research question, presents the results from the experiments and describes the analyses of these results. Finally, Section 6 concludes the work and points out some future directions to this research.

2 Previous Works

As mentioned earlier, very few works have been performed on the application of ACO to solve software engineering problems. Next, some of these researches are summarized.

An ACO-based algorithm for error tracing and model checking is designed and implemented in [8]. In [9], the ACOhg metaheuristic, an ACO algorithm proposed to deal with large construction graphs, is combined with partial order reduction to reduce memory consumption. This combination is employed to find safety property violations in concurrent models.

The first proposal for the application of ACO in requirement engineering, more specifically to tackle the NRP, appeared in [10]. This proposal was later fully developed in [11], where an ACS algorithm is established to search for a subset of requirements with maximum satisfaction and subject to a certain effort bound. When compared to the Simulated Annealing and the Genetic Algorithm metaheuristics, over a real software problem with 20 requirements, ACO was the only algorithm which found the known best solution to the problem every time.

3 The Software Release Planning Problem Definition

This section formally defines the Software Release Planning problem (SRP) as it will be considered on this paper.

Let $R = (r_1, r_2, \ldots, r_N)$ be the set of requirements to be implemented and allocated to some software release, with N representing the number of requirements. The implementation of each requirement r_i demands certain implementation cost, denoted by $cost_i$. In addition, each requirement r_i has an associated risk, given by $risk_i$. Let $C = (c_1, c_2, \ldots, c_M)$ be the set of clients, whose requirements should be delivered. Each client c_j has a given importance to the organization, defined as wt_j.

Consider, yet, $S = (s_1, s_2, \ldots, s_P)$ to be the set of software releases to be planned, with P representing the number of releases. Each release s_k has an available budget ($budgetRelease_k$) which should be respected. Additionally, different clients have different interests in the implementation of each requirement. Therefore, $importance(c_j, r_i)$ defines the importance, or business value, client c_j attributes to requirement r_i.

Therefore, the Software Release Planning problem can be mathematically formulated with the following objective and restriction functions:

$$Maximize \ \sum_{i=1}^{N}(score_i \cdot (P - x_i + 1) - risk_i \cdot x_i) \cdot y_i$$

subject to

$$\sum_{i=1}^{N} cost_i \cdot f_{i,k} \leq budgetRelease_k, \ for \ all \ k \in \{1, \ldots, P\}$$
$$x_b \leq x_a, \forall (r_a \rightarrow r_b), where \ r_a, r_b \in R$$

where the boolean variable y_i indicates whether requirement r_i will be implemented in some release, variable x_i indicates the number of the release where requirement r_i is to be implemented, and the boolean value $f_{i,k}$ indicates whether requirement r_i will be implemented in release k.

The first component of the objective function expresses the weighted overall satisfaction of the stakeholders, where

$$score_i = \sum_{j=1}^{M} wt_j . importance(c_j, r_i)$$

represents the aggregated business value for requirement r_i. The other component deals with risk management, expressing those requirements with higher risk should be implemented earlier. Finally, the two restrictions will, respectively, limit the implementation cost of requirements in each release and guarantee that the precedence among requirements will be respected. In this second restriction, $r_a \rightarrow r_b$ represents that requirement r_b is a precedent of requirement r_a, indicating that r_b should be implemented earlier or at the same release as r_a.

4   An ACO Algorithm for Software Release Planning

This section describes the main contribution of this work, the proposed ACO algorithm for the Software Release Planning problem. First, however, it outlines the problem encoding which will allow the application of such algorithm.

4.1   Problem Encoding

To be able to apply an Ant Colony Optimization strategy to the Software Release Planning problem, a proper encoding is required. For that purpose, a graph will be generated with the Release Planning problem instance information, as follows. Two types of edges will be created, representing mandatory and optional moves for a particular ant. Mandatory moves will be created to ensure that precedence constraints are respected.

This way, the problem will be encoded as a directed graph, $G = (V, E)$, where $E = E_m + E_o$, with E_m representing mandatory moves, and E_o representing optional ones.

    i.   each vertex in V represents a requirement r_i;
    ii. a directed mandatory edge $(r_i, r_j) \in E_m$, if $(r_i \rightarrow r_j)$;
    iii. a directed optional edge $(r_i, r_j) \in E_o$, if $(r_i, r_j) \notin E_m$ and $i \neq j$.

Consider $overall\_cost_i$ to represent the cost of implementing requirement r_i, that is, $cost_i$, in addition to the cost of implementing all unvisited precedent requirements of requirement r_i. That means, $overall\_cost_i = cost_i$ if requirement r_i has no precedent requirements and $overall\_cost_i = cost_i + \sum overall\_cost_j$, for all unvisited requirements r_j where $r_i \rightarrow r_j$, i.e, requirement r_j is a precedent of r_i.

When visiting a node r_i, an ant k, which will select requirements do release k, will define two sets, $mand\_vis_k(i)$ and $opt\_vis_k(i)$, representing, respectively, mandatory and optional moves. These two sets are defined as follows:

$$mand\_vis_k(i) = \{r_j | (r_i, r_j) \in E_m \text{ and } visited_j = False\}$$

That is, the set of mandatory moves for an ant k visiting node r_i will contain the requirements r_j in the graph which respect the two conditions below:

1. r_j can be reached from r_i using a mandatory edge, that is, $(r_i, r_j) \in E_m$;
2. node r_j has not been previously visited, i.e., $visited_j = False$.

Additionally, $opt\_vis_k(i)$ can be defined as:

$$opt\_vis_k(i) = \{r_j|(r_i,r_j) \in E_o, effort(k) + overall\_cost_j \le budgetRelease_k$$
$$\text{and } visited_j = False\}$$

Similarly, set $opt\_vis_k(i)$ is defined with the same rules above, except, in rule 1., node r_j can be reached from r_i using an optional edge, in other words, $(r_i,r_j) \in E_o$, and by the addition of a third rule, which verifies whether a new requirement can be added to the release without breaking the budget constraint, in a way that the added effort for implementing r_j, does not exceed the defined budget for release k, that is, $effort(k) + overall\_cost_j \le budgetRelease_k$.

The heuristic information of a particular node, represented by a productivity measure for the respective software requirement, is defined as:

$$w_i = \mu \cdot (score_i * risk_i)$$

where μ is a normalization constant.

At each step, in case the random value $q \le q_0$ (where q_0 is a parameter), an ant k visiting a node r_i will have the probability of moving to the node r_j given by:

$$p_{ij}^k = \frac{\tau_{ij}^{\alpha} \cdot w_j^{\beta}}{\sum_{r_j \in opt\_vis_k(i)} \tau_{ij}^{\alpha} \cdot w_j^{\beta}}$$

where τ_{ij} is the amount of pheromone in edge (r_i,r_j) and α and β are parameters controlling the relative importance of pheromone and requirement information. When $q > q_0$, ant k visiting a node r_i will move to r_j with higher value given by $\tau_{ij} \cdot w_j^{\beta}$.

Pheromone will be initially distributed, equally, only on optional edges. When crossing a particular optional edge (r_i,r_j), ant k will update the pheromone as follows:

$$\tau_{ij} = (1 - \varphi) \cdot \tau_{ij} + \varphi \cdot \tau_0$$

with $\varphi \in (0,1]$ representing the pheromone decay coefficient.

This encoding will allow us to generate an ACO adaptation to the Software Release Planning problem, as proposed in the next section.

4.2 The ACO Algorithm

The overall structure of the ACO Algorithm for the Software Release Planning problem is: each ant will be responsible for iteratively constructing a single release. At an iteration of the algorithm, k ants will be deployed, one at a time and in order, which will produce a complete release planning. A roulette procedure, considering the heuristic information measure of a node will be employed to select the initial node of each ant. Here, an ant can only be placed in a requirement that can fit, along with its precedent nodes, in that particular release. The first ant will travel through the generated graph, adding requirements to the first release until no more additions are allowed, due to budget constraints. Next, a second ant will be placed in an unvisited node, using the roulette procedure, and will start its traversal through the graph, constructing the second release. The process is repeated until all k ants have been delivered and produced their respective releases. At this point, a solution to the

Software Release Planning problem has been constructed. The process is repeated a number of times. At the end, the best found solution is returned.

Next, in Fig. 1, the general ACO algorithm for the Software Release Planning problem is presented.

OVERALL INITIALIZATION
$COUNT = 1$

MAIN LOOP
  REPEAT

    MAIN LOOP INITIALIZATION
    FOR ALL optional edges $(r_i r_j) \in E_o$, $\tau_{ij} \leftarrow \tau_0$
    FOR ALL vertices $r_i \in V$, $visited_i \leftarrow False$
    FOR ALL vertices $r_i \in V$, $current\_planning_i \leftarrow 0$

    SINGLE RELEASE PLANNING LOOP
    FOR EACH Release, k
        Place, using a roulette procedure, ant k in a vertex $r_i \in V$,
            where $visited_i = False$ and $overall\_cost_i \leq budgetRelease_k$
        ADDS (r_i, k)
        WHILE $opt\_vis_k(i) \neq \emptyset$ **DO**
            Move ant k to a vertex $r_j \in opt\_vis_k(i)$ with probability p_{ij}^k or
                         considering $max(\tau_{ij} \cdot w_j^\beta)$.
            Update pheromone in edge $(r_i r_j)$, with $\tau_{ij} = (1 - \varphi) \cdot \tau_{ij} + \varphi \cdot \tau_0$
            ADDS (r_j, k)
            $i \leftarrow j$

    MAIN LOOP FINALIZATION
    $best\_planning \leftarrow current\_planning$

  $COUNT + +$
  UNTIL $COUNT > MAX\_COUNT$

  RETURN $best\_planning$

  // **Besides r_i, adds to release k all of its dependent requirements, and, repeatedly,**
  their dependent requirements
  ADDS (r_i, k)
      ENQUEUE (Q, r_i)
      WHILE $Q \neq \emptyset$ **DO**
          $r_s \leftarrow$ DEQUEUE (Q)
          FOR EACH $r_t \in mand\_vis_k(s)$ **DO**
              ENQUEUE (Q, r_t)
          $visited_s \leftarrow True$
      $current\_planning_s \leftarrow k$

Fig. 1. ACO Algorithm for the Software Release Planning problem

This algorithm can, this way, be applied to solve the Software Release Planning problem. Such algorithm shows one way the ACO framework can be adapted to such a problem, thus answering our research question RQ1., as discussed earlier.

5   Experimental Evaluation

This section describes all aspects related to the design of the experiments aimed at evaluating the performance of the proposed ACO algorithm. It first presents the data employed in the experiments, followed by a description of the other metaheuristics employed in the experiments and the metrics used in the comparison.

5.1   The Data

For the experiments, synthetic instances were generated with different values, - indicated in the parentheses -, of *number of requirements* (50, 200, 500), *number of releases* (5, 20, 50), *number of clients* (5, 20), *density of the precedence table* (0%, 20%) and *overall budget available* (80%, 120%). The density of the precedence table indicates the percentage of requirements which will have precedence. In that case, the requirement will have, as precedents, between 1 and 5% of other requirements, which is established randomly. The value of the overall budget available is computed by adding the overall cost of all requirements in that particular instance and calculating the indicated percentage of this cost. With that overall budget value, each release budget is determined by dividing this value by the number of releases in that instance.

All combinations of values for all aspects were considered, generating a total of 72 instances. Table 1 below describes a small subset of the synthetically generated instances used in the experiments. Each instance is indicated with a label "I_A.B.C.D.E", where A represents the number of requirements, B represents the number of releases, C, the number of clients, D, the density of the precedence table and E represents the overall budget available.

Table 1. Sample of the 72 Synthetically Generated Evaluation Instances

Instance Name	Instance Features				
	Number of Requirements	Number of Releases	Number of Clients	Precedence Density	Overall Budget
I_50.5.5.80	50	5	5	0%	80%
I_50.5.5.120	50	5	5	0%	120%
...	...	...	...	...	...
I_200.50.20.20.80	200	50	20	20%	80%
...	...	...	...	...	...
I_500.50.20.20.120	500	50	20	20%	120%

The values of $cost_i$, w_j and $risk_i$, for each requirement, were randomly generated using scales from 10 to 20, 1 to 10 and 1 to 5, respectively. In addition, the importance that each costumer set to each requirement was randomly generated from 0 to 5.

In order to facilitate replication, all instances used in the experiments were described and made publicly available for download at the paper supporting material webpage - published at http://www.larces.uece.br/~goes/rp/aco/ -, which contains, additionally, several extra results that could not be presented here due to space constraints.

5.2 The Algorithms, Their Configurations and Comparison Metrics

In order to compare the performance of the proposed ACO approach to the Software Release Planning problem, the metaheuristics Genetic Algorithm and Simulated Annealing were considered, as described next.

- A. Genetic Algorithm (GA): it is a widely applied evolutionary algorithm, inspired by Darwin´s theory of natural selection, which simulates biological processes such as inheritance, mutation, crossover, and selection [16].
- B. Simulated Annealing (SA): it is a procedure for solving arbitrary optimization problems based on an analogy with the annealing process in solids [17].

The particular configurations for each metaheuristic were empirically obtained through a comprehensive experimentation process. First, 10 of the 72 instances were randomly selected to participate in the configuration process. For each algorithm, different configurations were considered, varying the values of each algorithm´s parameters, as shown in the Tables 2, 3 and 4. For ACO, different values of α (1, 3, 10) and β (1, 3, 10) were analyzed. Since all combinations were considered, a total of 9 configuration instances were created for ACO (see Table 2). For the Simulated Annealing, initial temperature (20, 50, 200) and cooling rate (0,1%, 1%, 5%) were examined. Once again, 9 instances were generated (Table 3). Finally, for the Genetic Algorithm, a total of 27 configuration instances were produced, varying the values for the population size (20, 50, 100), crossover (60%, 80%, 95%) and mutation (0,1%, 1%, 5%) rates (Table 4).

Table 2. ACO Configuration Instances   **Table 3.** SA Configuration Instances

Configuration Instance	Parameters		Configuration Instance	Parameters	
	α	β		Initial Temperature	Cooling Rate
C_ACO:1.1	1	1	C_SA:20.01	20	0.1%
C_ACO:1.3	1	3	C_SA:20.1	20	1%
...	....	...	...	..	...
C_ACO:1.10	10	10	C_SA:200.5	200	5%

With those configuration instances, the configuration process was performed as follows: each algorithm was executed over all 10 problem instances considering, one at a time, each configuration instance in order to determine which configuration was more suitable to that particular instance. Next, the number of times each configuration instance performed the best was counted.

Table 4. GA Configuration Instances

| Configuration | Parameters | | |
Instance	Population Size	Crossover Rate	Mutation Rate
C_GA:20.60.01	20	60%	0.01%
C_GA:20.60.1	20	60%	0.1%
...	...	...	...
C_GA:100.95.5	100	95%	5%

The selected configuration, for each algorithm, was the one which generated more frequently the best results over the 10 sample instances. Table 5 shows the selected configuration instances of each algorithm, which will be used in the comparison experiments described later on.

Table 5. Algorithms´ Configuration Instances

ACO	SA	GA
C_ACO:3.10	C_SA:50.01	C_GA:20.80.1

The paper supporting material webpage presents, with details, all results of this configuration process, showing, for each algorithm, which configuration instance performed best for each sample problem instance.

Additionally, for the Genetic Algorithm, a simple heuristic procedure was implemented to generate valid solutions to the initial population, and a single-point crossover and mutation operators were implemented, also producing only valid solutions. Here, binary tournament was used as selection method. Similarly, for the Simulated Annealing, a valid neighborhood operator was employed. For ACO, the normalization constant μ was set to 1, τ_0 to 10 and φ to 0.01.

In the experiments, this paper considers the following metrics to allow the comparison of the results generated by the different approaches: A) Quality: it relates to the quality of each generated solution, measured by the value of the objective function; B) Execution Time: it measures the required execution time of each strategy.

5.3 Experimental Results and Analyses

This section describes and discusses the results of the experiments carried out to compare the performance of the algorithms.

ACO (1k) x GA (1k) x SA (1k) (General Results)

The first set of experiments relates to the comparison of the algorithms using as stopping criterion the number of evaluated solutions. For that initial comparison, all algorithms were allowed to perform 1000 evaluations.

Table 6 below presents the results of a selected number of instances - 10 of 72 -, including the averages and standard deviations, over 10 executions, for the proposed ACO Algorithm - ACO (1k) -, Genetic Algorithm (GA) and Simulated Annealing (SA), regarding the quality of the generated solutions.

Table 6. Sample of the results, regarding the quality of the generated solutions and execution time (in milliseconds), for all algorithms executing 1000 evaluations, showing averages and standard deviations over 10 executions.

Instance		ACO (1k)	GA (1k)	SA (1k)
I_50.5.5.20.120	quality	11146.1±39.67	10869.8±182.51	9907.5±182.22
	exec. Time (ms)	1936.1±45.34	79.1±0.87	34.4±6.39
I_50.5.20.0.120		46161.4±253.83	44110.8±864.41	43777.9±751.19
		2194.1±14.68	123.2±0.78	46.8±0.42
I_50.20.20.20.80		93124±956.68	91606.7±5911.03	77506.7±3325.29
		1210±7.07	107.3±1.88	104.6±7.56
I_200.5.5.20.80		41953.8±101.28	37366.6±3455.83	29527.5±1139.68
		14723.5±277.3	623.1±57.44	447.7±7.39
I_200.5.5.20.120		43868.2±64.35	33205.7±2857.03	29718.1±765.27
		13579±181.42	626.9±28.17	400.9±10.49
I_200.5.20.20.120		147873.5±247.95	121931.6±4782.33	103197.6±4923.95
		13046.6±517.64	695.5±53.92	451±8.81
I_200.20.5.0.120		209290.1±396.24	157792.4±23691.97	158245.3±3364.83
		23665.6±301.9	919.2±38.9	460.2±13.33
I_200.20.20.0.120		501178.8±1682.89	442525±65014.99	428164.1±2801.25
		23012±33.43	1063.3±70.73	515.1±16.33
I_500.5.5.0.80		101377.6±317.28	95966±6044.53	83741.7±979.48
		136875±497.07	5376.9±274.98	2364.7±49.02
I_500.5.20.0.120		387081.6±157.18	342013.3±37472.1	331882.1±4308.78
		141801.3±1078.02	5551±314.3	2051.3±13.4

The complete description of all results, over all 72 instances, can be found in the paper supporting material webpage.

Overall, regarding the quality of the generated solutions, ACO performed better than GA and SA in all cases. Percentagewise, ACO generated solutions, in average, 78.27% better than those produced by GA and 96.77% than SA. Additionally, the expressively low standard deviations produced by the proposed approach demonstrates its stability, especially when compared to the results of the other algorithms.

However, in terms of execution time, ACO operated substantially slower than the other two metaheuristics when evaluation the same number of solutions. This may be attributed to the more complex constructive process performed by ACO in the building of each candidate solution. In average, for this metric, ACO required almost 60 times more than GA and more than 90 times more than SA.

ACO (1k) x GA (1k) x SA (1k) (Statistical Analyses)

In order to properly select the most appropriate statistical test, a normality test was performed over 20 samples - randomly chosen - generated throughout the whole experimentation process presented in this paper. The Shapiro-Wilk Normality Test was used for that purpose. The results suggest that normality should be accepted on 17 samples and rejected in the other 3 (the complete presentation of these tests can be found in the paper supporting material webpage). Therefore, since normality can be assumed to all generated samples, the nonparametric Wilcoxon Rank Sum Test was used to evaluate statistical significance.

Thus, the statistical significance of the differences between the results generated by each pair of algorithms was calculated using the Wilcoxon Rank Sum Test, considering the significance levels of 90%, 95% and 99%. Under these conditions, for all instances, the results generated by ACO were significantly better than those generated by GA and SA, in all three significance levels, except for the instances shown in Tables 7.

Table 7. Instances in which statistical confidence cannot be assured when comparing the quality of the solutions generated by ACO with GA and SA, with all algorithms executing 1000 evaluations, calculated with the Wilcoxon Ranked Sum Test.

	90% confidence level	95% confidence level	99% confidence level
GA	I_50.5.5.20.80, I_50.5.20.0.80, I_50.20.20.0.120, I_50.20.20.20.80, I_200.5.20.0.80,I_200.5.20.0.120,, I_500.5.5.0.80,I_500.5.20.0.80	I_50.5.5.20.80, I_50.5.20.0.80 I_50.20.20.0.120,I_50.20.20.20.80, I_200.5.20.0.80,I_200.5.20.0.120, I_500.5.5.0.80,I_500.5.20.0.80	I_50.5.5.20.80, I_50.5.20.0.80, I_50.20.20.0.120,I_50.20.20.20.80, I_200.5.20.0.80,I_200.5.20.0.120, I_200.50.20.0.80,I_500.5.5.0.80, I_500.5.20.0.80,I_500.5.20.0.120, I_500.20.20.0.80
SA	-	-	-

As can be seen, only for 8 instances - out of 72 -, statistical significance could be assured under the 95% confidence level when comparing ACO with GA. For SA, even within the 99% level, ACO performed significantly better in all cases.

The complete set of results, with all measures generated by the Wilcoxon Rank Sum Test can be found in the paper supporting material webpage, for this, and all other statistical significance evaluations.

ACO (1k) x GA (10k) x SA (10k) (General Results)

To evaluate whether the better performance of the proposed ACO algorithm can be attributed to the relatively small number of evaluations performed by GA and SA, a new set of experiments where performed, this time by allowing both GA and SA to evaluate 10000 solution. A sample of the results for these experiments can be found in Table 7.

On these experiments, the ACO algorithm did better than GA in 69 out of the 72 instances. Only for instances I_50.5.5.20.80, I_50.5.20.0.80 and I_200.5.20.0.80, the Genetic Algorithm produced solutions with higher fitness value in average. The exact same behavior occurred with SA, which outperformed ACO over the same 3 instances.

Regarding execution time, ACO was still substantially slower than GA and SA. This time, however, ACO performed around 9 times slower than both GA and SA.

ACO (1k) x GA (10k) x SA (10k) (Statistical Analyses)

Considering initially only the 3 instances where both GA and SA performed better than ACO, the Wilcoxon Rank Sum Test produced the following p-values when comparing ACO with GA: 0.1230000 for instance I_50.5.5.20.80, 0.0232300 for I_50.5.20.0.80 and 0.0015050 for I_200.5.20.0.80, and with SA: 0.0020890 for I_50.5.5.20.80, 0.0000217 for I_50.5.20.0.80 and 0.0000108 for I_200.5.20.0.80.

Table 8. Sample of the results, regarding the quality of the generated solutions and execution time (in milliseconds), with ACO executing 1000 evaluations, and GA and SA executing 10000 evaluations, showing averages and standard deviations over 10 executions.

Instance		ACO (1k)	GA (10k)	SA (10k)
I_50.5.5.20.120	*Quality*	11146.1±39.67	11038.7±197.86	10560.6±177.9
	exec. Time (ms)	1936.1±45.34	603.5±89.74	348.4±17.01
I_50.5.20.0.120		46161.4±253.83	45451.2±750.84	45605.4±352.43
		2194.1±14.68	1192±16.85	460.4±7.93
I_50.20.20.20.80		93124±956.68	91888.8±8920.19	83924.6±1604.32
		1210±7.07	1134.3±10.36	1028.4±71.77
I_200.5.5.20.80		41953.8±101.28	38398.7±3607.22	33473.9±895.87
		14723.5±277.3	7664.5±357.54	4978.5±88.11
I_200.5.5.20.120		43868.2±64.35	33471.4±1390.99	33951.4±2514.54
		13579±181.42	5514.5±225.92	4210±73.25
I_200.5.20.20.120		147873.5±247.95	134656.7±5846.67	124129.8±5285.18
		13046.6±517.64	7887.7±537.4	4841±131.76
I_200.20.5.0.120		209290.1±396.24	174431.4±8076.1	169316.3±2779.69
		23665.6±301.9	9760.1±65.68	6137.3±132.75
I_200.20.20.0.120		501178.8±1682.89	445685.5±15383.84	447483.6±6166.36
		23012±33.43	11255±89.76	7402.7±138.89
I_500.5.5.0.80		101377.6±317.28	100026.3±1221.57	95707±819.69
		136875±497.07	57316.1±284.37	31427.3±848.28
I_500.5.20.0.120		387081.6±157.18	367935±4991.23	375352.8±1660.25
		141801.3±1078.02	61106.9±1122.9	27498.4±315.2

Therefore, considering a confidence level of 95%, GA and SA had, respectively, two and three cases where they were able to produce significantly better solutions. In all other cases, ACO did significantly better, except for the instances presented below in Table 9.

Table 9. Instances in which statistical confidence cannot be assured when comparing the quality of the solutions generated by ACO with GA and SA, with ACO executing 1000 evaluations, and GA and SA executing 10000 evaluations, when ACO performed better, calculated with the Wilcoxon Ranked Sum Test.

	90% confidence level	95% confidence level	99% confidence level
GA	I_50.20.5.0.120,I_50.20.20.0.80, I_50.20.20.20.80,I_50.50.20.0.120, I_50.50.20.20.120,I_200.5.20.0.120 ,I_200.5.20.20.80,I_200.50.20.0.80, I_500.5.5.0.120, I_500.5.20.0.80	I_50.5.5.20.120,I_50.20.5.0.120, I_50.20.20.0.80,I_50.20.20.20.80, I_50.50.20.0.120,I_50.50.20.20.120 ,I_200.5.20.0.120,I_200.5.20.20.80, I_200.50.20.0.80,I_500.5.5.0.120, I_500.5.20.0.80	I_50.5.5.20.80,I_50.5.5.20.120, I_50.5.20.20.80,I_50.20.5.0.120, I_50.20.5.20.120,I_50.20.20.0.80, I_50.20.20.20.80,I_50.50.5.20.120, I_50.50.20.0.120,I_50.50.20.20.120, I_200.5.20.0.120,I_200.5.20.20.80, I_200.50.20.0.80,I_500.5.5.0.80, I_500.5.5.0.120,I_500.5.20.0.80
SA	I_50.5.20.20.120, I_500.5.20.0.80	I_50.5.20.20.120, I_500.5.20.0.80	I_50.5.20.20.80,I_50.5.20.20.120

As can be seen, under the 95% confidence level, ACO did significantly better than GA and SA in all 69 cases, expect for 11 and 1 instances, respectively.

ACO (Restricted Time) x GA (1k) x SA (1k) (General Results)

Even with the increased number of evaluation, both GA and SA performed much more time efficiently then ACO. In order to evaluate whether the increased performance of the proposed ACO approach can be attributed to the considerably high computations cost, a new set of experiments were designed. Here, the amount of time available to ACO was limited, to meet exactly the times required by GA and SA when evaluating 1000 solutions. The performance of ACO under this time restriction is sampled in Table 10.

Table 10. Sample of the results, regarding the quality of the generated solutions, with ACO with a time restriction, and GA and SA executing 1000 evaluations, showing averages and standard deviations over 10 executions.

Instance	ACO w/ Time GA (1k)	GA (1k)	ACO w/ Time SA (1k)	SA (1k)
I_50.5.5.20.120	11038.8±27.62	10869.8±182.51	11007.8±17.14	9907.5±182.22
I_50.5.20.0.120	45633.9±140.17	44110.8±864.41	45637±188.55	43777.9±751.19
I_50.20.20.20.80	91271.7±736.73	91606.7±5911.03	91469±951.19	77506.7±3325.29
I_200.5.5.20.80	41604.4±109.05	37366.6±3455.83	41525.4±93.41	29527.5±1139.68
I_200.5.5.20.120	43715.7±36.64	33205.7±2857.03	43681.8±34.35	29718.1±765.27
I_200.5.20.20.120	147478±351.54	121931.6±4782.33	147404.3±350.34	103197.6±4923.95
I_200.20.5.0.120	208845.6±290.21	157792.4±23691.97	209149.9±486.96	158245.3±3364.83
I_200.20.20.0.120	498434.1±1061.48	442525±65014.99	497747.4±1092.87	428164.1±2801.25
I_500.5.5.0.80	100880.4±216.46	95966±6044.53	100747±100.92	83741.7±979.48
I_500.5.20.0.120	386919.9±205.62	342013.3±37472.1	386785.2±135.83	331882.1±4308.78

Even with the time restriction, ACO continues to outperform both GA and SA, respectively, in 70 and 72 out of 72 cases. These results confirm the ability of the proposed ACO algorithm to find good solutions in little computational time.

ACO (Restricted Time) x GA (1k) x SA (1k) (Statistical Analyses)

When performing better, GA, over instances I_50.5.20.0.80 and I_50.20.20.20.80, could not obtain solutions significantly better than ACO (95% confidence level). However, over all other cases, under the 95% level, ACO did significantly better 63 times. Considering SA, ACO significantly outperformed this algorithm all but one case.

Since the ACO seemed to degrade very little with the time restrictions, a statistical analysis was performed to evaluate, with precision, this level of degradation. For that purposed, three correlation metrics (Pearson, Kendall and Spearman) where employed to estimate the correlation between the results generated by ACO before and after the time restriction. The results of these tests are shown in Table 11.

Table 11. Correlation metrics (Pearson, Kendall and Spearman) over the results generated by ACO before and after the time restriction

	Pearson Correlation	Kendall Correlation	Spearman Correlation
ACO (1k) vs ACO - Time GA (1k)	0.9999907	0.9929577	0.9993890
ACO (1k) vs ACO - Time SA (1k)	0.9999879	0.9866980	0.9987137

Therefore, these measurements demonstrate that those samples are highly correlated, indicating that ACO lost very little of its capacity when subjected to such time constraints. Additionally, using the fitness averages generated by the two versions (with and without time restriction) of ACO, the Wilcoxon Rank Sum Test was applied to measure the significance in the difference of these samples. The p-value 0.8183 was obtained when comparing ACO with its versions restricted by the time required by GA, and 0.7966, using the time used by SA. Those measurements confirm that there are no significant differences in the results produced by ACO before and after the time restrictions were employed.

Final Remarks

Therefore, all experimental results presented and discussed above indicate the ability of the proposed ACO approach for the Software Release Planning problem to generate precise solutions with very little computational effort relative to the results produced by Genetic Algorithm and Simulated Annealing. Thus, our research question RQ2., as described earlier, can be answered, pointing out to the competitive performance of the proposed approach, both in terms of accuracy as well as for time performance.

The main treat to the validity of the reported results is the fact that only synthetically generated data was considered, since no real-world data was available. Therefore, there is the possibility that some peculiarities of such real-world scenarios are not being considered.

6   Conclusion and Future Works

Very little has been done regarding the employment of the Ant Colony Optimization (ACO) framework to tackle software engineering problems modeled as optimization problems, which seems surprising given the large applicability and the significant results obtained by such approach.

This paper proposed a novel ACO-based approach for the Software Release Planning problem with the presence of dependent requirement. Experiments were designed to evaluate the effectiveness of the proposed approach compared to both the Genetic Algorithm and Simulated Annealing. All experimental results pointed out to the ability of the proposed ACO approach to generate precise solutions with very little computational effort.

As future works, the experiments could be extended to cover real-world instances, which should evoke other interesting insights as to the applicability of the proposed ACO algorithm to the Software Release Planning problem. Additionally, other types of dependencies among requirements (value-related, cost-related, and, or) could be considered.

References

1. Harman, M.: The Current State and Future of Search Based Software Engineering. In: Proc. of International Conference on Software Engineering / Future of Software Engineering 2007 (ICSE/FOSE 2007), pp. 342–357. IEEE Computer Society, Minneapolis (2007)
2. Dorigo, M., Stutzle, T.: The Ant Colony Optimization Metaheuristic: Algorithms, Applications, and Advances. In: Glover, F., Kochenberger, G. (eds.) Handbook of Metaheuristics, Norwell, MA (2002)
3. Dorigo, M., Maniezzo, V., Colorni, A.: The Ant System: Optimization by a Colony of Cooperating Agents. IEEE Trans. Systems, Man Cybernetics, Part B 26(1), 29–41 (1996)
4. Dorigo, M., Gambardella, L.M.: Ant Colony System: A Cooperative Learning Approach to the Traveling Salesman Problem. IEEE Trans. Evolutionary Computation 1(1), 53–66 (1997)
5. Bianchi, L., Birattari, M., Chiarandini, M., Manfrin, M., Mastrolilli, M., Paquete, L., Rossi-Doria, O., Schiavinotto, T.: Metaheuristics for the vehicle routing problem with stochastic demands. In: Yao, X., Burke, E.K., Lozano, J.A., Smith, J., Merelo-Guervós, J.J., Bullinaria, J.A., Rowe, J.E., Tiňo, P., Kabán, A., Schwefel, H.-P. (eds.) PPSN 2004. LNCS, vol. 3242, pp. 450–460. Springer, Heidelberg (2004)
6. Gambardella, L.M., Dorigo, M.: Ant Colony System hybridized with a new local search for the sequential ordering problem. Informs. J. Comput. 12(3), 237 (2000)
7. Socha, K., Sampels, M., Manfrin, M.: Ant algorithms for the university course timetabling problem with regard to the state-of-the-art. In: Raidl, G.R., Cagnoni, S., Cardalda, J.J.R., Corne, D.W., Gottlieb, J., Guillot, A., Hart, E., Johnson, C.G., Marchiori, E., Meyer, J.-A., Middendorf, M. (eds.) EvoIASP 2003, EvoWorkshops 2003, EvoSTIM 2003, EvoROB/EvoRobot 2003, EvoCOP 2003, EvoBIO 2003, and EvoMUSART 2003. LNCS, vol. 2611, pp. 334–345. Springer, Heidelberg (2003)
8. Mahanti, P.K., Banerjee, S.: Automated Testing in Software Engineering: using Ant Colony and Self-Regulated Swarms. In: Proc. of the 17th IASTED International Conference on Modelling and Simulation (MS 2006), pp. 443–448. ACTA Press, Montreal (2006)
9. Chicano, F., Alba, E.: Ant Colony Optimization with Partial Order Reduction for Discovering Safety Property Violations in Concurrent Models. Information Processing Letters 106(6), 221–231 (2007)
10. del Sagrado, J., del Águila, I.M.: Ant Colony Optimization for requirement selection in incremental software development. In: Proc. of 1st International Symposioum on Search Based Software Engineering (SSBSE 2009), Cumberland Lodge, UK (2009), http://www.ssbse.org/2009/fa/ssbse2009_submission_30.pdf (fast abstracts)
11. del Sagrado, J., del Águila, I.M., Orellana, F.J.: Ant Colony Optimization for the Next Release Problem: A Comparative Study. In: Proc. of the 2nd International Symposium on Search Based Software Engineering (SSBSE 2010), Benevento, IT, pp. 67–76 (2010)
12. Karlsson, J., Olsson, S., Ryan, K.: Improved practical support for large-scale requirements prioritising. Requirements Engineering 2(1), 51–60 (1997)
13. Bagnall, A., Rayward-Smith, V., Whittley, I.: The next release problem. Information and Software Technology 43(8), 883–890 (2001)
14. Zhang, Y., Harman, M., Mansouri, S.A.: The multiobjective next release problem. In: Proc. of the 9th Annual Conference on Genetic and Evolutionary Computation, pp. 1129–1137. ACM Press, New York (2007)

15. Greer, D., Ruhe, G.: Software release planning: an evolutionary and iterative approach. Information & Technology 46(4), 243–253 (2004)
16. Holland, J.: Adaptation in natural and artificial systems. Univ. of Michigan Press (1975)
17. Kirkpatrick, S., Gelatt, Jr., C.D., Vecchi, M.P.: Optimization by simulated annealing. Science 220, 671–680 (1983)
18. Alaya, I., Solnon, G., Ghedira, K.: Ant algorithm for the multidimensional knapsack problem. In: Proc. of the International Conference on Bio-inspired Optimization Methods and their Applications (BIOMA 2004), pp. 63–72 (2004)
19. Leguizamon, G., Michalewicz, Z.: A new version of Ant System for Subset Problem. In: Congress on Evolutionary Computation, pp. 1459–1464 (1999)
20. Fidanova, S.: Evolutionary Algorithm for Multidimensional Knapsack Problem. In: PPSNVII- Workshop (2002)

Optimizing the Trade-Off between Complexity and Conformance in Process Reduction

Alessandro Marchetto, Chiara Di Francescomarino, and Paolo Tonella

FBK-CIT, Trento, Italy
{marchetto,dfmchiara,tonella}@fbk.eu

Abstract. While models are recognized to be crucial for business process management, often no model is available at all or available models are not aligned with the actual process implementation. In these contexts, an appealing possibility is recovering the process model from the existing system. Several process recovery techniques have been proposed in the literature. However, the recovered processes are often complex, intricate and thus difficult to understand for business analysts.

In this paper, we propose a process reduction technique based on multi-objective optimization, which at the same time minimizes the process complexity and its non-conformances. This allows us to improve the process model understandability, while preserving its completeness with respect to the core business properties of the domain. We conducted a case study based on a real-life e-commerce system. Results indicate that by balancing complexity and conformance our technique produces understandable and meaningful reduced process models.

Keywords: Business Process Recovery, and Multi-Objective Optimization.

1 Introduction

Managing a business process and evolving the associated software system can be difficult without an accurate and faithful documentation (e.g., a model) of the underlying process. When such documentation is missing or inaccurate, it is possible to attempt to reconstruct it through process model recovery and mining.

Several works [1,2] in the literature propose techniques to recover process models starting from the analysis of different artifacts, such as the source code or execution logs. In our previous work [3], we used dynamic analysis to recover processes realized through Web systems.

The typical problems that are faced when process models are recovered from logs include: (i) the process size and complexity; (ii) under-generalization: models may describe only a subset of the actual system behaviors; and (iii) over-generalization: recovery algorithms may generalize the actual observations beyond the possible behaviors. The use of a large set of traces and of an appropriate algorithm can limit the impact of problems (ii) and (iii), but state of

M.B. Cohen and M. Ó Cinnéide (Eds.): SSBSE 2011, LNCS 6956, pp. 158–172, 2011.

the art techniques have still a hard time with problem (i). In fact, process recovery and mining tools tend to produce process models that are quite difficult to understand, because they are overly complex and intricate (they are also called "spaghetti" processes [4]).

Existing approaches dealing with the process model size and complexity problem belong to two groups: clustering and frequency based filtering. Clustering takes advantage of the possibility of modularization offered by sub-processes [3]. Frequency-based process filtering removes process elements that are rarely executed [5]. Empirical evidence [6] shows that modularity affects positively process understandability, but its effect may be negligible due to factors such as the process domain, structure and complexity. Pruning processes according to the execution frequency [5] is useful to remove noise, but may lead to overly simplified processes, that do not capture the core business properties and activities. No existing process reduction technique treats process reduction as an intrinsically multi-objective optimization problem. Rather, they focus on a single dimension (e.g., process size) and take the others into account only implicitly. However, the problem is multi-dimensional: reduced processes are expected to be simpler to understand and manage (having lower size and complexity), but at the same time they should maximize their capability to represent all possible process flows, in a way that is meaningful and expressive for the business analysts.

In this work, we propose a process reduction technique which considers the multiple dimensions involved in this problem explicitly. We use multi-objective optimization to minimize at the same time the process model complexity and its non-conformances (i.e., inability to represent some execution traces). The proposed technique has been implemented in a tool and has been applied to a real-life e-commerce process implemented by a software system with a Web interface. Results indicate that by balancing both complexity and conformance we improve existing process reduction techniques.

2   Business Process Reduction

Recovered process models are reduced by removing some process elements (e.g., sequence flows and activities), with the aim of limiting process size and complexity, while preserving a reasonable level of *conformance*, i.e., ability to fully describe the observed behaviors, enacted by the process under analysis.

By *business process reduction* we mean a sequence of *atomic reduction operations*, each basically consisting of the removal of a direct connection between a pair of process activities, possibly followed by a cascade of further process element removals, occurring whenever an entire sub-process becomes unreachable from the start due to the initial removal. To perform business process reduction, we rely upon an intermediate process representation, called *activity graph*. The mapping between the original process model P and the activity graph AG_P must be invertible, since we want to be able to convert the reduced activity graph back to the original process.

Under the assumption that the initial BPMN process has only exclusive gateways[1] (as in case of processes recovered by our tool, see Section 5), we can safely remove them in the activity graph and reintroduce only those actually needed in the reduced process. Specifically, in the activity graph AG_P there will be a node n_a for each process activity a and an edge (n_a, n_b) for each pair of activities (a, b) such that there exists a path connecting them not traversing other activities. AG_P can be easily converted back to the original process P, since the exclusive gateways to be reintroduced are associated with nodes having fanout or fanin greater than 1. Though the number of gateways of the inverted and original process may differ, the semantics is however preserved and the original structure is sometimes obtainable by applying some gateway simplification rules. If the original BPMN process contains other types of gateways, in addition to the exclusive ones, it will not be possible to remove them from the activity graph. They will be explicitly represented by typed activity graph nodes, with the type used to distinguish different kinds of BPMN elements.

The example in Figure 1 represents the process for an on-line submission system. The corresponding activity graph contains a node for each activity/gateway of the process and two nodes (named GS and GE) representing the start and end event of the process.

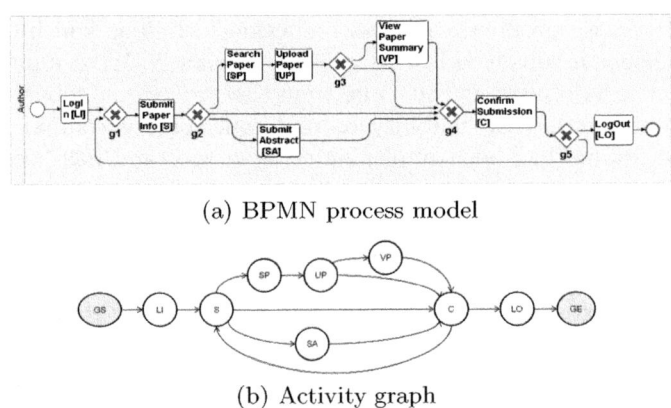

(a) BPMN process model

(b) Activity graph

Fig. 1. Paper submission system: BPMN process and activity graph

Atomic Reduction. An atomic reduction consists of the removal of an edge from AG_P, followed by the removal of the subgraph unreachable from the start event. When the removed edge (n_a, n_b) dominates its target n_b (i.e., it belongs to all the paths from the start node GS to n_b), n_b becomes unreachable from the start event. We hence perform a reachability analysis from the start node GS to determine the subgraph of AG_P that is no longer reachable from GS due to the removal of (n_a, n_b). Such subgraph is also removed from the activity

---

[1] Gateways are used for managing control flow branching (both splitting and merging) in BPMN. According to their type (exclusive, inclusive, parallel and complex), they enable a different control flow behaviour.

graph, in order to ensure that the graph obtained from the atomic reduction is still a meaningful process representation. This means that the impact of a single atomic reduction may range from an individual edge removal to the removal of a (possibly large) subgraph of AG_P. It can be easily shown that the atomic reduction operation is commutative, i.e., the same activity graph is obtained by applying the atomic reduction for e_1 and for e_2 or in the opposite order.

In the activity graph in Figure 1, the removal of the edge (S, C) does not leave any subgraph unreachable from GS ((S, C) is not a dominator of C). In the BPMN process corresponding to the reduced activity graph, the only sequence flow that is removed is $(g2, g4)$. On the contrary, the removal of the edge (S, SA), a dominator of SA, makes node SA unreachable from the start node. By reachability analysis, we can easily determine that node SA as well as its outgoing edge (SA, C) must be also removed, since unreachable from GS. The corresponding BPMN process is shown in Figure 2. Not only the sequence flow $(g2, SA)$ has been removed, but also the process activity *Submit Abstract* as well as its outgoing sequence flow $(SA, g4)$.

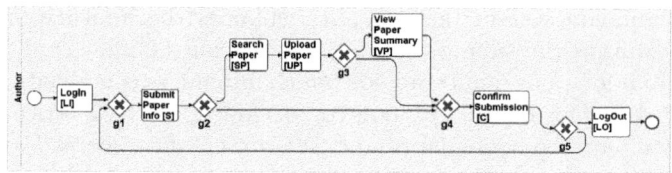

Fig. 2. Reduced process resulting after removing the edge (S, SA)

3   Process Complexity and Non-conformance

Three quality factors are dominant [7,8] concerning how to measure and evaluate the quality of (recovered) process models: *complexity*, *conformance* and *accuracy*. This work is focused on finding an optimal trade-off between the first two quality factors. Accuracy, which captures the ability of a process model to describe only feasible behaviors (i.e., executions admitted by the model should be also possible in reality), is not considered in this work for two reasons: (1) we apply process reduction to improve a single process mining technique, which has its own intrinsic accuracy level; (2) it is hard to get a precise and meaningful quantification of accuracy, since it is not possible to determine in an automated way which paths in the model are not possible in the real process implementation.

3.1   Process Complexity

The existing literature [7] proposes to measure the process complexity by resorting to the cyclomatic complexity, commonly used with software, and adapting it for processes. Hence, given a process model P, we measure its control-flow complexity $CFC(P)$ as follows:

$$CFC(P) = \sum_{g \in G(P) \wedge FOUT(g) > 1} FOUT(g) \qquad (1)$$

where $G(P)$ is the set of all process control-flow elements (gateways, in BPMN) and $FOUT(g)$ is the number of the sequence flows outgoing from g (fanout). We take into account only decision points of the process, i.e., elements with fanout greater than one. A high value of CFC indicates a high number of alternative execution flows, thus denoting a process potentially difficult to read and understand for the analyst.

For example, the online submission process in Figure 1 contains five gateways, one with fanout 3, two with fanout 2 and two with fanout 1. The resulting process CFC is hence 7. For the reduced process in Figure 2, the CFC is 6.

3.2   Process Conformance

The conformance of a process model is its ability to reproduce the execution traces (i.e., the traces should be admitted by the process model) [8]. A trace is a sequence of events executed during the run of a process and stored in a log file. Table 1 shows some examples of execution traces for the submission process in Figure 1. For instance, trace t_3 represents an execution in which the user logs into the submission system (activity LI), submits the information about the paper (S), confirms the submission (C) and logs out (LO).

Since we aim for an optimal trade-off which minimizes complexity, we take the complement of conformance, i.e., non-conformance, as the metrics to be minimized. To compute the non-conformance $NConf(P)$ for process P, we interpret the model as a parser that can either accept or refuse a trace, regarded as its input string. A process model parses a trace if there is an execution flow in the process model that complies with the process model semantics and consists of the sequence of events in the trace. We assume that the parser associated with a process model is a *robust* parser, i.e., it has a parsing resume strategy which allows the parser to skip an input subsequence that cannot be accepted and to resume parsing from a successive input symbol. Specifically, if the trace consists of three parts $t = <p, m, s>$, such that the prefix p can be parsed and brings the process model execution to state S while the subsequence m cannot be accepted from state S, a resume strategy is a rule that transforms the process state S into S', such that the suffix s can be parsed from S'. Usually, the resume strategies implemented by parsers are heuristic rules to modify the state S by performing minimal changes to it, until an accepting state S' is reached.

Given a process model P and a trace $t \in T$ (the set of traces), we start parsing t with P in the start state. When event $e \in t$ is provided as input to process P (in the execution state S), if there does not exist any transition $S \longmapsto_e S'$ in P and there does not exist any resume rule R such that $S \longmapsto_R S' \longmapsto_e S''$, we recognize a non conformance $\langle S, e \rangle$, which is added to the non-conformance

Table 1. Example of execution traces

Trace	Event sequence	Trace	Event sequence
t_1	< LI, S, SP, UP, C, LO >	t_2	< LI, S, SA, C, LO >
t_3	< LI, S, C, LO >	t_4	< LI, S, SP, UP, VP, C, S, SP, UP, C, LO >
t_5	< LI, S, SP, UP, C, S, SA, C, LO >		

set. The size of the non-conformance set after trying to reproduce all the traces in T is our non-conformance metrics $NConf$. It should be noticed that if the same non-conformance $\langle S, e \rangle$ occurs multiple times (it appears in many traces) it contributes only as a $+1$ to $NConf$.

Under the assumption that the process model being considered contains only exclusive gateways (which is the case of the process mining tool used in our case study), the state of the process model execution when event e is provided as input consists of the last accepted activity. Only one parsing resume rule is needed for this class of process models. When the input activity b cannot be accepted by P, the preceding input activity a in the trace is considered. If the process model P contains the edge (a, b), parsing is resumed from state a. Computation of the $NConf$ metrics is also simplified for this class of process models. Specifically, the following formula can be used:

$$NConf(P) = \left| \bigcup_{t \in T} \{(a,b)|(a,b) \in t \wedge dc(a,b) \notin P\} \right| \tag{2}$$

where $dc(a, b)$ indicates the existence of a *direct connection* (i.e., an edge or a path containing only gateways as intermediate elements) between a and b in the process model P. Hence, we measure the number of unique transitions in the traces that are not reproducible in the process model. Let us consider the trace $t_2 = \langle LI, S, SA, C, LO \rangle$ from Table 1. The reduced process model in Figure 2 accepts the first two events, but then SA is not even present in the reduced process model. Thus, $(S, SA), (SA, C)$ are non-conformances. However, when LO is considered as input, parsing can restart from C according to the resume rule given above, such that (C, LO) is accepted. The final value of $NConf$ is 2 for this reduced process. It should be clear from this example that instead of parsing the string $\langle LI, S, SA, C, LO \rangle$, we can more easily obtain $NConf$ by just counting the number of consecutive pairs of events in the trace that do not have a direct connection in the reduced process model. $NConf(P)$ is 0 if the process model reproduces all traces, while a high value of $NConf(P)$ indicates that the process model is not able to reproduce many transitions in the traces.

If the considered process model P contains other types of gateways, in addition to the exclusive ones, we need to resort to a more general definition of $NConf(P)$ and, in particular, to a more complex parser strategy which implements the resume rules such as the one proposed by Rozinat et al. [8].

4   Multi-objective Optimization

We use multi-objective optimization to produce a reduced process model that minimizes both process complexity and non-conformance. Specifically, we rely on the Non-dominated Sorting Genetic Algorithm II (NSGA-II, Deb et al. [9]).

NSGA-II uses a set of genetic operators (i.e., crossover, mutation, selection) to iteratively evolve an initial population of candidate solutions (i.e., processes). The evolution is guided by an objective function (called fitness function) that evaluates the quality of each candidate solution along the considered dimensions (i.e., complexity and non-conformance). In each iteration, the Pareto front of the best alternative solutions is generated from the evolved population. The front contains the set of non-dominated solutions, i.e., those solutions that are not inferior to any other solution in *all* considered dimensions. Population evolution is iterated until a (predefined) maximum number of iterations is reached.

The obtained Pareto front represents the optimal trade-off between complexity and non-conformance determined by the algorithm. The business analyst can inspect the Pareto front to find the best compromise between having a model that conforms to the observed traces, but is quite complex vs. having a simpler, probably more understandable, but less adherent to reality, model.

Solution Encoding: In our instantiation of the algorithm, a candidate solution is an activity graph in which some edges are kept and some are removed. We represent such a solution by means of a standard binary encoding, i.e., a binary vector. The length of the vector is the number of edges in the activity graph extracted from the unreduced process model. While the binary vector for the unreduced process is entirely set to 1, for a reduced process each binary vector element is set to 1 when the associated activity graph edge is kept; it is set to 0 otherwise. For instance, the encoding of the unreduced submission process (Figure 1) consists of a vector of 13 elements (i.e., all the edges of the activity graph), all set to 1. In the vector encoding the reduced process in Figure 2, three bits (representing the edges *(S, C)*, *(S, SA)* and *(SA, C)*) are zero.

Initialization: We initialize the starting population in two ways, either randomly or resorting to the frequency-based edge-filtering heuristics. Random initialization consists of the generation of random binary vectors for the individuals in the initial population. The frequency based edge-filtering heuristics consists of removing (i.e., flipping from 1 to 0) the edges that have a frequency of occurrence in the traces below a given, user-defined threshold [5]. An initial set population has been obtained by assigning the frequency threshold (used to decide which edges to filter) all possible values between minimum and maximum frequencies of edges in the initial process.

Genetic Operators: NSGA-II resorts to three genetic operators for the evolution of the population: mutation, crossover and selection. As mutation operator, we used the bit-flip mutation: one randomly chosen bit of the solution is swapped. The adopted crossover operator is the one-point crossover: a pair of solutions is recombined by cutting the two binary vectors at a randomly chosen (intermediate) point and swapping the tails of the two cut vectors. The selection operator we used is binary tournament: two solutions are randomly chosen and the fitter of the two is the one that survives in the next population.

Fitness Functions: Our objective functions are the two metrics CFC and $NConf$, measuring the complexity and non-conformance of the reduced processes. For each candidate solution in the population, the reduced activity graph is obtained by applying the atomic reduction operations encoded as bits set to 0 in the corresponding binary vector. Then, the resulting reduced activity graph is converted back to a reduced process, evaluated in terms of CFC and $NConf$.

5 Case Study

We implemented our process recovery algorithm in a set of tools[2]: *JWebTracer* [3] traces the run of a Web application; *JBPRecovery* [3] infers a BPMN model; *JBPFreqReducer* implements the frequency-based heuristics *Fbr* to reduce processes by removing their rarely executed elements [5]; and *JBPEvo* implements the multi-objective genetic algorithm (*MGA*) presented in Section 4. In *JBPEvo*, the initial population can be randomly generated or it can be generated by applying the frequency-based heuristics *Fbr*.

We have applied our tools to the process model recovered from execution traces of the Web application Softslate Commerce[3]. Softslate is a Java shopping cart application that allows companies to manage their on-line stores. It implements functionalities to support the online retail of products (e.g., cart, order and payment) and to handle customer accounts, product shipping and administrative issues. The application consists of more than 200k lines of code written in Java/JSP. It uses several frameworks (e.g., Struts, Wsdl4j, Asm, SaaJ) and it can be interfaced with several database managers (e.g., MySql, Postgresql).

The aim of the case study was answering the following research questions investigating effectiveness and viability of the process reduction techniques in making the recovered processes more understandable and manageable.

- *RQ1: Does the shape of the Pareto fronts offer a set of solutions which includes a wide range of tunable trade-offs between complexity and conformance?* It addresses the variety of different, alternative solutions produced by *JBPEvo*. In particular, the shape of the Pareto front and the density of the solutions in the front determine the possibility to choose among a wide range of interesting alternatives vs. the availability of a restricted number of choices. The Pareto front, in fact, might consist of points spread uniformly in the interesting region of the *CFC*, *NConf*-plane, or it may be concentrated in limited, possibly uninteresting regions of the plane (e.g., near the unreduced process).
- *RQ2: Does the genetic algorithm improve the initial solutions (both random and edge-filtered)?* It deals with the margin of optimization left by the initial population, generated randomly or by *Fbr*. We want to understand if the improvements achieved through *MGA* are substantial.
- *RQ3: Are the reduced processes in the Pareto front understandable and meaningful for business analysts?* It deals with the quality of the solutions produced by *MGA*, as perceived by the business analysts. We want to understand the quality of the processes produced by *MGA* in terms of their understandability and meaningfulness.
- *RQ4: Do the processes obtained by applying multi-objective optimization offer qualitative improvements over those obtained by applying the edge-filtering heuristics?* It deals with the quality of the solutions produced by *MGA* compared to those obtainable by means of the *Fbr* heuristics.

---

[2] The tools are available at `http://selab.fbk.eu/marchetto/tools/rebpmn`
[3] `http://www.softslate.com/`

The procedure followed in the experimentation consists of: (1) *JWebTracer* has been used to trace 50 executions of Softslate Commerce (involving, on average, 12 user actions per execution). These executions exercise each application functionality at least once. (2) *JBPRecovery* has been used to analyze the recorded traces and build the unreduced BPMN process model. (3) *JBPFreqReducer* has been used to reduce the initial process model by applying the *Fbr* heuristics. A set of solutions has been obtained by varying the frequency threshold. The maximum population size considered is 100 processes. (4) *JBPEvo* has been run with two different types of initial populations, one randomly generated (MGA_R) and the other generated by *JBPFreqReducer* (MGA_F).

The dataset and recovered processes are available online[4]. Note that we address the research questions by resorting to a quantitative analysis when possible (specifically, for *RQ1* and *RQ2*). Other questions (*RQ3* and *RQ4*) involve more subjective evaluations, hence a qualitative analysis is more appropriate for them.

5.1 Quantitative Results

Figures 3, 4 and 5 show the Pareto fronts at different iterations of MGA_R, MGA_F and with the best solutions found by MGA_R, MGA_F and *Fbr* (highlighting the 9 processes selected for the qualitative analysis).

- **RQ1.** While for a small number of iterations MGA_R and MGA_F produce a Pareto front with few solutions (as shown by the shape of the fronts in Figures 3 and 4), after a large enough number of iterations (at least 10,000), the Pareto fronts present a smooth shape covering uniformly the CFC and $NConf$ ranges. After 1,000,000 iterations, the Pareto front of MGA_R has several solutions in the regions $CFC > 50$ and $NConf > 180$, while a smaller number of alternative trade-offs is offered (compared to MGA_F) in the region $CFC < 50$ and $NConf < 180$. In the region $CFC < 50$ and $NConf < 100$ MGA_F offers a lot of alternative solutions, while *Fbr* finds no solution at all. We conclude that MGA can produce a Pareto front which includes a wide range of tunable solutions. However, this requires a high enough number of iterations and a carefully initialized starting population (via *Fbr*). Otherwise, the choices offered to the user are potentially limited and sub-optimal.

- **RQ2.** The Pareto fronts obtained by iterating MGA_R show substantial improvements with respect to the initial population. The improvement is particularly impressive in the first 10,000 iterations, when the initial random solutions start to converge to a front, but major improvements are achieved when moving from 100,000 to 1,000,000 iterations. Some improvements with respect to the initial *Fbr* population have been observed also for MGA_F, but the margin for improvement left by *Fbr* (line for iteration 0) is lower than that left by the random initial population. Hence, convergence to the final Pareto front is achieved more quickly than MGA_R as confirmed by the time values[5] (in minutes) required by MGA to perform a given number of iterations reported in Table 2

[4] http://selab.fbk.eu/marchetto/tools/rebpmn/opt_ext.zip
[5] Running times for all the algorithms have been computed on a desktop PC with an Intel(R) Core(TM) 2 Duo CPU working at 2.66GHz and with 3GB of RAM memory.

(last column). After 10,000 iterations, in fact, only minor improvements can be obtained by further increasing the iteration number (e.g., 1,000,000). However, the most notable difference between Fbr and MGA_F is the density of the solutions in the Pareto front. In fact, such density is extremely increased in the front produced by MGA_F compared to Fbr, the former offering more alternative trade-offs. Hence, we can conclude that MGA improves both random and Fbr solutions, the latter to a lower degree, but with a substantially higher density of solutions available.

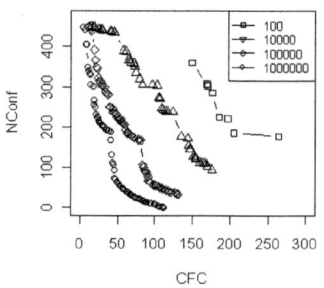

Fig. 3. Softslate: MGA_R Pareto fronts

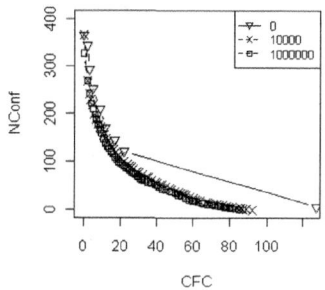

Fig. 4. Softslate: MGA_F Pareto fronts

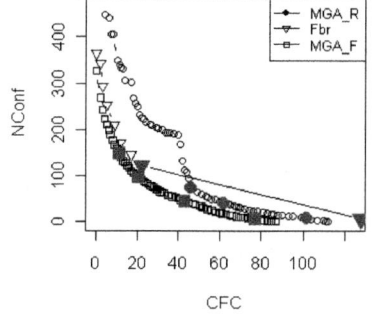

Fig. 5. Softslate: best Pareto fronts

Table 2. Unique processes and times in the Pareto fronts

Algo	Iter	Proc.	Unique Proc.	Time (min.)
MGA_R	100	9	8	1.18
MGA_R	10000	100	43	39.3
MGA_R	100000	100	68	294.2
MGA_R	1000000	100	67	2097.9
MGA_F	0	75	12	<0.2
MGA_F	100	83	14	1.24
MGA_F	10000	100	65	12.1
MGA_F	1000000	100	65	1077.2
Fbr	-	12	12	-

5.2 Qualitative Results

The points highlighted in Figure 5 represent the reduced processes randomly selected to be considered in the qualitative evaluation: $p4$ and $p15$ generated by Fbr; $p24$, $p25$, $p66$ generated by MGA_R; and $p23$ (Figure 6), $p27$, $p67$, $p41$ generated by MGA_F. Table 3 provides some structural metrics (number of activities, gateways and sequence flows), as well as complexity and non-conformance metrics, for the unreduced process model and for the 9 selected processes.

In terms of difficulty of understanding, a big difference can be observed between reduced and unreduced processes, confirmed by the metrics shown in Table 3: the 9 selected processes have substantially lower values of structural and complexity metrics. However, this is paid in terms of non-conformance, as apparent also from Table 3. The point is whether such non-conformances affect minor aspects of the process (noise), or core activities and properties.

Table 3. Metrics for the 9 selected processes

Pr. id	#Act	#G	#SF	CFC	NConf
unreduced					
-	213	105	581	502	0
MGA_R					
p24	31	25	104	46	74
p25	39	37	125	62	40
p66	48	50	168	102	7
MGA_F					
p23	21	8	52	11	148
p27	23	15	60	20	97
p67	36	25	97	43	44
p41	46	38	142	77	6
Fbr					
p4	19	16	51	22	122
p15	46	44	188	128	6

Table 4. Some core business activities and properties

Business activities
... a3.Add To Cart; ... a7.Clear This Cart; a8. Checkout; ... a10.Delete Item; a11.Log In; a12. Create New Account; ... a14.Confirm Order; ... a19.Reorder

	Business properties
pr2	Remove has to follow Add To Cart, Pick Up or Reorder
pr3	After Edit it has to be possible to Edit Item or to Delete Item
pr5	Delete Item has to follow Add To Cart, Pick Up or Reorder
pr15	After Pick Up it has to be possible to choose among Edit, Remove, Continue Shopping, Save This Cart, Clear This Cart and Checkout
pr19	Confirm Order has to follow Checkout
pr21	Checkout has to be executed after the Log In or the Creation of a New Account; otherwise it has to be possible to Log In or to Create a New Account immediately after the Checkout
. . .	

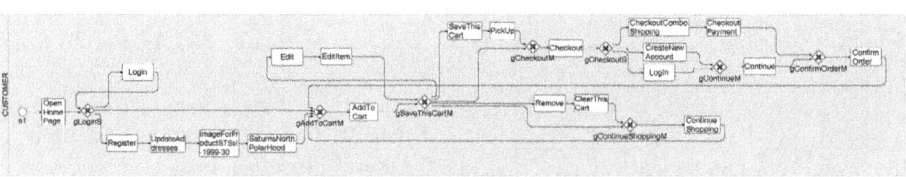

Fig. 6. Softslate: recovered reduced process

In order to assess the quality of the 9 selected processes from the point of view of the business analyst, we have identified 19 core business activities and 28 core business properties that pertain to the domain being modeled (Table 4 shows some examples). We assume that a good process model should represent explicitly all core business activities and should encode a process dynamics that complies with the core business properties. Core activities and properties have been defined by one of the authors not involved in the process recovery phase and without any knowledge about the recovered models (see Table 5). For instance, *Login* and *Checkout* (activities *a11* and *a8*) are core business activities, i.e., activities that any analyst would expect to be modeled explicitly. While an example of a core business property is: the user must be logged-in in order to be allowed to complete the Checkout operation (property *pr21*).

Table 5. Activities and properties modeled in the reduced processes

unreduced	MGA_R			Fbr		MGA_F			
	p24	p25	p66	p4	p15	p23	p27	p41	p67
Business Activities									
19	17	18	19	15	19	15	16	19	18
Business Properties									
19	19	21	25	18	24	19	22	25	25

- **RQ3**. Most of the 19 core activities are modeled in all 9 reduced processes (see Table 5). The highest number of missing core activities is 4 and is associated with the two processes (*p4* and *p23*) having among the lowest *CFC* values (22 and 11, respectively). The process *p27* has also low complexity (*CFC* = 20) and it misses 3 core activities (*a2*, *a16* and *a19*), missing in *p4* and *p23* too.

With regards to the business properties, something unexpected happened. Reduced processes tend to enforce the same number or more business properties than the initial, unreduced process recovered from the traces (note that the unreduced process covers 19 out of 28 identified properties). As shown in Table 5, there is only one exception: process *p4*, which enforces 1 property less than the unreduced process. Processes *p66*, *p41* and *p67* generated by *MGA* enforce 6 more core business properties than the unreduced process. Process *p15*, generated by *Fbr*, enforces 5 more properties. The explanation for this unexpected improvement is that the unreduced process was obtained by generalizing the behaviors observed in the execution traces, which contain noise and irrelevant details. This resulted in over-generalization of the possible execution paths, giving raise to extra behaviors, incompatible with the business domain. For instance, in the unreduced process we can find the following path: "⟨*Add To Cart*, ..., *Continue Shopping*, *Create New Account*, ..., *Confirm Order*⟩", which has never been traced in the logs and is forbidden by the Web application (core property *pr19*: "Confirm Order has to follow Checkout"). It appears as a consequence of the many complex paths combined together in a single model.

Moreover, it is possible to observe that even when properties do hold in the unreduced process, the process is so complex and intricate, that they can be hardly verified by humans, thus potentially becoming not much meaningful for the analysts. For example, while it is feasible for an analyst to check the failure of property *pr2* for process *p23* (see Figure 6), it is practically impossible for him to verify that the same property is true in the unreduced process.

We investigated also the reasons why none of the considered reduced processes realizes all 28 core business properties. We discovered three main problems: (1) one or more business activities involved in the property have been removed by the reduction algorithm (e.g., removal of activity *a10* from *p23* causes the failure of *pr3* and *pr5*); (2) a sequence flow that would allow to verify the business property has been removed by the reduction algorithm (e.g., removal of the sequence flow between the activities *Add To Cart* and *Clear This Cart* causes the failure of *pr15*); (3) over-generalization, which, as explained above, makes the unreduced process capable of enforcing only 19 out of 28 core business properties (e.g., the sequence of activities ⟨*Add To Cart*, *Continue Shopping*, *Continue*, ...⟩, possible in *p41*, is non-allowed by Softslate, as indicated also by property *pr18*). Cases 1 and 2 are instances of under-generalization, while 3 is the case of an over-generalized model. We analyzed the trend of under and over-generalization problems for the 9 selected processes, at decreasing complexity and increasing non-conformance (see Table 3). In these 9 cases, under-generalization problems grow at decreasing complexity (they are strictly related with the level of non-conformance), while over-generalization problems grow at increasing complexity, due to the excessive number of paths in the model.

Summarizing, a small number of business activities and properties are missing in the reduced processes, which make them meaningful to business analysts, especially in comparison to the unreduced process. Moreover, process reduction is almost always beneficial to the modeling of the core business properties, thanks to its implicit capability of reducing over-generalization.

- **RQ4.** To qualitatively compare the results achieved by Fbr and MGA_F, we consider the processes generated by the two algorithms that are within similar ranges of CFC and $NConf$: $p4$ vs. $p23$ and $p27$; $p15$ vs. $p67$ and $p41$. At lower complexity, the processes produced by MGA_F ($p23$ and $p27$) include the same or more business activities. They always comply with more business properties ($p23$ enforces 1 property more than $p4$; $p27$ 4 properties more). While process $p23$ produced by MGA_F is comparable to (actually, slightly better than) $p4$ in terms of modeled core business activities and properties, it has half the CFC complexity of $p4$. This clearly indicates that the multi-objective optimization performed by MGA is extremely effective in determining a trade-off able to keep complexity low (11 vs. 22), while at the same time minimizing the non-conformances, which allows the process model to be comparatively similar to the more complex process $p4$, obtained by means of frequency-based reduction. The benefits of multi-objective optimization are apparent when $p4$ and $p27$ are compared. In this case, the CFC complexity is similar (22 vs. 20, respectively), but process $p27$ has much less non-conformances (97 vs. 122), as a result of the multi-objective optimization. This can be appreciated in terms of properties that are meaningful for the business analyst. In fact, $p27$ models 4 core business properties more than $p4$ (22 vs. 18) and 1 more business activity.

When comparing $p15$ vs. $p67$ and $p41$, the number of business activities and properties is similar (differing by at most ±1). However, the process models produced by MGA are far less complex, with CFC respectively equal to 43 and 77, vs. $p15$ having CFC equal to 128. In the first case (process $p67$), multi-objective optimization is able to reduce the complexity of the model by a factor of around $1/3$ at almost unchanged core business activities and properties. In the second case (process $p15$), the exact same amount of non-conformance (namely, 6) is achieved by a process model having almost half complexity (77 vs. 128).

In conclusion, multi-objective optimization is overall effective in optimizing the trade-off reducing the complexity of the model while leaving unchanged the business properties captured by the model and its non-conformance, hence representing a substantial improvement over the models obtainable by means of Fbr. As remarked above, MGA offers also a wider range of alternative solutions.

5.3   Threats to Validity

It is always hard to generalize the results obtained on a single case study. The selected application, however, seems to be representative of the e-commerce domain, where Web applications are used to implement the trading processes.

Two threats to validity impact the procedure of the case study. The first concerns the used executions traces. Since different models can be recovered considering different sets of traces, we applied the functional coverage criterion for the selection of application executions to be used. The second threat concerns the stochastic nature of the MGA algorithm. We considered different runs of the algorithm and obtaining comparable results, we detailed only one of them.

Finally, the qualitative analysis could have been influenced by the limited number of processes analyzed and the strong subjectivity characterizing the analysis. To limit this latter threat, the person in charge of identifying the business information was not involved in the process recovery phase.

6   Related Works

Process recovery deals with the analysis of a process implementation to extract models of the underlying process. For instance, Zou et al. [2] presented a two-step approach to recover business processes from Web applications. Process mining techniques (e.g., [10], [5]) try to infer processes by analyzing the workflow logs, containing information about organizations and process executions. In this area, most of the effort has been devoted to control flow mining (e.g., see the α algorithm proposed by van der Aalst et al. [5]).

Mining techniques often produce large and intricate processes. Assuming that this is due to spurious information contained in the traces, some works prune the model by removing process elements having low execution frequencies [5]. In our case study, we made a direct comparison with the frequency-based process reduction, showing the superiority of our approach in reducing process complexity and non-conformance. Other works cluster segments of traces and mine a number of smaller process models, one for each different cluster [10]. We used clustering [3] to modularize the processes into sub-processes for improving their understandability. However, the effects of modularity can be limited by the process domain, structure and complexity [6]. Process reduction, hence, is applied after process recovery and after the application of existing techniques for reducing process complexity (e.g., noise pruning, modularization).

Some works propose the use of evolutionary algorithms to balance under and over-generalization when mining a process model. For instance, Alves de Medeiro et al. [11] apply a genetic algorithm to mine a process balancing the ability of reproducing behaviors traced in logs and extra-behaviors. Their algorithm optimizes a single-objective function which combines under and over-generalization. On the contrary, we aim at two objectives at the same time, complexity and non-conformance. The former (absent in [11]) descends from the analysts' understandability needs, while our notion of non-conformance corresponds to their of under-generalization.

7   Conclusion

We have presented a multi-objective process reduction technique for reducing large processes by balancing complexity and conformance. We conducted a case study involving a real-life process exposed as a Web application. Results indicate that: (1) MGA produces a rich, fine grained, evenly distributed set of alternatives; (2) MGA improves state of the art reduction techniques; (3) convergence of MGA depends on the choice of the initial population; (4) though reduced, processes produced by MGA include relevant business activities and properties (i.e., we deem them as meaningful for analysts); (5) MGA produces solutions that are optimal along multiple dimensions at the same time. Future works will be devoted to perform further experiments, involving additional case studies and including other process mining tools.

References

1. van der Aalst, W., Weijter, A., Maruster, L.: Workflow mining: Discovering process models from event logs. IEEE Transactions on Knowledge and Data Engineering 2004(16) (2003)
2. Zou, Y., Guo, J., Foo, K.C., Hung, M.: Recovering business processes from business applications. Journal of Software Maintenance and Evolution: Research and Practice 21(5), 315–348 (2009)
3. Di Francescomarino, C., Marchetto, A., Tonella, P.: Cluster-based modularization of processes recovered from web applications. Journal of Software Maintenance and Evolution: Research and Practice (to appear) doi: 10.1002/smr.518
4. Veiga, G.M., Ferreira, D.R.: Understanding spaghetti models with sequence clustering for prom. In: Proc. of Workshop on Business Process Intelligence (BPI), Ulm, Germany (2009)
5. van der Aalst, W., van Dongen, B., Herbst, J., Maruster, L., Schimm, G., Weijters, A.: Workflow mining: A survey of issues and approaches. Journal of Data and Knowledge Engineering 47(2), 237–267 (2003)
6. Reijers, H.A., Mendling, J.: Modularity in process models: Review and effects. In: Dumas, M., Reichert, M., Shan, M.-C. (eds.) BPM 2008. LNCS, vol. 5240, pp. 20–35. Springer, Heidelberg (2008)
7. Cardoso, J., Mendling, J., Neumann, G., Reijers, H.: A discourse on complexity of process models. In: Proc. of Workshop on Business Process Intelligence (BPI), Australia, pp. 115–126 (2006)
8. Rozinat, A., van der Aalst, W.: Conformance checking of processes based on monitoring real behavior. Information Systems 33(1), 64–95 (2008)
9. Deb, K., Pratap, A., Agarwal, S., Meyarivan, T.: A fast and elitist multiobjective genetic algorithm: NSGA-II. IEEE Transactions on Evolutionary Computation 6(2), 182–197 (2002)
10. Bose, R., van der Aalst, W.: Context aware trace clustering: Towards improving process mining results. In: Proc. of Symposium on Discrete Algorithms (SDM-SIAM), USA, pp. 401–412 (2009)
11. Alves de Medeiros, A., Weijters, A., van der Aalst, W.: Genetic process mining: An experimental evaluation. Journal of Data Mining and Knowledge Discovery 14(2), 245–304 (2006)

A Metaheuristic Approach to Test Sequence Generation for Applications with a GUI

Sebastian Bauersfeld, Stefan Wappler, and Joachim Wegener

Berner und Mattner Systemtechnik GmbH,
Gutenbergstr. 15, 10587 Berlin, Germany
{sebastian.bauersfeld,stefan.wappler,joachim.wegener}@berner-mattner.com
www.berner-mattner.com

Abstract. As the majority of today's software applications employ a graphical user interface (GUI), it is an important though challenging task to thoroughly test those interfaces. Unfortunately few tools exist to help automating the process of testing. Despite of their well-known deficits, scripting- and capture and replay applications remain among the most common tools in the industry. In this paper we will present an approach where we treat the problem of generating test sequences to GUIs as an optimization problem. We employ ant colony optimization and a relatively new metric called MCT (Maximum Call Tree) to search fault-sensitive test cases. We therefore implemented a test environment for Java SWT applications and will present first results of our experiments with a graphical editor as our main application under test.

Keywords: gui testing, search-based software testing, ant colony optimization.

1 Introduction

One reason why the test of applications with GUIs is often neglected, might be that this kind of testing is labour and resource intensive [14]. Capture and replay tools help the tester with recording input sequences that consist of mouse movements, clicks on widgets and keystrokes. These sequences can then be replayed on the software under test (SUT) to serve as regression tests. Unfortunately there are a few limitations to this approach:

1. It is difficult to find input sequences that are likely to expose errors of the SUT. The actions often need to be in a specific order, or have to appear in the context of certain other actions to provoke faults.
2. This kind of testing is laborious and takes a lot of time. One often needs several testers to compile an entire test suite.
3. Slight changes to the GUI of the SUT will break tests. For example removing a button that appears in a sequence as part of a click action, will cause this sequence to not be replayed properly on the updated application.

M.B. Cohen and M. Ó Cinnéide (Eds.): SSBSE 2011, LNCS 6956, pp. 173–187, 2011.

```
clickMenu("File"), clickMenu("Print"), pressKey(Tab),
type("22"), pressKey(Tab), type("44"), clickButton("OK")
```

Fig. 1. Input sequence that causes Microsoft Word to print pages 22 to 44 of the current document

Considering these difficulties, techniques for automatic test case generation are quite desirable. One way to deal with the task of finding test data, is to treat it as an optimization problem. This means that one tries to find solutions with the highest quality with respect to the chosen criteria. Since the input space is large and has a complex structure, one could try to exploit metaheuristic techniques. There has been a lot of research about this in a field commonly known as Search-based Software Engineering [12,17,1]. Recently, some of these techniques have also been applied to GUI testing [7,6,16,9]. The problem of finding input sequences or test suites is difficult. Some of the challenges are:

GUI Model. Throughout the optimization process it is necessary to generate new sequences which have to be assessed. An input sequence of length n is a tuple $s = (a_1, a_2, \ldots, a_n) \in A^n$ where A denotes the set of all actions that are executable on the SUT. Some actions are only available in certain states, so not all input sequences are *feasible*. Since many sequences are infeasible, it can be helpful to employ a model of the GUI. Many of the current approaches use an Event Flow Graph (EFG) which is a directed graph whose nodes are the actions that a user can perform. A transition between action x and action y means: *y is available after execution of x*. By traversing the edges of this graph one can generate sequences offline, i.e. without starting the SUT. It is possible to automatically obtain an EFG by employing a *GUI-Ripper* [13]. Unfortunately the generated EFG is not guaranteed to be complete and needs manual verification.

Since the model is only an approximation, it is still possible to generate infeasible sequences. E.g. in Figure 2 we could generate $s = (Edit, Paste)$. However, since in most applications the *Paste* menu entry is disabled or invisible until a *Copy* action has occurred, the execution of s is likely to fail.

Appropriate Adequacy Criteria. Before one can apply optimization techniques, it has to be defined what constitutes a good test sequence. Several criteria have been proposed for GUI testing. In addition to classic ones like code coverage, covering arrays [3] and criteria based on the EFG (e.g. all nodes / all edges) [15] have been employed. Choosing the right criteria is criticial to finding faults.

Exercising the GUI. Modern GUIs are quite complex, have lots of different kinds of widgets and allow various types of actions to be performed by the user. It takes a lot of effort to implement a tool that is able to obtain the state of the GUI and can derive a set of sensible actions. One first has to determine the position of all visible widgets and the state they are in. E.g. if a button is disabled, it would not make sense to perform a click, since the event handler would not be

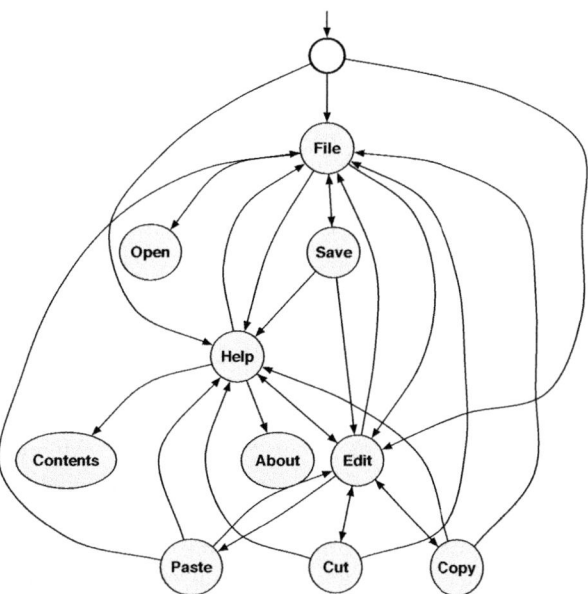

Fig. 2. Part of an Event Flow Graph of a typical GUI based application. The nodes correspond to clicks on menu items.

invoked. Likewise if a message box is on top of all windows and blocks input to them, it would not be effective to perform actions on controls other than the ones within the message box.

This paper proposes a new approach to input sequence generation for GUI testing, based on ant colony optimization. Our work differs from the existing approaches in that we use a relatively new criterion to direct our optimization process. We try to generate sequences that induce a large call tree within the SUT. The maximum call tree criterion (MCT) has been used by McMaster et al. [11] to minimize existing test suites. Similar to Kasik et al. [7] we generate our sequences online, i.e. by executing the SUT. Thus we do not need a model and do not have to deal with infeasibility. We developed a test execution environment, which allows a rich set of action types to be performed (clicks, drag and drop operations, input via keyboard). This way we can exercise even very complex SUTs like graphical editors.

In the following section we will look at related work. Section 3 discusses the adequacy criterion, presents our test execution environment and the search algorithm. In section 4 we present first results by comparing our technique to random sequence generation. Section 5 concludes the paper and reviews the approach.

2   Related Work

Kasik et al.[7] try to find novice user sequences by employing genetic algorithms. Their implementation captures the widget tree of the GUI at any given time. They consider only actions that are executable on the current widget tree and can thus generate arbitrary feasible input sequences. They reward actions that cause the GUI to stay on the same dialog based on the observation that novice users learn the behaviour of a GUI's functions through experimentation with different parameters within the same dialog. Their program usually starts with an existing input sequence, where the tester may insert a *DEVIATE* command. It then deviates this part of the sequence and tries to make it look like it was created by a novice user. By supplying just a single *DEVIATE* command, the program generates an entire sequence from scratch. However, according to the authors this gives quite random results which do not resemble novice user sequences. There are two possible modes: meander and pullback. Meander mode simply turns over control to the genetic algorithm whenever it encounters a *DEVIATE* command. It does not return to the remainder of the sequence, that follows the *DEVIATE* command. In Pullback mode the authors give reward for returning to the rest of the sequence, e.g. when an action reaches the same window of the action that the program tries to return to (the first action of the rest of the sequence). It is not mentioned how the crossover and mutation operators work and what type of subject applications have been used. Thus it is hard to say how well their implementation will perform on real world subject applications.

Memon et al. [6] use genetic algorithms to fix broken test suites. They create an EFG for the GUI and try to find a *covering array* to sample from the sequence space. A covering array $CA(N, t, k, v)$ is an $N \times k$ array (N sequences of length k over v symbols). In such an array all t-tuples over the v symbols are contained within every $N \times t$ sub-array. A covering array makes it possible to sample from the sequence space. Instead of trying all permuations of actions (which are exponentially many) only the set of sequences that contains all t-length tuples in every position are considered. The parameter t determines the strength of the sampling process.

Their array is constrained by the EFG (certain combinations of actions are not permitted). Since it is hard to find such a constrained covering array, they employ a special metaheuristic based on simulated annealing [5]. This way they get their initial test suite which, due to the fact that the EFG is only an approximation of the GUI, contains infeasible input sequences. Their next step is to identify these sequences and drop them. By doing that, they lose coverage regarding the coverage array. Thus they use a genetic algorithm which utilizes the EFG to generate new sequences offline, which will then be executed and rewarded depending on how many of their actions are executable and on how much coverage they restore. Infeasible sequences are penalized by adding a large static value. They pair the individuals in descending order to process a one-point-crossover, mutate them and use elitism selection. Their stopping criteria are: maximum number of generations and maximum number of bad moves (if the best individual of the current population is worse than the best of the last one, it is considered a bad move). The algorithm also stops if the best individual of the population already contains the maximum number of t-tuples. The authors tested their approach on small subject applications with 3 to 5 different *"button click"* actions.

Rauf et al. [16] use a similar technique, also employing an EFG. They have a set of short handcrafted input sequences, from which they want to generate a longer one that contains the short ones as subsequences. A possible use case for this approach is not mentioned within the paper.

Yongzhong et al. [9] seem to take a similar approach, except that they use ant colony optimization instead. Their work is hard to evaluate since they do not provide information on their fitness function.

3   Our Approach

In this section we will first explain the employed MCT metric and the motivation behind it. We will proceed with a quick insight into our execution environment and conclude with a pseudocode listing of our optimization algorithm. This listing will also present our fitness function.

3.1   Adequacy Criterion

For this work, we adopt a relatively new criterion that McMaster et al. [11] used to reduce the size of existing test suites. They instrumented the Java virtual machine of an application to obtain method call trees (see Figure 4) for runs of their SUT. They started with an existing test suite which they executed, to obtain the method call tree for each sequence. They merged all these trees into a single large tree and determined the number of its leaves. Then they went on to remove those test cases which did not cause the tree to shrink significantly. This means that they kept only the sequences which contributed the majority of the leaves. After this process, the reduced versions of the test suites still revealed most of the known faults. Thus we think that this strategy could be suitable for sequence generation. Our goal will be to find sequences that generate a call tree with a maximal number of leaves upon execution on the SUT. Throughout the rest of this paper, we will refer to this metric as MCT.

Figures 3 and 4 show a Java program and its corresponding method call tree. The tree is just a simplification of the much larger original version, which would also contain the methods of classloaders and Java library code. In fact there would be several thread call trees for the given program, since different threads are used for virtual machine initialization, cleanup, the garbage collector etc. In order to obtain the MCT metric, we merge all these thread trees into a single program call tree and count its leaves. Figure 5 illustrates this process. We introduce a new root node and merge threads with the same run() method into the same subtrees.

The idea behind the MCT metric is as follows: The larger the program call tree, the more contexts the methods of the SUT are tested in. For example: If

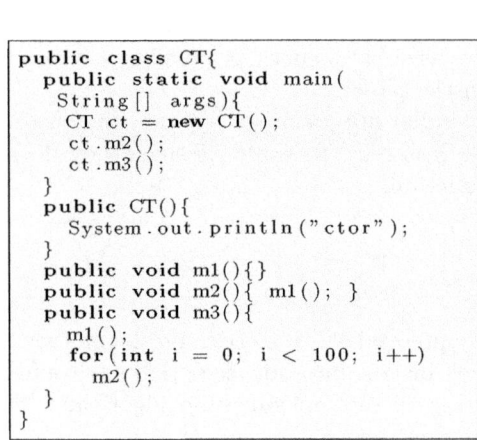

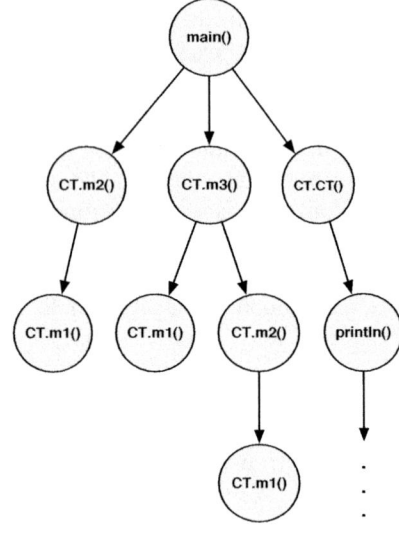

Fig. 3. Java program

Fig. 4. Simplified call tree for the main thread of the program in Figure 3 (library code partly omitted)

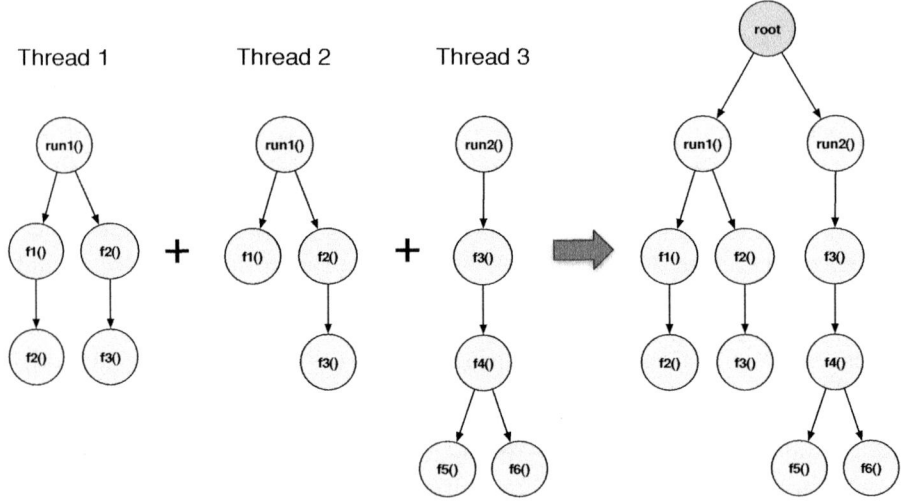

Fig. 5. Merging thread call trees into a single program call tree

we look at Figure 4 we can see that the method m1() appears in three different contexts. The ancestor methods, namely m2(), m3() and main() establish the context that m1() is invoked in, because they potentially modify variables that m1() might depend on directly or indirectly and thus affect its behaviour. So the premise is: The larger the call tree, the more aspects of the SUT are tested. The experiment of McMaster et al. gave first evidence of this.

One of the advantages of the MCT metric is, that no source code is required to obtain it. In addition the metric tracks activities within third-party modules and thus is suitable for testing the SUT as a whole. McMaster et al. [11] provide an implementation that is able to obtain the call tree generated by an input sequence. They developed solutions for Java- and C- based applications[1]. Their Java version employs the *Java Virtual Machine Tool Interface* (JVMTI), which provides callbacks for various events, like Thread-Start / -End, Method-Entry / -Exit. This way a call tree can be generated for every thread. Table 1 shows the results of applying their implementation to three simple programs. We can see that the MCT metric captures activities within third-party modules (here the Java library). Depending on the parameters supplied to println(), different methods are invoked and hence different call trees are generated.

Unfortunately the JVMTI prevents the virtual machine from doing important optimizations [8]. This not only degrades runtime performance, but might destabilize the SUT and thus introduce artificial faults. Since we encountered slowdowns of up to factor 30 and crashes with our main SUT, we developed our own solution using byte code instrumentation. We insert static method calls at the beginning and end of each method to obtain the call tree. This technique is frequently used by Java profilers [2].

Table 1. Three simple programs (main class and main method omitted) and the corresponding MCT metric. The programs have been executed on a Sun JVM on Windows XP.

Code	# Call Tree Leaves
System.out.println("");	716
System.out.println("Hello World!");	748
System.out.println("Hello\nWorld!");	750

3.2   Test Environment

This section gives a short introduction to our test environment, which enables us to operate the SUT, i.e. click on controls, type in text and perform drag and drop operations. In order to do this, it needs to be able to

1. scan the GUI of the SUT to obtain all visible widgets and their properties (size, position, focus etc.),
2. derive a set of interesting actions (e.g. a visible, enabled button on a foreground window, is clickable),

---

[1] http://sourceforge.net/projects/javacctagent/

3. give these actions unique names, so that we can refer to them in subsequent runs of the SUT,

4. execute sequences of these actions.

One could try to take advantage of the various commercial and open-source scripting and capture and replay tools. We tested *TestComplete*[2], *SWT-Bot*[3] and *WindowTester*[4]. Unfortunately all of these tools lack the capabilities outlined in 2. and 3.[5] They are good at recording and replaying, but expect the user to supply the right actions. Thus we implemented our own tool, which is able to exercise nearly all types of SWT widgets.

Figure 6 outlines the process of generating a feasible input sequence. 1. We start the SUT and 2. perform the byte code instrumentation, which is necessary to obtain the method call tree at the end of the execution cycle. 3. Then we scan the GUI to obtain all widgets and their properties. That means we determine the bounding rectangles of buttons, menus and other widgets and detect whether they are enabled, have the focus etc. From this information we are able to 4. compile a set of possible actions. In Figure 8 we can see a selection of actions that can be performed within our main SUT, the *Classification Tree Editor*[6]. We only consider "interesting actions". For example: A click on a greyed out, i.e. disabled, menu item would not make sense since no event handler would be invoked. 5. Our optimization algorithm then selects an appropriate action and 6. executes it. We repeat steps 3 to 6 until we generated a sequence of a specified length. 7. Then we stop the SUT and count the number of leaves of our call tree.

Figure 7 shows the components of our test environment. All of the above functionality is packaged in a so called JavaAgent, which is attached to the virtual machine of the SUT. Thus it has access to each loaded class and object, including the widget objects. It obtains the necessary information and sends it to the optimization component which selects the actions that are to be performed. At the end of a sequence the optimization component retrieves the MCT metric from the agent.

Our implementation is also able to obtain the thrown exceptions during a run. If these exceptions are "suspicious" or caused the SUT to crash, the corresponding sequence will be stored in a special file for later inspection.

3.3 The Algorithm

We will now describe our search-algorithm. We consider fixed-length input sequences of the form $s = (a_1, a_2, a_3, \ldots, a_n) \in A^n$ where A denotes the set of all actions within the SUT. We are trying to find a sequence $s^* \in A^n$ such that

---

[2] http://smartbear.com/products/qa-tools/automated-testing/

[3] http://www.eclipse.org/swtbot/

[4] http://code.google.com/javadevtools/wintester/html/index.html

[5] TestComplete has a naming scheme, but it doesn't work for all SWT widgets.

[6] http://www.berner-mattner.com/en/berner-mattner-home/products/cte/index-cte-ueberblick.html

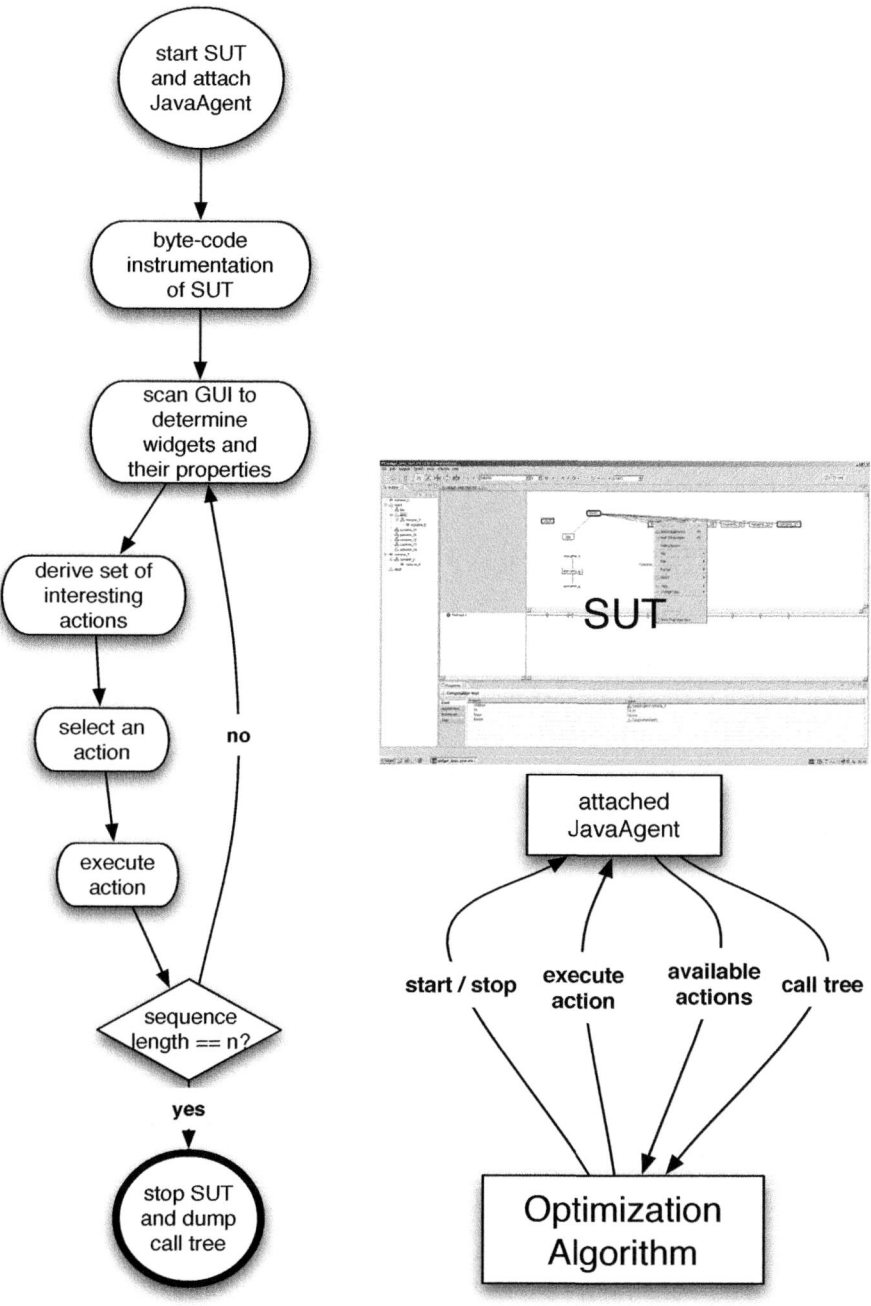

Fig. 6. Sequence generation   **Fig. 7.** Components of our framework

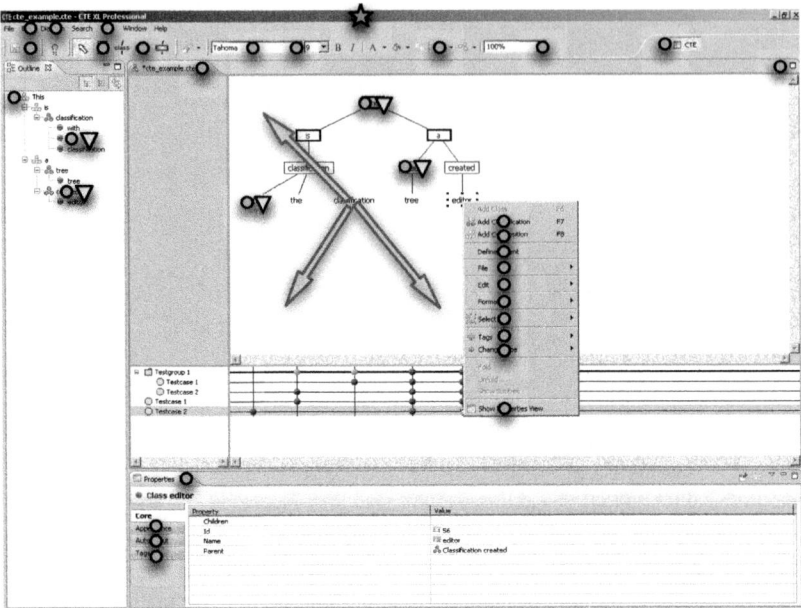

Fig. 8. Possible actions that can be performed on our SUT (green circles: left clicks, yellow triangles: right clicks, blue arrows: drag and drop operations, green stars: double clicks). These are not all possible actions, but only a selection, to preserve clarity.

$q^* = fitness(s^*) = max\{fitness(s)|s \in A^n\}$, where $fitness(s)$ returns the size of the method call tree generated by s, i.e. the MCT metric.

Due to the fact that not every action a is available at all states of the SUT, we cannot arbitrarily combine actions, but have to make sure that our algorithm produces feasible permutations. Classical metaheuristics like simulated annealing or genetic algorithms make use of a mutation operator which, depending on certain parameters, makes small or large changes to candidate solutions. The first issue here is, that in our case the operator has to maintain closure, i.e. its application should not affect the feasibility of sequences. Due to the unknown dependencies among the actions, it is hard to implement such an operator. Furthermore it is unclear what constitutes a *small* or *large* change of a sequence. If we substitute an action at position i, the rest of the sequence might have to undergo a complete change too, in order to maintain feasibility.

Thus we would like to bypass the implementation of such an operator and rather use metaheuristics where it is not necessary. This led us to consider ant colony optimization (ACO), which is an approach to combinatorial optimization [10]. Since ACO does not make use of a mutation operator, we think it is more suitable for the generation of input sequences than for example genetic algorithms.

ACO is a population-oriented metaheuristic, that means in contrast to methods such as hill climbing or simulated annealing, which constantly tweak a single candidate solution, ACO maintains an entire pool of so called ant trails which correspond to our input sequences. Each generation it builds several trails by selecting components from a set C (in our case $C = A$). The likelihood of a component $c \in C$ being chosen, is determined by its pheromone value p_c. After assessing the fitness of each trail, the pheromones of the components contained within that trail are updated according to the fitness value. Thus the pheromones tell us about the history of a component and how often it participated in high-quality solutions.

Algorithm 1. $maximizeSeq(popsize, seqlength)$

Output: Sequence that generates a large call tree upon execution.
begin
    $p \leftarrow \langle p_1, \ldots, p_l \rangle$;   `/* initialize pheromones */`
    $best \leftarrow \square$;   `/* best trail discovered so far */`
    $bestValue \leftarrow 0$;   `/* fitness of best trail */`

    while $\neg stoppingCriteria()$ **do**
        for $i = 1$ *to popsize* **do**
            startSUT()
            for $j = 1$ *to seqlength* **do**
                $E \leftarrow$ scanGuiForActions()
                $t_{ij} \leftarrow pseudoProportionateActionSelection(p, E)$
            shutdownSUT()
            $q_i \leftarrow fitness(t_i)$
            if $bestValue < q_i$ **then**
                $bestValue \leftarrow q_i$
                $best \leftarrow t_i$
        $p \leftarrow adjustPheromones(t, q, p)$
    return best
end

Algorithm 2. fitness(seq)

Input: sequence seq to evaluate
Output: fitness value of the sequence seq.
begin
    return number of leaves of the call tree generated by seq
end

Algorithm 1 outlines our overall strategy. It does the optimization work and tries to find a sequence that generates a large call tree. At the end of each generation we pick the k best rated trails and use them to update the pheromones of the contained actions. Our pheromone update rule for an action a_i is as follows: $p_i = (1 - \alpha) \cdot p_i + \alpha \cdot r_i$, where r_i is the average fitness of all trails that a_i appeared in and α the evaporation rate, as described in [4].

During the construction of a trail, we select the components (the available actions) according to the pseudo random proportional rule described by Dorigo et al.[4]. With probability ρ we select the action with the highest pheromone value, with probability $1 - \rho$ we perform a random proportionate selection.

At the moment our stopping criterion is a fixed limit on the number of generations. In the future we will employ more sophisticated criteria like for example the number of bad moves.

4   Experiment

To get a first impression of how well the optimization algorithm performs, we compared it to a random generation strategy. The *Classification Tree Editor*, a graphical editor for classification trees, served as our SUT. Table 2 shows the parameters and results of the random and ACO runs. k is the number of top-k sequences in every generation, which were used for the pheromone update. ρ is the probability parameter for the pseudo proportional random selection rule, and α is the pheromone evaporation rate. Both runs generated 6000 sequences. Figures 9 and 10 show the course of the optimization processes. The ACO algorithm eventually found a sequence with $MCT_{ACO} = 144082$, whereas the best sequence found by the random algorithm has $MCT_{Random} = 91587$. Although the quality of the candidate solutions significantly improved towards the end of

Table 2. Parameters and results of the runs

desc	k	α	ρ	popsize	generations	seqlength	pheromone default	best MCT	duration
ACO	15	0.3	0.7	20	300	10	30000	144082	12.5 h
Random	all	0.0	0.0	20	300	10	30000	91587	12.5 h

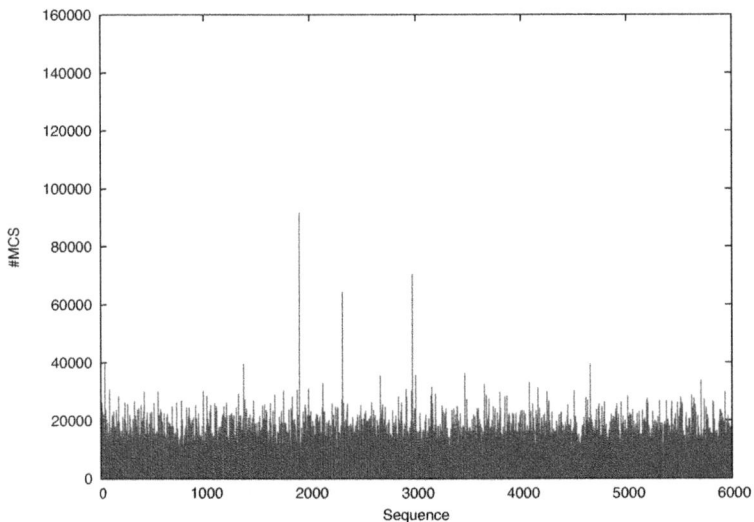

Fig. 9. Random run

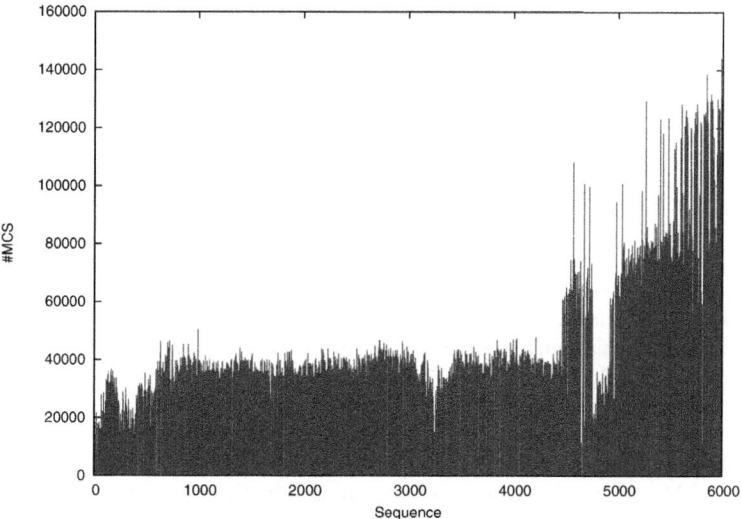

Fig. 10. ACO run

the ACO run, the algorithm might have performed better, but due to our rather simple stopping criterion (fixed number of generations) the optimization process probably terminated prematurely. In future experiments we will employ more sophisticated criteria to determine when to stop.

5   Conclusion

In this paper we proposed an approach to automatic generation of input sequences for applications with a GUI. Our approach differs from earlier works in the way we tackle the optimization problem. We use dynamic feedback from the SUT in the form of the MCT metric to direct the search process. Since we forgo the application of a GUI model, we do not have the problem of generating infeasible sequences. We implemented a test environment which enables us to generate arbitrary input sequences for Java SWT applications. Our optimization algorithm employs ant colony optimization with the pseudo proportional random selection rule. A first experiment showed that the implementation worked, that the algorithm continuously improved the candidate solutions and eventually found a better sequence than the random strategy. In future works we will carry out additional experiments to analyze the fault revealing capabilities of the generated sequences. Our goal is to take a set of different applications with known faults and generate test suites for them. We will then determine the amount of faults discovered by these test suites.

186   S. Bauersfeld, S. Wappler, and J. Wegener

Acknowledgements. This work is supported by EU grant ICT-257574 (FITTEST).

References

1. Baresel, A., Sthamer, H., Schmidt, M.: Fitness function design to improve evolutionary structural testing. In: Langdon, W.B., Cantú-Paz, E., Mathias, K.E., Roy, R., Davis, D., Poli, R., Balakrishnan, K., Honavar, V., Rudolph, G., Wegener, J., Bull, L., Potter, M.A., Schultz, A.C., Miller, J.F., Burke, E.K., Jonoska, N. (eds.) GECCO, pp. 1329–1336. Morgan Kaufmann, San Francisco (2002)
2. Binder, W., Hulaas, J., Moret, P., Villazón, A.: Platform-independent profiling in a virtual execution environment. Software: Practice and Experience (2008)
3. Cohen, M.B., Gibbons, P.B., Mugridge, W.B., Colbourn, C.J.: Constructing test suites for interaction testing. In: Proceedings of the 25th International Conference on Software Engineering, ICSE 2003, pp. 38–48. IEEE Computer Society Press, Washington, DC, USA (2003)
4. Dorigo, M., Blum, C.: Ant colony optimization theory: a survey. Theor. Comput. Sci. 344, 243–278 (2005)
5. Garvin, B.J., Cohen, M.B., Dwyer, M.B.: An improved meta-heuristic search for constrained interaction testing. In: Proceedings of the 2009 1st International Symposium on Search Based Software Engineering, SSBSE 2009, pp. 13–22. IEEE Computer Society Press, Washington, DC, USA (2009)
6. Huang, S., Cohen, M.B., Memon, A.M.: Repairing gui test suites using a genetic algorithm. In: ICST 2010: Proceedings of the 2010 Third International Conference on Software Testing, Verification and Validation, pp. 245–254. IEEE Computer Society Press, Washington, DC, USA (2010)
7. Kasik, D.J., George, H.G.: Toward automatic generation of novice user test scripts. In: CHI 1996: Proceedings of the SIGCHI conference on Human factors in computing systems, pp. 244–251. ACM, New York (1996)
8. Kurzyniec, D., Sunderam, V.: Efficient cooperation between java and native codes – jni performance benchmark. In: The 2001 International Conference on Parallel and Distributed Processing Techniques and Applications (2001)
9. Lu, Y., Yan, D., Nie, S., Wang, C.: Development of an improved gui automation test system based on event-flow graph. In: International Conference on Computer Science and Software Engineering, vol. 2, pp. 712–715 (2008)
10. Luke, S.: Essentials of Metaheuristics. Lulu (2009), http://cs.gmu.edu/~sean/book/metaheuristics/
11. McMaster, S., Memon, A.: Call-stack coverage for gui test suite reduction. IEEE Transactions on Software Engineering 34, 99–115 (2008)
12. McMinn, P.: Search-based software test data generation: a survey: Research articles. Softw. Test. Verif. Reliab. 14, 105–156 (2004)
13. Memon, A., Banerjee, I., Nagarajan, A.: Gui ripping: Reverse engineering of graphical user interfaces for testing. In: Proceedings of the 10th Working Conference on Reverse Engineering, WCRE 2003, IEEE Computer Society Press, Washington, DC, USA (2003)
14. Memon, A.M.: A comprehensive framework for testing graphical user interfaces. Ph.D, Advisors: Mary Lou Soffa and Martha Pollack; Committee members: Prof. Rajiv Gupta (University of Arizona), Prof. Adele E. Howe (Colorado State University), Prof. Lori Pollock (University of Delaware) (2001)

15. Memon, A.M., Soffa, M.L., Pollack, M.E.: Coverage criteria for gui testing. In: ESEC/FSE-9: Proceedings of the 8th European Software Engineering Conference held Jointly with 9th ACM SIGSOFT International Symposium on Foundations of Software Engineering, pp. 256–267. ACM, New York (2001)
16. Rauf, A., Anwar, S., Jaffer, M.A., Shahid, A.A.: Automated gui test coverage analysis using ga. In: Third International Conference on Information Technology: New Generations, pp. 1057–1062 (2010)
17. Wappler, S., Wegener, J.: Evolutionary unit testing of object-oriented software using strongly-typed genetic programming. In: Cattolico, M. (ed.) GECCO, pp. 1925–1932. ACM, New York (2006)

Integration Test of Classes and Aspects with a Multi-Evolutionary and Coupling-Based Approach

Thelma Elita Colanzi, Wesley Klewerton Guez Assunção,
Silvia Regina Vergilio, and Aurora Pozo*

DInf - Federal University of Paraná, CP: 19081, CEP 19031-970, Curitiba, Brazil
{thelmae,wesleyk,silvia,aurora}@inf.ufpr.br

Abstract. The integration test of aspect-oriented systems involves the determination of an order to integrate and test classes and aspects, which should be associated to a minimal possible stubbing cost. To determine such order is not trivial because different factors influence on the stubbing process. Many times these factors are in conflict and diverse good solutions are possible. Due to this, promising results have been obtained with multi-objective and evolutionary algorithms that generally optimize two coupling measures: number of attributes and methods. However, the problem can be more effectively addressed considering as many as coupling measures could be associated to the stubbing process. Therefore, this paper introduces MECBA, a Multi-Evolutionary and Coupling-Based Approach to the test and integration order problem, which includes the definition of models to represent the dependency between modules and to quantify the stubbing costs. The approach is instantiated and evaluated considering four AspectJ programs and four coupling measures. The results represent a good trade-off between the objectives and an example of use of the obtained results shows how they can be used to reduce test effort and costs.

Keywords: Integration testing, aspect-oriented software, multi-objective evolutionary algorithms.

1 Introduction

Similarly to object-oriented (OO) software test, the test of aspect-oriented (AO) programs comprises different phases [19,29]. A first phase includes the test of each class, by testing its methods and crosscutting concerns. After this, in the integration test phase, the interactions among classes and aspects are tested, and to do this, different strategies have been proposed in the last years [6,19,29]. These strategies are derived from the knowledge acquired from the OO context and due to this, as it happens with other activities in AOSD (Aspect-Oriented Software Development), we find similar integration problems in both contexts.

---

* We thank to CNPq and CAPES for financial support and to Edison K. Fillus.

M.B. Cohen and M. Ó Cinnéide (Eds.): SSBSE 2011, LNCS 6956, pp. 188–203, 2011.

An example of an inherited problem is known as CITO (Class Integration and Test Order) problem [1], which involves to determine an optimal order to integrate and test classes that minimizes stub creation costs. In the AO context, it is called CAITO (Class and Aspect Integration and Test Order) problem [12]. To determine such sequences different factors that influence on the stubbing process should be considered and this is not always a trivial task, mainly due to the existence of dependency cycles among modules (either a class or aspect). A recent study shows that is very common to find complex dependency cycles in Java programs [20]. In the AO context many researches [25] found crosscutting concerns that are dependent of other crosscutting concerns, which imply in dependency between aspects, and between classes and aspects. Hence, this fact motivated studies to solve the problem in both contexts.

Most existing strategies are graph-based and consider characteristics of OO software [1,4,18,26,27]. These strategies have been recently extended to the AO context [24,25], however, graph-based strategies are not satisfactory because in many cases sub-optimal solutions are found. Furthermore, they need some adaptation to consider different possible factors and measures that affect the stub construction. To reduce such limitations, in the OO context, bio-inspired strategies are very promising [3,5], particularly that one based on Multi-Objective Evolutionary Algorithms (MOEAs), which presented the best results [2,22].

The use of evolutionary algorithms in the AO context is recent. Galvan et al [12] introduced a Genetic Algorithm (GA) to solve the CAITO problem. The algorithm obtained better results than the traditional graph-based strategies. The GA allows the use of different factors to establish the test orders by using a fitness function based on an aggregation of objectives to be minimized (a weighted average of number of operations and number of attributes). However, this fitness function requires the tester adjusts the weight of each objective, and the choice of the more adequate weights for the GA is a labor intensive task for complex cases and makes difficult the use of the GA-based strategy in practice. To overcome this limitation, in a previous work [9] we explored the use of two MOEAs to the CAITO problem: NSGA-II and SPEA2. These algorithms have achieved solutions of minimal effort to test, considering two objectives: number of attributes and methods to be handled by the created stubs.

Motivated by the results obtained in previous works from the OO context [2,22] and AO context with two objectives [9], this work introduces an approach, named MECBA (Multi-Evolutionary and Coupling-Based Approach) to solve the integration order problem. The approach consists of some generic steps that include the definition of models to represent the dependency between modules and to quantify the stubbing costs, and the optimization through multi-objective algorithms. At the end, a set of good solutions is produced and used by the tester according to test goals and resources.

The approach is instantiated and evaluated considering specific dependency relations of the AO context, with four real AspectJ programs and four coupling measures. Nevertheless, it is important to know the MOEAs behavior for the CAITO problem with several objectives. It is known that they are efficient to solve this problem with two objectives [9], but in some cases the performance of MOEAs significantly deteriorates with more than two objectives. So, this is also a research question to be evaluated in the present work.

The paper is organized as follows. Section 2 reviews related works. Section 3 introduces the MECBA approach and shows how it was applied in our study. Section 4 describes an empirical evaluation. Section 4.3 contains some examples of how to use the achieved solutions. Finally, Section 5 concludes the paper and points out future research works.

2 The Class and Aspect Integration Test Order Problem

The CAITO problem has been solved from adaptations of existing strategies proposed to the similar problem in OO context. In general, they are based on directed graphs, named Object Relation Diagrams (ORDs) [18]. In such graphs the vertexes represent the classes, and their relations are edges. When there are no dependency cycles in the graph, the solution is found with a simple reverse topological ordering of classes considering their dependency. However, in most cases, when dependency cycles are present, this ordering can not be applied. Hence, strategies were proposed to break the cycles and produce an order that minimizes stubbing costs [1,4,18,26,27]. A disadvantage of all the graph-based solutions is that they are very hard to be adapted to consider many factors that are involved in the stub creation, such as number of calls or distinct methods, constraints related to organizational or contractual reasons, etc [3]. Other limitation is that they work to reduce broken cycles, but, there are cases where breaking two dependencies has a lower cost than breaking only one, and the solutions can be sub-optimal.

To overcome these limitations, Briand et al [3] explore the use of a GA and use fitness functions based on two coupling measures besides the dependency factor: the number of methods and attributes necessary for the stubbing process. Cabral et al [5] investigated a solution based on the Ant Colony algorithm by using Pareto concepts [21] to treat the CITO problem as multi-objective. In multi-objective problems, the objectives to be optimized are usually in conflict, which means that they do not have a single solution. The goal is to find a good trade-off of solutions representing a possible compromise among the objectives. These solutions are named non-dominated and form the Pareto front [21]. Given a set of possible solutions to the problem, the solution A dominates a solution B if A is better than B at least in one objective, and A is not worse than B in any other remaining objectives. In most applications, the search for the Pareto optimal is NP-hard [16], then the optimization focuses on finding an approximation set to the Pareto front. Multi-objective optimization algorithms are being widely applied in several areas, such as Search Based Software Engineering [13,14,15], to solve problems with many interdependent interests (objectives).

The multi-objective approach presents better solutions than the function based on aggregation of Briand et al. Furthermore, this approach does not need weights adjustments and generates a set of good solutions to be used by the tester. In [22] the authors evaluate the multi-objective approach with three different algorithms, and NSGA-II, the evolutionary one, obtained the best results. This algorithm was also used with different coupling measures [2].

In the AO context, these strategies have been extended for integration of classes and aspects. In such context, other relations and ways to combine the aspects are necessary. The work of Ceccato et al [6] uses a strategy in which the classes are first tested without integrating aspects. After this, the aspects are integrated and tested with the classes, and, at the end, the classes are tested in the presence of the aspects. Solutions based on graphs were investigated by Ré et al [24,25]. The authors propose an extended ORD to consider dependency relations between classes and aspects, and different graph-based strategies to perform the integration and test of AO software. They are: i) Combined: aspects and classes are integrated and tested together; ii) Incremental+: first only classes are integrated and tested, and after only aspects are integrated and tested; iii) Reverse: applies the reverse combined order; and iv) Random: applies a random selected order. As a result of the study, the Combined and Incremental+ strategies performed better than the others, producing a lower number of stubs.

The use of evolutionary algorithms in the AO context is recent. Galvan et al [12] introduced a simple and mono-objective GA that uses an aggregation of functions to the CAITO problem. This algorithm presented better solutions than the strategies based on graphs proposed by Ré et al. We did not find works exploring the use of multi-objective algorithms in the AO context, despite of its promising use in the OO context [2,5,22]. Because of this, we explored in a previous work [9] the use of MOEAs to establish integration test orders for AO programs. However, we used only two objectives, traditionally used in the related works. To investigate the use of other measures and the MOEAs performance in such situation, in the next section, we describe an approach based on multi-objective optimization and Pareto's concepts to solve the CAITO problem.

3   The MECBA Approach

As mentioned before, in a previous work [9], we explored the use of two MOEAs to establish integration test orders of aspects and classes considering two objectives: number of attributes and methods. The ideas explored in that work serve as basis for the approach, named here Multi-Evolutionary and Coupling-Based Approach (MECBA). MECBA includes a set of steps that produce artifacts that can be used in a generic way, and allows the use of different coupling measures for solving the integration order problem. Next, these steps are described and possible entries and artifacts produced in each step are illustrated. This instantiation example for MECBA is used in its evaluation presented in Section 4.

3.1   Construction of the Dependency Model

This step produces a representation of the dependency relations to be considered; they can be between classes, between aspects and between classes and aspects. Different restrictions to some kind of dependency can also be represented. The

dependency model used in our evaluation is the extended ORD proposed by
Ré et al [24,25] with the Combined strategy. This strategy seems to be more
practical and realistic than the other ones, since classes and aspects probably
are tested together if both are under development. An example of extended ORD
is presented in Figure 1. To a better visualization, classes are on the left side of
the figure and aspects are on the right.

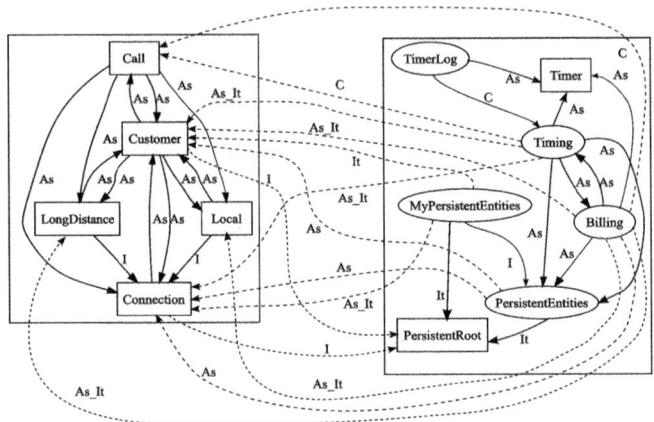

Fig. 1. Extended ORD (extracted from [25])

Considering the aspects mechanisms, the following new relationships between
vertexes are possible:

- Crosscutting Association (C) represents the association generated by a point-
  cut with a class method or other advice. In Figure 1 it is illustrated between
  the aspect `Billing` and class `Call`;
- Use Dependency (U) is generated by a relation between advices and pointcuts, and between pointcuts;
- Association Dependency (As) occurs between objects involved in pointcuts.
  This is shown in Figure 1 by the relationship between `Timing` and `Customer`;
- Inter-type Declaration Dependency (It) occurs when there are inter-type relationships between aspects and the base class. For example an aspect Aa
  declares that class A extends B. In the example there is this kind of dependency between `Billing` and `Local`; and among `MyPersistentEntities`,
  `PersistentRoot` and `Connection`;
- Inheritance Dependency (I) represents inheritance relationships among aspects or among classes and aspects. An example in Figure 1 is the aspects
  `PersistentEntities` and `MyPersistentEntities`.

3.2   Definition of the Cost Model

This step defines a cost model. Different coupling measures that qualify a dependency can be used, such as coupling, cohesion and time constraints. They are

in fact the objectives to be minimized that contribute to increase costs. In this work, we use four coupling measures, adapted from related works [1,2,3,9,12,25]. Considering that: (i) m_i and m_j are two coupled modules and m_i depends on m_j, (ii) modules are either classes or aspects, and (iii) the *operation* term represents class methods, aspect methods and aspect advices. The measures are defined as:

Attribute Coupling (A): number of attributes locally declared in m_j when references or pointers to instances of m_j appear in the argument list of some operations in m_i, as the type of their return value, in the list of attributes (data members) of m_i, or as local parameters of operations of m_i. It counts the (maximum) number of attributes that would have to be handled in the stub if the dependency were broken. In the case of inheritance, we do not count the number of attributes inherited from the ancestor classes, as in [3].

Operation Coupling (O): number of operations (including constructors) locally declared in m_j which are invoked by operations of m_i. It counts the number of operations that would have to be emulated in the stub if the dependency were broken. In the case of inheritance, we count the number of operations declared in the ancestor modules.

Number of distinct return types (R): number of distinct return types of the operations locally declared in m_j that are called by operations of m_i. Returns of type void are not counted as return type, since they represent the absence of return. In the case of inheritance, we count the number of operations declared in the ancestor modules.

Number of distinct parameter types (P): number of distinct parameters of operations locally declared in m_j and called by operations of m_i. When there is overloading operations, the number of parameters is equals to the sum of all distinct parameter types among all implementations of each overloaded operation. The worst case is considered, represented by situations in which the coupling consists of calls to all implementation of a given operation. Again, we count the number of operations declared in the ancestor modules.

The measures A and O are commonly used in the related works. In the other hand, the measures R and P allow to consider different factors related directly to the stub complexity. Furthermore, O, R and P are interdependents.

3.3   Multi-Objective Evolutionary Algorithm

This step is the application of a MOEA to solve the problem. The use of any metaheuristics includes some points. The first one is the representation chosen for the problem, which influences on the implementation of all MOEA stages. Since the CAITO problem is related to permutations of modules (classes and aspects), which form testing orders, the chromosome is represented by a vector of integers where each vector position corresponds to a module. The size of the chromosome is equal to the number of modules of each system. Thus, being each module represented by a number, an example of a valid solution for a problem with 5 modules is $(2, 4, 3, 1, 5)$. In this example, the first module to be tested and integrated would be the module represented by number 2. This representation is the same one used in our previous work [9].

The second point is related to the fitness function (objectives). It is calculated from five matrices that are inputs to the algorithms, associated to (i) dependencies between modules; (ii) measure A; (iii) measure O; (iv) measure R; and (v) measure P. Based on the dependency matrices, the precedence constraints are defined. In this work, Inheritance and Inter-types declarations dependencies cannot be broken. This means that base modules must precede child modules in any test order t. The sum of the dependencies between the modules for each measure corresponds to an objective, and the goal is to minimize all objectives.

Another point is the selection of an algorithm. In this work we use two variants of GAs adapted to multi-objective optimization that adopt different evolution and diversification strategies. They are: NSGA-II (Non-dominated Sorting Genetic Algorithm) [10] and SPEA2 (Strength Pareto Evolutionary Algorithm) [30]. This choice is supported by the results found in the OO context [2,22]. For each generation NSGA-II sorts the individuals, from parent and offspring populations, considering the non-dominance relation, creating several fronts and, after the sorting, solutions with lower dominance are discarded. These fronts characterize the elitism strategy adopted by NSGA-II. This algorithm also uses a diversity operator (crowding distance) that sorts the individuals according to their distance from the neighbors of the border for each objective, in order to ensure greater spread of solutions. SPEA2 maintains an external archive that stores non-dominated solutions in addition to its regular population. Some of them are selected for the evolutionary process. For each solution in the archive and in the population, a strength value is calculated, which is used as fitness of the individuals. The strength value of a solution i corresponds to the number j of individuals, belonging to the archive and to the population, dominated by i. The archive size s is fixed, then, when the number n of solutions exceeds s, a clustering algorithm is used to reduce n [8].

3.4   Order Selection

In this step, illustrated in Section 4.3, the tester selects an order from the Pareto front of non-dominated solutions produced by the algorithms. This selection should be based on restrictions and priorities related to the software development, such as test goals, available resources, contractual restrictions, etc.

4   MECBA Empirical Evaluation

4.1   Empirical Study Description

The methodology of our empirical study is similar to that one adopted in [9]; we use the same systems and parameters to configure the MOEAs. Differently, we adopted four quality indicators to compare the algorithms: Coverage [17] and the Euclidean Distance (ED) from an ideal solution [7], Generational Distance (GD) [28] and Inverted Generational Distance (IGD) [23]. Considering that the

MOEAs deteriorate their performance with more than two objectives, we decided to add two other quality indicators: GD and IGD, because they allow to analyze the convergence and diversity of the algorithms regarding to the Pareto front.

Four real AO systems developed in AspectJ were used in the study[1]. Table 1 presents some information about these systems, such as number of classes, aspects and dependencies. They are larger and more complex than the programs used in related works. The used objective functions consist in minimize four objectives related to the coupling measures. These measures are generally calculated during the software design, however it is difficult to obtain architectural design documentation of complex systems in order to execute empirical studies. So, reverse engineering was performed to identify the existing dependencies between modules from programs code. A parser based on AJATO[2] (AspectJ and Java Assessment Tool) was developed to do this. It uses the Java/AspectJ code as entry and returns the syntactic tree code. From this tree, all dependencies were identified. The dependency and complexity matrices were obtained after combining classes and aspects. So, the parser generated as output the five input matrices for the MOEAs.

Table 1. Used Systems

System	LOC	# Classes	# Aspects	# Dependencies						
				I	U	As	It	PointCuts	Advices	Total
AJHotDraw	18586	290	31	234	1177	140	40	0	1	1592
AJHSQLDB	68550	276	25	107	960	271	0	0	0	1338
HealthWatcher	5479	95	22	64	290	34	3	1	7	399
Toll System	2496	53	24	24	109	46	4	0	5	188

We use the NSGA-II and SPEA2 versions available at JMetal [11] with the same parameters values adopted in our previous work [9]. Such values are: population size = 300; number of fitness evaluation = 20000; mutation rate = 0.02; crossover rate = 0.95; and archive size = 250 (required only by SPEA2). Both MOEAs executed the same number of fitness evaluation in order to analyze whether they can produce similar solutions when they are restricted to the same resources (number of fitness evaluations). Furthermore, they were executed in the same computer. Each algorithm was executed 30 runs for each AO system. In each run, each MOEA found an approximation set of solutions named PF_{approx}. Furthermore, for each MOEA it is obtained a set, called PF_{known}, formed by all non-dominated solutions achieved in all runs. Considering that PF_{true} is not known, in our study, it was obtained by the union of the non-dominated solutions from all PF_{approx} found by NSGA-II and SPEA2 [31]. PF_{true} and PF_{known} were used for quality indicators GD, IGD and ED.

---

[1] Available at: AJHotDraw (version 0.4): http://sourceforge.net/projects/ajhotdraw/; AJHSQLDB (version 18): http://sourceforge.net/projects/ajhsqldb/files/; TollSystem (version 9): http://www.comp.lancs.ac.uk/~greenwop/tao/; HealthWatcher(version 9): http://www.aosd-europe.net/

[2] http://www.teccomm.les.inf.puc-rio.br/emagno/ajato/

The Generational Distance (GD) indicator [28] is used to calculate the distance from PF_{known} to PF_{true}. So, GD is an error measure used to examine the convergence of an algorithm to the PF_{true}. Inverted Generational Distance (IGD) [23] is an indicator based on GD, but with goal of evaluating the distance from PF_{true} to PF_{known}, i.e., the inverse of GD. Figure 2(a) presents an example of GD and IGD indicators. For these indicators, values closer to 0 are desired, since 0 indicates that all points of PF_{known} are points on PF_{true} for GD or PF_{known} found all the points on PF_{true} for the IGD indicator.

The Coverage (C) indicator [17] is used to measure the dominance between two sets of solutions. C(PF_a, PF_b) represents a value between 0 e 1 according to how much the set PF_b is dominated by set PF_a. Similarly, we compare C(PF_b, PF_a) to obtain how much PF_a is dominated by PF_b. Figure 2(b) presents an example of C indicator involving the analysis of two sets, for a minimization problem with two objectives. For instance, C(P_a, P_b) corresponds to 0.5 because the P_b set has two of its four elements dominated by P_a set. Value 0 for C indicates that the solutions of the former set do not dominate any element of the latter set; on the other hand, value 1 indicates that all elements of the latter set are dominated by elements of the former set.

Euclidean Distance from the Ideal Solution (ED) is used to find the closest solution to the best objectives. An ideal solution has the minimum value of each objective, considering a minimization problem [7]. These minimum values are obtained from all PF_{true}'s solutions. Figure 2(c) shows an example of calculating the ED for a minimization problem with two objectives. The purpose of this quality indicator is to find the closest solution to the ideal solution.

The results of GD, IGD and C were analyzed through Wilcoxon test in order to verify if the MOEAs are considered statistically different ($p-value <= 0.05$).

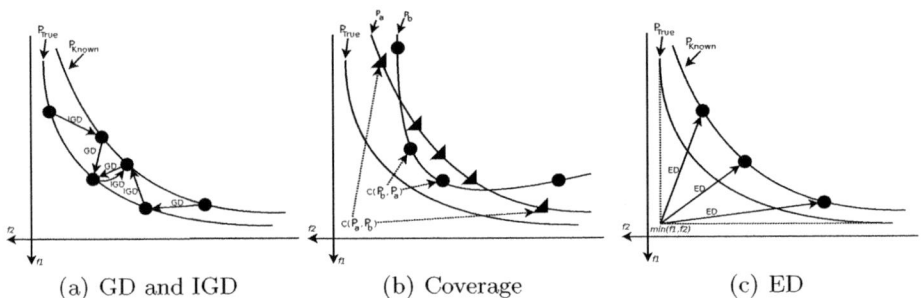

(a) GD and IGD   (b) Coverage   (c) ED

Fig. 2. Quality Indicators

4.2   Results and Analysis

Table 2 presents the number of solutions found by each MOEA and the runtime for all systems: at Column 2, the cardinality of the PF_{true} found after running all algorithms 30 times; and at Column 4, the total of different solutions of PF_{approx} returned by each algorithm. From these results, it is possible to estimate the complexity of solving the CAITO problem for each system.

Table 2. Number of solutions found and runtime

Software	PF_{true} Cardinality	MOEA	PF_{approx} Cardinality	Runtime Average	Runtime Standard Deviation
AJHotDraw	95	NSGA-II	120	35781.83	344.71
		SPEA2	51	54605.90	958.26
AJHSQLDB	105	NSGA-II	153	28209.90	200.06
		SPEA2	40	40874.07	553.38
HealthWatcher	1	NSGA-II	1	5599.70	99.18
		SPEA2	1	190734.60	47541.36
TollSystem	1	NSGA-II	1	2971.40	102.52
		SPEA2	1	223473.43	59979.78

For HealthWatcher and TollSystem both algorithms found a single and equal solution. Maybe the objectives in question are not interdependent and conflicting for these cases. The MOEAs achieved the optimal solution for HealthWatcher, i.e., an order of modules that does not need any stub. This system has only 8 cycles. Regarding to TollSystem, with only one cycle, the value achieved for the measures are A=12, O=2, R=0 and P=1. However, considering that this system has 53 classes and 24 aspects, to find the best order is not trivial for any tester. Sure, the use of a MOEA in this activity contributes to reduce efforts. In both cases, the initial solutions generated by the MOEAs were not optimal. Initially the fitness values were high and, over generations, they decreased until the discovery of the optimal solutions.

In the case of AJHotDraw and AJHSQLDB the PF_{true} has larger cardinality. For both systems, NSGA-II found more different solutions than SPEA2. Furthermore, it is notable that SPEA2 requires a higher runtime with a greater standard deviation than NSGA-II. However, it seems that there is not a direct relationship between the number of modules/dependencies and the size of solution sets found by the algorithms, since AJHotDraw has more modules and more dependencies than AJHSQLDB but the algorithms found a lower number of solutions to the former.

Regarding to the similarity of the solutions found, NSGA-II and SPEA2 achieved solutions that are located in the same area of the solution space for AJHSQLDB. In the case of AJHotDraw, the solutions are a little more spread in the solution space as it can be observed in Figures 3(a) and 3(b). Despite the algorithms minimize four objectives, the representation in graph form is possible only for two or three dimensions. Figure 3(a) represents the measures A and O, and Figure 3(b) represents measures O, R and P.

NSGA-II and SPEA2 are effective even when four objectives are used, since, they achieved similar results despite the use of different evolution strategies. Both produced a variety of good solutions that represent a good trade-off between the used coupling measures, even for complex cases.

Considering the quality indicators, it is possible to realize in Table 3 that SPEA2 dominates NSGA-II for the AJHotDraw and AJHSQLDB systems. Only values above 0.5 point out dominance and are significant. However, Wilcoxon

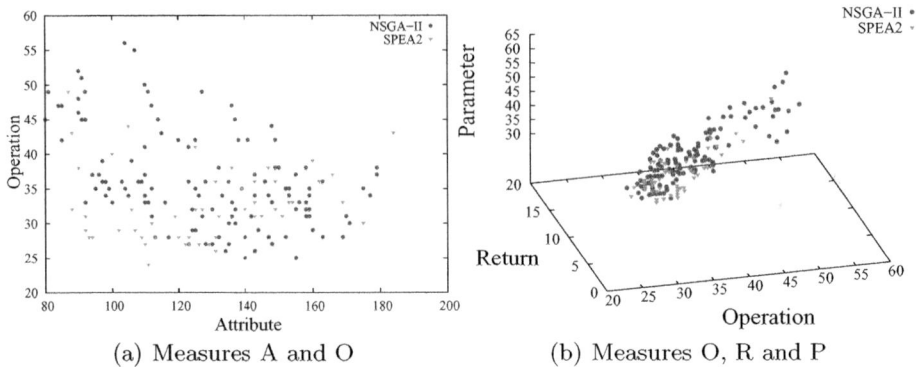

(a) Measures A and O   (b) Measures O, R and P

Fig. 3. Solution Space for AJHotDraw

Table 3. NSGA-II and SPEA2 coverages

System	C(NSGA-II,SPEA2)	C(SPEA2,NSGAII)
AJHotDraw	0.137255	0.575
AJHSQLDB	0.25	0.509804

test point out that there is not significant difference between these MOEAs when observed the Coverage indicator because the $p-values$ returned for AJHotDraw and AJHSQLDB were 0.9407 and 0.964, respectively.

For GD and IGD, the algorithms produced very similar values of average among the 30 runs (Table 4) but NSGA-II reached better average for AJHotDraw and AJHSQLDB systems. For the systems with only one solution, the values of GD and IGD are 0 because in all runs the two MOEAs achieved the same solution. The $p-values$ returned by the Wilcoxon for GD are: AJHotDraw = 0.0008203 and AJHSQLDB = 8.315e-10. For IGD the $p-values$ are: AJHotDraw = 6.264e-05 and AJHSQLDB = 1.875e-06. This indicates that there is significant difference between the algorithms for these two systems.

The costs of the ideal solutions achieved by the algorithms are presented in the second column of the Table 5. This table also presents, for each system, the lowest ED and the fitness of the associated solution. The MOEA that achieved

Table 4. Average and Standard Deviation for GD and IGD

Indicator	System	NSGA-II		SPEA2	
		Average	Standard Deviation	Average	Standard Deviation
GD	AJHotDraw	**0.043509**	0.019905	0.056029	0.017677
	AJHSQLDB	**0.042257**	0.019723	0.107550	0.061781
IGD	AJHotDraw	**0.049335**	0.025848	0.075230	0.038058
	AJHSQLDB	**0.035771**	0.014831	0.072917	0.064175

Table 5. Costs of Ideal Solution and the shortest distances found

Software	Cost of Ideal Solution	MOEA	Lowest Achieved ED	Fitness of the Solution
AJHotDraw	(80,24,0,31)	NSGA-II	24.617	(94,37,4,46)
		SPEA2	**18.385**	**(93,28,3,43)**
AJHSQLDB	(1877,446, 189,308)	NSGA-II	205.842	(2008,569,273,363)
		SPEA2	**189.365**	**(1960,562,256,413)**
HealthWatcher	(0,0,0,0)	NSGA-II	0	(0,0,0,0)
		SPEA2	0	(0,0,0,0)
Toll System	(12,2,0,1)	NSGA-II	0	(12,2,0,1)
		SPEA2	0	(12,2,0,1)

the lowest ED is typed in boldface. We can note that SPEA2 achieved the solutions with the lowest ED for AJHotDraw and AJHSQLDB. In the case of HealthWatcher and TollSystem both MOEAs achieved the ideal solution since they found a single solution.

Figure 4 shows ED from ideal solution of each solution found by MOEAs. For AJHotDraw, SPEA2 found a greater number of solutions with lower ED. For AJHSQLDB, both MOEAs have similar results, although SPEA2 has a higher number of solutions located in the left region of the graph. Thus, despite NSGA-II and SPEA2 explore the solution space in different ways, they achieve feasible solutions. Due to the great diversity of solutions, NSGA-II has the best distribution of solutions in the search space related to PF_{true}. Thus it has better performance than SPEA2 for GD and IGD indicators. In the other hand, in spite of SPEA2 has a smaller diversity of solutions, it has a good concentration of solutions near to the ideal solution, as the ED indicator shows. So, these solutions with lower ED cover some NSGA-II solutions improving the coverage rate of SPEA2 on NSGA-II. These informations can be also corroborated by analyzing Figure 3. Often, decision makers prefer solutions near to the ideal solution. So, in this case the SPEA2 should be chosen.

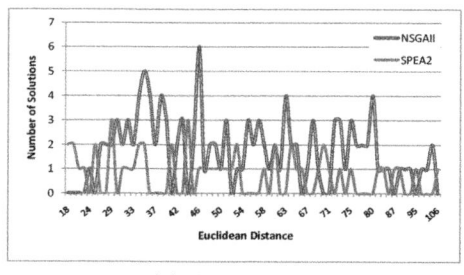

(a) AJHotDraw

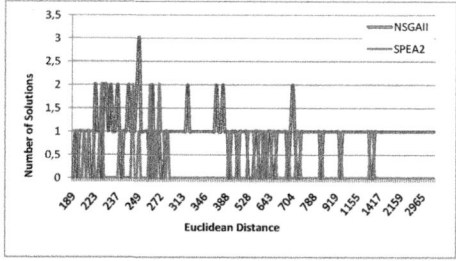

(b) AJHSQLDB

Fig. 4. Number of Solutions X Euclidean Distance

4.3   Selecting Orders

To illustrate an use of the solutions found by the MOEAs and the influence of the coupling measures, consider two solutions a and b, generated by NSGA-II for AJHotDraw, and the cost of each measure being $c(a)$ = (A=84; O=47; R=7; P=59) and $c(b)$ = (A=85; O=47; R=3; P=53). We can observe that, for the traditional measures (A and O), the solution a is better than solution b because it needs one attribute less, but considering the other measures we verify that a requires the emulation of four distinct return types and six distinct parameter types more than b. So, the cost of stub construction for the solution a is greater than for the solution b considering R and P.

The selection of a solution should be based on the measure that the tester needs to prioritize, the characteristics of the system, or other factors associated to the development process. To illustrate this, consider some SPEA2 solutions with the lowest cost for each measure for AJHotDraw and AJHSQLDB, presented in Table 6. The column Ranking corresponds to the solution position according to the ED from the ideal solution.

Table 6. Costs of Solutions achieved by SPEA2

	AJHotDraw						AJHSQLDB					
	A	**O**	**R**	**P**	Ranking	Costs		**A**	**O**	**R**	**P**	Ranking	Costs
a	**87**	49	11	52	18°		a	**1932**	675	302	424	23°	
b	111	**24**	1	43	14°		b	2436	**470**	225	335	27°	
c	102	29	**0**	44	7°	(80,24,0,31)	c	2596	493	**212**	345	36°	(80,24,0,31)
d	184	43	14	**31**	51°		d	3235	522	253	**311**	40°	
e	93	28	3	43	**1°**		e	1960	562	256	413	**1°**	

If AJHotDraw and AJHSQLDB have complex attributes to be emulated, the solutions a from Table 6 should be selected because they have the lowest complexity of attributes. If the greater complexity of the system is emulation of operations, solutions b should be selected. Likewise solutions c and d prioritize R and P, respectively. If the tester does not want to prioritize a specific measure, the best option is to use the solutions e, that are the closest solutions to the ideal solution and present the best compromise between the four objectives. It is important to note that due to the interdependence between the measures, to decrease the cost related to an objective involves to increase another one.

5   Conclusions

This paper presented MECBA, a multi-evolutionary and coupling-based approach for the integration test order problem. This approach was used for integration of classes and aspects by using a dependency model that considers specific characteristics of aspect-oriented programs, and a cost model that uses besides the traditional measures, attribute and operation coupling, two other measures: number of distinct return types and distinct parameter types. Furthermore two multi-objective algorithms, NSGA-II and SPEA were evaluated.

The empirical results point out that the MECBA approach can be efficiently used to solve the CAITO problem with more than two objectives, without requiring any priori information on the problem or weights to combine the objectives. The MOEAs achieved solutions of minimal effort to test, for instance, test orders that do not require stub creation were found for HealthWatcher system. For the AJHotDraw and AJHSQLDB, the algorithms find a set of different solutions containing different alternatives of compromise relation among the objectives. From this set, the tester can select the best solution according to the test priorities.

From all the presented results, it is possible to affirm that the two MOEAs have similar performance for the CAITO problem, but it seems that SPEA2 is more appropriated to generate solutions that are closer to the ideal solution and present the best compromise between all the objectives.

In our study, the Combined strategy was used with our approach to solve the CAITO problem. So, all solutions contain test orders to integrate classes and aspects together. However, another strategy could be used, for instance, the integration of only classes and, after this, aspects. Then the tester could use the solutions in a different way. As future work we intend to perform empirical studies with other AO systems and/or considering other strategies for integrating classes and aspects to confirm the evidences found in the present work. It is also interesting to analyze the efficiency of other MOEAs to solve the same problem.

References

1. Abdurazik, A., Offutt, J.: Coupling-based class integration and test order. In: International Workshop on Automation of Software Test, ACM, New York (2006)
2. Assunção, W., Colanzi, T., Pozo, A., Vergilio, S.: Establishing integration test orders of classes with several coupling measures. In: GECCO 2011, pp. 1867–1874 (2011)
3. Briand, L.C., Feng, J., Labiche, Y.: Using genetic algorithms and coupling measures to devise optimal integration test orders. In: 14th SEKE (July 2002)
4. Briand, L.C., Labiche, Y.: An investigation of graph-based class integration test order strategies. IEEE Trans. on Software Engineering 29(7), 594–607 (2003)
5. da Veiga Cabral, R., Pozo, A., Vergilio, S.: A Pareto Ant Colony Algorithm Applied to the Class Integration and Test Order Problem. In: Petrenko, A., Simão, A., Maldonado, J.C. (eds.) ICTSS 2010. LNCS, vol. 6435, pp. 16–29. Springer, Heidelberg (2010)
6. Ceccato, M., Tonella, P., Ricca, F.: Is AOP code easier or harder to test than OOP code. In: First Workshop on Testing Aspect-Oriented Program (WTAOP), Chicago, Illinois (2005)
7. Cochrane, J., Zeleny, M.: Multiple Criteria Decision Making. University of South Carolina Press, Columbia (1973)
8. Coello, C.A.C., Lamont, G.B., Veldhuizen, D.A.V.: Evolutionary algorithms for solving multi-objective problems. In: GECCO 2006 (2006)

9. Colanzi, T., Assunção, W., Vergilio, S., Pozo, A.: Generating integration test orders for aspect-oriented software with multi-objective algorithms. In: Latin American Workshop on Aspect-Oriented Software Development (2011) (to appear)

10. Deb, K., Pratap, A., Agarwal, S., Meyarivan, T.: A fast and elitist multiobjective genetic algorithm: NSGA-II. IEEE Trans. on Evolutionary Computation 6(2), 182–197 (2002)

11. Durillo, J., Nebro, A., Alba, E.: The jMetal framework for multi-objective optimization: Design and architecture. In: CEC 2010., pp. 4138–4325 (July 2010)

12. Galvan, R., Pozo, A., Vergilio, S.: Establishing Integration Test Orders for Aspect-Oriented Programs with an Evolutionary Strategy. In: Latinamerican Workshop on Aspect Oriented Software (2010)

13. Harman, M.: The current state and future of search based software engineering. In: Future of Software Engineering, FOSE, pp. 342–357 (May 2007)

14. Harman, M., Mansouri, A.: Special issue on search based software engineering. IEEE Transactions on Software Engineering 36(6) (2010)

15. Harman, M., Mansouri, S.A., Zhang, Y.: Search based software engineering: A comprehensive analysis and review of trends techniques and applications. Tech. Rep. TR-09-03 (April 2009)

16. Knowles, J., Thiele, L., Zitzler, E.: A tutorial on the performance assessment of stochastic multiobjective optimizers. Tech. rep., Computer Engineering and Networks Laboratory (TIK), ETH Zurich, Switzerland (fevereiro 2006) (revised version)

17. Knowles, J.D., Corne, D.W.: Approximating the nondominated front using the Pareto archived evolution strategy. Evol. Comput. 8, 149–172 (2000)

18. Kung, D.C., Gao, J., Hsia, P., Lin, J., Toyoshima, Y.: Class firewall, test order and regression testing of object-oriented programs. J. of Object-Oriented Progr. (1995)

19. Lemos, O.A.L., Vincenzi, A.M.R., Maldonado, J.C., Masiero, P.C.: Control and data flow structural testing criteria for aspect-oriented programs. The Journal of Systems and Software 80, 862–882 (2007)

20. Melton, H., Tempero, E.: An empirical study of cycles among classes in Java. Empirical Software Engineering 12, 389–415 (2007)

21. Pareto, V.: Manuel D'Economie Politique. Ams Press, Paris (1927)

22. Pozo, A., Bertoldi, G., Árias, J., Cabral, R., Vergilio, S.: Multi-objective optimization algorithms applied to the class integration and test order problem. Software Tools for Technology Transfer (2011) (submitted)

23. Radziukyniene, I., Zilinskas, A.: Evolutionary Methods for Multi-Objective Portfolio Optimization. In: World Congress on Engineering (July 2008)

24. Ré, R., Lemos, O.A.L., Masiero, P.C.: Minimizing stub creation during integration test of aspect-oriented programs. In: 3rd Workshop on Testing Aspect-Oriented Programs, Vancouver, British Columbia, Canada, pp. 1–6 (March 2007)

25. Ré, R., Masiero, P.C.: Integration testing of aspect-oriented programs: a characterization study to evaluate how to minimize the number of stubs. In: Brazilian Symposium on Software Engineering, pp. 411–426 (October 2007)

26. Tai, K.C., Daniels, F.J.: Test order for inter-class integration testing of object-oriented software. In: 21st International Computer Software and Applications Conference, pp. 602–607. IEEE Computer Society Press, Los Alamitos (1997)

27. Traon, Y.L., Jéron, T., Jézéquel, J.M., Morel, P.: Efficient object-oriented integration and regression testing. IEEE Transactions on Reliability, 12–25 (2000)

28. van Veldhuizen, D.A., Lamont, G.B.: Multiobjective evolutionary algorithm test suites. In: Proceedings of the 1999 ACM Symposium on Applied Computing (SAC 1999), pp. 351–357. ACM, New York (1999)
29. Zhao, J.: Data-flow based unit testing of aspect-oriented programs. In: 27th Conference on Computer Software and Applications, Washington, DC (2003)
30. Zitzler, E., Laumanns, M., Thiele, L.: SPEA2: Improving the Strength Pareto Evolutionary Algorithm. Tech. rep., Zurich, Switzerland (2001)
31. Zitzler, E., Thiele, L., Laumanns, M., Fonseca, C.M., da Fonseca, V.G.: Performance assessment of multiobjective optimizers: An analysis and review. IEEE Transactions on Evolutionary Computation 7, 117–132 (2003)

Divide-by-Zero Exception Raising
via Branch Coverage

Neelesh Bhattacharya, Abdelilah Sakti, Giuliano Antoniol
Yann-Gaël Guéhéneuc, and Gilles Pesant

Department of Computer and Software Engineering
École Polytechnique de Montréal, Québec, Canada
{neelesh.bhattacharya,abdelilah.sakti,giuliano.antoniol,yann-gael.
gu`eheneuc,gilles.pesant}@polymtl.ca

Abstract. In this paper, we discuss how a search-based branch coverage approach can be used to design an effective test data generation approach, specifically targeting divide-by-zero exceptions. We first propose a novel testability transformation combining *approach level* and *branch distance*. We then use different search strategies, *i.e.*, hill climbing, simulated annealing, and genetic algorithm, to evaluate the performance of the novel testability transformation on a small synthetic example as well as on methods known to throw divide-by-zero exceptions, extracted from real world systems, namely Eclipse and Android. Finally, we also describe how the test data generation for divide-by-zero exceptions can be formulated as a constraint programming problem and compare the resolution of this problem with a genetic algorithm in terms of execution time. We thus report evidence that genetic algorithm using our novel testability transformation out-performs hill climbing and simulated annealing and a previous approach (in terms of numbers of fitness evaluation) but is out-performed by constraint programming (in terms of execution time).

Keywords: Exception raising, test input data generation, evolutionary testing.

1 Introduction

Consequences of uncaught or poorly-managed exception may be dire: program crashes and/or security breaches. For embedded systems, an exception can be caused by, for example, unexpected values read from a sensor and can cause catastrophic effects. Indeed, poorly-managed exceptions are at the root of the 1996 Arianne 5 incident during which an uncaught floating-point conversion exception led to the rocket self-destruction 40 seconds after launch. In aerospace, as in other domains requiring highly-dependable systems such as medical systems, poorly-managed exceptions may have severe consequences to human beings or lead to great economic losses.

In software engineering, testing have traditionally been one of the main activities to obtain highly-dependable systems. Testing activities consume about

M.B. Cohen and M. Ó Cinnéide (Eds.): SSBSE 2011, LNCS 6956, pp. 204–218, 2011.

50% of software development resources [14] and any technique reducing testing costs is likely to reduce the software development costs as a whole. Although, exhaustive and thorough testing is often infeasible because of the possibly infinite execution-space and its high costs with respect to tight budget limitations, other techniques, such as code inspection are even costlier, though more effective. Therefore, testing activities should focus on the kinds of defects that, if were to slip into some deployed safety or mission-critical systems, may lead the systems to crash with possibly catastrophic consequences.

Consequently, we follow the work by Tracey *et al.* [19] on the generation of test data to raise exceptions and by others [13,20,2] on branch coverage criteria to propose a novel approach to generate test data for raising divide-by-zero exceptions for integers. In [19], the authors proposed to transform a target system so that the problem of generating test data to raise some exceptions becomes equivalent to a problem of branch coverage. They transform statements possibly leading to exceptions into branches with sufficient guard conditions. They then applied evolutionary testing to the transformed system to generate test data by traversing the branches and firing the exceptions. However, in their proposal, the search was solely guided by its *branch distance* [11], *i.e.*, the number of traversed control nodes, which may lead the search to behave like a random search.

In this paper, we propose to apply both *branch distance* as well as *approach level* [11] to generate test data to raise divide-by-zero exceptions for integers. The use of both guiding criteria, *i.e.*, *branch distance* and *approach level*, in an additive fitness function similar to previous work [20], to fire divide-by-zero exceptions yields to a reduction of the number of fitness evaluations needed to reach a given target statement [13,11]. To the best of our knowledge, this paper presents the first use of such a fitness function to generate test data to raise divide-by-zero exceptions.

We apply the novel testability transformation to generate test input data leading to divide-by-zero exceptions on the exemplary code presented in [19] and on two methods extracted from Eclipse and Android. We report the comparison of several meta-heuristic search techniques, *i.e.*, hill climbing (HC), simulated annealing (SA), and genetic algorithm (GA), with a random search (RND) and with constraint programming (CSP) on the three exemplary code samples. We thus show that the GA technique out-performs the other techniques but performs worse than the CSP technique.

Thus, the contributions of this paper are as follows:

- We propose to adopt both *branch distance* and *approach level* to generate test input data to fire divide-by-zero exceptions.
- We report the performance of HC (in three variants), SA, GA, and CSP on three systems, one synthetic and two real-world, from which we extracted three and two divide-by-zero exception-prone methods respectively.

The remainder of the paper is organized as follows: Section 2 describes the novel testability transformation. Section 3 describes the empirical study along with its settings. Sections 4 and 5 describe and discuss the results of the study. Section 6 summarizes related work. Section 7 concludes with some future work.

2   The Approach

We now present our approach, the novel testability transformation and the different techniques that we will use to generate test input data.

2.1   Example and Fitness Function

We follow previous work [19] to transform the problem of generating test input data to raise divide-by-zero exceptions into a branch coverage problem. This transformation essentially consists of wrapping divide-by-zero prone statements with a branch statement (an *if*), whose condition corresponds to the expression containing the possible division by zero. Consequently, satisfying the *if* through some branch coverage is equivalent to raising the divide-by-zero exception. For example, let us consider the following fragment of code:

```
1     int z, x=4;
2     if (Z>1 AND Z<=5)
3            return z;
4     else
5            return (x*4)/(z-1);
```

a divide-by-zero exception would be raised when z equals to 1 at line 5.

It is usually difficult to generate test data targeting a specific condition by obtaining appropriate variable values. We transform the code fragment above into a semantically-equivalent fragment in which the expression possibly leading to an exception becomes a condition. Then, it is sufficient to satisfy the new condition to obtain test input data raising the exception, as in the following fragment:

```
1     int z, x=4;
2     if (Z>1 AND Z<=5)
3            return z;
4     else
5.1          if (Z == 1)
5.2                 print "Exception raised";
5.3          else
5.4                 return (x*4)/(z-1);
```

where we transform the divide-by-zero prone statement at line 5 into the lines 5.1 to 5.4.

In general, such a transformation may not be trivial and different types of exceptions may require different types of transformations. Defining the types of transformations for various types of exceptions similarly to a Harman *et al.* framework [6] is future work.

To efficiently generate test data to expose the exception, it is not sufficient to reach line 5.1 using the *approach level* because between two test input data, both reaching line 5.1, we would prefer the data making the condition at line 5.1 true and thus reaching line 5.2.

Consequently, our fitness function is an additive function using both the *approach level* and the normalized *branch distance* [1,8], where the normalized branch distance is defined by Equation 1 and used in the fitness function defined by Equation 2.

$$Normalized\ branch\ distance = 1 - 1.001^{-branch\_distance} \qquad (1)$$

$$Fitness\ function = Approach\ level +$$
$$Normalized\ branch\ distance \qquad (2)$$

2.2 Search Techniques to Generate Test Input Data

Once the code fragments under test are transformed and instrumented to collect run-time variable values needed to compute the *approach level* and normalized *branch distance*, we can generate test input data using several techniques, such as hill climbing (HC), simulated annealing (SA), and genetic algorithms (GA), or simply by a random search (RND). In the following section, we briefly describe the settings of the various techniques as well as the use of constraint programming for structural software testing (CP-SST)[16].

We assume that the input values are integers. Other more structured data types will be investigated as part of our future works, following the strategy proposed in [5].

Hill Climbing. Hill climbing (HC) is the simplest, widely-used, and probably best-known search technique. HC is a local search method, where the search proceeds from a randomly chosen point (solution) in the search space by considering the neighbours (new solutions obtained by mutating the previous solution) of the point. Once a fitter neighbour is found, this becomes the current point in the search space and the process is repeated. If, after mutating a given x number of times no fitter neighbour is found, then the search terminates and a maximum has been found (by definition). Often, to avoid local optima, the hill climbing algorithm is restarted multiple times from a random point (also called stochastic hill climbing). We have drawn inspiration from this idea and proposed three strategies.

Strategy 1: The HC1 strategy generates, for any input variable involved in the denominator of the exceptions raising statements, an immediate neighbour of the input data as the sum of the the current value of the variable with a randomly-generated value drawn from a Gaussian distribution with zero mean and an initial standard deviation (SD) of ten, which we choose after several trials to have neighbourhoods that are not too small or large.

If after a given number of moves in the neighbourhoods, the fitness values of the neighbours are always worse than the current fitness value, then we change the value of the SD to a larger value to expand the neighbourhood and give the algorithm an opportunity to get out of the, possible local optimum.

Strategy 2: In the HC1 strategy, the values of the SD may change at run-time. We observed that HC1 does not always improve the search and may lead to a slow search-space exploration. Thus, to avoid getting "trapped" in a specific region of the space, we define the HC2 strategy that forces the search to take a jump away from unsuccessful neighbourhood in an attempt to move into a more favourable neighbourhood, similarly to HC with random restarts.

For a given SD value, if the search does not improve for a given number of iterations, instead of changing SD, we force a jump to another neighbourhood using a large value and HC reiterates its process. The "length" of a jump and the number of jumps depend on the search space. For example, a search space of $[-10,000; +10,000]$ would be likely covered with 40 jumps of lengths 500. As with the previous strategy, this strategy goes on until it reaches a maximum number of iterations or generates test data firing the targeted exception.

Strategy 3: The HC3 strategy is a combination of HC1 and HC2. With HC3, we store the fitness values of the best neighbour of all previously-visited neighbourhoods before jumping to another neighbourhood. After having visited a given number of neighbourhoods as in HC2, HC3 returns to the "best" one, *i.e.*, the neighbourhood with the best fitness value among all recorded values, and then increases the SD by 25 (making the SD 35), as in HC1, to visit more of this neighbourhood. As with the previous strategies, this strategy goes on until it reaches a maximum number of iterations or generates test data firing the targeted exception.

Simulated Annealing. SA like hill climbing, is a local search method. However, simulated annealing has a 'cooling mechanism' that initially allows moves to less fit solutions if $p < m$, where p is a random number in the range $[0 \ldots 1]$ and m, acceptance probability, is a value that decays ('cools') at each iteration of the algorithm. The effect of 'cooling' on the simulation of annealing is that the probability of following an unfavourable move is reduced. This (initially) allows the search to move away from local optima in which the search might be trapped. As the simulation 'cools' the search becomes more and more like a simple hill climb. The choice of the parameters of SA are guided by two equations [21]:

$$Final\ temperature = Initial\ temperature \times \alpha^{Number\ of\ iterations}$$
$$Acceptance\ probability = e^{\frac{-Normalized\ fitness\ function}{Final\ temperature}}$$

where *Acceptance probability* if the probability that the algorithm decides to accept solution or not: if the current neighbour is "worse" than previous ones, it can still be accepted (in contrary to hill climbing) if the probability is greater than a randomly-selected value; α and *Number of iterations* are chosen constants.

Genetic Algorithms. A GA starts by creating an initial population of n sets of test input data, chosen randomly from the domain D of the program being tested. Each chromosome represents a test set; genes are values of the input variables. In an iterative process, the GA tries to improve the population from one generation to another using the fitness of each chromosome to perform reproduction, *i.e.*, cross-over and–or mutation. The GA creates a new generation with the l fittest test sets of the previous generation and the offspring obtained from cross-overs and mutations. It keeps the population size constant by retaining only the n best test sets in each new generation. It stops if either some test set satisfies the condition or after a given number of generations.

We implemented our GA algorithm using *JMetal*[1]. We use the binary tournament selection operator. Once parents are selected, they undergo a single point cross-over. To diversify the population, the off-springs (after cross-overs) may be mutated. We use bit-flip mutation, in which, based on a probability, the variable values are replaced with values selected randomly.

Random Search. Not using any heuristics to guide the search, this technique relies on generating initial input variable data randomly to execute the transformed program and to try firing the targeted exception. It stops if either the generated test data fires the exception or after a given number of iterations.

Constraint Programming. Constraint programming for software structural testing (CP-SST) is a generic technique for test-data generation to reach a specific target or to satisfy a test coverage criteria, for proof post-condition, or for counter-example generation.

The main idea of CP-SST is to convert the program under test and the test target into a constraint solving problem (CSP) and to solve the resulting CSP to obtain test input data. The first step of CP-SST consists of transforming the program under test into the static single assignment (SSA) form. The second step consists of modelling the program control flow graph (CFG) as a preliminary CSP. CP-SST begins by generating the CFG that features an independent node for each parameter and global variable, each control statement, each block of statements, and each join point. CP-SST labels edges among nodes depending on the origin node: an edge outgoing from a statement node is labelled by 1, an edge outgoing from a condition node is labelled by 1 if the decision is positive and -1 if the decision is negative. Then, CP-SST generates the preliminary CSP by translating each node into a CSP variable whose domain is the set of labels of its outgoing edges, except for join nodes that take their domains from the joint nodes.

In the third step, CP-SST uses the preliminary CSP, the SSA form, and the relationships among nodes and their statements to create a new global CSP, which it then solves to generate test input data or return a failure if no solution can be reached.

3   Empirical Study

The *goal* of our empirical study is to compare our novel testability transformation against previous work and identify the best technique among the five

---
[1] http://jmetal.sourceforge.net/

Table 1. Details of the systems under test and tested units

Systems	Versions	Class Names	LOCs	Numbers of Exceptions	Bug Tracking Numbers
Tracey's code	N/A	F	13	2	N/A
Eclipse	2.0.1	GridCanvas	10	2	205772
Android	2.0	ProcessStats	41	3	Unavailable

presented in Section 2 using synthetic as well as real systems to generate integer test input data to fire divide-by-zero exceptions. The *quality focus* is the performance of the proposed hill climbing strategies and other meta-heuristics and constraint programming techniques to raise divide-by-zero exceptions. The *perspective* includes researchers and software engineers working in search-based software testing looking to generate test data for firing exceptions in the code. The *context* of our research includes three case studies: one synthetic program and two real software systems, namely, *Eclipse* and *Android*. Table 1 summarizes the three software systems and the selected methods/functions for testing and the corresponding class names having two, two, and three divide-by-zero exception statements, respectively.

We seek answers to four research questions:

RQ1: Based on the fitness function we use, which of the three proposed hill climbing strategies is best suited to raise a divide-by-zero exception and what is the measure of its effectiveness?

RQ2: Which of all the meta-heuristic techniques is best suited to raise a divide-by-zero exception and what is the measure of its effectiveness? (Retaining the best-suited hill climbing strategy from RQ1.)

RQ3: Which of Tracey's fitness function and the fitness function we used, is best suited to raise a divide-by-zero exception and what is the measure of its effectiveness? (Retaining the best-suited meta-heuristic from RQ2.)

RQ4: Which of the best-suited meta-heuristic technique and of the CP-SST is best suited to raise a divide-by-zero exception and what is the measure of its effectiveness? (Retaining the best-suited meta-heuristic from RQ2.)

3.1   Choice of the Comparison Measure

HC (in the three variants), SA, GA, and RND can be compared with one another using their numbers of fitness evaluations to fire some divide-by-zero exception. CP-SST is based on a completely different paradigm than the meta-heuristic techniques. Thus, CP-SST cannot be compared with the other techniques using the numbers of fitness evaluations and we use execution times of the different techniques for comparison. We consider the approach requiring less execution time to reach a target to be "better" to generate test data for firing divide-by-zero exceptions.

3.2   Choice of the Targeted Exceptions

We selected three methods in three classes of three different systems, for a total of seven possible target exceptions. For the sake of space, we only report in the following the results of our empirical study for three target exceptions, chosen to lead to the worst performance for all the techniques, among the seven possible targeted exceptions and called in the following units-under-test, UUT. All results and data for replication are available on-line[2].

3.3 General Parameters of the Techniques

We chose different ranges of values for each input variable to analyse the performance of all the techniques to deal with values ranging from very small to very large. The domains have been varied from $[-100; +100]$ to $[-50,000; +50,000]$ for all the input variables. Reaching a success, *i.e.*, raising the targeted divide-by-zero exception in the UUT, is the stopping criterion as well as a number of evaluations of 1000000. We repeated each computations 20 times to analyse the diversity in the observed values and conduct statistical tests. Table 2(a) details the values used.

Table 2. Parameters

(a) General Parameters

Input Domain	$[-100; +100]$ - $[-50,000; +50,000]$
Max # iterations	1000000
# Computations	20

(b) Hill Climbing

Strategies	CS	SD
S1	100	-
S2	100	-
S3	100	35

(c) Simulated Annealing

Params.	Inspected Values (Chosen)
Temper.	0.5-50 (20)
α	0.8-0.995 (0.99)
# Iter.	10-500 (100)

(d) Genetic Algorithm

Operators	Type	Prob.
Crossover	Single Point	0.9
Mutation	Bit Flip	0.09
Selection	Binary Tournament	-

3.4 Specific Parameters of the Techniques

We use the following parameters for the techniques (we do not report techniques which do not use any particular parameters):

Hill Climbing: For the first strategy, we use a parameter *checkStagnation* to control the number of iterations before changing neighbourhood. We use 100, *i.e.*, if no improvement occurs in a neighbourhood after 100 iterations, HC1 changes neighbourhood. We use 100 as SD because it led to better performance than other values.

In the second strategy, we also use *checkStagnation* parameter. We use two other important parameters: *gaussianJumpLength* and *numberOfJumps* depicting the length of the "jump" and the number of jumps, respectively. We found the values of these two parameters by trial-and-error runs.

In the third strategy, we also use *deviationValue*, the value of SD when the technique returns to the best neighbourhood. Table 2(b) depicts the parameter values.

---

[2] http://web.soccerlab.polymtl.ca/ser-repos/public/div_by_zero.tar.gz

Simulated Annealing: We base our choice of the initial temperature, α, and the number of iterations on several experiments in which we varied the initial temperature. Table 2(c) shows the values used.

Genetic Algorithm: We used single-point cross-over, bit-flip mutation, and binary-tournament selection. We choose the binary-tournament selection because its complexity is lower than that of any other selections and provides more population diversity to the cross-over operator than others [23]. Table 2(d) shows the various values.

4   Study Results

Figure 1, 2, and 3 reports the box plots of the number of fitness evaluation needed to raise a divide-by-zero exception for the Tracey exemplary code, Eclipse, and Android UTTs, respectively. We did not include results for RND as it performs always substantially worse then even the slowest HC1 strategy.

We observe that HC3 is, in all cases, better then the other two hill climbing strategies but in all cases is also performing substantially worse than SA and GA. Overall, Figure 1, 2, and 3 support the observation that GA is the most effective meta-heuristic technique as far as these UTTs are concerned.

Table 3, 4, and 5 reports the t-test values comparing the numbers of fitness evaluations needed by the different search techniques as well as the Cohen d effect size [4]. The effect size is defined as the difference between the means of two groups, divided by the pooled standard deviation of both groups. The effect size is considered small for $0.2 \leq d < 0.5$, medium for $0.5 \leq d < 0.8$, and large for $d \geq 0.8$ [4]. We chose the Cohen d effect size because it is appropriate for our variables (ratio scales) and given its different levels (small, medium, large) easy to interpret.

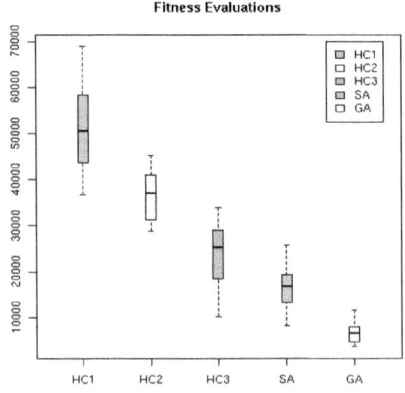

Fig. 1. Comparison on Tracey [19] UUT of the different search techniques (input domain $[-50,000; +50,000]$)

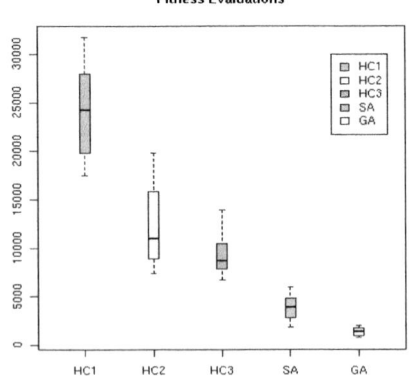

Fig. 2. Comparison on Eclipse UUT of the different search techniques (input domain $[-50,000; +50,000]$)

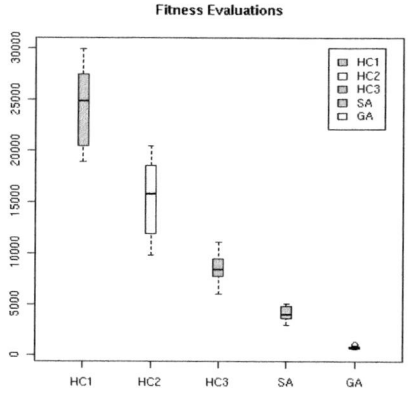

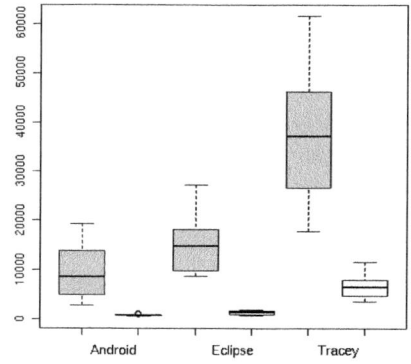

Fig. 3. Comparison on Android UUT of the different search techniques (input domain $[-50,000; +50,000]$)

Fig. 4. GA comparison against Tracey's original fitness [19] versus the fitness function we used (input domain $[-50,000; +50,000]$)

Table 3. Results of t-test and Cohen d effect size for Tracey [19] UUT

Comparisons	p-values	Cohen d values
HC1-HC2	9.261e-10	2.55246
HC1-HC3	6.376e-16	5.951003
HC2-HC3	6.868e-08	2.428475
HC3-SA	7.049e-14	4.147889
HC3-GA	2.2e-16	8.223645
SA-GA	8.763e-15	6.254793

Table 4. Results of t-test and Cohen d effect size for Eclipse UUT

Comparisons	p-values	Cohen d values
HC1-HC2	3.245e-10	2.682195
HC1-HC3	7.167e-13	4.111778
HC2-HC3	0.003998	0.9912142
HC3-SA	2.387e-11	3.239916
HC3-GA	1.933e-13	5.258295
SA-GA	9.989e-09	2.694495

Table 5. Results of t-test and Cohen d effect size for Android UUT

Comparisons	p-values	Cohen d values
HC1-HC2	1.438e-06	1.894204
HC1-HC3	2.981e-12	3.345377
HC2-HC3	7.438e-08	2.12037
HC3-SA	0.0003169	1.266088
HC3-GA	1.283e-10	3.481401
SA-GA	4.531e-09	2.696728

Table 6. Comparison of GA against CP-SST in terms of average execution times (ms) and standard deviations for all UUTs

	Tracey's Code	Eclipse	Android
GA	8.067/1.439	2.129/1.149	1.926/1.177
CP	1.035/0.0135	0.01/0	0.01/0

As expected from Figures 1, 2, and 3, the t-test and Cohen d effect size results support with very strong statistical evidence the superiority of HC3 over HC1 and HC2 as well as the superiority of GA over SA and HC3.

Box-plots as well as tables clearly support the superiority of GA over the other techniques. Overall, **we answer RQ1 by stating that HC3 performs better than HC1 and HC2 with a large effect size.** Furthermore, **we answer RQ2 by stating, with a large effect size also, that GA outperforms the other techniques.**

214 N. Bhattacharya et al.

We compare our fitness function with that proposed by Tracey *et al.* [19] by using two GA implementations, one using Tracey's fitness function and another using the fitness function explained before. We compare the two fitness functions in terms of the required numbers of fitness evaluations for all the UUTs in Figure 4 to reach the targeted exceptions. Figure 4 shows that our novel testability transformation allows the GA to reach the targeted exceptions in much less numbers of evaluations. Consequently, **we answer RQ3 by stating that, in comparison to Tracey's fitness function, our novel testability transformation dramatically improves the performance of a GA technique.**

Finally, Table 6 reports average and standard deviations of the execution times for twenty experiments on the three UUTs for both GA and CP. For the given UUTs, it is clear that CP out-performs GA in term of execution times. This result may be due to the size of the UUTs, which are relatively small, and to the structure of the condition to satisfy. More evidence is needed to verify if the averages in Table 6 represent a general trend. Yet, on the selected UUTs, **we answer RQ4 by claiming that the CP-SST technique out-performs the best of the meta-heuristic techniques, GA.**

5 Study Discussions

5.1 Discussions

We presented the results of three UUTs to answer the four research questions. The other four UUTs from the same systems exhibit the same trends as the ones reported in this paper, thus adding more evidence to our answers.

We also evaluated the performance of our novel testability transformation with respect to the one proposed by Tracey *et al.* [19] in terms of required numbers of fitness evaluations. The results showed the importance of having both *approach level* and *branch distance* in the fitness function, as opposed to the one proposed by Tracey *et al.* [19] which uses only the *approach level*.

5.2 Threats to the Validity

We now discuss the threats to the validity of our study.

Threats to *construct validity* concern the relationship between theory and observation. In our study, these threats can be due to the fact that one of the UUT is a synthetic code, even though previously-used to exemplify and study the divide-by-zero exception [19], and thus might represent real code. However, we extracted the two other UUTs from real-world systems (Eclipse and Android) and the method containing the divide-by-zero exceptions has been documented in the Eclipse issue tracking system. Finally, the code excerpt [19] as well as the Eclipse and Android studied methods contain multiple possible divide-by-zero statements and, in all cases, we focused on the statements leading to the worst performances, *i.e.*, the most deeply-nested statements.

Threats to *internal validity* concern external factors that may affect an independent variable. We limited the bias of intrinsic randomness of our results by repeating each experiment 20 times and using proper statistics to compare the results. We have calibrated the HC (*i.e.*, HC1, HC2, and HC3), SA, and GA settings using a trial-and-error procedure. We chose the values of the parameters of the techniques, such as *checkStagnation*, *gaussianJumpLength* and so on, after executing the techniques several times and evaluating their performance on a toy program. We also chose the cross-over and mutation operators by doing a small study on the same toy program: although we found evidence of the superiority of specific operators, it could happen that (1) studies on different systems would lead to a different choice of cross-over and mutation operators and (2) the obtained calibration may not be the most suitable for our subject systems.

Threats to *conclusion validity* involve the relationship between the treatment and the outcome. To overcome this threat, we inspected box-plots, performed *t*-tests, and evaluated the Cohen *d* effect sizes.

Threats to *external validity* involve the generalization of our results. We evaluated the novel testability transformation on UUTs from the work of Tracey *et al.* [19] and two different Java systems. The sample size is small and, although for Eclipse code it corresponds to a documented bug, a larger evaluation is be highly desirable.

Finally, for all divide-by-zero conditions listed in Table 1 and all applied search techniques, including random search, a replication package is available on-line[3] to promote replication.

6   Related Work

Our approach stems from the work of Tracey *et al.* [19]. They proposed an approach to automatically generate test data for exceptions by (1) transforming the statements containing exceptions into a branch with guard conditions derived from the possible exception and the statement structure and (2) generating test data to traverse the added branch and thus fire the exception. The fitness function used in [19] is in essence oriented to structural coverage and uses only the *branch distance*.

Automation of structural coverage criteria and structural testing have been the most-widely investigated subjects. Local search was first used by Miller and Spooner [12] with the goal of generating input data to cover particular paths in a system. This work was later extended by Korel [10]. In brief, to cover a particular path, the system is initially executed with some arbitrary input. If an undesired branch is taken, an objective function derived from the predicate of the desired branch is used to guide the search. The objective function value, referred to as *branch distance* [8], measures how close the predicate is to being true. Baresel *et al.* [1] proposed a normalization of the *branch distance* between in [0, 1] to better guide the search avoiding *branch distance* making *approximation level* useless. The idea of minimizing such an objective function was refined and extended by several researchers to satisfy coverage criteria of certain given procedural-program structures like branches, statements, paths, or conditions.

---

[3] http://web.soccerlab.polymtl.ca/ser-repos/public/div_by_zero.tar.gz

To overcome the limitations associated with local search techniques, Tracey *et al.* [?] applied simulated annealing and defined a more sophisticated objective function for relational predicates. The genetic algorithm was first used by Xanthakis [22] to generate input data satisfying the all branch predicate criterion. Evolutionary approaches, where search algorithms, in particular genetic algorithm, are tailored to automate and support testing activities, *i.e.*, to generate test input data [9,18,20] are often referred to as evolutionary-based software testing or simply evolutionary testing. A survey of evolutionary testing and related techniques is beyond the scope of this paper; the interested reader may refer to the survey published by McMinn [11].

In the last few years, researchers have focused on static, dynamic and hybrid approaches to identify and handle various types of exceptions in object-oriented systems. Sinha *et al.* [17] proposed an approach to reduce the complexity of a program in the presence of implicit control flow. The approach, based on static and dynamic analysis of constructs, provides information to developers in an IDE. Ryder *et al.* [15] studied the tool *JESP* and evaluated the frequency with which exception-handling constructs are used in Java programs. Their analysis found that exception-handling constructs were used in 16% of the methods that they examined. Chatterjee *et al.* [3] proposed an approach for data-flow testing. They identified the definition–use associations arising along with the exceptional control-flow paths. Jang *et al.* [7] proposed an exception analysis approach for Java, both at the expression and method level, to overcome the dependence of JDK Java compiler on developers' declarations for checking against uncaught exceptions.

Our work shares many commonalities with previous work, as we apply structural evolutionary testing developed for branch coverage to generate test input data exposing divide-by-zero exceptions in a unit under test transformed as proposed by Tracey *et al.* [19].

7   Conclusion

In this paper, we presented a novel testability transformation to generate test input data to raise divide-by-zero exceptions in software systems. We compared the performance of hill climbing, simulated annealing, genetic algorithm, random search, and constraint programming when using this fitness function. The novel testability transformation used by hill climbing, simulated annealing, and genetic algorithm is based on both *approach level* and *branch distance*. Further, we also proposed three hill climbing strategies to improve basic hill climbing search. Finally, we chose the best meta-heuristic technique (genetic algorithm) and compared its performance with that of constraint programming in terms of execution time.

We validated our novel testability transformation and compared the search technique on three software units: one synthetic code fragment taken from [19] and two methods extracted from Eclipse and Android, respectively. While comparing the meta-heuristic techniques, genetic algorithm performed best in terms of the number of required fitness evaluations to reach the desired target for all the three units under test. Then, constraint programming out-performed the genetic algorithm in terms of execution times for all the three case studies.

In the future, we will validate our fitness function and choice of search technique with more complex input data types and different types of exceptions. We will also extend the validation part to other software systems. We would also like to integrate a chaining approach to better deal with data dependencies and study the testability transformations required to simplify and make it efficient to generate test input data to raise exceptions.

References

1. Baresel, A.: Automatisierung von strukturtests mit evolutionren algorithmen. Diploma Thesis, Humboldt University, Berlin, Germany (2000)
2. Baresel, A., Sthamer, H., Schmidt, M.: Fitness function design to improve evolutionary structural testing. In: Proceedings of the Genetic and Evolutionary Computation Conference, pp. 1329–1336 (July 2002)
3. Chatterjee, R., Ryder, B.G.: Data-flow-based testing of object-oriented libraries. Tech. Rep. DCS-TR-382, Department of Computer Science, Rutgers University (1999)
4. Cohen, J.: Statistical power analysis for the behavioral sciences, 2nd edn. Lawrence Earlbaum Associates, Hillsdale (1988)
5. Romano, D., Massimiliano Di Penta, G.A.: An approach for search based testing of null pointer exceptions. In: Proceedings of the Fourth International Conference on Software Testing, Verification and Validation, pp. 160–169 (March 2011)
6. Harman, M., Baresel, A., Binkley, D., Hierons, R.M., Hu, L., Korel, B., McMinn, P., Roper, M.: Testability transformation – program transformation to improve testability. In: Hierons, R.M., Bowen, J.P., Harman, M. (eds.) FORTEST. LNCS, vol. 4949, pp. 320–344. Springer, Heidelberg (2008)
7. Jo, J.W., Chang, B.M., Yi, K., Choe, K.M.: An uncaught exception analysis for java. Journal of System Software 72, 59–69 (2004), http://portal.acm.org/citation.cfm?id=1005486.1005491
8. Joachim Wegener, A.B., Sthamer, H.: Evolutionary test environment for automatic structural testing. Information and Software Technology 43(14), 841–854 (2001)
9. Jones, B., Sthamer, H., Eyres, D.: Automatic structural testing using genetic algorithms. Software Engineering Journal 11(5), 299–306 (1996)
10. Korel, B.: Dynamic method of software test data generation. Softw. Test, Verif. Reliab. 2(4), 203–213 (1992)
11. McMinn, P.: Search-based software test data generation: a survey. Software Testing Verification and Reliability 14(2), 105–156 (2004)
12. Miller, W., Spooner, D.L.: Automatic generation of floating-point test data. IEEE Transactions on Software Engineering 2(3), 223–226 (1976)
13. Mresa, E.S., Bottaci, L.: Efficiency of mutation operators and selective mutation strategies: An empirical study. Software Testing Verification and Reliability 9(4), 205–232 (1999)
14. Pressman, R.S.: Software Engineering: A Practitioner's Approach, 3rd edn. McGraw-Hill, New York (1992)

15. Ryder, B.G., Smith, D.E., Kremer, U., Gordon, M.D., Shah, N.: A static study of java exceptions using JESP. In: Watt, D.A. (ed.) CC 2000. LNCS, vol. 1781, pp. 67–81. Springer, Heidelberg (2000), http://portal.acm.org/citation.cfm?id=647476.727763

16. Sakti, A., Guéhéneuc, Y.G., Pesant, G.: Cp-sst: approche basée sur la programmation par contraintes pour le test structurel du logiciel. Septitièmes Journées Francophones de Programmation par Contraintes (JFPC), 289–298 (June 2011)

17. Saurabh Sinha, R.O., Harrold, M.J.: Automated support for development, maintenance, and testing in the presence of implicit control flow. In: ICSE 2004, pp. 336–345. IEEE Computer Society Press, Washington, DC, USA (2004)

18. Tracey, N., Clark, J.A., Mander, K., McDermid, J.A.: Automated test-data generation for exception conditions. Software Practice and Experience 30(1), 61–79 (2000)

19. Tracey, N., Clark, J.A., Mander, K.: Automated program flaw finding using simulated annealing. In: ISSTA, pp. 73–81 (1998)

20. Wegener, J., Baresel, A., Sthamer, H.: Evolutionary test environment for automatic structural testing. Information & Software Technology 43(14), 841–854 (2001)

21. Wright, M.: Automating parameter choice for simulated annealing. Tech. Rep. 32, Lancaster University Management School, UK (2010)

22. Xanthakis, S., Ellis, C., Skourlas, C., Gall, A.L., Katsikas, S., Karapoulios, K.: Application des algorithmes genetiques au test des logiciels. In: 5th Int. Conference on Software Engineering and its Applications, pp. 625–636 (1992)

23. Zhang, B.T., Kim, J.J.: Comparison of selection methods for evolutionary optimization. Evolutionary Optimization 2(1), 55–70 (2000)

Highly Scalable Multi Objective Test Suite Minimisation Using Graphics Cards

Shin Yoo[1], Mark Harman[1], and Shmuel Ur[2]

[1] University College London
[2] University of Bristol

Abstract. Despite claims of "embarrassing parallelism" for many optimisation algorithms, there has been very little work on exploiting parallelism as a route for SBSE scalability. This is an important oversight because scalability is so often a critical success factor for Software Engineering work. This paper shows how relatively inexpensive General Purpose computing on Graphical Processing Units (GPGPU) can be used to run suitably adapted optimisation algorithms, opening up the possibility of cheap scalability. The paper develops a search based optimisation approach for multi objective regression test optimisation, evaluating it on benchmark problems as well as larger real world problems. The results indicate that speed–ups of over 25x are possible using widely available standard GPUs. It is also encouraging that the results reveal a statistically strong correlation between larger problem instances and the degree of speed up achieved. This is the first time that GPGPU has been used for SBSE scalability.

1 Introduction

There is a pressing need for scalable solutions to Software Engineering problems. This applies to SBSE work just as much as it does to other aspects of Software Engineering. Scalability is widely regarded as one of the key problems for Software Engineering research and development [1, 2]. Furthermore, throughout its history, lack of scalability has been cited as an important barrier to wider uptake of Software Engineering research [3–5]. Without scalable solutions, potentially valuable Software Engineering innovations may not be fully exploited.

Many search based optimisation techniques, such as evolutionary algorithms are classified as 'embarrassingly parallel' because of their potential for scalability through parallel execution of fitness computations [6]. However, this possibility for significant speed–up (and consequent scalability) has been largely overlooked in the SBSE literature. The first authors to suggest the exploitation of parallel execution were Mitchell et al. [7] who used a distributed architecture to parallelise modularisation through the application of search-based clustering. Subsequently, Mahdavi et al. [8] used a cluster of standard PCs to implement a parallel hill climbing algorithm. More recently, Asadi et al. [9] used a distributed architecture to parallelise a genetic algorithm for the concept location problem.

M.B. Cohen and M. Ó Cinnéide (Eds.): SSBSE 2011, LNCS 6956, pp. 219–236, 2011.
© Springer-Verlag Berlin Heidelberg 2011

Of 763 papers on SBSE[10] only these three present results for parallel execution of SBSE. Given the 'embarrassingly parallel' nature of the underlying approach and the need for scalability, it is perhaps surprising that there has not been more work on SBSE parallelisation. One possible historical barrier to wider application of parallel execution has been the high cost of parallel execution architectures and infrastructure. All three previous results cited in the previous paragraph used a cluster of machines to achieve parallelism. While commodity PCs have significantly reduced the cost of such clusters, their management can still be a non-trivial task, restricting the potential availability for developers.

Fortunately, recent work [11] has shown how a newly emerging parallelism, originally designed for graphics, can be exploited for non–graphical tasks using General Purpose computing on Graphical Processing Unit (GPGPU) [12]. Modern graphics hardware provides an affordable means of parallelism: not only the hardware is more affordable than multiple PCs but also the management cost is much smaller than that required for a cluster of PCs because it depends on a single hardware component. GPGPU has been successfully applied to various scientific computations [13, 14]. However, these techniques have never been applied to Search-Based Software Engineering problems and so it remains open as to whether large-scale, affordable speed–up is possible for Software Engineering optimisations using GPGPU to parallelise SBSE.

Fast regression test minimisation is an important problem for practical software testers, particularly where large volumes of testing are required on a tight build schedule. For instance, the IBM middleware product used as one of the systems in the empirical study in this paper is a case in point. While it takes over four hours to execute the entire test suite for this system, the typical smoke test scenario performed after each code submit is assigned only an hour or less of testing time, forcing the tester to select a subset of tests from the available pool. If the computation involved in test suite minimisation requires more than one hour itself, then the tester cannot benefit from such a technique; the smoke test will be highly suboptimal as a result. Using the GPGPU approach introduced in this paper, this time was reduced from over an hour to just under 3 minutes, thereby allowing sophisticated minimisation to be used on standard machines without compromising the overall build cycle.

The paper presents a modified evolutionary algorithm for the multi-objective regression test minimisation problem. The algorithm is modified to support implementation on a GPU by transforming the fitness evaluation of the population of individual solutions into a matrix-multiplication problem, which is inherently parallel and renders itself very favourably to the GPGPU approach. This transformation to matrix-multiplication is entirely straightforward and may well be applicable to other SBSE problems, allowing them to benefit from similar scale-ups to those reported in this paper.

This algorithm has been implemented using OpenCL technology, a framework for GPGPU. The paper reports the results of the application of the parallelised GPGPU algorithm on 13 real world programs, including widely studied, but relatively small examples from the Siemens' suite [15], through larger more realistic real world examples from the Software-Infrastructure Repository (SIR) for testing [16], and on a very large IBM middleware regression testing problem.

The primary contributions of the paper are as follows:

1. The paper is the first to develop SBSE algorithms for GPGPU as a mechanism for affordable massive parallelism.
2. The paper presents results for real world instances of the multi objective test suite minimisation problem. The results indicate that dramatic speed–up is achievable. For the systems used in the empirical study, speed–ups over 20x were observed. The empirical evidence suggests that, for larger problems where the scale up is the most needed, the degree of speed–up is the most dramatic; a problem that takes over an hour using conventional techniques, can be solved in minutes using the GPGPU approach. This has important practical ramifications because regression testing cycles are often compressed: overnight build cycles are not uncommon.
3. The paper studies multiple evolutionary algorithms and both GPU- and CPU-based parallelisation methods in order to provide robust empirical evidence for the scalability conferred by the use of GPGPU. The GPGPU parallelisation technique maintained the same level of speed–up across all algorithms studied. The empirical evidence highlights the limitations of CPU-based parallelisation: with smaller problems, multi-threading overheads erode the speed–up, whereas with larger problems it fails to scale as well as GPU-based parallelisation.
4. The paper explores the factors that influence the degree of speed–up achieved, revealing that both program size and test suite size are closely correlated to the degree of speed–up achieved. The data have a good fit to a model for which increases in the degree of scale up achieved are logarithmic in both program and test suite size.

The rest of the paper is organised as follows. Section 2 presents background and related work in test suite minimisation and GPGPU-based evolutionary computation. Section 3 describes how the test suite minimisation problem is re-formulated for a parallel algorithm, which is described in detail in Section 4. Section 5 describes the details of the empirical study, the results of which are analysed in Section 6. Section 7 discusses the related work and Section 8 concludes.

2   Background

Multi-Objective Test Suite Minimisation: The need for test suite minimisation arises when the regression test suite of an existing software system grows to such an extent that it may no longer be feasible to execute the entire test suite [17]. In order to reduce the size of the test suite, any *redundant* test cases in the test suite need to be identified and removed. More formally, test suite minimisation problem can be defined as follows [18]:

Test Suite Minimisation Problem

Given: A test suite of m tests, T, a set of l test goals $R = \{r_1, \ldots, r_l\}$, that must be satisfied to provide the desired 'adequate' testing of the program, and subsets of T, T_is, one associated with each of the r_is such that any one of the test cases t_j belonging to T_i can be used to achieve requirement r_i.

Problem: Find a representative set, T', of test cases from T that satisfies R.

The testing criterion is satisfied when every test-case requirement in R is satisfied. A test-case requirement, r_i, is satisfied by any test case, t_j, that belongs to T_i, a subset of T. Therefore, the representative set of test cases is the hitting set of T_is. Furthermore, in order to maximise the effect of minimisation, T' should be the minimal hitting set of T_is. The minimal hitting-set problem is an NP-complete problem as is the dual problem of the minimal set cover problem [19].

The NP-hardness of the problem encouraged the use of heuristics and meta-heuristics. The greedy approach [20] as well as other heuristics for minimal hitting set and set cover problem [21, 22] have been applied to test suite minimisation but these approaches were not cost-cognisant and only dealt with a single objective (test coverage). With the single-objective problem formulation, the solution to the test suite minimisation problem is one subset of test cases that maximises the test coverage with minimum redundancy.

Since the greedy algorithm does not cope with multiple objectives very well, Multi-Objective Evolutionary Algorithms have been applied to the multi-objective formulation of the test suite minimisation [23, 24]. While this paper studies three selected MOEAs, the principle of parallelising fitness evaluation of multiple solutions in the population of an MOEA applies universally to any MOEA.

GPGPU and Evolutionary Algorithms: Graphics cards have become a compelling platform for intensive computation, with a set of resource-hungry graphic manipulation problems that have driven the rapid advances in their performance and programmability [12]. As a result, consumer-level graphics cards boast tremendous memory bandwidth and computational power. For example, ATI Radeon HD4850 (the graphics card used in the empirical study in the paper), costing about \$150 as of April 2010, provides 1000GFlops processing rate and 63.6GB/s memory bandwidth. Graphics cards are also becoming faster more quickly compared to CPUs. In general, it has been reported that the computational capabilities of graphics cards, measured by metrics of graphics performance, have compounded at the average yearly rate of 1.7x (rendered pixels/s) to 2.3x (rendered vertices/s) [12]. This significantly outperforms the growth in traditional microprocessors; using the SPEC benchmark, the yearly rate of growth for CPU performance has been measured at 1.4x by a recent survey [25].

The disparity between two platforms is caused by the different architecture. CPUs are optimised for executing sequential code, whereas GPUs are optimised for executing the same instruction (the graphics shader) with data parallelism (different objects on the screen). This Single-Instruction/Multiple-Data (SIMD) architecture facilitates hardware-controlled massive data parallelism, which results in the higher performance.

It is precisely this massive data-parallelism of General-Purpose computing on Graphics Processing Units (GPGPU) that presents GPGPU as an ideal platform for parallel evolutionary algorithms. Many of these algorithms require the calculation of fitness (single instruction) for multiple individual solutions in the population pool (multiple data). Early work has exploited this potential for parallelism with both single- and multi-objective evolutionary algorithms [26–28]. However, most existing evaluation has been performed on benchmark problems rather than practical applications.

3   Parallel Formulation of MOEA Test Suite Minimisation

Parallel Fitness Evaluation: The paper considers, for parallelisation, a multi objective test suite minimisation problem from existing work [24]. In order to parallelise test suite minimisation, the fitness evaluation of a generation of individual solutions for the test suite minimisation problem is re-formulated as a matrix multiplication problem. Instead of computing the two objectives (i.e. coverage of test goals and execution cost) for each individual solution, the solutions in the entire population are represented as a matrix, which in turn is multiplied by another matrix that represents the trace data of the entire test suite. The result is a matrix that contains information for both test goal coverage and execution cost. While the paper considers structural coverage as test goal, the proposed approach is equally applicable to other testing criteria, such as dataflow coverage and functional coverage provided that there is a clear mapping between tests and the test objectives they achieve.

More formally, let matrix A contain the trace data that capture the test goals achieved by each test; the number of rows of A equals the number of test goals to be covered, l, and the number of columns of A equals the number of test cases in the test suite, m. Entry $a_{i,j}$ of A stores 1 if the test goal f_i was executed (i.e. covered) by test case t_j, 0 otherwise.

The multiplier matrix, B, is a representation of the current population of individual solutions that are being considered by a given MOEA. Let B be an m-by-n matrix, where n is the size of population for the given MOEA. Entry $b_{j,k}$ of B stores 1 if test case t_j is selected by the individual p_k, 0 otherwise.

The fitness evaluation of the entire generation is performed by the matrix multiplication of $C = A \times B$. Matrix C is a l-by-n matrix; entry $c_{i,k}$ of C denotes the number of times test goal f_i was covered by different test cases that had been selected by the individual p_k.

Cost and Coverage. In order to incorporate the execution cost as an additional objective to the MOEA, the basic reformulation is extended with an extra row in matrix A. The new matrix, A', is an $l + 1$ by m matrix that contains the cost of each individual test case in the last row. The extra row in A' results in an additional row in C' which equals to $A' \times B$ as follows:

$$A' = \begin{pmatrix} a_{1,1} & \cdots & a_{1,m} \\ a_{2,1} & \cdots & a_{2,m} \\ & \cdots & \\ a_{l,1} & \cdots & a_{l,m} \\ cost(t_1) & \cdots & cost(t_m) \end{pmatrix} \qquad C' = \begin{pmatrix} c_{1,1} & \cdots & c_{1,n} \\ c_{2,1} & \cdots & c_{2,n} \\ & \cdots & \\ c_{l,1} & \cdots & c_{l,n} \\ cost(p_1) & \cdots & cost(p_n) \end{pmatrix}$$

By definition, an entry $c_{l+1,k}$ in the last row in C' is defined as $c_{l+1,k} = \sum_{j=1}^{m} a_{l+1,j} \cdot b_{j,k} = \sum_{j=1}^{m} cost(t_j) \cdot b_{j,k}$. That is, $c_{l+1,k}$ equals the sum of costs of all test cases selected by individual solution p_k, i.e. $cost(p_k)$. Similarly, after the multiplication, the k-th column of matrix C' contains the coverage of test goals achieved by individual solution p_k. However, this information needs to be summarised into a percentage coverage, using a step function f as follows: $coverage(p_k) = \frac{\sum_{i=1}^{m} f(c_{i,k})}{m}$, $f(x) = 1$ $(x > 0)$ or 0 (otherwise).

While the cost objective is calculated as a part of the matrix multiplication, the coverage of test goals requires a separate step to be performed. Each column of C' contains the number of times individual testing goals were *covered* by the corresponding solution; in order to calculate the coverage metric for a solution, it is required to iterate over the corresponding column of C'. However, the coverage calculation is also of highly parallel nature because each column can be independently iterated over and, therefore, can take the advantage of GPGPU architecture by running n threads.

4   Algorithms

This section presents the parallel fitness evaluation components for CPU and GPU and introduces the MOEAs that are used in the paper.

Parallel Matrix Multiplication Algorithm: Matrix multiplication is inherently parallelisable as the calculation for an individual entry of the product matrix does not depend on the calculation of any other entry. Algorithm 1 shows the pseudo-code of the parallel matrix multiplication algorithm using the matrix notation in Section 3.

Algorithm 1 uses one thread per element of matrix C', resulting in a total of $(l + 1) \cdot n$ threads. Each thread is identified with unique thread id, tid. Given a thread id, Algorithm 1 calculates the corresponding element of the resulting matrix, $C'_{y,x}$ given the width of matrix A, w_A, i.e., $y = \frac{tid}{w_A}$ and $x = tid \mod w_A$.

Coverage Collection Algorithm: After matrix-multiplication using Algorithm 1, coverage information is collected using a separate algorithm whose pseudo-code is shown in Algorithm 2. Unlike Algorithm 1, the coverage collection algorithm only requires n threads, i.e. one thread per column in C'.

The loop in Line (3) and (4) counts the number of structural elements that have been executed by the individual solution p_{tid}. The coverage is calculated by dividing this number by the total number of structural elements that need to be covered.

While coverage information requires a separate collection phase, the sum of costs for each individual solution has been calculated by Algorithm 1 as a part of the matrix multiplication following the extension in Section 3.

Algorithm 1. Matrix Multiplication

Input: The thread id, *tid*, arrays containing $l + 1$ by m and m by n matrices, A and B, the width of matrix A and B, w_A and w_B

Output: An array to store an $l + 1$ by n matrix, C

MATMULT(*tid*, A, B, w_A, w_B)

(1) $x \leftarrow tid \mod w_A$

(2) $y \leftarrow \frac{tid}{w_A}$

(3) $v \leftarrow 0$

(4) **for** $k = 0$ **to** $w_A - 1$

(5) $v \leftarrow v + A[y \cdot w_A + k] \cdot B[k \cdot w_B + x]$

(6) $C'[y * w_B + x] \leftarrow v$

Algorithm 2. Coverage Collection

Input: The thread id, *tid*, an array containing the result of matrix-multiplication, C', the width of matrix A, w_A and the height of matrix A, h_A

Output: An array containing the coverage achieved by each individual solution, *coverage*

COLLECTCOVERAGE(*tid*, C', w_A, h_A)

(1) $e \leftarrow 0$

(2) **for** $k = 0$ **to** $w_A - 1$

(3)   **if** $C'[k \cdot w_A + tid] > 0$ **then**
         $e \leftarrow e + 1$

(4) $coverage[tid] \leftarrow e/h_A$

5 Experimental Setup

5.1 Research Questions

This section presents the research questions studied in the paper. **RQ1** and **RQ2** concern the scalability achieved by the speed-up through the use of GPGPU:

RQ1. Speed–up: what is the speed–up factor of GPU- and CPU-based parallel versions of MOEAs over the untreated CPU-based version of the same algorithms for multi-objective test suite minimisation problem?

RQ2. Correlation: what are the factors that have the highest correlation to the speed–up achieved, and what is the correlation between these factors and the resulting speed–up?

RQ1 is answered by observing the dynamic execution time of the parallel versions of the studied algorithms as well as the untreated single-threaded algorithms. For **RQ2**, two factors constitute the size of test suite minimisation problem: the number of test cases in the test suite and the number of test goals in System Under Test (SUT) that need to be covered. The speed–up values measured for **RQ1** are statistically analysed to investigate the correlation between the speed–up and these two size factors.

RQ3. Insight: what are the realistic benefits of the scalability that is achieved by the GPGPU approach to software engineers?

RQ3 concerns the practical implications of the speed-up and the consequent scalability to the practitioners. This is answered by analysing the result of test suite minimisation obtained for a real-world testing problem.

5.2 Subjects

Table 1 shows the subject programs for the empirical study. 12 of the programs and test suites are from the Software Infrastructure Repository (SIR) [16]. In order to obtain test suites with varying sizes ranging from a few hundred to a few thousand test cases, the study includes multiple test suites for some subject programs. For printtokens and schedule, smaller test suites are coverage-adequate test suites, whereas larger test suites include all the available test cases. To avoid selection bias, four small test suites were randomly selected from the pool of available tests for each program. In the case of space, SIR contains multiple coverage-adequate test suites of similar sizes; fout test suites were selected randomly.

The subjects also include a large system-level test suite from IBM. For this subject, the coverage information was maintained at the function level. The test suite contains only 181 test cases, but these test cases are used to cover 61,770 functions in the system.

Each test suite has an associated execution cost dataset. For the subject programs from SIR, the execution costs were measured by observing the number of instructions required by the execution of tests. This was performed using a well-known profiling tool, valgrind [29], which executes the given program on a virtual processor. For ibm, physical wall-clock time data, measured in seconds, were provided by IBM. The entire test suite for ibm takes more than 4 hours to execute.

Table 1. Subject programs used for the empirical study

Subject	Description	Program Size	Test Suite Size
printtokens	Lexical analyser	188	315-319[2]
			4,130
printtokens2	Lexical analyser	199	4,115
schedule	Priority scheduler	142	224-227[2]
			2,650
schedule2	Priority scheduler	142	2,710
tcas	Aircraft collision avoidance system	65	1,608
totinfo	Statistics computation utility	124	1,052
replace	Pattern matching & substitution tool	242	5,545
space	Array Definition Language (ADL) interpreter	3,268	154-160[3]
flex	Lexical analyser	3,965	103
gzip	Compression utility	2,007	213
sed	Stream text editor	1,789	370
bash	Unix shell	6,167	1,061
ibm	An IBM middleware system	61,770[1]	181

[1] For the IBM middleware system, the program size represents the number of functions that need to be covered. Others are measured in LOC.

[2] For schedule and printtokens, four randomly selected, coverage-adequate test suites were used as well as the complete test suite in SIR.

[3] For space, four randomly selected, coverage-adequate test suites were used.

5.3   Implementation and Hardware

Implementation: The paper uses NSGA-II implementation from the open source Java MOEA library, jMetal [30, 31] as the untreated version of MOEA. The GPGPU-based parallel version of NSGA-II is implemented in the OpenCL GPGPU framework using a Java wrapper called JavaCL [32]. The CPU-based parallel version of NSGA-II uses a parallel programming library for Java called JOMP [33]. JOMP allows parameterised configuration of the number of threads to use. In both cases, the parallelisation is only applied to the fitness evaluation step of the basic jMetal implementation of NSGA-II, because it is not clear whether certain steps in NSGA-II, such as sorting, may yield sufficient efficiency when performed in parallel.

NSGA-II is configured with population size of 256 following the standard recommendation to set the number of threads to multiples of 32 or 64 [34]. The stopping criterion is to reach the maximum number of fitness evaluations, which is set to 64,000, allowing 250 generations to be evaluated. Individual solutions are represented by binary strings that form columns in matrix B in Section 3. The initial population is generated by randomly setting the individual bits of these binary strings so that the initial solutions are randomly distributed in the phenotype space.

NSGA-II uses the binary tournament selection operator and the single-point crossover operator with probability of crossover set to 0.9 and the single bit-flip mutation operator with the mutation rate of $\frac{1}{n}$ where n is the length of the bit-string (i.e. the number of test goals).

Hardware: All configurations of NSGA-II have been evaluated on a machine with a quad-core Intel Core i7 CPU (2.8GHz clock speed) and 4GB memory, running Mac OS X 10.6.5 with Darwin Kernel 10.6.0 for x86_64 architecture. The Java Virtual Machine used to execute the algorithms is Java SE Runtime with version 1.6.0_22. The GPGPU-based version of NSGA-II has been evaluated on an ATI Radeon HD4850 graphics card with 800 stream processors running at 625MHz clock speed and 512MB GDDR3 onboard memory.

5.4   Evaluation

The paper compares five different configurations of NSGA-II: the untreated configuration (hereafter refered to CPU), the GPGPU configuration (GPU) and the JOMP-based parallel configurations with 1, 2, and 4 threads (JOMP1/2/4). The configuration with one thread (JOMP1) is included to observe the speed-up achieved by evaluating the fitness of the entire population using matrix multiplication, instead of evaluating the solutions one by one as in the untreated version. Any speed–up achieved by JOMP1 over CPU is, therefore, primarily achieved by the optimisation that removes the method invocation overheads. On the other hand, JOMP1 does incur an additional thread management overhead.

For each subject test suite, the five configurations were executed 30 times in order to cater for the inherent randomness in dynamic execution time. The observation of algorithm execution time ($Time_{total}$) is composed of the following three parts:

- Initialisation ($Time_{init}$): the time it takes for the algorithm to initialise the test suite data in a usable form; for example, GPU configurations of MOEAs need to transfer the test suite data onto the graphics card.
- Fitness Evaluation ($Time_{fitness}$): the time it takes for the algorithm to evaluate the fitness values of different generations during its runtime.
- Remaining ($Time_{remaining}$): the remaining parts of the execution time, most of which is used for archive management, genetic operations, etc.

Execution time is measured using the system clock. The speed-up is calculated by dividing the amount of the time that the CPU configuration required by the amount of the time parallel configurations required.

6   Results

Speed–up: Table 2 contains the speed–up data in more detail, whereas the statistical analysis of the raw information can be obtained from the appendix.[1] Overall, the observed paired mean speed–up ranges from 1.43x to 25.09x. The speed–up values below 1.0 show that the overhead of thread management and the additional data structure manipulation can be detrimental for the problems of sufficiently small size. However, as the problem size grows, JOMP1 becomes faster than CPU with all algorithms, indicating that the amount of reduced method call overhead eventually becomes greater that the thread management overhead. With the largest dataset, ibm, the GPU configuration of NSGA-II reduces the average execution time of CPU, 4,347 seconds (1 hour 12 minutes and 27 seconds), into the average of 174 seconds (2 minutes and 54 seconds). The speed–up remains consistently above 5.0x if the problem size is larger than that of flex, i.e. about 400,000 (103 tests × 3,965 test goals).

To provide more detailed analysis, the observed execution time data have been compared using The Mann-Whitney 'U' test. The Mann-Whitney 'U' test is a non-parametric statistical hypothesis test, i.e. it allows the comparison of two samples with unknown distributions. The execution time data observed with JOMP1/2/4 and GPU configurations were compared to those from CPU configuration. The null hypothesis is that there is no difference between the parallel configurations and CPU configuration; the alternative hypothesis is that the execution time of the parallel configurations is smaller than that of CPU configuration.

Table 3 contains the resulting p-values. With JOMP1 configuration, the alternative hypothesis is rejected for 15 cases at the confidence level of 95%, providing evidence that the parallel configurations required more time than the untreated configuration(CPU). With all other configurations, the null hypothesis is universally rejected for all subjects, providing strong evidence that the parallel configurations required less time than the untreated configuration(CPU). The particular

---

[1] The detailed statistical data can be viewed at
http://www.cs.ucl.ac.uk/staff/s.yoo/gpgpu

Table 2. Speed–up results

Subject	S_{JOMP1}	S_{JOMP2}	S_{JOMP4}	S_{GPU}
printtokens-1	0.83	1.21	1.54	2.14
printtokens-2	0.83	1.23	1.56	2.20
printtokens-3	0.82	1.21	1.53	2.13
printtokens-4	0.84	1.22	1.54	2.19
schedule-1	0.97	1.22	1.40	1.56
schedule-2	0.96	1.22	1.41	1.46
schedule-3	0.96	1.22	1.39	1.45
schedule-4	0.95	1.20	1.37	1.43
printtokens	0.76	1.24	1.44	4.52
schedule	0.69	1.08	1.26	3.38
printtokens2	0.72	1.18	1.37	4.38
schedule2	0.71	1.09	1.27	3.09
tcas	0.84	1.10	1.30	1.94
totinfo	0.90	1.28	1.61	2.50
flex	1.58	2.76	4.19	6.82
gzip	1.19	2.15	3.31	8.00
sed	1.02	1.87	3.04	10.28
space-1	1.77	3.22	5.10	10.51
space-2	1.86	3.34	5.19	10.88
space-3	1.80	3.27	5.16	10.63
space-4	1.76	3.25	5.12	10.54
replace	0.73	1.23	1.44	5.26
bash	1.54	2.90	4.87	25.09
ibm	3.01	5.55	9.04	24.85

Table 3. Mann-Whitney U test

Subject	p_{JOMP1}	p_{JOMP2}	p_{JOMP4}	p_{GPU}
printtokens-1	1.00e+00	1.51e-11	8.46e-18	1.51e-11
printtokens-2	1.00e+00	1.51e-11	8.46e-18	1.51e-11
printtokens-3	1.00e+00	1.51e-11	8.46e-18	8.46e-18
printtokens-4	1.00e+00	1.51e-11	1.51e-11	1.51e-11
schedule-1	1.00e+00	1.51e-11	1.51e-11	1.51e-11
schedule-2	1.00e+00	1.51e-11	8.46e-18	1.51e-11
schedule-3	1.00e+00	1.51e-11	1.51e-11	1.51e-11
schedule-4	1.00e+00	1.51e-11	1.51e-11	1.51e-11
printtokens	1.00e+00	8.46e-18	8.46e-18	8.46e-18
schedule	1.00e+00	1.51e-11	1.51e-11	8.46e-18
printtokens2	1.00e+00	1.51e-11	8.46e-18	1.51e-11
schedule2	1.00e+00	1.51e-11	8.46e-18	8.46e-18
tcas	1.00e+00	8.46e-18	8.46e-18	8.46e-18
totinfo	1.00e+00	1.51e-11	8.46e-18	8.46e-18
flex	8.46e-18	8.46e-18	1.51e-11	1.51e-11
gzip	1.51e-11	1.51e-11	1.51e-11	1.51e-11
sed	2.56e-07	8.46e-18	8.46e-18	1.51e-11
space-1	8.46e-18	8.46e-18	1.51e-11	1.51e-11
space-2	8.46e-18	8.46e-18	1.51e-11	1.51e-11
space-3	8.46e-18	8.46e-18	8.46e-18	1.51e-11
space-4	8.46e-18	8.46e-18	8.46e-18	1.51e-11
replace	1.00e+00	8.46e-18	1.51e-11	8.46e-18
bash	8.46e-18	8.46e-18	8.46e-18	8.46e-18
ibm	1.51e-11	8.46e-18	8.46e-18	1.51e-11

results are naturally dependent on the choice of the graphics card that has been used for the experiment. However, these results, taken together, provide strong evidence that, for test suite minimisation problems of realistic sizes, the GPGPU approach can provide a speed–up of at least 5.0x. This finding answers **RQ1**.

Correlation: Regarding **RQ2**, one important factor that contributes to the level of speed–up is the speed of each individual computational unit in the graphics card. The HD4850 graphics card used in the experiment contains 800 stream processor units that are normally used for the computation of geometric shading. Each of these stream processors execute a single thread of Algorithm 1, of which there exist more than 800. Therefore, if the individual stream processor is as powerful as a single core of the CPU, the absolute upper bound of speed–up would be 800. In practice, the individual stream processors run with the clock speed of 625MHz, which makes them much slower and, therefore, less powerful than a CPU core. This results in speed–up values lower than 800.

In order to answer **RQ2**, statistical regression analysis was performed on the correlation between the observed speed–up and the factors that characterise the size of problems.

Three size factors have been analysed for the statistical regression: the number of test goals and the number of test cases are denoted by l and m respectively, following the matrix notation in Section 3: l denotes the number of threads the GPGPU-version of the algorithm has to execute (as the size of the matrix C' is l-by-n and n is fixed); m denotes the amount of computation that needs to be performed by a single thread (as each matrix-multiplication kernel computes a

Table 4. Spearman's rank correlation coefficients between three size factors and speed–ups

Config	ρ_z	ρ_l	ρ_m
JOMP1	0.2257	0.6399	-0.8338
JOMP2	0.4908	0.7800	-0.6423
JOMP4	0.4788	0.8227	-0.6378
GPGPU	0.8760	0.8617	-0.2299

Table 5. Regression Analysis for NSGA-II

Config	Model	α	β	γ	R^2
JOMP1	$S_p \sim z$	1.56e-07	N/A	1.00e+00	0.4894
	$S_p \sim \log z$	2.01e-01	N/A	-1.34e+00	0.3423
	$S_p \sim l + m$	3.27e-05	-1.13e-04	1.17e+00	0.7060
	$S_p \sim \log l + m$	2.69e-01	-4.83e-05	-4.79e-01	0.8487
	$S_p \sim l + \log m$	3.12e-05	-1.78e-01	2.15e+00	0.7600
	$S_p \sim \log l + \log m$	2.62e-01	-6.83e-02	-6.15e-02	0.8509
JOMP2	$S_p \sim z$	3.24e-07	N/A	1.58e+00	0.5009
	$S_p \sim \log z$	4.78e-01	N/A	-4.05e+00	0.4606
	$S_p \sim l + m$	6.64e-05	-1.82e-04	1.87e+00	0.6367
	$S_p \sim \log l + m$	6.00e-01	-2.84e-05	-1.83e+00	0.9084
	$S_p \sim l + \log m$	6.35e-05	-3.07e-01	3.58e+00	0.6836
	$S_p \sim \log l + \log m$	5.96e-01	-4.04e-02	-1.59e+00	0.9086
JOMP4	$S_p \sim z$	5.80e-07	N/A	2.15e+00	0.5045
	$S_p \sim \log z$	8.72e-01	N/A	-8.13e+00	0.4814
	$S_p \sim l + m$	1.16e-04	-3.42e-04	2.70e+00	0.6199
	$S_p \sim \log l + m$	1.08e+00	-5.93e-05	-4.00e+00	0.9322
	$S_p \sim l + \log m$	1.11e-04	-5.49e-01	5.74e+00	0.6611
	$S_p \sim \log l + \log m$	1.08e+00	-5.50e-02	-3.72e+00	0.9313
GPU	$S_p \sim z$	2.25e-06	N/A	4.13e+00	0.7261
	$S_p \sim \log z$	3.45e+00	N/A	-3.66e+01	0.7178
	$S_p \sim l + m$	3.62e-04	-1.63e-04	5.33e+00	0.4685
	$S_p \sim \log l + m$	3.53e+00	7.79e-04	-1.66e+01	0.8219
	$S_p \sim l + \log m$	3.62e-04	-1.34e-01	5.98e+00	0.4676
	$S_p \sim \log l + \log m$	3.85e+00	1.69e+00	-2.82e+01	0.8713

loop with m iterations). In addition to these measurement, another size factor $z = l \cdot m$ is considered to represent the *perceived* size of the minimisation problem. Table 4 shows the results of Spearman's rank correlation analysis between size factors and observed speed–ups.

Spearman's rank correlation is a non-parametric measure of how well the relationship between two variables can be described using a monotonic function. As one variable increases, the other variable will tend to increase monotonically if the coefficient is close to 1, whereas it would decrease monotonically if the coefficient is close to -1.

Size factor l shows the strongest overall positive correlation with speed–ups in all configurations. The correlation coefficients for z are weaker than those for l, whereas correlation for m remains negative for all algorithms and configurations.

To gain further insights into the correlation between size factors and speed–ups, a regression analysis was performed. Factor z is considered in isolation, whereas l and m are considered together; each variable has been considered in its linear form (z, l and m) and logarithmic form ($\log z, \log l$ and $\log m$). This results in 6 different combinations of regression models. Table 5 presents the results of regression analysis for four configurations respectively.

With a few exceptions of very small margins (JOMP4), the model with the highest r^2 correlation for all configurations is $S_p = \alpha \log l + \beta \log m + \gamma$. Figure 1 shows the 3D plot of this model for the GPU and JOMP4 configurations.

Plot of regression model

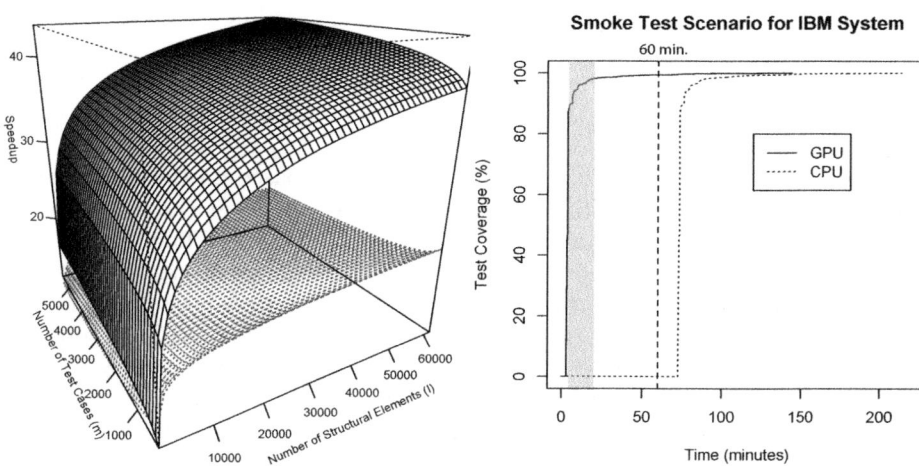

Fig. 1. 3D-plot of regression model $S_p = \alpha \log l + \beta \log m + \gamma$ for GPU(solid line) and JOMP4(dotted line) configurations.

Fig. 2. Comparison of smoke test scenarios for IBM System (`ibm`). The solid line shows the trade-offs between time and test coverage when `GPU` configuration of NSGA-II is used, whereas the dotted line shows that of `CPU`. The grey area shows the interesting trade-off that the `CPU` configuration fails to exploit within 60 minutes.

The observed trend is that the inclusion of $\log l$ results in higher correlation, whereas models that use l in its linear form tend to result in lowest correlation. This confirms the results of Spearman's rank correlation analysis in Table 4. The coefficients for the best-fit regression model for `GPU`, $S_p = \alpha \log l + \beta \log m + \gamma$, can explain why the speed–up results for `space` test suites are higher than those for test suites with similar z values such as `tcas`, `gzip` and `replace`. Apart from `bash` and `ibm`, `space` has the highest l value. Since α is more than twice larger than β, a higher value of l has more impact to S_p than m.

Based on the analysis, **RQ2** is answered as follows: the observed speed–up shows a strong linear correlation to the log of the number of test goals to cover and the log of the number of test cases in the test suite. The positive correlation provides a strong evidence that GPU-based parallelisation scales up.

Furthermore, within the observed data, the speed–up continues to increase as the problem size grows, which suggests that the graphics card did not reach its full computational capacity. It may be that for larger problems, if studied, the speed–up would be even greater than those observed in this paper; certainly the correlation observed indicates that this can be expected. The finding that the scalability factor increases with overall problem size is a very encouraging finding; as the problem gets harder, the solutions are obtained faster.

Insights: This section discusses a possible real-world scenario in which the parallelisation of multi-objective test suite minimisation can have a high impact. A smoke test is a testing activity that is usually performed in a very short window of time to detect the most obvious faults, such as system crashes. IBM's smoke test practice is to allow from 30 to 60 minutes of time to execute a subset of tests from a large test suite that would require more than 4 hours to execute in its entirety.

Figure 2 shows two possible smoke test scenarios based on the results of CPU and GPU configurations of NSGA-II. The solid line represents the scenario based on the GPU configuration of the algorithm, whereas the dotted line represents the scenario based on the CPU configuration. The flat segment shows the time each configuration spends on the optimisation process; the curved segment shows the trade-off between time and test coverage achieved by the optimised test suite. Since the CPU configuration of NSGA-II takes longer than 60 minutes to terminate, it cannot contribute to any smoke test scenario that must be completed within 60 minutes. On the other hand, the GPU configuration allows the tester to consider a subset of tests that can be executed under 30 minutes. If the grey region was wider than Figure 2, the difference between two configurations would have been even more dramatic.

This answers **RQ3** as follows: a faster execution of optimisation algorithms enables the tester not only to use the algorithms but also to exploit their results more effectively. This real world smoke test example from IBM demonstrates that scale–ups accrued from the use of GPU are not only sources of efficiency improvement, they can also make possible test activities that are simply impossible without this scalability.

The ability to execute a sophisticated optimisation algorithm within a relatively short time also allows the tester to consider state-of-the-art regression testing techniques with greater flexibility. The greater flexibility is obtained because the cost of the optimisation does not have to be amortised across multiple iterations. Many state-of-the-art regression testing techniques require the use of continuously changing sets of testing data, such as recent fault history [24] or the last time a specific test case has been executed [35, 36]. In addition to the use of dynamic testing data, the previous work also showed that repeatedly using the same subset of a large test suite may impair the fault detection capability of the regression testing [37].

7   Related Work

Test suite minimisation aims to reduce the number of tests to be executed by calculating the minimum set of tests that are required to satisfy the given test requirements. The problem has been formulated as the minimal hitting set problem [21], which is NP-hard [19].

Various heuristics for the minimal hitting set problem, or the minimal set cover problem (the duality of the former), have been suggested for the test suite minimisation [20, 38]. However, empirical evaluations of these techniques have reported conflicting views on the impact on fault detection capability: some reported no impact [39, 40] while others reported compromised fault detection capability [17, 41].

One potential reason why test suite minimisation has negative impact on the fault detection capability is the fact that the criterion for minimisation is structural coverage; achieving coverage alone may not be sufficient for revealing faults. This paper uses the multi-objective approach based on Multi-Objective Evolutionary Algorithm (MOEA) introduced by Yoo and Harman [24]; the paper also presents the first attempt to parallelise test suite minimisation with sophisticated criteria for scalability.

Population-based evolutionary algorithms are ideal candidates for parallelisation on graphics cards [12] and existing work has shown successful implementations for classical problems. Tsutsui and Fujimoto implemented a single-objective parallel Genetic Algorithm (GA) using GPU for the Quadratic Assignment Problem (QAP) [26]. Wilson and Banzaf implemented a linear Genetic Programming (GP) algorithm on XBox360 game consoles [27]. Langdon and Banzaf implemented GP for GPU using an SIMD interpreter for fitness evaluation [11]. Wong implemented an MOEA on GPU and evaluated the implementation using a suite of benchmark problems [28]. Wong's implementation parallelised not only the fitness evaluation step but also the parent selection, crossover & mutation operator as well as the dominance checking.

Despite the highly parallelisable nature of many techniques used in SBSE, few parallel algorithms have been used. Mitchell et al. used a distributed architecture for their clustering tool Bunch [7]. Asadi et al. also used a distributed Server-Client architecture for Concept Location problem [9]. However, both approaches use a distributed architecture that requires multiple machines; this paper is the first work on SBSE that presents highly affordable parallelism based on GPGPU.

8   Conclusion

This paper presents the first use of GPGPU-based massive parallelism for improving scalability of regression testing, based on Search-Based Software Engineering (SBSE). The advances in GPGPU architecture and the consequent availability of parallelism provides an ideal platform for improving SBSE scalability.

The paper presents an evaluation of the GPGPU-based test suite minimisation for real-world examples that include an industry-scale test suite. The results show that the GPGPU-based optimisation can achieve a speed–up of up to 25.09x compared to a single-threaded version of the same algorithm executed on a CPU. The highest speed–up achieved by the CPU-based parallel optimisation was 9.04x. Statistical analysis shows that the speed–up correlates to the logarithmic of the problem size, i.e. the size of the program under test and the size of the test suite. This finding indicates that as the problem becomes larger, the scalability of the proposed approach increases; a very attractive finding.

References

1. Sommerville, I.: Software Engineering, 6th edn. Addison-Wesley, Reading (2001)
2. Pressman, R.: Software Engineering: A Practitioner's Approach, 3rd edn. McGraw-Hill Book Company Europe, Maidenhead (1992); european adaptation (1994); Adapted by Darrel Ince
3. Cordy, J.R.: Comprehending reality - practical barriers to industrial adoption of software maintenance automation. In: IEEE International Workshop on Program Comprehension (IWPC 2003), pp. 196–206. IEEE Computer Society, Los Alamitos (2003)
4. Chau, P.Y.K., Tam, K.Y.: Factors affecting the adoption of open systems: An exploratory study. MIS Quarterly 21(1) (1997)
5. Premkumar, G., Potter, M.: Adoption of computer aided software engineering (CASE) technology: An innovation adoption perspective. Database 26(2&3), 105–124 (1995)
6. Cantú-Paz, E., Goldberg, D.E.: Efficient parallel genetic algorithms: theory and practice. Computer Methods in Applied Mechanics and Engineering 186(2-4), 221–238 (2000)
7. Mitchell, B.S., Traverso, M., Mancoridis, S.: An architecture for distributing the computation of software clustering algorithms. In: IEEE/IFIP Proceedings of the Working Conference on Software Architecture (WICSA 2001), pp. 181–190. IEEE Computer Society Press, Amsterdam (2001)
8. Mahdavi, K., Harman, M., Hierons, R.M.: A multiple hill climbing approach to software module clustering. In: IEEE International Conference on Software Maintenance, pp. 315–324. IEEE Computer Society Press, Los Alamitos (2003)
9. Asadi, F., Antoniol, G., Guéhéneuc, Y.-G.: Concept locations with genetic algorithms: A comparison of four distributed architectures. In: Proceedings of 2nd International Symposium on Search based Software Engineering (SSBSE 2010). IEEE Computer Society Press, Benevento (2010) (to appear)
10. Zhang, Y.: SBSE repository (February 14, 2011),
    http://www.sebase.org/sbse/publications/repository.html
11. Langdon, W.B., Banzhaf, W.: A SIMD interpreter for genetic programming on GPU graphics cards. In: O'Neill, M., Vanneschi, L., Gustafson, S., Esparcia Alcázar, A.I., De Falco, I., Della Cioppa, A., Tarantino, E. (eds.) EuroGP 2008. LNCS, vol. 4971, pp. 73–85. Springer, Heidelberg (2008)
12. Owens, J.D., Luebke, D., Govindaraju, N., Harris, M., Krüger, J., Lefohn, A.E., Purcell, T.J.: A survey of general-purpose computation on graphics hardware. Computer Graphics Forum 26(1), 80–113 (2007)
13. Boyer, M., Tarjan, D., Acton, S.T., Skadron, K.: Accelerating leukocyte tracking using cuda: A case study in leveraging manycore coprocessors. In: Proceedings of the 23rd IEEE International Parallel and Distributed Processing Symposium (IPDPS) (May 2009)
14. Govindaraju, N.K., Gray, J., Kumar, R., Manocha, D.: Gputerasort: High performance graphics coprocessor sorting for large database management. In: ACM SIGMOD (2006)
15. Hutchins, M., Foster, H., Goradia, T., Ostrand, T.: Experiments of the effectiveness of dataflow- and controlflow-based test adequacy criteria. In: Proceedings of the 16th International Conference on Software Engineering (ICSE 1994), pp. 191–200. IEEE Computer Society Press, Los Alamitos (1994)

16. Do, H., Elbaum, S.G., Rothermel, G.: Supporting controlled experimentation with testing techniques: An infrastructure and its potential impact. Empirical Software Engineering 10(4), 405–435 (2005)
17. Rothermel, G., Harrold, M., Ronne, J., Hong, C.: Empirical studies of test suite reduction. Software Testing, Verification, and Reliability 4(2), 219–249 (2002)
18. Yoo, S., Harman, M.: Regression testing minimisation, selection and prioritisation: A survey. Software Testing, Verification, and Reliability (2010) (to appear)
19. Garey, M.R., Johnson, D.S.: Computers and Intractability: A guide to the theory of NP-Completeness. W. H. Freeman and Company, New York (1979)
20. Offutt, J., Pan, J., Voas, J.: Procedures for reducing the size of coverage-based test sets. In: Proceedings of the 12th International Conference on Testing Computer Software, pp. 111–123. ACM Press, New York (1995)
21. Harrold, M.J., Gupta, R., Soffa, M.L.: A methodology for controlling the size of a test suite. ACM Transactions on Software Engineering and Methodology 2(3), 270–285 (1993)
22. Chen, T., Lau, M.: Heuristics towards the optimization of the size of a test suite. In: Proceedings of the 3rd International Conference on Software Quality Management, vol. 2, pp. 415–424 (1995)
23. Maia, C.L.B., do Carmo, R.A.F., de Freitas, F.G., de Campos, G.A.L., de Souza, J.T.: A multi-objective approach for the regression test case selection problem. In: Proceedings of Anais do XLI Simpòsio Brasileiro de Pesquisa Operacional (SBPO 2009), pp. 1824–1835 (2009)
24. Yoo, S., Harman, M.: Pareto efficient multi-objective test case selection. In: Proceedings of International Symposium on Software Testing and Analysis, pp. 140–150. ACM Press, New York (2007)
25. Ekman, M., Warg, F., Nilsson, J.: An in-depth look at computer performance growth. SIGARCH Computer Architecture News 33(1), 144–147 (2005)
26. Tsutsui, S., Fujimoto, N.: Solving quadratic assignment problems by genetic algorithms with GPU computation: a case study. In: Proceedings of the 11th Annual Conference Companion on Genetic and Evolutionary Computation Conference (GECCO 2009), pp. 2523–2530. ACM Press, New York (2009)
27. Wilson, G., Banzhaf, W.: Deployment of cpu and gpu-based genetic programming on heterogeneous devices. In: Proceedings of the 11th Annual Conference Companion on Genetic and Evolutionary Computation Conference (GECCO 2009), pp. 2531–2538. ACM Press, New York (2009)
28. Wong, M.L.: Parallel multi-objective evolutionary algorithms on graphics processing units. In: Proceedings of the 11th Annual Conference Companion on Genetic and Evolutionary Computation Conference (GECCO 2009), pp. 2515–2522. ACM Press, New York (2009)
29. Nethercote, N., Seward, J.: Valgrind: A program supervision framework. In: Proceedings of ACM Conference on Programming Language Design and Implementation, pp. 89–100. ACM Press, New York (2007)
30. Durillo, J.J., Nebro, A.J., Luna, F., Dorronsoro, B., Alba, E.: jMetal: A Java Framework for Developing Multi-Objective Optimization Metaheuristics. Departamento de Lenguajes y Ciencias de la Computación, University of Málaga, E.T.S.I. Informática, Campus de Teatinos, Tech. Rep. ITI-2006-10 (December 2006)
31. Durillo, J.J., Nebro, A.J., Alba, E.: The jmetal framework for multi-objective optimization: Design and architecture. In: Proceedings of Congress on Evolutionary Computation 2010, Barcelona, Spain, pp. 4138–4325 (July 2010)

32. Chafik, O.: JavaCL: opensource Java wrapper for OpenCL library (2009), code.google.com/p/javacl/ (accessed June 6, 2010)
33. Bull, J.M., Westhead, M.D., Kambites, M.E., Obrzalek, J.: Towards OpenMP for java. In: Proceedings of the European Workshop on OpenMP, pp. 98–105 (2000)
34. ATI Stream Computing: OpenCL Programming Guide Rev. AMD Corp. (August 2010)
35. Kim, J.-M., Porter, A.: A history-based test prioritization technique for regression testing in resource constrained environments. In: Proceedings of the 24th International Conference on Software Engineering, pp. 119–129. ACM, New York (2002)
36. Engström, E., Runeson, P., Wikstrand, G.: An empirical evaluation of regression testing based on fix-cache recommendations. In: Proceedings of the 3rd International Conference on Software Testing Verification and Validation (ICST 2010), pp. 75–78. IEEE Computer Society Press, Los Alamitos (2010)
37. Yoo, S., Harman, M., Ur, S.: Measuring and improving latency to avoid test suite wear out. In: Proceedings of the Interntional Conference on Software Testing, Verification and Validation Workshop (ICSTW 2009), pp. 101–110. IEEE Computer Society Press, Los Alamitos (2009)
38. Chen, T.Y., Lau, M.F.: Dividing strategies for the optimization of a test suite. Information Processing Letters 60(3), 135–141 (1996)
39. Wong, W.E., Horgan, J.R., London, S., Mathur, A.P.: Effect of test set minimization on fault detection effectiveness. Software Practice and Experience 28(4), 347–369 (1998)
40. Wong, W.E., Horgan, J.R., Mathur, A.P., Pasquini, A.: Test set size minimization and fault detection effectiveness: A case study in a space application. The Journal of Systems and Software 48(2), 79–89 (1999)
41. Rothermel, G., Elbaum, S., Malishevsky, A., Kallakuri, P., Davia, B.: The impact of test suite granularity on the cost-effectiveness of regression testing. In: Proceedings of the 24th International Conference on Software Engineering (ICSE 2002), pp. 130–140. ACM Press, New York (2002)

Bytecode Testability Transformation

Yanchuan Li and Gordon Fraser

Saarland University, Saarbruecken-66123, Germany
yanchuan@st.cs.uni-saarland.de, fraser@cs.uni-saarland.de

Abstract. Bytecode as produced by modern programming languages is well suited for search-based testing: Different languages compile to the same byte-code, bytecode is available also for third party libraries, all predicates are atomic and side-effect free, and instrumentation can be performed without recompilation. However, bytecode is also susceptible to the flag problem; in fact, regular source code statements such as floating point operations might create unexpected flag problems on the bytecode level. We present an implementation of state-of-the-art testability transformation for Java bytecode, such that all Boolean values are replaced by integers that preserve information about branch distances, even across method boundaries. The transformation preserves both the original semantics and structure, allowing it to be transparently plugged into any bytecode-based testing tool. Experiments on flag problem benchmarks show the effectiveness of the transformation, while experiments on open source libraries show that although this type of problem can be handled efficiently it is less frequent than expected.

1 Introduction

Search-based testing can efficiently generate test inputs that trigger almost any desired path through a program. At the core of these techniques is the fitness function, which estimates how close a candidate solution comes to satisfying its objective. Traditionally, this fitness is based on distances in the control flow and distance estimates for predicate evaluation. The latter are sensitive to Boolean flags, in which the distance information is lost on the way to the target predicate, thus giving no guidance during the search.

Traditionally, search-based testing requires that the source code of the program under test (PUT) is instrumented to collect information required for the distance estimation during execution. The instrumented program is compiled and repeatedly executed as part of fitness evaluations. The fitness evaluation is hindered by problems such as Boolean flags, in which information that could be used for fitness guidance is lost. Testability transformation [8] has been introduced as a solution to overcome this problem, by changing the source code such that information lost at flag creation is propagated to the predicates where flags are used.

If Boolean flags are created outside the scope of the PUT, the source code for these might not be available (e.g., third party libraries), traditional testability transformation is not possible. In contrast, languages based on bytecode interpretation such as Java or C# have the advantage that the bytecode is mostly available even for third party libraries (except for some cases of calls to native code). Bytecode is well suited for search based testing: Complex predicates in the source code are compiled to atomic predicates based

M.B. Cohen and M. Ó Cinnéide (Eds.): SSBSE 2011, LNCS 6956, pp. 237–251, 2011.

on integers in the bytecode. These atomic predicates are always side-effect free, and instrumenting the bytecode to measure branch distances at these predicates is straight forward. In addition, bytecode instrumentation can be done during class loading or even in memory, thus removing the need to recompile instrumented code.

In this paper, we present a bytecode testability transformation which allows us to retain the information traditionally lost when Booleans are defined, thus improving the guidance during search-based testing. In detail, the contributions of this paper are:

Bytecode Instrumentation: Based on previous work in testability transformation [15], we present a semantics preserving transformation of bytecode, which improves the search landscape with respect to traditional Boolean flags as well as those introduced during the compilation to bytecode.

Testability Transformation for Object Oriented Code: The transformation is interprocedural, preserving the information across method calls and interfaces. In addition, the transformation applies to object-oriented constructs, transforming all class members, while preserving validity with respect to references to and inheritance from non-transformable classes (e.g., `java.lang.Object`).

Evaluation: We apply the transformation to a set of open source libraries, thus allowing us to measure the effects of the flag problem in real world software.

This paper is organized as follows: First, we give all the necessary details of search-based testing based on bytecode (Section 2). Then, we describe the details of our transformation in Section 3. Finally, we present the results of evaluating the transformation on a set of case study examples and open source libraries in Section 4.

2   Background

2.1   Search-Based Testing

Search-based testing applies efficient meta-heuristic search techniques to the task of test data generation [10]. For example, in a genetic algorithm a population of candidate solutions (i.e., potential test cases) is evolved towards satisfying a chosen coverage criterion. The search is guided by a fitness function that estimates how close a candidate solution is to satisfying a coverage goal.

The initial population is usually generated randomly, i.e., a fixed number of random numbers for the input values is generated. The operators used in the evolution of this initial population depend on the chosen representation. For example, in a bitvector representation, crossover between two individuals would split the parent bitvectors at random positions and merge them together, and mutation would flip bits.

A fitness function guides the search in choosing individuals for reproduction, gradually improving the fitness values with each generation until a solution is found. For example, to generate tests for branch coverage a common fitness function [10] integrates the *approach-level* (number of unsatisfied control dependencies) and the *branch distance* (estimation of how close the deviating condition is to evaluating as desired).

In this paper we consider object oriented software, for which test cases are essentially small programs exercising the classes under test. Search-based techniques have been applied to test object oriented software using method sequences [3, 7, 13] and strongly typed genetic programming [12, 16].

2.2   Bytecode and Bytecode Instrumentation

Modern programming languages such as Java or those of the .NET framework do not follow the traditional process of compilation to machine code, but are compiled to an intermediate format (bytecode) which is interpreted by virtual machines. The main advantage of such an approach is that the same bytecode can be executed on any platform for which there is a virtual machine available. In addition, it is possible to compile source code of different languages to the same bytecode: For example, all .NET languages (e.g., C# or VB) compile to the same bytecode, and many languages such as Ada, Groovy or Scala can be compiled to Java bytecode. Although machine independent, bytecode is traditionally very close to machine code while retaining some of the information traditionally only available in the source code. As such, it is well suited for different types of analyses even when source code is not available.

An important feature of languages that are based on interpreting bytecode is that they conveniently allow manipulation of the bytecode during class loading, such that instrumentation can be performed without recompilation. In addition, bytecode is at a lower level of abstraction, where the choice of different bytecode instructions is usually smaller than the possible syntactic constructs at source code level, thus making analysis much simpler.

In this paper, we focus on the Java language and bytecode. A detailed description of Java bytecode is out of the scope of this paper; we give the details necessary to understand the transformation, and refer the interested reader to the specification of the Java virtual machine [9]. Java bytecode is based on a stack machine architecture, which retains the information about classes and methods. Each method is represented as a sequence of bytecode instructions, where dedicated registers represent the method parameters and the special value `this`.

The most interesting aspect for search-based testing is that all predicates in source code are translated to simple but potentially nested jump conditions in the bytecode. These conditions operate only integer values, and are free of side effects. Each jump condition consists of an op-code that denotes the type of condition, and a target label. If the condition evaluates to true, then execution jumps to the position in the instruction sequence labelled with the target label, else it proceeds with the next bytecode instruction in sequence. There are different categories of jump conditions; for example, Table 1 lists the conditional jump instructions that compare integer values. Each of the operations in the left half of the table pops a value from the stack and compares it to 0. Similar operations are available to compare identity of object references (IF_ACMPEQ, IF_ACMPNE) and comparison of an object reference to the special value null (IF_NULL, IF_NONNULL). Finally, there is also an unconditional jump operation (GOTO), which always jumps to the target label.

The Java API provides an instrumentation interface, where each class is passed on to different instrumentation classes when loaded. There are several libraries available which allow this instrumentation to be done very conveniently. In our experiments, we used the library ASM[1].

A straight forward approach to search-based testing is to instrument the target program with additional calls that track information about the control flow and branch

---

[1] http://asm.ow2.org/

Table 1. Branch instructions in Java bytecode based on integer operators; top denotes the top value on the stack, top' denotes the value below top

Operator	Description	Operator	Description
IFEQ	$top = 0$	IF_ICMPEQ	$top' = top$
IFNE	$top \neq 0$	IF_ICMPNE	$top' \neq top$
IFLT	$top < 0$	IF_ICMPLT	$top' < top$
IFLE	$top \leq 0$	IF_ICMPLE	$top' \leq top$
IFGT	$top > 0$	IF_ICMPGT	$top' > top$
IFGE	$top \geq 0$	IF_ICMPGE	$top' \geq top$

distances — such instrumentation can easily be done at the bytecode level. For example, our recent EVOSUITE [6] prototype adds a method call before each conditional branch in the bytecode, which keeps track of the top elements on the stack and the op-code of the branch instruction, thus allowing the calculation of precise fitness values.

2.3 Testability Transformation

The success of search-based testing depends on the availability of appropriate fitness functions that guide towards an optimal solution. In practice, the search landscape described by these fitness functions often contains problematic areas such as local optima, i.e., candidate solutions may have better fitness than their neighbors but are not globally optimal, thus inhibiting exploration. Another problem are plateaux in the search landscape, where individuals have the same fitness as their neighborhood, which lets the search degrade to random search. A typical source of such problems are Boolean flags or nested predicates, and a common solution is testability transformation [8], which tries to avoid the problem by altering the source code in a way that improves the search landscape before applying the search.

Harman et al. [8] categorize different instances of the flag problem and present transformations to lift instances to easier levels, until the flag problem disappears at level 0. For example, a flag problem of level 1 defines a Boolean flag (`boolean flag = x > 0;`) and then uses the flag (`if(flag) ...`) without any computation on the flag in between definition and use. In its original form, this transformation only works in an intraprocedural setting, and the structure of the program may be changed.

Recently, Wappler et al. [15, 17] presented a solution for function assigned flags. This technique consists of three different tactics: branch completion, data type substitution, and local instrumentation. Data type substitution replaces Boolean values with floating point variables, where positive values represent true and negative values represent false, and these values are calculated by the local instrumentation. Our approach applies these tactics, and extends the approach to apply to bytecode instrumentation.

In this paper, we are mainly focusing on the problem of Boolean flags. Testability transformation has been successfully applied to solve other related problems. For example, a special case of the flag problem is when Boolean flags are assigned within loops [4, 5] and nested predicates [11] can cause local optima even when there are no Boolean flags.

3   Bytecode Testability Transformation

The idea of bytecode testability transformation is to transform bytecode during load-time, such that the information loss due to Booleans is reduced. Ideally, we want this transformation to be transparent to the user, such that the transformation can be plugged into any search-based testing tool without requiring any modifications. In particular, this means that the transformation should not introduce new branches in the source code. While testability transformation as it was defined originally [8] explicitly allows that the semantics of the program are changed by the transformation, as long as the resulting test cases apply to the original program, we want our transformation to preserve the original semantics.

3.1   Boolean Flags In Bytecode

In general, a flag variable is a Boolean variable that results from some computation such that information is necessarily lost. In Java bytecode, there is no dedicated Boolean datatype, but Booleans are compiled to integers that are only assigned the values 0 (ICONST_0 for false) and 1 (ICONST_1 for true). The typical pattern producing such a flag looks as follows:

```
boolean flag = x <= 0;

L0:
  IFLE L1
  ICONST_0
  GOTO L2
L1:
  ICONST_1
L2:
  // ...
```

```
boolean flag = x > 0;

L0:
  IFLE L1
  ICONST_1
  GOTO L2
L1:
  ICONST_0
L2:
  // ...
```

It is interesting to note that even though there is no branch here in the source code, at bytecode level we do have a branching instruction when defining a Boolean flag. When such a flag is used in a predicate, this predicate checks whether the flag equals to 0 (IFEQ) or does not equal to 0 (IFNE):

```
if(flag)
    // some code

L0:
  IFEQ L1
  // some code
  GOTO L2
L1:
  // flag is false
L2:
  // ...
```

```
if(!flag)
    // some code

L0:
  IFNE L1
  // some code
  GOTO L2
L1:
  // flag is true
L2:
  // ...
```

These examples show how flags are defined and used, but much of the difficulty of Boolean flags at bytecode level arises from how the Booleans are propagated from their definition to their usage. In the simplest case, the Boolean flag would be stored in a register for a local variable (ISTORE), and then loaded immediately before usage (ILOAD). However, Boolean values may also be passed via method calls (e.g., IN-VOKEVIRTUAL, INVOKESTATIC) or via fields (e.g., SETSTATIC, SETFIELD), or they may not be stored explicitly at all but simply exist on the operand stack.

3.2 Testability Transformation

The general principle of our transformation is similar to that presented by Wappler et al. [17]: We replace Boolean variables with values that represent "how" true or false a particular value is. In Java bytecode, all (interesting) branching operations act on integers, and we therefore replace all Boolean values with integers. Positive values denote true, and the larger the value is, the "truer" it is. Negative values, on the other hand, denote different grades of false. We further define a maximum value K, such that a transformed Boolean is always in the range $[-K,K]$.

When a flag is defined, we need to keep track of the distance value that the condition creating the flag represents, such that this value is used instead of the Boolean value for assignment to a local variable, class variable, as a parameter, or anonymously (e.g., if the flag usage immediately follows the definition). To achieve this, the transformation consists of two parts: First, we have to keep track of distance values at the predicates where Boolean flags are created, and second we need to replace Boolean assignments with integer values based on these distance values.

To keep track of distance values, we insert method calls before predicate evaluation as follows:

```
L0:                         L0:
  IFLE L1                     DUP
  // false branch             INVOKESTATIC push
  GOTO L2                       IFLE L1
L1:                            // false branch
  // true branch               GOTO L2
L2:                          L1:
  // ...                       // true branch
                             L2:
                               // ...
```

The special method push keeps a stack of the absolute values of the distance values observed, as predicates can be nested in the bytecode. This way, the top of the stack will always contain the most recently evaluated predicate, and will also tell us how many predicates were evaluated on the way to this predicate. The distance of a predicate essentially equals the distance between the two elements of the comparison. In the case of comparisons to 0, we therefore have to duplicate the top element on the stack (DUP), and this value already represents $top - 0$. For comparisons of two integer values, we have to duplicate the top two elements (DUP2) and then calculate their difference

(`ISUB`), which is then passed to the method (`push`). Another reason why we need the value stack is that all conditions in bytecode are atomic – even simple conjunctions or disjunctions in bytecode are compiled to nested predicates.

As a method may call other methods after which execution returns to the first method, each method has its own such stack. This essentially means there is a stack of stacks: Each time a method is called, a new value stack is put on this stack, and when the method is left via a return or throw statement, the value stack is removed again.

To complete the transformation, the distance values need to be checked when a Boolean value is assigned. To achieve this, we insert a call to the GETDISTANCE function (see Algorithm 1), which is a variant of the method used by Wappler et al. [15], before an assignment to a Boolean variable, i.e., whenever a Boolean value is assigned to a local variable (ISTORE), a Boolean field value (PUTSTATIC, PUTFIELD), used as a Boolean parameter of a method call (INVOKEVIRTUAL, INVOKESTATIC), or used as return value of a method. This function takes the Boolean value resulting from the flag definition, and replaces it with an integer value based on the distance of the last predicate evaluation. GETDISTANCE creates a normalized value in the range $[0,1]$, and scales it across the range $[0,K]$. If the original value was *false*, then the value is multiplied with -1. The call is inserted at the end of a nested predicate evaluation, and the stack depth represents how far evaluation in the predicate has evaluated.

```
L0:                              L0:
  // Flag definition               // Flag definition
  IFNE  L1                         IFNE  L1
  ICONST_1                         ICONST_1
  GOTO  L2                         GOTO  L2
L1:                              L1:
  ICONST_0                         ICONST_0
L2:                              L2:
  // Store flag                    INVOKESTATIC getDistance
  ISTORE 1                         ISTORE 1
```

Whenever a Boolean flag is used in a branch condition (IFNE or IFEQ), we have to replace the comparison operators acting on transformed values to check whether the value is greater than 0 or not (IFGT/IFLE).

```
// load flag                   // load transformed flag
  ILOAD 0                        ILOAD 0
  IFEQ L1                        IFLE L1
  // flag is true                // flag is true
  // ...                         // ...
  GOTO  L2                       GOTO  L2
L1:                            L1:
  // flag is false               // flag is false
  // ...                         // ...
L2:                            L2:
  // ...                         // ...
```

Algorithm 1. Get distance value

Require: Boolean value $orig$
Require: Predicate distance stack $stack$
Ensure: Transformed Boolean value d

1: **procedure** GETDISTANCE($orig$)
2:      **if** stack is empty **then**
3:           distance $\leftarrow K$
4:      **else**
5:           distance $\leftarrow$ stack.$pop()$
6:      **end if**
7:      $d \leftarrow K \times (1.0 + \text{normalize}(distance))/2^{\text{size of stack}}$
8:      **if** orig ≤ 0 **then**
9:           $d \leftarrow -d$
10:     **end if**
11:     stack.$clear()$
12:     **return** d;
13: **end procedure**

When a Boolean value is negated, in bytecode this amounts to a branching structure assigning true or false depending on the value of the original Boolean. This case is automatically handled by the already described transformations.

There are some branch conditions that do not operate on integers (see Table 2). While these operators themselves do not need to be transformed, they are part of the branching structure and we therefore add their representative truth values on to the value stack. In principle, this amounts to adding either $+K$ or $-K$, depending on the outcome of the comparison.

Table 2. Non-integer comparisons

Operator	Description
IF_ACMPEQ	Top two references on the stack are identical
IF_ACMPNE	Top two references on the stack are not identical
IF_NULL	Top value on stack equals null reference
IF_NONNULL	Top value on stack does not equal null

Furthermore, there is the `instanceof` operation that checks whether an object is an instance of a given class, and returns the result of this comparison as a Boolean. We simply replace any instanceof operations with calls to a custom made call that returns $+K$ or $-K$ depending on the truth value of `instanceof`.

Another type of operator that needs special treatment as an effect of the transformation are bitwise operators (arithmetic operations on Booleans are not allowed by the compiler): For example, a bitwise and of Boolean true (1) and false (0) is false (0), whereas a bitwise and of a negative and a positive integer might very well return a number that is not equal to 0. We therefore have to replace bitwise operations performed on transformed Booleans using replacement functions as follows: A binary AND (IAND) of two transformed Booleans returns the minimum of the two values; A binary XOR

(IXOR) of two transformed values a, b returns $-|a - b|$ if both a and b are greater than 0 or both are smaller than 0, else it returns maximum of a and b (i.e., the positive number). Finally, a binary OR (IOR) returns the largest positive number if there is at least one, or the smallest negative number in case both values are negative.

3.3 Instrumenting Non-integer Comparisons

Except for those listed in Table 2, branch instructions in Java bytecode are exclusively defined on integers. Non-integer variables (long, float, double) are first compared with each other (using the operators LCMP, DCMPL, DCMPG, FCMPL, FCMPG) and the result is stored as an integer -1, 0, or 1 representing that the first value is smaller, equal, or larger than the second value of the comparison. This integer is then compared with 0 using standard operators such as IFLE. This is also an instance of a flag problem, as the branch distance on the branching predicate gives no guidance at all to the search.

To avoid this kind of flag problem, we replace the non-integer comparison operator with an operator to calculate the difference (DSUB, LSUB, FSUB), and then pass the difference of the operators on to a function (fromDouble) that derives an integer representation of the value:

```
DLOAD 1                 DLOAD 1
DLOAD 2                 DLOAD 2
DCMPL                   DSUB
IFLE L1                 INVOKESTATIC fromDouble
// ...                  IFLE L1
                        // ...
```

When calculating the integer representation one has to take care that longs and doubles can be larger than the largest number representable as an integer (usually, an integer is a 32 bit number, while longs and doubles are 64 bit numbers). In addition, for floats and doubles guidance on the decimal places is less important the larger the distance value is, but gets more important the smaller the distance value is. Therefore, we normalize the distance values in the range $[0,1]$ using the normalization function $x = x/(x+1)$, which does precisely this (cf. Arcuri [1]), and then multiply the resulting floating point number x with the possible range of integer values. This means that the fromDouble function returns $(int)round(K * signum(d) * abs(d)/(1.0 + abs(d)))$ for the difference d.

3.4 Instrumenting Interfaces

Object oriented programs generally follow a style of many short methods rather than large monolithic code blocks. This means that very often, flags do not only exist within a single method but across method boundaries. As we are replacing Boolean flags with integer values, we also have to adapt method interfaces such that the transformation applies not only in an intra-method scenario, but also in an inter-method scenario.

To adapt the interfaces, we have to change both field declarations and method and constructor signatures. There is a possibility that changing the signature of a method results in a conflict with another existing method in the case of method overloading. If such a conflict occurs, then in addition to the signature the method name is also changed. Furthermore, in addition to the interface declarations every single call to a transformed method or access to a transformed field in the bytecode has to be updated to reflect the change in the signature or name.

It is important to ensure that the transformation is also consistent across inheritance hierarchies, such that overriding works as expected. However, there are limits to the classes and interfaces that can be transformed: Some base classes are already loaded in order to execute the code that performs the bytecode transformation. In addition, it might not be desirable to instrument the code of the test generator itself. Therefore we only instrument classes that are in the package that contains the unit under test, or any other user specified packages.

This, however, potentially creates two problems: First, some essential interfaces define Boolean return values and are used by all Java classes. For example, the `Object.equals` class cannot be changed, but is a potential source of Boolean flags. Second, a called method might receive a transformed Boolean value as parameter, but expects a real Boolean value. In these cases, a transformed Boolean is transformed back to a normal Boolean value representing whether the transformed value is greater than 0 or not, such that the normal Boolean comparisons to 0 and 1 work as expected. Similarly, we have to transform Boolean values received from non-transformed methods and fields back to the integer values $+K$ or $-K$.

3.5   Instrumenting Implicit Else Branches

Often, a Boolean value is only assigned a new value if a predicate evaluates in one way, but not if it evaluates the other way. In this case, if the value is not assigned, we have no guidance on how to reach the case that the condition evaluates to the other value. To overcome this problem, we add implicit else branches; this technique is referred to as *branch completion* by Wappler et al. [17], who introduced it to ensure that a guiding distance value can always be calculated.

```
ILOAD  0                    ILOAD  0
IFLE L1                     IFLE L1
ICONST_0                    ICONST_0
ISTORE 1                    ISTORE 1
L1:                         GOTO L2
   // ...                   L1:
                               ILOAD 1
                               INVOKESTATIC GetDistance
                               ISTORE 1
                            L2:
                               // ...
```

We add such an implicit else branch whenever a Boolean value is assigned to a field or a local variable (PUTSTATIC, PUTFIELD, ISTORE), such that we can easily add the else branch. In the example, the value is assigned to local variable 1, therefore in the implicit else branch we first load this variable (`ILOAD 1`) and then store a transformed Boolean value based on the current predicate (`GetDistance`) again (`ISTORE 1`).

4   Evaluation

We have implemented the described bytecode transformation as part of our evolutionary test generation tool EVOSUITE [6]. To measure the effects of the transformation with as little as possible side-effects, we ignored collateral coverage in our experiments, i.e., we only count a branch as covered if EVOSUITE was able to create a test case with this branch as optimization target. We deactivated optimizations such as reusing constants in the source code, and limited the range of numbers to $\pm 2,048,000$. EVOSUITE was configured to use a (1+1)EA search algorithm, for details of the mutation probabilities and operators please refer to [6]. EVOSUITE was further configured to derive test cases for individual branches, such that individuals of the search equal to sequences of method calls. The length of these sequences is dynamic, but was limited to 40 statements. Each experiment was repeated 30 times with different random seeds; to allow a fair comparison despite the variable length of individuals we restricted the search budget in terms of the number of executed statements.

4.1   Flag Problem Examples

To study the effects of the transformation, we first use a set of handwoven examples that illustrate the effectiveness of the transformation, and run test generation with a search limit of 300,000 statements[2]:

```
// Intra-method flags          // Nested predicates          // Example for doubles
class FlagTest1 {              class FlagTest2 {             // and conjunction
                                void coverMe(int x,          class FlagTest3 {
  boolean flag1 = false;                     int y) {
                                  boolean flag1 =              void coverMe(double x) {
  boolean flagMe(int x) {             x == 2904;                 if(x > 251.63 &&
    return x == 762;             boolean flag2 = false;            x < 251.69)
  }                             if(flag1) {                        // target branch
                                  if(y == 23598)                }
  void coverMeFirst(int x) {      flag2 = true;               }
    if(flagMe(x))               }
       flag1 = true;            else {
  }                               if(y == 223558)
                                  flag2 = true;
  void coverMe() {              }
    if(flag1)                   if(flag2)
      // target branch            // target branch
  }                             }
}                             }
```

In addition to these three examples, we also use the `Stack` example previously used by Wappler et al. [15] to evaluate their testability transformation approach. The target branch in this example is in the method `add`, which throws an exception if flag method `isFull` returns true. The other examples used by Wappler et al. [15] are in principle also covered by our other examples.

---

[2] As individuals in EVOSUITE are method sequences and can have variable length we count the number of executed statements rather than fitness evaluations.

Table 3. Results of the transformation on case study examples

Example	Without transformation			With transformation		
	Success Rate	Statements	Time/Test	Success Rate	Statements	Time/Test
FlagTest1	0/30	300,001.07	0.06ms	30/30	154,562.40	0.09ms
FlagTest2	0/30	300,001.53	0.06ms	30/30	154,142.37	0.08ms
FlagTest3	0/30	300,000.93	0.07ms	30/30	99,789.53	0.13ms
Stack	0/30	300,001.00	0.07ms	30/30	4,960.40	1.40ms

The first question we want to analyze is whether the transformation has the potential to increase coverage. The four examples clearly show that this is the case (see Table 3): Out of 30 runs, the target branches could not be covered a single time for any of the examples without transformation. With the transformation applied, on the other hand, every single run succeeded, with convergence between 100,000-200,000 executed statements, except for the Stack example which converges already around 5,000 executed statements. This improvement comes at a cost, as can be seen in the average test execution time: The average execution time increases by 34%, 25%, 44%, and 95% for each of the examples, respectively. An average increase of 50% in the execution time can be significant, as every single test case has to be executed as part of the search. Note that our implementation is not optimized in any way, so the 50% increase could likely be reduced by optimizations. However, the question is whether flag problems occur frequently in real software, such that the overhead of the transformation is justified.

4.2 Open Source Libraries

To study whether the potential improvement as observed on the case study subjects also holds on "real" software, we applied EVOSUITE and the transformation to a set of open source libraries. We chose four different libraries with the intent to select a wide range of different applications: First, we selected the non-abstract container classes of the java.util library. Furthermore, we selected the non-abstract top level classes of the JDom XML library, and all classes of the Apache Commons Codec and Command Line Interface libraries. We used a search limit of 100,000 executed statements for each branch. Statistical difference has been measured with the Mann-Whitney U test, following the guidelines on statistical analysis described by Arcuri and Briand [2]. To quantify the improvement in a standardized way, we used the Vargha-Delaney $\hat{A}_{12}$ effect size [14]. In our context, the $\hat{A}_{12}$ is an estimation of the probability that EVOSUITE with testability transformation can cover more branches than without. When the two types of tests are equivalent, then $\hat{A}_{12} = 0.5$. A high value $\hat{A}_{12} = 1$ would mean that the testability transformation satisfied more coverage goals in *all* cases.

The results of the analysis are summarized in Table 4. In total, we obtained p-values lower than 0.05 in 36 out of 43 comparisons in which $\hat{A}_{12} \neq 0.5$. In all four libraries, we observed classes where sometimes the transformation seems to decrease the coverage slightly. In particular, this happens when a method takes a Boolean parameter and is therefore transformed to take an integer as input. When mutating a Boolean value, EVOSUITE replaces the value with a new random Boolean value. For integers, however,

Table 4. Results of the $\hat{A}_{12}$ effect size on open source libraries. $\hat{A}_{12} > 0.5$ denotes the probability that the transformation leads to higher coverage.

Case Study	Classes	$\#\hat{A}_{12} < 0.5$	$\#\hat{A}_{12} = 0.5$	$\#\hat{A}_{12} > 0.5$	$\oslash\hat{A}_{12}$
Commons Codec	21	4	11	6	0.53
Commons CLI	14	2	7	5	0.51
Java Collections	16	4	1	11	0.59
JDom	18	5	7	6	0.52
Σ	69	15	26	28	0.53

EVOSUITE only replaces the value with a low probability (0.2 in our experiments), but else adds a small (random) delta in the range [-20,20]. It can therefore happen that such a transformed Boolean parameter only sees positive values during the evaluation, while a negative value (i.e., false) would be needed to take a certain branch. We expect that this behavior would disappear for example if the number of generations were increased, or if an algorithm with larger population sizes than the single individual of the (1+1)EA would be used.

In 28 out of 69 cases, the transformation resulted in higher coverage, which is a good result. However, on average over all classes and case study subjects, the $\hat{A}_{12}$ value is 0.53, which looks like only a small improvement. To understand this effect better, we take a closer look at the details of the results. In the Commons Codec library, the coverage with and without the transformation has identical results on 11/21 classes, and only very small variation on the remaining classes except one particular class: language.DoubleMetaphone has 502 branches on bytecode, and is the most complex class of the library. With testability transformation, on average 402,5 of these branches are covered; without transformation, the average is 386,8. Testability transformation clearly has an important effect on this class. In the Commons CLI library the picture is similar: On most classes, the coverage is identical or comparable. However, in the CommandLine (39.0 out of 45 branches with transformation, 37.6 without) and Option (86.3 out of 94 branches with transformation, 85.3 without) classes there seems to be an instance of the flag problem. The Java container classes have several classes where the transformation increases coverage slightly by 1–2 branches each (several HashMap, Hashtable, and HashSet variants. Interestingly, the Stack class in the java.util library has no flag problem). Finally, JDom also has mainly comparable coverage, with the main exception being the Attribute class, which has a clear coverage improvement (50.9 out of 65 branches with transformation, 49.8 without).

In summary, this evaluation shows that the transformation can effectively overcome the flag problem in real-world software — however, the flag problem seems to be less frequent than expected, so when performance is critical, testability transformation might only be activated on-demand when analysis or problems in the search show that there is a flag problem in a class. Potentially, static analysis could be used to identify sections in the bytecode where transformation is necessary, such that the transformation would only need to be applied selectively, thus reducing the overhead of the instrumentation. In general, the increase in the effort may be acceptable as it leads to higher coverage. Furthermore, our evaluation on the open source subjects only considers whether the coverage has increased or not; the testability transformation might also achieve that branches are covered *faster* than without the transformation, i.e., with fewer iterations of the search algorithm. We plan to investigate this as future work.

5 Threats to Validity

Threats to *construct validity* are on how the performance of a testing technique is defined. Our focus is on the achieved coverage of the test generation. However, our experiments show a clear disadvantage with respect to performance, and we did not evaluate any effects on secondary objectives such as the size of results.

Threats to *internal validity* might come from how the empirical study was carried out. To reduce the probability of defects in our testing framework, it has been carefully tested. In addition, to validate the correctness of our transformation, we used the test suites provided by the open source projects we tested and checked whether the test results were identical before and after the transformation. As in any empirical analysis, there is the threat to *external validity* regarding the generalization to other types of software. We tried to analyze a diverse range of different types of software, but more experiments are definitely desirable.

6 Conclusions

Bytecode as produced by modern languages is well suited for search-based testing, as bytecode is simple, instrumentation is easy and can be done on-the-fly, and predicates are atomic and use mainly integers. However, bytecode is just as susceptible to the flag problem as source code is. In fact, the compilation to bytecode even adds new sources of flags that need to be countered in a transformation. In this paper, we presented such a transformation, and showed that it can overcome the flag problem.

Experiments showed that the transformation is effective on the types of problems it is conceived for, but it also adds a non-negligible performance overhead. Our experiments on open source software revealed that the flag problem is also less frequent than one would expect, although it can be efficiently handled by the transformation if it occurs. Clearly our experiments in this respect can only be seen as an initial investigation, and further and larger experiments on real software will be necessary to allow any definite conclusions about the frequency of the flag problem. Furthermore, we only analyzed the basic case where the search tries to cover a single target; it is likely that new techniques such as optimization with respect to all coverage goals at the same time, as is also supported by EVOSUITE , can affect the flag problem. However, the conclusion we can draw from our experiments is that the presented transformation does overcome the flag problem as expected, but it probably makes most sense to use it on-demand rather than by default, or to identify and focus the transformation only on problematic parts or the program under test.

Acknowledgments. Gordon Fraser is funded by the Cluster of Excellence on Multi-modal Computing and Interaction at Saarland University, Germany.

References

1. Arcuri, A.: It really does matter how you normalize the branch distance in search-based software testing. Software Testing, Verification and Reliability (2011)
2. Arcuri, A., Briand, L.: A practical guide for using statistical tests to assess randomized algorithms in software engineering. In: IEEE International Conference on Software Engineering, ICSE (2011)
3. Arcuri, A., Yao, X.: Search based software testing of object-oriented containers. Information Sciences 178(15), 3075–3095 (2008)
4. Baresel, A., Binkley, D., Harman, M., Korel, B.: Evolutionary testing in the presence of loop-assigned flags: a testability transformation approach. In: Proceedings of the 2004 ACM SIGSOFT International Symposium on Software Testing and Analysis, ISSTA 2004, pp. 108–118. ACM Press, New York (2004)
5. Binkley, D.W., Harman, M., Lakhotia, K.: Flagremover: A testability transformation for transforming loop assigned flags. ACM Transactions on Software Engineering and Methodology 2(3), 110–146 (2009)
6. Fraser, G., Arcuri, A.: Evolutionary generation of whole test suites. In: International Conference On Quality Software, QSIC (2011)
7. Fraser, G., Zeller, A.: Mutation-driven generation of unit tests and oracles. In: ISSTA 2010: Proceedings of the ACM International Symposium on Software Testing and Analysis, pp. 147–158. ACM, New York (2010)
8. Harman, M., Hu, L., Hierons, R., Wegener, J., Sthamer, H., Baresel, A., Roper, M.: Testability transformation. IEEE Trans. Softw. Eng. 30, 3–16 (2004)
9. Lindholm, T., Yellin, F.: Java Virtual Machine Specification, 2nd edn. Addison-Wesley Longman Publishing Co., Inc., Amsterdam (1999)
10. McMinn, P.: Search-based software test data generation: a survey: Research articles. Software Testing Verification Reliability 14(2), 105–156 (2004)
11. McMinn, P., Binkley, D., Harman, M.: Testability transformation for efficient automated test data search in the presence of nesting. In: Proceedings of the 3rd UK Software Testing Research Workshop (UKTest 2005), Sheffield, UK, September 5-6, pp. 165–182 (2005)
12. Ribeiro, J.C.B.: Search-based test case generation for object-oriented Java software using strongly-typed genetic programming. In: GECCO 2008: Proceedings of the 2008 GECCO Conference Companion on Genetic and Evolutionary Computation, pp. 1819–1822. ACM, New York (2008)
13. Tonella, P.: Evolutionary testing of classes. In: ISSTA 2004: Proceedings of the ACM International Symposium on Software Testing and Analysis, pp. 119–128. ACM, New York (2004)
14. Vargha, A., Delaney, H.D.: A critique and improvement of the CL common language effect size statistics of McGraw and Wong. Journal of Educational and Behavioral Statistics 25(2), 101–132 (2000)
15. Wappler, S., Baresel, A., Wegener, J.: Improving evolutionary testing in the presence of function-assigned flags. In: Proceedings of the Testing: Academic and Industrial Conference Practice and Research Techniques - MUTATION, pp. 23–34. IEEE Computer Society Press, Washington, DC, USA (2007)
16. Wappler, S., Lammermann, F.: Using evolutionary algorithms for the unit testing of object-oriented software. In: GECCO 2005: Proceedings of the 2005 Conference on Genetic and Evolutionary Computation, pp. 1053–1060. ACM, New York (2005)
17. Wappler, S., Wegener, J., Baresel, A.: Evolutionary testing of software with function-assigned flags. J. Syst. Softw. 82, 1767–1779 (2009)

A Fast Algorithm to Locate
Concepts in Execution Traces

Soumaya Medini[1], Philippe Galinier[1], Massimiliano Di Penta[2],
Yann-Gaël Guéhéneuc[1], and Giuliano Antoniol[1]

[1] DGIGL, École Polytechnique de Montréal, Canada
[2] RCOST, University of Sannio, Italy
soumaya.medini@polymtl.ca, philippe.galinier@polymtl.ca,
dipenta@unisannio.it, yann-gael.gueheneuc@polymtl.ca, antoniol@ieee.org

Abstract. The identification of cohesive segments in execution traces is an important step in concept location which, in turns, is of paramount importance for many program-comprehension activities. In this paper, we reformulate concept location as a trace segmentation problem solved via dynamic programming. Differently to approaches based on genetic algorithms, dynamic programming can compute an exact solution with better performance than previous approaches, even on long traces. We describe the new problem formulation and the algorithmic details of our approach. We then compare the performances of dynamic programming with those of a genetic algorithm, showing that dynamic programming reduces dramatically the time required to segment traces, without sacrificing precision and recall; even slightly improving them.

Keywords: Concept identification, dynamic analysis, information retrieval, dynamic programming.

1 Introduction

Program comprehension is an important activity that may require half of the effort devoted to software maintenance and evolution. An important task during program comprehension is concept location, which aims at identifying concepts (*e.g.*, domain concepts, user-observable features) and locating them within code regions or, more generally, into software artifact chunks [8,15]. The literature reports concept location approaches built upon static [1] and dynamic [24,25] analyses; information retrieval (IR) [20]; and hybrid (static and dynamic) [3,5,12] techniques. Dynamic and hybrid approaches rely on execution traces.

A typical scenario in which concept location takes part is the following. Let us suppose that (1) a failure has been observed in a software system under certain execution conditions, (2) unfortunately, such execution conditions are hard to reproduce, but (3) one execution trace was saved during such a failure. Maintainers then face the difficult and demanding task of analyzing the one execution trace of the system to identify in the trace the set(s) of methods pertaining to the failure, *i.e.*, some unexpected sequence(s) of method invocations, and then to relate the invoked methods to some features producing the failure.

M.B. Cohen and M. Ó Cinnéide (Eds.): SSBSE 2011, LNCS 6956, pp. 252–266, 2011.
© Springer-Verlag Berlin Heidelberg 2011

Inspired by the above scenario where a developer must identify methods likely responsible for a system failure, a step of the (hybrid) concept location process has been recently defined as the *trace segmentation problem*, where the textual content of the methods contained in execution traces is used to split the traces into segments that likely participate in the implementation of some concepts related to some features [4,5]. The underlying assumption of this step is that, if a specific feature is being executed within a complex scenario (*e.g.*, "Open a Web page from a browser" or "Save an image in a paint application"), then the set of methods being invoked is likely to be conceptually cohesive, decoupled from those of other features, and invoked in sequence. Going back to the system crash scenario, we are interested in splitting a trace into segments one of which may be implementing the unwanted feature *i.e.*, is responsible for the system failure. Unfortunately, despite the use of meta-heuristic techniques, *e.g.*, genetic algorithms [5] and their parallelization [4], segmenting a trace is a computationally intensive step and published approaches do not scale up to thousands of methods.

This paper extends our previous work [4,5] and reformulates the trace segmentation problem as a dynamic programming (DP) problem. Differently to approaches based on meta-heuristic techniques, in particular Genetic Algorithms (GA), the DP approach can compute an exact solution to the trace segmentation problem with better performance that previous approaches, which would possibly make this approach more scalable. The DP approach relies on the same representation and fitness function as proposed for a previous approach based on a GA [4,5], however, the trace segmentation problem is reformulated as an optimization problem taking advantage of (1) the order of the methods in the trace, (2) the additive property of the fitness function, and (3) the Bellman's Principle of Optimality [7].

Thus, the contributions of this paper are as follows. First, we present a novel formulation of the trace segmentation problem as a DP problem and its algorithmic details. Second, we report an empirical study comparing the DP approach with a previous GA approach [4,5]. We show that the DP approach can segment traces in a few seconds, at most, while the GA approach takes several minutes/hours. Despite such a drastic improvement of performances, precision and recall do not decrease; they even slightly increase.

The remainder of the paper is organized as follows. Section 2 summarizes a previous trace-segmentation approach for the sake of completeness [4,5]. Section 3 explains trace segmentation using GA and DP approaches. Section 4 describes the empirical study and reports and discusses the obtained results. Section 5 recalls related work. Section 6 concludes the paper with future work.

2   The Trace Segmentation Problem

This section summarizes essential details of a previous trace segmentation approach [4,5], which problem we reformulate as a dynamic programming problem. Therefore, the five steps of the two approaches are identical, with the only difference that the trace segmentation was previously performed using a GA algorithm and that we describe the use of DP in Section 3.

2.1   Steps 1 and 2 – System Instrumentation and Trace Collection

First, a software system under study is instrumented using the *instrumentor* of MoDeC to collect traces of its execution under some scenarios. MoDeC is an external tool to extract and model sequence diagrams from Java systems [23], implemented using the Apache BCEL bytecode transformation library[1]. The tool also allows to manually label parts of the traces during executions of the instrumented systems, which we did to produce our oracle. In this paper MoDeC is simply used to collect and manually tag traces.

2.2   Step 3 – Pruning and Compressing Traces

Usually, execution traces contain methods invoked in most scenarios, *e.g.*, methods related to logging or GUI events. Yet, it is unlikely that such invocations are related to any particular concept, *i.e.*, they are utility methods. We build the distribution of method invocation frequency and prune out methods having an invocation frequency greater than $Q3 + 2 \times IQR$, where $Q3$ is the third quartile (75% percentile) of the invocation frequency distribution and IQR is the interquartile range because these methods do not provide useful information when segmenting traces and locating concepts.

Finally, we compress the traces using a Run Length Encoding (RLE) algorithm to remove repetitions of method invocations. We introduced this compression to address scalability issues of the GA approach [4,5]. We still apply the RLE compression to compare segments obtained with the DP approach with those obtained using the GA approach when segmenting the same traces.

2.3   Step 4 – Textual Analysis of Method Source Code

Trace segmentation aims at grouping together subsequent method invocations that form conceptually cohesive groups. The conceptual cohesion among method is computed using the Conceptual Cohesion metric defined by Marcus *et al.* [16].

We first extract terms from source code, split compound identifiers separated by camel case (*e.g.*, `getBook` is split into `get` and `book`), remove programming language keywords and English stop words, and perform stemming [19]. We then index the obtained terms using the *tf-idf* indexing mechanisms [6]. We obtain a term–document matrix, and finally, we apply Latent Semantic Indexing (LSI) [11] to reduce the term–document matrix into a concept–document[2] matrix, choosing, as in previous work, a LSI subspace size equal to 50.

---

[1] http://jakarta.apache.org/bcel/

[2] In LSI "concept" refers to orthonormal dimensions of the LSI space, while in the rest of the paper "concept" means some abstraction relevant to developers.

2.4   Step 5 – Trace Splitting Through Optimization Techniques

The final step consists of applying some optimization techniques to segment the obtained trace. Applying an optimization technique requires a representation of the trace and of a trace segmentation and a means to evaluate the quality of a trace segmentation, *i.e.*, a fitness function. In the following paragraphs, we reuse where possible previous notations and definitions [5] for the sake of simplicity.

We represent a problem solution, *i.e.*, a trace segmentation, as a bit-string as long as the execution trace in number of method invocations. Each method invocation is represented as a "0", except the last method invocation in a segment, which is represented as a "1". For example, the bit-string $\underbrace{00010010001}_{11}$ repre-

sents a trace containing 11 method invocations and split into three segments: the first four method invocations, the next three, and the last four.

The fitness function drives the optimization technique to produce a (near) optimal segmentation of a trace into segments likely to relate to some concepts. It relies on the software design principles of cohesion and coupling, already adopted in the past to identify modules in software systems [18], although we use conceptual (*i.e.*, textual) cohesion and coupling measures [16,21], rather than structural cohesion and coupling measures.

Segment cohesion (COH) is the average (textual) similarity between the source code any pair of methods invoked in a given segment l. It is computed using the formulas in Equation 1 where $begin(l)$ is the position of the first method invocation of the lth segment and $end(l)$ the position of the last method invocation in that segment. The similarity σ between methods m_i and m_j is computed using the cosine similarity measure over the LSI matrix from the previous step. COH is the average of the similarity [16,21] of all pairs of methods in a segment.

Segment coupling (COU) is the average similarity between a segment l and all other segments in the trace, computed using Equation 2, where N is the trace length. It represents, for a given segment, the average similarity between methods in that segment and those in different ones.

Thus, we compute the quality of the segmentation of a trace split into K segments using the fitness function (fit) defined in Equation 3, which balances segment cohesion and their coupling with other segments in the split trace.

$$COH_l = \frac{\sum_{i=begin(l)}^{end(l)-1} \sum_{j=i+1}^{end(l)} \sigma(m_i, m_j)}{(end(l) - begin(l) + 1) \cdot (end(l) - begin(l))/2} \tag{1}$$

$$COU_l = \frac{\sum_{i=begin(l)}^{end(l)} \sum_{j=1, j<begin(l) \text{ or } j>end(l)}^{l} \sigma(m_i, m_j)}{(N - (end(l) - begin(l) + 1)) \cdot (end(l) - begin(l) + 1)} \tag{2}$$

$$fit(segmentation) = \frac{1}{K} \cdot \sum_{i=1}^{K} \frac{COH_i}{COU_i + 1} \tag{3}$$

3 Segmenting Traces Using a Genetic Algorithm and Dynamic Programming

We now use previous notations and definitions to describe the use of a GA algorithm to segment traces and the reformulation of the trace segmentation problem as a dynamic programming problem.

3.1 Trace Segmentation Using a Genetic Algorithm

Section 2 described the representations of a trace and its segmentation and a fitness function. We now define the mutation, crossover, and selection operators, used by a GA to segment traces [4,5].

The mutation operator randomly chooses one bit in the trace representation and flips it over. Flipping a "0" into a "1" means splitting an existing segment into two segments, while flipping a "1" into a "0" means merging two consecutive segments. The crossover operator is the standard 2-points crossover. Given two individuals, two random positions x, y, with $x < y$, are chosen in one individual's bit-string and the bits from x to y are swapped between the two individuals to create a new offspring. The selection operator is the roulette-wheel selection. We use a simple GA with no elitism, *i.e.*, it does not guarantee to retain best individuals across subsequent generations.

3.2 Trace Segmentation Using Dynamic Programming

Dynamic Programming (DP) is a technique to solve search and optimization problems with overlapping sub-problems and an optimal substructure. It is based on the divide-and-conquer strategy where a problem is divided into sub-problems, recursively solved, and where the solution of the original problem is obtained by combining the solutions of the sub-problems [7,10].

Sub-problems are overlapping if the solving of a (sub-)problem depends on the solutions of two or more other sub-problems, *e.g.*, the computation of the Fibonacci numbers. The original problem must have a particular structure. First, it must be possible to recursively break it down into sub-problems up to some elementary problem easily solved; second, it must be possible to express the solution of the original problem in term of the solutions of the sub-problems; and, third, the Bellman's principle of optimality must be applicable. For our trace segmentation problem, we interpret this principle as follows. When computing a trace segmentation, at a given intermediate method invocation in the trace and for a given number of segments ending with that invocation, only the best among those possible partial splits, will be, possibly, part of the final optimal solution. Thus, we must record only the best fitness for any segmentation and we must expand only the corresponding best segment to include more method invocation, possibly including the entire trace. In other words, when extending an existing solution two things can happen: either a new segment is added or the method is attached to the last solution segment. Given a trace of $1, \ldots, N$ calls, suppose we compute and store all possible optimal splits of a trace into two segments.

For example, for the sub-trace of the first nine method invocations, we compute its optimal (in terms of fitness function) split into two segments. Clearly there are several ways to split the nine methods into two segments, however we only consider the best in term of fitness function. The same can be done for a sub-trace of length ten, eleven, twelve and so. When we reach N we will have the best segmentation of N into two parts. When computing the segmentation into three parts, there is no need to redo all computations. For example, three segments ending at position eleven can be computed in terms of two segments ending at any previous position (e.g., position nine), and forming a third segment with the remaining methods. Thus, a possible solution consists of the two segments ending at position nine, plus a segment of length two.

More formally, let $\mathcal{A} = \{1, 2, \ldots, n\}$ be an alphabet of n symbols, *i.e.*, method invocations, and $T[1 \ldots N]$ be an array of method invocations of $\mathcal{A}$, *i.e.*, an execution trace. Given an interval $T[p \ldots q]$ $(1 \leq p \leq q \leq N)$ of $T[1 \ldots N]$, as explained Section 2, we compute COH as the average similarity between the elements of $T[p \ldots q]$ and the interval coupling, COU, as the average similarity between any element of $T[p \ldots q]$ (methods between p and q) and any element of $T[1 \ldots N] - T[p \ldots q]$. We compute the *score of an interval* as COH/COU.

A segmentation S of $T[1 \ldots L](L \leq N)$ is a partition S of $T[1 \ldots L]$ in k_S intervals: $S = \{T[1 \ldots a_1], T[a_1 + 1 \ldots a_2] \ldots T[a_{k-1} + 1 \ldots a_k = N]\}$. We denote such a segmentation by $(a_0 = 0, a_1, \ldots, a_{k_S} = L)$. We then define the segmentation score (*e.g.*, fitness) of an array as the average score of its intervals. Therefore, the *trace segmentation problem* consists to find a segmentation of $T[1 \ldots N]$ maximizing the score fit, as defined in 2.

We introduce the definitions D1–D4 to explain our DP approach:

(D1) $A(p,q) = \Sigma_{i=p}^{q-1} \Sigma_{j=i+1}^{q} \sigma(i,j)$

(D2) $B(p,q) = \Sigma_{i=p}^{q} \Sigma_{j=1 \ldots N(j \notin [p,q])} \sigma(i,j)$

(D3) $f(p,q) = \frac{2 \times (N-(q-p+1))}{(q-p)} \times \frac{A(p,q)}{B(p,q)}$

(D4) $fit(k,L) = max_{\{(a_i)_{i=0..k}:a_0=0, a_i<a_{i+1}, a_k=L\}} \Sigma_{i=1..k} f(a_{i-1}+1, a_i)$

We notice that the COH and COU of an interval $T[p \ldots q]$ correspond to $\frac{2 \times A(p,q)}{(q-p) \times (q-p+1)}$ and $\frac{B(p,q)}{(N-(q-p+1)) \times (q-p+1)}$, respectively. Thus $f(p,q)$ represents the score of the interval $T[p \ldots q]$. It also represents the contribution of the interval to a solution and $fit(k,L)$ corresponds to the maximum score of a (k,L)-segmentation, *i.e.*, a segmentation of $T[1 \ldots L]$ in k intervals. Therefore, the optimum segmentation score is $max_{k=1}^{N/2} \frac{fit(k,N)}{k}$.

If we consider a solution ending at p (sub-trace $T[1 \ldots p]$) and made up by k segments, then its score is $fit(k,p)$ and we have multiple optimum segmentations: one for each possible k in $1 < k < p/2$. When we extend the sub-trace to q, $T[1 \ldots p \ldots q]$ and given a solution made up of k segments ending in p, we seek the solution $fit(k+1, q)$ into $max_{p=k \ldots q}(fit(k,p) + f(p+1, q))$, where $1 \leq k < q \leq N$. If we pre-compute and store $fit(k,p)$ in a table, we do not need to recompute the expensive COH and COU every time to evaluate $fit(k+1, q)$.

However, we still must compute $f(p+1, q)$ for every sub-problems and we perform this computation efficiently using the following definitions:

(D5) $\Delta(p, q) = \Sigma_{i=p}^{q-1} \sigma(T[i], T[q])$
(D6) $\Theta(p) = \Sigma_{i=1..N (i \neq p)} \sigma(T[i], T[p])$

It can be proved that $\Delta(p, q) = \Delta(p+1, q) + \sigma(T[p], T[q])$ and, thus, $A(p, q) = A(p, q-1) + \Delta(p, q)$ and $B(p, q+1) = B(p, q) + \Theta(q+1) - 2 \times \Delta(p, q+1)$ and thus we can recursively update $A(p, q)$ and $B(p, q+1)$. We choose $q = p + 1$, which means that we extend the current solution one method at the time from left-to-right and that $A(p, q)$ becomes $A(p, p+1)$ and $B(p, q+1)$ becomes $B(p, p+2)$, which we can pre-compute (from previous values) and stored into two arrays.

To conclude, we can compute $fit(k+1, p+1)$ using $fit(k, i)$ and the sum of the values of $f(i+1, p+1)$, which we can compute by dividing $A(i+1, p+1)$ by $B(i+1, p+1)$, both already pre-computed. The DP approach is thus fast because it goes left-to-right and reuses as much as possible of previous computation.

We show below the pseudo-code of (a basic version of) the algorithm at the core of the DP approach.

Algorithm DP split
Input:
integers n and N, matrix of similarities $Sim[1..n][1..n]$, array $T[1..N]$
Output: matrix of fitness values $fit[1..N][1..N]$

```
1.    For L=1..N do
2.        Theta := comp_theta(L)
3.        Delta := 0
4.        A[L] := 0
5.        B[L] := Theta
6.        For p=L-1..1 do
7.            Delta := Delta + Sim[T[p]][T[L]]
8.            A[p] := A[p-1] + Delta
9.            B[p] := B[p-1] + Theta − 2 × Delta
10.   For L=1..N do
11.       fit[1][L] := comp_f(1,L)
12.       For k=2..L do
13.           F_max := 0
14.           For p=k..L-1 do
15.               F_max:=max(F_max, fit[k-1][p] + comp_f(p+1))
16.           fit[k][L] := F_max
17.   Return fit
```

where the input matrices $Sim[1..n][1..n]$ and $T[1..N]$ contain the similarities between methods and the trace encoding, respectively. The function $comp\_f()$ computes the value of f based on definition $D3$ and $comp\_theta$ recursively evaluates $\Theta(p)$. The most expensive part of the algorithm are the nested loops at lines 10, 12, and 14. The algorithm, in this basic formulation, has a complexity of $\mathcal{O}(N^3)$, which is also the (worst case) complexity of the evaluation of the GA fitness function as both COH and COU have worst case complexity of $\mathcal{O}(N^2)$

Table 1. Data of the empirical study

(a) Statistics of the two systems.

Systems	NOC	KLOC	Release Dates
ArgoUML v0.18.1	1,267	203	30/04/05
JHotDraw v5.4b2	413	45	1/02/04

(b) Statistics of the collected traces.

Systems	Scenarios	Original Size	Cleaned Sizes	Compressed Sizes
ArgoUML	Start, Create note, Stop	34,746	821	588
	Start, Create class, Create note, Stop	64,947	1,066	764
JHotDraw	Start, Draw rectangle, Stop	6,668	447	240
	Start, Add text, Draw rectangle, Stop	13,841	753	361
	Start, Draw rectangle, Cut rectangle, Stop	11,215	1,206	414
	Start, Spawn window, Draw circle, Stop	16,366	670	433

and in the worst case must be evaluated for $N/2$ segments. Thus, a single step of the GA approach equates the entire calculation of the DP approach.

4   Empirical Study

This section reports an empirical study comparing the GA approach proposed by Asadi *et al.* [5] with our novel DP approach. The *goal* of this study is to analyze the performances of the trace segmentation approaches based on GA and DP with the *purpose* of evaluating their capability to identify meaningful concepts in traces. The *quality focus* is the accuracy and completeness of the identified concepts. The *perspective* is that of researchers who want to evaluate which of the two techniques (GA or DP) better solves the trace segmentation problem. The *context* consists of two trace segmentation approaches, one based on GA and one on DP, and of the same execution traces used in previous work [5] and extracted from two open-source systems, ArgoUML and JHotDraw.

ArgoUML[3] is an open-source UML modelling tool with advanced features, such as reverse engineering and code generation. The ArgoUML project started in September 2000 and is still active. We analyzed release 0.19.8. *JHotDraw*[4] is a Java framework for drawing 2D graphics. JHotDraw started in October 2000 with the main purpose of illustrating the use of design patterns in a real context. We analyzed release 5.1. Table 1(a) summarizes the systems statistics. We generated traces by exercising various scenarios in the two systems. Table 1(b) summarizes the scenarios and shows that the generated traces include from 6,000 to almost 65,000 method invocations. The compressed traces include from 240 up to more than 750 method invocations.

---

[3] http://argouml.tigris.org

[4] http://www.jhotdraw.org

This study aims at answering the three following research questions:

- **RQ1.** *How do the performances of the GA and DP approaches compare in terms of fitness values, convergence times, and number of segments?*
- **RQ2.** *How do the GA and DP approaches perform in terms of overlaps between the automatic segmentation and the manually-built oracle, i.e., recall?*
- **RQ3.** *How do the precision values of the GA and DP approaches compare when splitting execution traces?*

4.1   Study Settings and Analysis Method

The GA approach iss implemented using the *Java GA Lib*[5] library. We use a simple GA with no elitism, *i.e.*, it does not guarantee to retain best individuals across subsequent generations. We set the population size to 200 individuals and a number of generations of 2,000 for shorter traces (those of JHotDraw) and 3,000 for longer ones (those of ArgoUML). The crossover probability is set to 70% and the mutation to 5%, which are values used in many GA applications.

The DP approach scans the trace from left-to-right building the exact solution and in its current formulation does not have any configuration parameter.

In previous work, the results of the GA approach were reported for for multiple (10) runs of the algorithm to account for the nondeterministic nature of the technique. We only report the results of the DP approach for one of its run per traces because it is by nature deterministic and multiple runs would produce exactly the same results. Also, we compare DP results with the best result achieved among the 10 GA runs.

To address **RQ1**, we compare the value of the fitness function reached by the GA approach with the value of the segmentation score obtained by the DP approach. The values of the fitness function and segmentation score *per se* do not say anything about the quality of the obtained solutions. Yet, we compare these values to assess, given a representation and a fitness function/segmentation score, which of the GA or DP approach obtain the best value. We also compare the execution times of the GA and DP approaches. We finally report the number of segments that the two approaches create for each execution trace.

For **RQ2**, we compare the overlap between a manually-built oracle and segments identified by the GA and DP approaches. We build an oracle by manually assigning a concept to trace segments—using the tagging feature of the instrumentor tool—while executing the instrumented systems. Given the segments determined by the tags in the oracle and given the segments obtained by an execution of either of the approaches, we compute the Jaccard overlap [14] between each manually-tagged segment in the oracle and the closest, most similar segment obtained automatically. Let us consider a (compressed) trace composed of N method invocations $T \equiv m_1, \ldots m_N$ and partitioned in k segments $s_1 \ldots s_k$. For each segment s_x, we compute the maximum overlap between s_x and the manually-tagged segments so_y as $max(Jaccard(s_x, so_y)), y \in \{1 \ldots k\}$ where:

$$Jaccard(s_x, so_y) = \frac{|s_x \cap so_y|}{|s_x \cup s_y|}$$

---

[5] http://sourceforge.net/projects/java-galib/

and where union and intersection are computed considering method invocations occurring at a given position in the trace.

For **RQ3**, we evaluate (and compare) the precision of both the GA and DP approaches in terms of precision, which is defined as follows:

$$Precision(s_x, so_y) = \frac{|s_x \cap so_y|}{|s_y|}$$

where s_x is a segment obtained by an automatic approach (GA or DP) and so_y is a segment in the corresponding trace of the oracle.

For **RQ1**, **RQ2**, and **RQ3**, we statistically compare results obtained with the GA and DP approaches using the non-parametric, paired Wilcoxon test. We also compute the magnitude of the differences using the non-parametric effect-size Cliff's δ measure [13], which, for dependent samples, as in our study, is defined as the probability that a randomly-selected member of one sample DP has a higher response than a randomly-selected member of the second sample GA, minus the reverse probability:

$$\delta = \frac{\left|DP^i > GA^j\right| - \left|GA^j > DP^i\right|}{|DP|\,|GA|}$$

The effect size δ is considered small for $0.148 \leq \delta < 0.33$, medium for $0.33 \leq \delta < 0.474$ and large for $\delta \geq 0.474$ [13].

4.2   Results

This section reports the results of the empirical study. Data sets are available for replication[6].

Table 2. Number of segments, values of fitness function/segmentation score, and times required by the GA and DP approaches

System	Scenario	# of Segments GA	DP	Fitness GA	DP	Time (s) GA	DP
ArgoUML	(1)	24	13	0.54	0.58	7,080	2.13
	(2)	73	19	0.52	0.60	10,800	4.33
JHotDraw	(1)	17	21	0.39	0.67	2,040	0.13
	(2)	21	21	0.38	0.69	1,260	0.64
	(3)	56	20	0.46	0.72	1,200	0.86
	(4)	63	26	0.34	0.69	240	1.00

Regarding **RQ1**, Table 2 summarizes the obtained results using both the GA and DP approaches, in terms of (1) number of segments in which the traces were split, (2) achieved values of fitness function/segmentation score, and (3) times needed to complete the segmentations (in seconds). The DP approach tends to segment the trace in less segments than the GA one, with the exception of Scenario (1) of JHotDraw, composed of one feature only and for which the number of segments is 21 for both approaches, and of Scenario 3 of JHotDraw,

---

[6] http://web.soccerlab.polymtl.ca/ser-repos/public/dp_sp.tar.gz

for which the DP approach creates 21 segments whereas GA creates only 17 segments. The difference of the number of segments is not statistically significant (p-value=0.10), although Cliff's δ effect size is high (1.16) and in favor of the GA approach.

Looking at the values of the fitness function/segmentation score, the DP approach always produces better values than the GA one. The Wilxocon test indicates that the difference is statistically significant (p-value=0.03) and the Cliff's δ effect size is high (0.76): the DP approach performs significantly better than the GA approach, given the representations described in Section 2. The better convergence of the DP also explains the smaller number of segments obtained; that is, DP is able to converge to better solutions that—according to the fitness function of equation (3)—favor a smaller number of segments.

Finally, the convergence times of the GA approach are by far higher than that of the DP one: from several minutes or hours (for ArgoUML) to seconds. The difference between the GA and DP approaches is statistically significant (p-value=0.03) and the effect size high (1.05). We thus answer **RQ1** by stating that *in terms of fitness values, convergence time, and number of segments, the DP approach out-performs the GA approach.*

Table 3. Jaccard overlaps and precision values between segments identified by the GA and DP approaches

System	Scenario	Feature	Jaccard		Precision	
			GA	DP	GA	DP
ArgoUML	(1)	Create Note	0.33	0.87	1.00	0.99
	(2)	Create Class	0.26	0.53	1.00	1.00
	(2)	Create Note	0.34	0.56	1.00	1.00
JHotDraw	(1)	Draw Rectangle	0.90	0.75	0.90	1.00
	(2)	Add Text	0.31	0.33	0.36	0.39
	(2)	Draw Rectangle	0.62	0.52	0.62	1.00
	(3)	Draw Rectangle	0.74	0.24	0.79	0.24
	(3)	Cut Rectangle	0.22	0.31	1.00	1.00
	(4)	Draw Circle	0.82	0.82	0.82	1.00
	(4)	Spawn window	0.42	0.44	1.00	1.00

To address **RQ2**, we evaluate the Jaccard overlap between the manually-identified segments corresponding to each feature of the execution scenarios and the segments obtained using the GA and DP approaches. Columns 4 and 5 of Table 3 report the results. Jaccard scores are always higher for the GA approach than for the DP one, with the only exception of the *Draw Rectangle* feature in JHotDraw, for which the Wilcoxon paired test indicates that there is no significant difference between Jaccard scores (p-value=0.56). The obtained Cliff's δ (0.11) is small, although slightly in favor of the DP approach. We thus answer **RQ2** by stating that *in terms of overlap, segments obtained with the GA and DP approaches do not significantly differ and the DP approach has thus a recall similar to that of the GA one.*

Regarding **RQ3**, Columns 6 and 7 of Table 3 compare the precision values obtained using the GA and DP approaches. Consistently with results reported in previous work [5], precision is almost always higher than 80%, with some exceptions, in particular the *Add Text* and *Draw Rectangle* features of JHotDraw.

There is only one case for which the DP approach exhibits a lower precision than the GA one: for the *Draw Rectangle* feature of JHotDraw (Scenario 3) where the DP approach has a precision of 0.24 whereas the GA one has a precision of 0.79. Yet, in general, the Wilcoxon paired test indicates no significant differences between the GA and DP approaches (p-value=0.52) and the Cliff's δ (0.04) indicates a negligible difference between the two approaches. In conclusion, we answer **RQ3** by stating that *the precision obtained using the DP approach does not significantly differ from the one obtained using the GA approach.*

4.3   Threats to Validity

We now discuss the threats to the validity of our empirical study.

Threats to *construct validity* concern the relation between theory and observation. In this study, they are mainly due to measurement errors. To compare the GA and DP approaches, other than considering the achieved fitness function values and the computation times, we used precision and Jaccard overlap, already used in a previous work [5] as well as in the past [22]. While in this paper, due to the lack of space, we cannot report a qualitative analysis of the obtained segments, previous work [5] already showed that a segmentation with high overlap and precision produces meaningful segments. Finally, we cannot compare the times required by the GA and DP approaches to achieve the a same fitness value/segmentation score because the DP approach always reaches, by construction, the global optimum while the GA approach does not. Moreover, even if the achieved fitness values and segmentation scores are different, we showed that the DP approach is able to reach a better score in a shorter time.

Threats to *internal validity* concern confounding factors that could affect our results. These could be due to the presence, in the execution traces, of extra method invocations related to GUI events or other system events. The frequency-based pruning explained in Step 3 of Section 2 mitigates this threat.

Threats to *conclusion validity* concern the relationship between treatment and outcome. We statistically compared the performances of the GA and DP approaches using the non-parametric Wilcoxon paired test and used the non-parametric Cliff's δ effect size measure.

Threats to *external validity* concern the possibility to generalize our results. Although we compared the GA and DP approaches on traces from two different systems, further studies on larger traces and more complex systems are needed, especially to better demonstrate the scalability of the DP approach. Indeed, we showed that the DP approach out-performs the GA one in terms of computation times to segment traces but did not show that, differently from the GA approach, its computation time does not exponentially increase with trace size.

5   Related Work

As sketched in the introduction, concept location approaches can be divided into static, dynamic, and hybrids approaches.

Static approaches relies on information statically collected from the program under analysis. Anquetil and Lethbridge [1] proposed techniques to extract concepts from a very simple source of information, *i.e.*, file names. Chen and Rajilich [9] developed an approach to locate concepts using only Abstract System-Dependency Graph (ASDG). The ASDG is constructed using a subset of the information of a system-dependency graph (SDG). Finally, Marcus *et al.* [17] performed concept location using an approach based on information retrieval. As Marcus *et al.*, our approach strongly relies on the textual content of the program source code.

Dynamic approaches. use one or more execution traces to locate concepts in the source code. In their seminal work, Wilde and Scully [25] used test cases to produce execution traces; concepts location was performed by comparing different traces: one in which the concept is executed and another without concept. Similarly, Poshyvanyk *et al.* [20] used multiple traces from multiple scenarios.

Hybrid approaches. have been introduced to overcome the limitations of dynamic and static approaches. Static approaches often fail to properly capture a system behavior, while dynamic approaches are sensitive to the chosen execution traces. Antoniol and Guéhéneuc [2] presented a hybrid approach to concept location and reported results for real-life large object-oriented multi-threaded systems. They used knowledge filtering and probabilistic ranking to overcome the difficulties of collecting uninteresting events. This work was improved [3] by using the notion of epidemiology of diseases in locating the concepts.

We share with previous works the general idea of concept location and with hybrid approaches. This work extends our previous work [5,4] by reformulating the trace segmentation problem as a DP problem and comparing the previous results with the new ones.

6   Conclusions and Future Work

In this paper we reformulate the trace segmentation problem as a dynamic programming (DP) problem and, specifically, as a particular case of the string splitting problem. We showed that we can benefit from the overlapping sub-problems and an optimal substructure of the string splitting problem to reuse computed scores of intervals and segmentation scores and, thus, to obtain dramatic gains in performances without loss in precision and recall. Indeed, differently from the GA approach, the DP approach reuses pre-computed cohesion and coupling values among subsequent segments of an execution trace, which is not possible using genetic algorithms, due to their very nature. We believe that other problems, such as segmenting composed identifiers into component terms, could be modelled in a similar way and, thus, that we, as a community, should be careful when analyzing a problem: a different, possibly non-orthodox, problem formulation may lead to surprisingly good performances.

We empirically compared the DP and GA approaches, using the same data set from previous work [4,5]. Our empirical study consisted in the execution traces from ArgoUML and JHotDraw, which were previously used to validate the GA approach. Results indicated that the DP approach can achieve results similar to the GA approach in terms of precision and recall when its segmentation is compared with a manually-built oracle. They also show that the DP approach has significantly better results in terms of the optimum segmentation score vs. fitness function. More important, results showed that the DP approach significantly out-performed the GA approach in terms of the times required to produce the segmentations: where the GA approach would take several minutes, even hours; the DP approach just takes a few seconds.

Work-in-progress aims at further validating the scalability of the DP trace segmentation approach as well as at complementing the approach with segment labelling to make the produced segments better suitable for program-comprehension activities. Finally, we would like to further explore sub-optimal solutions of the DP problem with lower bound complexity, and evaluate their impact on the solution accuracy.

References

1. Anquetil, N., Lethbridge, T.: Extracting concepts from file names: a new file clustering criterion. In: Proceedings of the International Conference on Software Engineering, pp. 84–93. IEEE Computer Society Press, Los Alamitos (1998)
2. Antoniol, G., Guéhéneuc, Y.G.: Feature identification: a novel approach and a case study. In: Proceedings of the International Conference on Software Maintenance, pp. 357–366. IEEE Computer Society Press, Los Alamitos (2005)
3. Antoniol, G., Guéhéneuc, Y.G.: Feature identification: An epidemiological metaphor. IEEE Transactions on Software Engineering 32(9), 627–641 (2006)
4. Asadi, F., Antoniol, G., Guéhéneuc, Y.G.: Concept locations with genetic algorithms: A comparison of four distributed architectures. In: Proceedings of the International Symposium on Search Based Software Engineering, pp. 153–162. IEEE Computer Society Press, Los Alamitos (2010)
5. Asadi, F., Di Penta, M., Antoniol, G., Guéhéneuc, Y.G.: A heuristic-based approach to identify concepts in execution traces. In: Proceedings of the European Conference on Software Maintenance and Reengineering, pp. 31–40. IEEE Computer Society Press, Los Alamitos (2010)
6. Baeza-Yates, R., Ribeiro-Neto, B.: Modern Information Retrieval. Addison-Wesley, Reading (1999)
7. Bellman, R.E., Dreyfus, S.E.: Applied Dynamic Programming, vol. 1. Princeton University Press, Princeton (1962)
8. Biggerstaff, T., Mitbander, B., Webster, D.: The concept assignment problem in program understanding. In: Proceedings of the International Conference on Software Engineering, pp. 482–498 (1993)
9. Chen, K., Rajlich, V.: Case study of feature location using dependence graph. In: Proceedings of the International Workshop on Program Comprehension, pp. 241–249. IEEE Computer Society Press, Los Alamitos (2000)
10. Cormen, T.H., Leiserson, C.E., Rivest, R.L.: Introductions to Algorithms. MIT Press, Cambridge (1990)
11. Deerwester, S., Dumais, S.T., Furnas, G.W., Landauer, T.K., Harshman, R.: Indexing by latent semantic analysis. Journal of the American Society for Information Science 41(6), 391–407 (1990)

12. Eaddy, M., Aho, A.V., Antoniol, G., Guéhéneuc, Y.G.: Cerberus: Tracing require-
    ments to source code using information retrieval, dynamic analysis, and program
    analysis. In: Proceedings of the International Conference on Program Comprehen-
    sion, pp. 53–62. IEEE Computer Society Press, Los Alamitos (2008)
13. Grissom, R.J., Kim, J.J.: Effect sizes for research: A broad practical approach, 2nd
    edn. Lawrence Earlbaum Associates, NJ (2005)
14. Jaccard, P.: Paul jaccard. etude comparative de la distribution florale dans une por-
    tion des alpes et des jura. Bulletin del la Socit Vaudoise des Sciences Naturelles 37,
    547–549
15. Kozaczynski, V., Ning, J.Q., Engberts, A.: Program concept recognition and trans-
    formation. IEEE Transactions on Software Engineering 18(12), 1065–1075 (1992)
16. Marcus, A., Poshyvanyk, D., Ferenc, R.: Using the conceptual cohesion of classes
    for fault prediction in object-oriented systems. IEEE Transactions on Software
    Engineering 34(2), 287–300 (2008)
17. Marcus, A., Sergeyev, A., Rajlich, V., Maletic, J.I.: An information retrieval ap-
    proach to concept location in source code. In: Proceedings of the Working Con-
    ference on Reverse Engineering, pp. 214–223. IEEE Computer Society Press, Los
    Alamitos (2004)
18. Mitchell, B.S., Mancoridis, S.: On the automatic modularization of software sys-
    tems using the bunch tool. IEEE Transactions on Software Engineering 32(3),
    193–208 (2006)
19. Porter, M.F.: An algorithm for suffix stripping. Program 14(3), 130–137 (1980)
20. Poshyvanyk, D., Guéhéneuc, Y.G., Marcus, A., Antoniol, G., Rajlich, V.: Feature
    location using probabilistic ranking of methods based on execution scenarios and
    information retrieval. Transactions on Software Engineering 33(6), 420–432 (2007)
21. Poshyvanyk, D., Marcus, A.: The conceptual coupling metrics for object-oriented
    systems. In: Proceedings of the International Conference on Software Maintenance,
    pp. 469–478. IEEE Computer Society Press, Los Alamitos (2006)
22. Salah, M., Mancordis, S., Antoniol, G., Penta, M.D.: Towards employing use-cases
    and dynamic analysis to comprehend mozilla. In: Proceedings of the International
    Conference on Software Maintenance, pp. 639–642. IEEE Press, Los Alamitos
    (2005)
23. Ka-Yee Ng, J., Guéhéneuc, Y.G., Antoniol, G.: Identification of behavioral and cre-
    ational design motifs through dynamic analysis. Journal of Software Maintenance
    and Evolution: Research and Practice 22(8), 597–627 (2010)
24. Tonella, P., Ceccato, M.: Aspect mining through the formal concept analysis of
    execution traces. In: Proceedings of Working Conference on Reverse Engineering,
    pp. 112–121 (2004)
25. Wilde, N., Scully, M.C.: Software reconnaissance: Mapping program features to
    code. Journal of Software Maintenance - Research and Practice 7(1), 49–62 (1995)

Evaluating Modularization Quality as an Extra Objective in Multiobjective Software Module Clustering

Márcio de Oliveira Barros

Post-graduate Information Systems Program – PPGI/UNIRIO
Av. Pasteur 458, Urca – Rio de Janeiro, RJ – Brazil
marcio.barros@uniriotec.br

Abstract. The application of multiobjective optimization to address Software Engineering problems is a growing trend. Multiobjective algorithms provide a balance between the ability of the computer to search a large solution space for valuable solutions and the capacity of the human decision-maker to select an alternative when two or more incomparable objectives are presented. However, when more than a single objective is available to be taken into account in a search process, the number of objectives to be considered becomes part of the decision. We have examined the effectiveness of using modularization quality (MQ) as an objective function in the context of the software module clustering problem. We designed and executed a set of experiments using both randomly-generated and real-world instances of varying size and complexity and a fixed calculation budget set in a per instance basis. Results collected from these experiments show that using MQ as an extra objective can improve search results for small instances (few modules to be clustered), while it decreases search quality for larger instances (more than 100 modules to be clustered). Search quality was measure both in terms of the number of distinct solutions found and on their coverage of the solution space, according to the spread and hypervolume quality indicators. We correlated problem characteristics (number of modules, clusters, and dependencies), instance attributes (module dependency distribution patterns), and algorithmic measures (MQ conflict with cohesion and coupling) and found that these elements can only partially explain the effectiveness of using MQ as an extra objective.

Keywords: multiobjective optimization, software clustering, coupling, cohesion, genetic algorithms.

Acknowledgements. The author would like to express his gratitude for FAPERJ and CNPq, the research agencies that financially supported this project.

M.B. Cohen and M. Ó Cinnéide (Eds.): SSBSE 2001, LNCS 6956, p. 267, 2011.

A Survey of Empirical Investigations on SSBSE Papers

Márcio de O. Barros[1] and Arilo Claudio Dias-Neto[2]

[1] Postgraduate Information Systems Program – UNIRIO
Av. Pasteur 458, Urca – Rio de Janeiro, RJ – Brazil
marcio.barros@uniriotec.br
[2] Computer Science Department – Postgraduate Program in Informatics – UFAM
R. Gen. Rodrigo Octávio Jordão Ramos, 3000 – Setor Norte – Manaus, AM – Brazil
arilo@dcc.ufam.edu.br

Abstract. We present a survey based on papers published in the first two editions of the Symposium on Search-Based Software Engineering (2009 and 2010). The survey addresses how empirical studies are being designed and used by researchers to support evidence on the effectiveness and efficiency of heuristic search techniques when applied to Software Engineering problems. The survey reuses the structure and research questions proposed by a systematic review published in the context of search-based software testing and covering research papers up to 2007. A list of validity threats for SBSE experiments is also proposed and the extent to which the selected research papers address these threats is evaluated. We have compared our results with those presented by the former systematic review and observed that the number of Search-based Software Engineering (SBSE) research papers supported by well-designed and well-reported empirical studies seems to be growing over the years. On the other hand, construct, internal, and external validity threats are still not properly addressed in the design of many SBSE experiments.

Keywords: survey, empirical studies, meta-heuristic algorithms, search-based software engineering.

Acknowledgements. The authors would like to express their gratitude for FAPERJ, CNPq, INCT-SEC, and FAPEAM, the research agencies that financially supported this project.

Subgroup Discovery for Defect Prediction

Daniel Rodríguez[1], R. Ruiz[2], J.C. Riquelme[3], and Rachel Harrison[4]

[1] Univ. of Alcalá, 28871 Alcalá, Spain
daniel.rodriguezg@uah.es*
[2] Pablo de Olavide Univ., 41013 Seville, Spain
robertoruiz@upo.es
[3] Univ. of Seville, 41012 Seville, Spain
riquelme@us.es
[4] Oxford Brookes Univ., Oxford OX33 1HX, UK
rachel.harrison@brookes.ac.uk

Although there is extensive literature in software defect prediction techniques, machine learning approaches have yet to be fully explored and in particular, Subgroup Discovery (SD) techniques. SD algorithms aim to find subgroups of data that are statistically different given a property of interest [1,2]. SD lies between predictive (finding rules given historical data and a property of interest) and descriptive tasks (discovering interesting patterns in data). An important difference with classification tasks is that the SD algorithms only focus on finding subgroups (e.g., inducing rules) for the property of interest and do not necessarily describe all instances in the dataset.

In this preliminary study, we have compared two well-known algorithms, the Subgroup Discovery algorithm [3] and CN2-SD algorithm [4], by applying them to several datasets from the publicly available PROMISE repository [5], as well as the Bug Prediction Dataset created by D'Ambros *et al.* [6]. The comparison is performed using quality measures adapted from classification measures. The results show that generated models can be used to guide testing effort. The parameters for the SD algorithms can be adjusted to balance the specificity and generality of a rule so that the selected rules can be considered *good enough* for software engineering standards. The induced rules are simple to use and easy to understand. Further work with more datasets and other SD algorithms that tackle the discovery of subgroups using different approaches (e.g., continuous attributes, discretization, quality measures, etc.) is needed.

References

1. Wrobel, S.: An algorithm for multi-relational discovery of subgroups. In: Proceedings of the 1st European Symposium on Principles of Data Mining, pp. 78–87 (1997)
2. Herrera, F., Carmona del Jesus, C.J., González, P., del Jesus, M.J.: An overview on subgroup discovery: Foundations and applications. Knowl. Inf. Syst. (2010)

* Research supported by Spanish Ministry of Education MEC TIN 2007-68084-C02.

M.B. Cohen and M. Ó Cinnéide (Eds.): SSBSE 2011, LNCS 6956, pp. 269–270, 2011.
© Springer-Verlag Berlin Heidelberg 2011

3. Gamberger, D., Lavrac, N.: Expert-guided subgroup discovery: methodology and application. Journal of Artificial Intelligence Research 17, 501–527 (2002)
4. Lavrač, N., Kavšek, B., Flach, P., Todorovski, L.: Subgroup discovery with CN2-SD. The Journal of Machine Learning Research 5, 153–188 (2004)
5. Boetticher, G., Menzies, T., Ostrand, T.: Promise repository of empirical software engineering data. West Virginia University, Department of Computer Science (2007)
6. D'Ambros, M., Lanza, M., Robbes, R.: An extensive comparison of bug prediction approaches. In: IEEE Mining Software Repositories (MSR), pp. 31–41 (2010)

Search-Based Parallel Refactoring Using Population-Based Direct Approaches

Hurevren Kilic[1], Ekin Koc[2], and Ibrahim Cereci[2]

[1] Computer Engineering Department, Gediz University, Menemen, Izmir, Turkey*
Hurevren.kilic@gediz.edu.tr
[2] Department of Computer Engineering, Atilim University, Incek, Ankara, Turkey
antimon@gmail.com, icereci@atilim.edu.tr

Abstract. Automated software refactoring is known to be one of the "hard" combinatorial optimization problems of the search-based software engineering field. The difficulty is mainly due to candidate solution representation, objective function description and necessity of functional behavior preservation of software. The problem is formulated as a combinatorial optimization problem whose objective function is characterized by an aggregate of object-oriented metrics or pareto-front solution description. In our recent empirical study, we have reported the results of a comparison among alternative search algorithms applied for the same problem: pure random, steepest descent, multiple first descent, simulated annealing, multiple steepest descent and artificial bee colony searches. The main goal of the study was to investigate potential of alternative multiple and population-based search techniques. The results showed that multiple steepest descent and artificial bee colony algorithms were most suitable two approaches for an efficient solution of the problem. An important observation was either with depth-oriented multiple steepest descent or breadth-oriented population-based artficial bee colony searches, better results could be obtained through higher number of executions supported by a lightweight solution representation. On the other hand different from multiple steepest descent search, population-based, scalable and being suitable for parallel execution characteristics of artificial bee colony search made the population-based choices to be the topic of this empirical study. 1In this study, we report the search-based parallel refactoring results of an empirical comparative study among three population-based search techniques namely, artificial bee colony search, local beam search and stochastic beam search and a non-populated technique multiple steepest descent as the baseline. For our purpose, we used parallel features of our prototype automated refactoring tool A-CMA written in Java language. A-CMA accepts bytecode compiled Java codes as its input. It supports 20 different refactoring actions that realize searches on design landscape defined by an adhoc quality model being an aggregation of 24 object-oriented software metrics. We experimented 6 input programs written in Java where 5 of them being open source codes and one student project code. The empirical results showed that for almost all of the considered input programs with different run parameter settings, local beam

---

* In partof the study, the author H.Kilic has been with Atilim University, Ankara, Turkey.

M.B. Cohen and M. Ó Cinnéide (Eds.): SSBSE 2001, LNCS 6956, pp. 271–272, 2011.
© Springer-Verlag Berlin Heidelberg 2011

search is the most suitable population-based search technique for the efficient solution of the search-based parallel refactoring problem in terms of mean and maximum normalized quality gain. However, we observed that the computational time requirement for local beam search becomes rather high when the beam size exceeds 60. On the other hand, even though it is not able to identify high quality designs for less populated search setups, time-efficiency and scalability properties of artificial bee colony search makes it a good choice for population sizes ≥ 200.

Search-Based Functional Test Data Generation Using Data Metamodel

János Oláh and István Majzik

Department of Measurement and Information Systems
Budapest University of Technology and Economics
Magyar Tudósok körútja 2., Budapest, Hungary
{janos.olah,majzik}@mit.bme.hu

Software testing is the process of evaluating the quality of the *software under test* (SUT) by controlled execution, with the primary aim to reveal inadequate behavior. Despite the automation offered by modern development environments, the process of *test data generation* remains a largely manual task. In this paper we present a model-based approach for the generation of test data, using search-based software engineering technique.

Search-based software engineering (SBSE) is the use of search-based optimization algorithms to software engineering problems. Software testing is probably the most important domain of SBSE [1]. Most studies, however, have applied SBSE for structural testing, while the use of such techniques for functional testing is rarely addressed. The main reason is probably the implicit nature of the software specifications and the complexity of their mapping to fitness functions.

The key ingredients for the application of search-based optimization to test data generation is the choice of candidate representation and the definition of the fitness function. In our proposed approach we utilize the *metamodel* constructed to describe the *context* of the SUT. Parts of the program data, their relations and the constraints among their values are represented by the metamodel. Candidate test data are *model instances* conforming to this metamodel.

We focus on functional specifications that describe the expected behaviour of the SUT in case of a certain context. In order to test the accomplishment of a specification, we need test data that contain particular configuration of objects as input described by the specification. We refer to these as *context patterns*, and our goal is to generate test data that contain these patterns. The fitness function formulated to guide the test data generation rewards model instances that cover the model patterns.

The iterative manipulation of instances and pattern matching in order to calculate the fitness are executed with popular *model transformation frameworks*, which usually apply rule based manipulation of models [2].

References

1. McMinn, P.: Search-based software test data generation: A survey. Software Testing, Verification and Reliability 14, 105–156 (2004)
2. Rozenberg, G. (ed.): Handbook of Graph Grammars and Computing by Graph Transformation, vol. 1. World Scientific, Singapore (1997)

M.B. Cohen and M. Ó Cinnéide (Eds.): SSBSE 2011, LNCS 6956, p. 273, 2011.

How Multi-Objective Genetic Programming Is Effective for Software Development Effort Estimation?

Filomena Ferrucci, Carmine Gravino, and Federica Sarro

Via Ponte Don Melillo, 84084 Fisciano (SA), Italy
{fferrucci,gravino,fsarro}@unisa.it

The idea of exploiting search-based methods to estimate development effort is based on the observation that the effort estimation problem can be formulated as an optimization problem. As a matter of fact, among possible estimation models, we have to identify the best one, i.e., the one providing the most accurate estimates. Nevertheless, in the context of effort estimation there does not exist a unique measure that allows us to compare different models and consistently derives the best one [1]. Rather, several evaluation criteria (e.g., MMRE and Pred(25)) covering different aspects of model performances (e.g., underestimating or overestimating) are used to assess and compare estimation models [1]. Thus, considering the effort estimation problem as an optimization problem we should search for the model that optimizes several measures. From this point of view, the effort estimation problem is inherently multi-objective. Nevertheless, all the studies that have been carried out so far on the use of search-based techniques for effort estimation exploited single objectives (e.g., [2][3]). Those studies have also revealed that the use of some measures as fitness function (e.g., MMRE) decreased a lot the accuracy in terms of other summary measures [2]. A first attempt to take into account different evaluation criteria has been reported by Ferrucci *et al.* [3], where Genetic Programming (GP) exploited a combination of two measures (e.g., Pred(25) and MMRE) in a single fitness function, providing encouraging results. Obviously, an approach based on combination of measures is the simplest way to deal with the multi-objective problem but this can determine biases since there is no defined way of aggregating different objectives. Thus, we investigated the use of a Multi-Objective Genetic Programming (MOGP) approach with the aim to verify its effectiveness. To the best of our knowledge this is the first attempt to apply a MOGP approach in this field. In particular, we designed and experimented an adaptation to GP of the Non dominated Sort Genetic Algorithm-II (NSGA-II) exploiting multi-objective functions based on a different number and type of evaluation criteria. Moreover, we compared the performance of MOGP with GP using different fitness functions. The preliminary empirical analysis, carried out with some publicly available datasets included in the PROMISE repository [4], revealed that the choice of the evaluation criteria employed in the definition of the fitness function affects the overall accuracy of both MOPG and GP. Nevertheless, no significant statistical difference has been found between the best results achieved with MOGP and GP. Thus, the use of a more sophisticated technique, such as MOGP, seems to be not cost/effective in this context. However, this is a preliminary analysis

M.B. Cohen and M. Ó Cinnéide (Eds.): SSBSE 2001, LNCS 6956, pp. 274–275, 2011.
© Springer-Verlag Berlin Heidelberg 2011

that needs to be deepen also using more data. Moreover, the use of other multi-objective optimization approaches could be exploited to investigate whether there are improvements in the accuracy of the obtained estimation models.

References

[1] Kitchenham, B., Pickard, L., MacDonell, S., Shepperd, M.: What accuracy statistics really measure. IEEE Procs. Software 148(3), 81–85 (2001)
[2] Burgess, C., Lefley, M.: Can Genetic Programming Improve Software Effort Estimation: A Comparative Evaluation. Inform. and Softw. Technology 43(14), 863–873 (2001)
[3] Ferrucci, F., Gravino, C., Oliveto, R., Sarro, F.: Genetic Programming for Effort Estimation: An Analysis of the Impact of Different Fitness Functions. In: Procs. of SSBSE 2010, pp. 89–98 (2010)
[4] PROMISE Repository of Emp. Softw. Engine. data,
   http://promisedata.org/repository

On the Applicability of Exact Optimization in Search Based Software Engineering

Fabrício Freitas, Thiago Silva, Rafael Carmo, and Jerffeson Souza

Optimization in Software Engineering Group (GOES.UECE)
Natural and Intelligent Computing Lab (LACONI)
State University of Ceará (UECE) - Avenue Paranjana, 1700, Ceará, Brazil
{fabriciogf.uece,thi.nepo,carmorafael}@gmail.com,
jeff@larces.uece.br

Abstract. The Search Based Software Engineering (SBSE) field has emerged as an exciting and promising area by proposing the formulation of software engineering problems as optimization problems. Hitherto, metaheuristics have been widely employed for solving these problems, whilst little work has been done regarding the use of exact techniques in the area. This paper aims to fulfil this lack by presenting a comprehensive study on the theory and practice of the application of exact optimization in SBSE. A conceptual comparison of both optimization approaches in the software engineering context is presented. Problems' aspects are analysed regarding suitability for use of exact techniques. As illustration, comparison experiments with exact technique and metaheuristics are conducted over a well-known SBSE problem. The results reveal the overall behaviour of exact techniques, regarding efficacy and efficiency, in the SBSE context considered, indicating its potential use.

Keywords: exact optimisation, theoretical work, empirical study, SBSE applications, optimisation techniques comparison.

M.B. Cohen and M. Ó Cinnéide (Eds.): SSBSE 2001, LNCS 6956, pp. 276, 2011.
© Springer-Verlag Berlin Heidelberg 2011

Automatic Evolution of Java-Written Game Heuristics

Michael Orlov*, Carmel Bregman†, and Moshe Sipper

Department of Computer Science, Ben-Gurion University
PO Box 653, Beer-Sheva 84105, Israel
{orlovm,carmelbr,sipper}@cs.bgu.ac.il

FINCH is a methodology for evolving Java bytecode, enabling the evolution of extant, unrestricted Java programs, or programs in other languages that compile to Java bytecode. The established approach in genetic programming (GP) involves the definition of functions and terminals appropriate to the problem at hand, after which evolution of expressions using these definitions takes place. FINCH evolutionarily improves actual, extant software, which was *not intentionally written* for the purpose of serving as a GP representation in particular, nor for evolution in general. In this work we show how several game heuristics that are taken as real-world Java programs are effortlessly and automatically improved by FINCH.

We have developed a powerful tool [1,2,3] by which extant software, written in the Java programming language, or in a language that compiles to Java bytecode, can be evolved directly, without an intermediate genomic representation, and with no restrictions on the constructs used. We provide an overview of this system, some previous results, its usability, and the application of FINCH to evolving Java-written game heuristics.

References

1. Orlov, M., Sipper, M.: Genetic programming in the wild: Evolving unrestricted bytecode. In: Raidl, G., et al. (eds.) Proceedings of the 11th Annual Conference on Genetic and Evolutionary Computation, Montréal Québec, Canada, July 8-12, pp. 1043–1050. ACM Press, New York (2009)
2. Orlov, M., Sipper, M.: FINCH: A system for evolving Java (bytecode). In: Riolo, R., McConaghy, T., Vladislavleva, E. (eds.) Genetic Programming Theory and Practice VIII, GPTP 2010, Genetic and Evolutionary Computation, Ann Arbor, Michigan, USA, May 20-22, vol. 8, ch. 1, pp. 1–16. Springer, New York (2010)
3. Orlov, M., Sipper, M.: Flight of the FINCH through the Java wilderness. IEEE Transactions on Evolutionary Computation 15(2), 166–182 (2011)

---

* M. Orlov is supported by the Adams Fellowship Program of the Israel Academy of Sciences and Humanities, and is partially supported by the Lynn and William Frankel Center for Computer Sciences.
† C. Bregman is supported by the Lynn and William Frankel Center for Computer Sciences.

M.B. Cohen and M. Ó Cinnéide (Eds.): SSBSE 2011, LNCS 6956, p. 277, 2011.

Author Index

GPSR Compliance

The European Union's (EU) General Product Safety Regulation (GPSR) is a set of rules that requires consumer products to be safe and our obligations to ensure this.

If you have any concerns about our products, you can contact us on ProductSafety@springernature.com

In case Publisher is established outside the EU, the EU authorized representative is:

Springer Nature Customer Service Center GmbH
Europaplatz 3
69115 Heidelberg, Germany

Batch number: 09490872

Printed by Printforce, the Netherlands